MAJOR LEAGUE WINNERS

WINNERS

Using Sports and Cultural Centers as Tools for Economic Development

American Society for Public Administration
Book Series on Public Administration & Public Policy

Editor-in-Chief
Evan M. Berman, Ph.D.
National Chengchi University, Taiwan
evanmberman@gmail.com

Mission: Throughout its history, ASPA has sought to be true to its founding principles of promoting scholarship and professionalism within the public service. The ASPA Book Series on Public Administration and Public Policy publishes books that increase national and international interest for public administration and which discuss practical or cutting edge topics in engaging ways of interest to practitioners, policy-makers, and those concerned with bringing scholarship to the practice of public administration.

Major League Winners: Using Sports and Cultural Centers as Tools for Economic Development, Mark S. Rosentraub

The Formula for Economic Growth on Main Street America, Gerald L. Gordon

The New Face of Government: How Public Managers Are Forging a New Approach to Governance, David E. McNabb

The Facilitative Leader in City Hall: Reexamining the Scope and Contributions, James H. Svara

American Society for Public Administration
Series in Public Administration and Public Policy

MAJOR LEAGUE WINNERS

Using Sports and Cultural Centers as Tools for Economic Development

MARK S. ROSENTRAUB

CRC Press
Taylor & Francis Group
Boca Raton   London   New York

CRC Press is an imprint of the
Taylor & Francis Group, an **informa** business

CRC Press
Taylor & Francis Group
6000 Broken Sound Parkway NW, Suite 300
Boca Raton, FL 33487-2742

© 2010 by Mark S Rosentraub
CRC Press is an imprint of Taylor & Francis Group, an Informa business

No claim to original U.S. Government works

Printed in the United States of America on acid-free paper
10 9 8 7 6 5 4 3 2 1

International Standard Book Number: 978-1-4398-0159-8 (Hardback)

Library of Congress Cataloging-in-Publication Data

Rosentraub, Mark S., 1950-
   Major league winners : using sports and cultural centers as tools for economic development / Mark S. Rosentraub.
      p. cm. -- (American Society for Public Administration book series on public administration and public policy)
   Includes bibliographical references and index.
   ISBN 978-1-4398-0159-8
   1. Sports--Economic aspects--United States. 2. Sports facilities--United States--Planning. 3. Civic centers—United States--Planning. 4. Urban renewal--United States. 5. City planning--United States. 6. Sports--Economic aspects—United States--Case studies. 7. Sports facilities—United States--Planning--Case studies. 8. Civic centers—United States--Planning--Case studies. 9. Urban renewal--United States—Case studies. 10. City planning--United States--Case studies. I. Title. II. Series.

GV716.R673 2009
338.4'77960973--dc22   2009009016

For Brooklyn, Ian, Jackson, and Graycen; they are my
next generation, joined by Alex and Jessica.

This book is G-Pop's gift to you for the inspiration and
joy I get from the love of life I see in your eyes.

Contents

Preface.. xiii

Acknowledgments xvii

The Author xxi

**1. Urban Change, a Loss of Centrality, and New Destinies for
   Downtowns** 1
    I. Introduction 1
        A. The Era of Subsidies and Hope 2
        B. What Can New Facilities Do for a Region? 3
        C. Subsidies and Strategic Investments: The Difference
           Defined...3
    II. Sports, Entertainment, and Culture for Image, Attracting
       Human Capital, and Economic Development 4
    III. The Beginning of an End to the Need for Central Cities.................5
        A. Population Change 5
        B. Rise, Decline, and Lessons Learned from Festival
           Marketplaces 7
        C. Indianapolis and a Civic Image Strategy............................8
        D. Rise of Sports and Culture for Revitalization 9
    IV. Why Should Cities Care about Sports, Entertainment, and
       Culture?..10
        A. Human Capital and Amenities...12
        B. Are Sports, Entertainment, and Culture a City's Fool's
           Gold? 13
    V. Sports, Entertainment, and Culture: The Trinity for
       Redevelopment 16
        A. Cities, Sports Facilities, and Subsidies 16
        B. Franchise Values and Changing the System 20
    VI. Misplaced Revenues, Misplaced Values 22
    VII. Goal and Organization of This Book..24
    Endnotes...26

2. Teams, Cities, Elites, and the Real Value of "Big-Ticket" Amenities..**31**
   I. A General Framework for Investments in Big-Ticket Items............31
   II. The Value and Appropriateness of Big-Ticket Items 35
      A. A City's Image 35
      B. Amenities and the "Creative Class"...................................36
      C. Amenities or Neighborhood Development? 38
   III. Amenities, Human Capital, and Economic Development 39
      A. Supply of Amenities... 42
      B. Importance of Amenities 43
   IV. Organic Urban Change versus Planned Redevelopment................. 44
      A. Delayed Development or Stagnation? 45
      B. Growth Poles 47
   V. Business Leaders and Urban Redevelopment 49
   VI. The Unbalanced Playing Field between Teams and Cities 51
      A. What Are Teams Worth?...51
      B. Implications of the Leagues' Control of the Supply of Teams 54
      C. How Did the Leagues Amass Their Economic Power?............56
   VII. Challenging the Leagues in Court, at the Statehouse, or in Congress...58
   VIII. Revitalization and Development as an Alternative to Subsidies 60
   IX. Summary..60
   Endnotes...61

3. Indianapolis as the Broker City **65**
   I. The Indianapolis Plan: Goals, Objectives, and History...................65
   II. Indianapolis, Sports, and Redevelopment: What Was Built, How Much Was Invested, and Whose Dollars Were Spent?...........69
      A. What Was Built?...70
      B. Who Paid How Much for the New Downtown?......................72
   III. Has Indianapolis Been Changed by the Sports and Downtown Redevelopment Strategy? 75
      A. Maintaining Downtown Indianapolis 75
      B. Regional Economic Changes and the Centrality of Downtown Indianapolis...78
      C. Image of Indianapolis: Intangible Benefits and the Journey from "Indiana-No-Place" to Super Bowl Host City 87
   IV. Challenges on the Horizon: Subsidies and Revenues 90
   V. Indianapolis: The Broker City to Be a Major League Winner..........94
   Endnotes...96

4. **Shared Risk, Shared Returns: San Diego's Unique Partnership for a Ballpark, Convention Center Hotel, and a New Downtown Neighborhood** 99
  I. Introduction 99
    A. Fiscal Challenges for the Padres....................................100
    B. "Poisoned Environment" for Sports Subsidies........................100
  II. The Padres and the "Need" for a New Ballpark 101
  III. Politics of San Diego's Sports World 102
  IV. Task Force II and the Generation of Substantial Public Benefits ...107
  V. Public Benefits and the Stigma of Subsidies...........................107
  VI. Scorecard on the Ballpark District: What Was Built 112
  VII. The Scorecard: Taxes Generated 115
  VIII. The Ballpark District: Development, Land Use, and the Best
       Use of Urban Land 117
  IX. The Ballpark District and San Diego: Mutual Risk in a New
      Model for Public/Private Partnerships 124
  Endnotes..128

5. **A White Elephant, an Arena, and Revitalization: Using Location and the Glitz of *L.A. LIVE* to Rebuild a Downtown Area** 129
  I. Introduction 129
  II. Thinking Outside the Box: Bringing the Lakers and Kings
      Downtown 130
    A. The Lakers, the Kings, and the "Fabulous Forum" 131
    B. The "Fabulous Forum" and Its Limitations........................132
    C. Arena Economics and the Appeal of Downtown Los
       Angeles 133
  III. Downtown Los Angeles: Liabilities and Assets 136
  IV. Sealing and Selling the Deal..140
  V. Los Angeles' Investment and Returns.................................141
    A. Were the Taxpayers Protected?....................................144
    B. Rebuilding Downtown: Housing.....................................146
  VI. Rebuilding Downtown Los Angeles: L.A. LIVE 148
  VII. Rebuilding Downtown: Other Iconic Projects.........................153
  VIII. Conclusions 154
  Endnotes...157

6. **Columbus, Major League Sports, and a New Downtown Neighborhood: A Failed Initiative and a Privately Built Arena** 161
  I. Introduction 161
  II. Fighting for a Toe Hold in Professional Sports 163

    A.   Sports Leagues and Their Placement of Teams in
        Cincinnati and Cleveland 164
    B.   An Effort to Make Columbus Home to a Major League
        Team 165
  III. A Privately Built Arena, Real Estate Development, and a
      Unique Public/Private Partnership 166
    A.   The Arena District Plan 167
    B.   Financing the Arena District 168
  IV. Columbus' Arena District: An Early Assessment 171
   V. Columbus' Arena District: What Was Built 176
  VI. Conclusions 177
Endnotes 182

**7. Can a City Win When Losing? Cleveland and the Building of
    Sports, Cultural, and Entertainment Facilities in the Midst of
    Population Declines and Job Losses 185**
    I. Introduction 185
   II. The Crisis of Confidence 188
    A.   Racial Conflict and White Flight 188
    B.   Economic Contraction and Fiscal Default 190
  III. Cleveland's "Hail Mary" Pass: Downtown Revitalization as
      Symbols of Confidence 191
    A.   Playhouse Square and a Citizen-Driven Public/Private
        Partnership 191
    B.   Public/Private Partnership Mayoralty of George Voinovich
        and the Reinvigoration of a Regime[6] 192
    C.   Mayor Michael White and the Ballpark and Arena
        Proposal's Redux 194
    D.   Large Subsidies and the Dispersion of Assets 196
  IV. Results of Cleveland's "Hail Mary" Pass 198
    A.   Private Investment Levels in Cleveland: Nonresidential
        Projects 199
    B.   Private Investment in Residential Properties 200
    C.   Tax Revenue Changes 202
    D.   Job Retention and Employment Changes 205
   V. Extra Benefits from Building Amenities: Regional Cooperation 207
  VI. Amending Cleveland's Major League Loser Status: New Leases ... 208
    A.   Provision of Extraordinary Subsidies 208
    B.   New Owners, New Possibilities 210
    C.   New Leases for the Ballpark and Arena 213
 VII. Business Leaders and Downtown and Community
      Development 215

VIII. Conclusions 217
Endnotes 220

8. Stagnation, Crime, and Population Change: Reading's Volunteer Leadership Group and a Focus on Sports, Entertainment, the Arts, and Culture to Revitalize a Small City 223
   I. Introduction: Economic Change in a Small City 223
  II. Changes in a Small City: Economic and Racial Separation 224
     A. Reading in Brief 224
     B. Reading and Berks County Today 226
 III. Into the Breach: A Volunteer Leadership Group and Its Focus on Entertainment 230
  IV. Reimaging Reading: From the Outlet Capital to a Mid-Atlantic Arts Center 235
   V. Reading's Leadership Group and Community Development 238
  VI. Measures of Success 239
 VII. Conclusions 241
Endnotes 243

9. Sports, Culture, Entertainment and Revitalization: Turning Subsidies into Strategic Investments 245
   I. Introduction 245
  II. Subsidies to Investments in the Aftermath of the Credit Crisis 246
     A. Value of Amenities for Economic Development and Revitalization 248
     B. Urban Tourism 248
 III. Lessons Learned: Similarities within Differences 249
  IV. Lessons Learned: Advice for Other Cities Looking to Sports, Entertainment, and Cultural Amenities for Revitalization 250
     A. Recommendation 1: Value of Advertising 250
     B. Recommendation 2: Concentrate Amenities and Make Detailed Plans 252
     C. Recommendation 3: Build Neighborhoods or Iconic Architecture 254
     D. Recommendation 4: Link Private Sector Investments to a Commitment of Tax Money 256
     E. Recommendation 5: Organizations Needed to Succeed as a Broker City 258
     F. Recommendation 6: Prudent Risk-Taking for Confidence Building 260
       What Lesson Does This Offer? 260

G. Recommendation 7: "Über-Plans" Unifying Public and
     Private Capital 261
H. Recommendation 8: Constructively Involve Business
     Leaders in Downtown and Community Development 262
I.   Recommendation 9: Level the Negotiating Table 264
V. Conclusion 265
Endnotes.. 266

References **267**
Index **277**

Preface

Any book appearing in the midst of a severe recession discussing the use of sports and culture to rebuild cities might seem to be either irrelevant or insensitive. Some could consider it irrelevant because its focus seemingly ignores the quintessential issue of our day: "How does America restart its economy?" Other people might consider the book insensitive in that it analyzes sports, culture, and entertainment—what some might consider frivolous luxuries—at a time when millions of people have lost their jobs and homes. When I began this book, I, like many of my academic colleagues, did not believe a complete collapse of the nation's financial system was imminent. We did not expect to see job losses of 500,000 or more per month for several months, and we did not think mayors and community leaders would be struggling to provide basic services while engaging in the work to rebuild local economies. As this book appears, however, it is my conviction that what is described in the pages that follow makes a definite (and important) contribution to the fundamental issue of rebuilding the economies of America's cities.

How does this book make its contribution? I have been involved in the study of sports and cities, sports economics, and sports management since 1976. Every study, academic article, op-ed piece, book, or assignment with civic leaders focused on keeping or bringing sports and culture to a downtown area was driven by one over-arching policy directive. How can a city and region (or our city and region when I worked directly with community leaders or as a public official in Cleveland) diversify its economic base, attract the human capital needed by emerging industries, and retain entrepreneurs without sports and culture? That policy question or issue always raised two others. One question came from those opposed to investments or subsidies for sports and culture. The other question came from a particular project's strongest supporters. The first question was: "Can sports and culture really matter for a city's economic and social development?" The second question—the one from projects supporters—was: "Can you help us do it at the least cost to taxpayers"?

I would submit the answers to these questions are even more relevant today. The economic crisis that grips America will impact each region differently. No region will be unaffected. But those areas that will feel the effects least and recover fastest will be those that have succeeded in building the most diversified economic bases and have the largest concentration of human capital with the widest sets of skills. As Richard Florida points out, New York City was the epicenter of the financial crisis and those employed in money and banking produced more than one-fifth of the region's income. Yet, only 8 percent of the workforce was employed in what was the overblown and excessively compensated financial sector. Regions in other parts of the country actually had larger concentrations of their workforce employed in the financial services sector. As a result, Florida recommends that New Yorkers fasten their seatbelt for the rocky ride ahead as lower salaries and fewer jobs in the financial sector lead to declining property values and far fewer expensive meals at five-star restaurants. Yet, he also argues that New York will recover far more quickly than many realize.[1] Why? New York has a mix of human capital that is far more diversified than the mixes that exist in most other regions of North America.

What that says to me is that the mayors and community leaders that I have worked with through the past decades "got it" and understood what needed to be done long before many academicians gave them credit. They understood that their states were making large investments in human capital through their state university systems. They also understood that America's private universities were also producing high-skilled human capital, as were the hundreds of excellent community college systems throughout the country. Their task as mayors and local community leaders was to attract and retain this human capital. To be sure, they also wanted to make investments in workers, but they knew if their regions did not have the assets (like sports and culture) that make communities a great place to live and raise a family, their cities and regions would, in the long run, be destined to a second or third tier economic status.

These community leaders never lost sight of their responsibility to produce safe streets, quality public schools, and livable neighborhoods. But, they also recognized something that sociologists studying sports and culture well understood. For thousands of years, people have yearned for safe streets and good places for their families to live. But, they also loved and wanted sports and culture. Those cities and regions that could meet the basic requirements of safety and quality education and offer an environment where sports and culture also existed would thrive. Other areas that failed to offer sports and culture (along with the basic requirements of a safe environment) would fall to the side and be characterized by slower growth rates, fewer economic opportunities to attract and retain younger workers, and, in the event of a severe recession, far longer recovery periods.

In the 1980s and 1990s, many regions provided extraordinary subsidies to ensure that sports teams and cultural facilities were part of the civic fabric of their community. Those costs rose into the billions of dollars and prompted leaders in other communities to ask two very simple questions. First, "Is there a better and cheaper way to ensure that our region has a piece of America's premier sports and cultural life?" Second, "How can our region effectively use sports, culture, and any other asset to rebuild downtown areas and make them desirable places to live, work, and play?"

This book is a response to those questions and a follow-up to my earlier work that chronicled the creation of the great sports welfare machine that produced the subsidies paid by governments for professional sports. *Major League Losers: The Real Cost of Sports and Who's Paying for It* (Basic Books, 1997, 1999) presented the case for changing the laws that govern the sports industry to make it less able to extract subsidies. *Major League Winners* is about the lessons learned and success of cities that could not wait for Congress or their states to change the laws that governed sports. Pressured by forces that drive economic development, these cities and their leaders tried different tools, policies, and plans to rebuild downtown areas with sports and culture by turning any subsidies into strategic investments. The lessons learned and the prescription for the future is more relevant now than when this book project began.

The cities and regions that recover fastest from the credit and financial crisis that now threatens families and the quality of life in America will be those that took the strides to differentiate their economy and produce a rich and varied pool of local labor resources. That talent is concentrated in the areas with safe and high quality of life neighborhoods that are part of the regions firmly anchored to the mainstream of American sports and culture. The lessons that unfold in the chapters ahead should be part of each region's stimulus plan. Curing what ails America does not lie with more sports and culture. It lies with building the most creative and productive workforce possible. Yet sports and culture will continue to contribute to the decisions made by these creative workers when they choose where they want to live. The companies that will propel America from this recession will locate where they know they can attract and retain the human capital they need to meet their clients' needs. Cities that fail to learn from the efforts of places such as San Diego and Columbus, Ohio or from the risks, successes, and setbacks endured by places like Indianapolis and Cleveland will not build the infrastructure needed to survive the next fiscal crisis our nation will face. America will survive the current fiscal crisis—just as it did all of the others in our past—and despite new safeguards, market tendencies will produce other crises for future generations. Designing cities that are magnets for human capital will make future recoveries far less painful and the fallout from future recessions far less destructive.

Endnote

1. Florida, R. 2009. How will the crash reshape America? *Atlantic Monthly* (March): 44–56.

Acknowledgments

This book grew from a presentation I made at the University of Pennsylvania's Institute for Urban Research in 2007 discussing successful downtown revitalization efforts anchored by sports facilities. Professor Eugenie Birch smiled during my remarks and wryly suggested a book on these successes would be an appropriate complement to my *Major League Losers*. That earlier book focused on the excessive subsidies provided by different cities to teams that had created a perverse welfare system. Eugenie, thank you for helping me see the value of this project.

I wrote this book after stepping out of my position as Dean of the Maxine Goodman Levin College of Urban Affairs at Cleveland State University. In my transition year, several colleagues showed me the support that made them into life-long friends. I will continue to owe them more than words can express. In this book, I want to acknowledge and thank Richard Bingham, Bill Bowen, Scott Cummings, Rene Hearns, Brad Humphreys, Dennis Keating, Norm Krumholz, Seong Kyu Ha, Myung-Jin Jun, Kenna Quinet, Dan Mason, Brian Mikelbank, Eran Razin, Noam Shoval, Jessica Sowa, and Mark Tumeo for their kindness. I will remember always how lucky I am to have had each of you in my life.

In the Greater Cleveland area, Khalid Bakhur, David and Brenda Goldberg, Anita Gray, Sam Mohammad, Albert and Audrey Ratner, and Marc Silverstein became even stronger friends and I will treasure each of you in my heart. Your support, kindness, wisdom, and friendship at a time when all four were needed leaves me in your debt.

Students are always a source of inspiration for their professors and I am thankful Akram Ijla, Wasim Al-Habil, Mijin Joo, Jerry Rugley, Dafna Sholomovich, and Holly Whisman allowed me to be part of their education and career. The time I was able to spend with each of you was a great source of support and inspiration, and, after this book, the best medicine possible.

In every city, different people provided me with more research help than I deserved. Dr. Charles Isgar's probing questions, insights, and biting sense of humor sharpened my focus. His jokes pushed me to make this book and the Los Angeles chapter far better products. I am also very lucky to be able to call Steve Soboroff a friend and to learn from him. He is a part of Los Angeles's economic leadership who lives the meaning of community development each day. In San Diego, Mike Aguirre is the driving critic and community leader who forces everyone to consider how to avoid subsidies. Eric Judson of the San Diego Padres also shared his ideas and visions for how teams can and should work with cities. He is a leader in the next generation of sports corporate executives who understand what teams can and should do for their home cities. In Indianapolis—a city I still call home—Susan Williams and a score of public and community leaders have always been a great help to me in my research. There are too many to name from my adopted home, but I want to thank the leadership of the Indianapolis Colts and Indiana Pacers for a lifetime of insights. Anthony Schoettle of the *Indianapolis Business Journal* was also willing to help chase down even the smallest details of Indianapolis' revitalization efforts. In Cleveland, a special thanks is owed to the Greater Cleveland Partnership and its staff for providing access to their records and history. The leadership of the Gateway Economic Redevelopment Corporation—Todd Greathouse and Brian Kelly—helped uncover the data I needed. Mike Ehlerman and Al Boscov in Reading were not only invaluable sources, but their commitment to the city's future is an extraordinary inspiration. I have been infected by their love of Reading and now find myself hoping that *goggleWorks* leads an unprecedented revitalization. Richard Sandomir of *The New York Times*, a friend for more than 40 years, is now someone who I am privileged to call a colleague. I know our parents are still amazed that our playground games turned into lifetime pursuits and permanent bonds of friendship.

Books like this are not done without a great deal of family support. Sabrina, my youngest daughter, attended law school in Cleveland when this book was written and was a rock of support in a trying year. A father should not need to depend on a daughter, but I will be forever grateful for her help. Her words of support and her advice meant more to and for me than I can express. My journey to the University of Michigan began because of her advice and instincts even though she remains a most loyal member of The Ohio State University's Buckeye Nation. Natalie, Alexa, and David—my other three adult children—always expressed their confidence and applauded the change in my life. They convinced me that stepping away from administration and focusing on research and my students was the best thing for me. This book is the proof they were right. I learned that fathers should listen carefully to their adult children, as their advice is, more often than not, the best course of action. Karen, my wife, shared every minute of the trouble, conflict, frustrations, and successes in 2007 and 2008, and was also able to share in the joy of this book's emergence and my journey to Ann Arbor. I am very lucky to have had her to stand by and with me. I will never be able to repay her for that help and support.

Evan Berman's faith in this project is gratefully acknowledged and the special friends and colleagues who read drafts of each chapter made this book a far better product. Particular thanks are due Jay Margolis, project editor at Taylor & Francis, whose love of Cleveland led him to pay special attention to this book. I am indebted to each of these people for their help and probing questions. Without the investment of their time, this book would not be as easy to read. Any errors that remain are solely my responsibility. The administrative sabbatical offered by Cleveland State University provided the time needed to finish this book.

It is a great honor to have this book appear during my first year as the Bickner Chair in the School of Kinesiology at the University of Michigan. It is an extraordinary privilege for me to be part of this distinguished faculty and I trust this book adds to the luster of our programs and helps us launch a new set of initiatives.

The Author

Mark Rosentraub, PhD, has been studying and writing about the economics and management of professional sports and the relationship between sports and cities for more than 30 years. *Major League Losers: The Real Cost of Sports and Who's Paying For It,* published in 1997 (Basic Books), analyzed the perverse subsidy system that involved taxpayer support for facilities and the lack of economic benefits from these sports facilities built with their money, which were not part of redevelopment strategies. In addition to a second and revised edition of this book (1999), he is co-author of *The Economics of Sports: An International Perspective* and 30 other academic articles and book chapters on different aspects of sports economics and urban development.

Dr. Rosentraub's work on sports and economic development has not been limited to academic studies. He worked with the San Diego Padres in helping to secure support for the Ballpark District plan and assisted Los Angeles in its efforts to bring sports teams back to the downtown area. He has also advised two different mayors of Indianapolis for more than a decade on their sports strategy, and has been a consultant for several other cities. He has presented expert testimony on the economics of sports and the effects of teams on economies before Congressional and state legislative committees and numerous city and county councils.

In 2003, the Cuyahoga County Commissioners appointed Dr. Rosentraub to the board of the Gateway Economic Development Corporation, the public agency responsible for Progressive Field, home to the Cleveland Indians, and Quicken Loans Arena, home to the Cleveland Cavaliers. He served as a commissioner renegotiating the leases with the teams, which is saving taxpayers more than $4 million each year for the life of the new leases.

In 2009, Professor Rosentraub became the University of Michigan's first holder of the Bickner Chair in the School of Kinesiology's Department of Sports Management. Previously, he was dean and professor at the Levin College of Urban Affairs at Cleveland State University and an associate dean and professor in the School of Public and Environmental Affairs, Indiana University (Indianapolis campus).

Chapter 1

Urban Change, a Loss of Centrality, and New Destinies for Downtowns

I. Introduction

As suburban areas grew and downtown centers lost department stores, theaters, and jobs, many cities paid for new ballparks, arenas, stadiums, theaters, and museums to lead the revitalization of deteriorating core areas. For some cities that were devastated by economic transformations, which led to the loss of thousands of manufacturing jobs and the movement of Fortune 500 companies to larger cities, new sports, entertainment, and cultural centers were larger-than-life efforts to restore tarnished images and confidence in a better future. The 1980s and 1990s launched an unprecedented era of the building of taxpayer-financed sports facilities in downtown areas from Baltimore to San Diego and from Miami to Seattle. New or renovated theaters and museums were joined to these sports facilities, and the public sector often paid most or all of the costs for these new entertainment centers as well. Why? It was hoped the billions of dollars invested by state and local governments in sports, cultural, and entertainment centers would make central cities more attractive places to live and work. Elected leaders also hoped these new venues would bring visitors from suburban areas and other tourists so that downtown areas would again

1

be "the place to be" and the years of decline would soon be replaced by crowds eager to live, work, and play in comeback cities and new downtowns.

A. The Era of Subsidies and Hope

This latest wave of public investments was not the first time local governments had paid for sports, cultural, and entertainment facilities in efforts to improve the quality of life and enhance their economic futures.[1] What made this new wave of public investments unique was that state and local governments agreed to build and maintain these new facilities while permitting team owners, producers, and other investors to retain all the revenues generated *and* pay little or no rent. Team owners were offered state-of-the-art facilities that included luxury seating and numerous new advertising opportunities including the right to sell a name for the facility to the highest bidder. Airlines, high tech firms, and banks frequently placed their names on sports facilities and some long-term deals often delivered $100 million to a team's bottom line. In addition, the new designs provided improved sight lines for fans, meeting areas to socialize, and expansive retail centers for the sale of memorabilia. Food and beverage services and choices were expanded and the profits earned by teams that called these new sports palaces home soared. Performing arts centers followed the lead with regard to naming rights and soon facilities from Austin, Texas, to Estes Park, Colorado and from Durham, North Carolina, to Livermore and Los Angeles, California, were adorned with the names of corporations and other benefactors, and these facilities also required large taxpayer investments.

In the debates over the appropriateness of using tax dollars to build sports, cultural, and entertainment facilities, the most pointed criticism has been directed at the financing plans for ballparks, stadiums, and arenas. With control over all revenue streams and little of their own money involved in paying for the new facilities, the value of teams soared. When some owners sold their teams, the profits earned were in excess of $200 million, and the 100 and 200 percent return on their investments was a direct result of the use of tax dollars to build the new facilities that contained new ways for teams to earn more and more revenue from fans. Team owners were not the only ones to benefit. Some of the higher profits found their way to the players and many more of them became millionaires. But fans continued to buy tickets and attendance levels soared. So, what was the cause of all the criticism?

While owners, players, and fans benefited and enjoyed the new facilities, the cities that made the investments found themselves with higher levels of debt and taxes as well as frustrated dreams of revitalized downtowns. What went wrong for cities in these "public/private partnerships" with team owners to ensure new facilities were built? The combination of sports, entertainment, and culture was the three-pronged approach used to rebuild downtown areas and create new images for a city and its center. However, sports facilities and entertainment and cultural centers by themselves are unlikely to change a region's economy.[2] Most of the spending that takes places at these venues would occur within the region even if the new facilities were not built. In the absence of attending games, shows, or other live performances, people spend money on other things.[3] As a result sports facilities and cultural centers generate little regional economic development and only a few regions attract sufficient numbers of tourists to change overall development levels.[4] The hope that sports and other cultural facilities would create new jobs and generate revenues to improve cities was crushed by the reality of new debt levels and higher taxes.

B. What Can New Facilities Do for a Region?

New sports and cultural facilities do change where people spend money.[5] That change provides community leaders with a strategic opportunity to capitalize on the attraction of large crowds and use the new location for that economic activity to leverage development. Sports facilities, entertainment complexes, and cultural facilities that are part of large-scale redevelopment efforts involving substantial levels of private investment can renew downtown areas, creating new images, and generating real economic development. But, outcomes like that require plans and a substantial investment of private capital.[6]

Many communities in the 1980s and 1990s invested tax money in sports, entertainment, and cultural facilities hoping improvements would follow. It was then again hoped that new buildings would attract scores of young professionals and new companies to their downtown areas. Simply put, too many cities did more "hoping" than they did planning a strategy or establishing partnerships with private capital to achieve success.[7] Some cities, however, did just what was necessary to turn subsidies into shrewd investments. What made these cities different from others and what can community leaders and public officials learn that can turn tax dollars from subsidies to investments?

C. Subsidies and Strategic Investments: The Difference Defined

In some cities voters and community leaders refused to support higher taxes to pay for sports or performing arts venues without detailed redevelopment strategies or substantial private sector investments. In these communities, voters and leaders were willing to make strategic investments, but wanted to avert anything that appeared to be a subsidy. What is the difference between a strategic investment and a subsidy? A subsidy is when the public sector pays for most or all of the cost of building (and maintaining) a sports, entertainment, and cultural center while team owners, organizations, or other entrepreneurs retain all or most of the revenues from the staging of events *without* any substantial investment from these beneficiaries in redevelopment activities. An investment by the public sector, in contrast, would be defined by: (1) increased tax revenues that *substantially* offset the tax dollars spent, (2) the building of a new or revitalized neighborhood as a result of private investment, or (3) more jobs or higher salaries for residents that produces more tax revenues.[8] To be sure there is risk for the public sector in these investments when private capital is committed. Assuming a level of risk when private investors do the same is far different from subsidizing a facility without requiring similar levels of investment and risk by private sector partners. This book is about changing public subsidies into investments in partnerships where equal and appropriate risks were assumed by the private sector.

II. Sports, Entertainment, and Culture for Image, Attracting Human Capital, and Economic Development

Why did voters, elected officials, and community leaders continue to raise taxes to subsidize sports and other cultural facilities when the initial warnings were that there would be no economic benefits?[9] The reasons vary, but the themes, in every instance, are quite familiar. When it comes to sports, many argue that large cities or regions without teams did not have a "major league image" and that second-rate images meant businesses and high-skilled workers would choose to locate elsewhere.[10] One St. Louis leader when asked why he favored a subsidy to convince the National Football League's (NFL) Rams to move from California to Missouri replied that too many people thought the city's best days were behind it (because they had lost their football team to Phoenix). The Rams would make St. Louis "big league" again in ways the St. Louis Cardinals (baseball team) or Washington University could not.[11] By extension, smaller cities, in an effort to elevate and distinguish themselves to businesses and create an image of a higher quality of life sought to attract minor league teams, so they too were part of the sports culture of the country.[12] And regardless of size, if a city did not have a venue to attract concerts and host shows and plays, it too risked being seen as too quaint and boring (too few concerts, shows, or other events) to attract and retain the human capital twenty-first century businesses need.

Most cities also looked to new sports facilities and cultural centers as tools to help rebuild deteriorating downtown areas or town squares. Leaders hoped the crowds and excitement of games and shows or other events would convince some people to think about living downtown and attract some of the retail and commercial businesses that were heading to expanding suburban areas. Some cities even hoped an exciting downtown could reduce the exodus of residents and businesses heading to other parts of the country or cities, such as Boston, Chicago, and New York, that seemed to have a diverse set of sports, entertainment, and cultural amenities that contributed to regional economic development. For other cities, entertainment venues were ways of convincing people that cities and their downtown areas were safe places to visit, dine, and enjoy an evening's entertainment. In areas where riots or large-scale demographic changes had taken place, just getting people to come downtown was a lofty goal. For many cities, the excitement of "Play Ball" or "It's Showtime" were efforts to recapture the years when central cities were the economic, social, and entertainment capitals of their regions and seen as safe and alluring places to visit and spend a day.

To be sure, sports teams are treasured assets; when tens of millions of fans will pay billions of dollars for tickets, it is clear that sports are important to people. That importance would not lead to tax subsidies if the major sports leagues were not given the ability to control the supply and location of teams. Antitrust exemptions and special laws allow the leagues to create auctions where cities compete to host teams.[13] If any city does not meet an owner's demands, teams have the ability to move elsewhere and the leagues—more often than not—would only replace the team if an even larger subsidy were provided in later years. However, to understand why cities turned to sports and entertainment to change economic development patterns, a bit more history is needed.

III. The Beginning of an End to the Need for Central Cities

When Americans began their mass movement to suburban areas in the post-World War II years, central city leaders initially took passing interest in the changing population patterns. The country was enjoying an extraordinary movement of people from rural to metropolitan areas and there were still new waves of foreign immigrants. Central cities and their suburbs *both* grew through the late 1940s and into the 1950s and there was no reason for America's central cities to fret about their stature or the growth of suburban cities. Baltimore, Cleveland, Detroit, and St. Louis, like New York, Boston, and Chicago dominated their regions' economies and social life; these were salad days for America's cities.

A. *Population Change*

By 1960, however, an ominous trend had emerged. The proportion of people choosing to live in the suburbs instead of a central city had dramatically shifted. By 1960, 31 percent of the U.S. population lived in suburban cities, a proportion virtually equal to the 32 percent living in central cities. Within a decade, the central cities that used to define their regions would account for less than one-third of the nation's residents while suburban areas had become home to 37.6 percent of the nation's population. The gap continued to grow and suburban cities accounted for 44.8 percent of the U.S. population in 1980, 46.2 percent in 1990, and fully half of the nation's population by the 2000 Census.[14] Complacency turned to panic for the leadership in America's central cities as these areas no longer dominated or defined their regions. Indeed, in some areas, the central cities were losing so many middle and upper class families that the average income of families in center cities was less than half of the average income of families in the suburbs. The economic and social leadership of many regions seemed to pass, overnight, from the larger cities that had dominated for more than a century to the suburban communities that surrounded aging and decaying core cities. Even Boston, Chicago, and New York lost residents. The percentage declines were particularly substantial for St. Louis, Cleveland, and Detroit where more than a third of each city's 1950 population base was lost. City–county consolidation in Indianapolis led to the higher population number in 1970, but out-migration continued with a decline for the merged city–county in 1980. The loss of residents does not necessarily mean that wealth or centrality is not being maintained. In the long run, however, declining population numbers usually leads to economic contraction and then longer-term declines. The overall pattern was clear and the fear of higher proportions of lower income residents concentrated in central cities and far fewer high-paying jobs in downtown areas focused the attention of the leaders of central cities on the ways their communities could compete with suburban areas for residents (Table 1.1).

With so many households relocating to the suburbs, new retail centers followed. Several center cities could do little more than watch as numerous large department stores that from the 1940s and 1950s defined the holiday season and the vibrant life of downtown areas closed their doors in the 1970s and 1980s. With changing transportation and communication costs, businesses found they, too, could easily (and more profitably) locate in suburban areas. By 1996, across the 100 largest metropolitan areas, just 22 percent of the region's jobs were within three miles of the center city's core area, and, in 34 of the largest regions, at least 40 percent of all jobs were located 10 miles or more from the downtown center. Included in this group were Baltimore, Cleveland, Cincinnati, Detroit, Phoenix, and San Diego, cities that would or had focused on building downtown sports facilities to slow suburbanization. Columbus and Indianapolis, two state capitals, which also focused on downtown sports development, both had more than a third of their region's jobs located 10 miles or more from their downtown centers.[15] With more and more people living farther and farther from downtown areas, entertainment and cultural centers began a suburban exodus as well. In virtually every city in the United States, the grand downtown theaters built in the 1920s were closed and, in some instances, razed. From cities as small as Reading (Pennsylvania) to the mid-sized, such as Indianapolis, Cleveland, Fort Worth, and Dallas, to larger ones like Detroit, the grand theaters were fading as fast as downtown department stores.

The smugness with which center city leaders watched the initial growth of suburban areas was replaced by an urgency to compete first with suburban areas and then with faster growing regions for a share of residents and businesses. The initial focus of this competition included a reinvigoration of retail trade based on the festival marketplace designs of James W. Rouse. His legendary designs tried to

Table 1.1   Population Changes in Selected Central Cities, 1950 to 1980

Central City	1950	1960	1970	1980	Change 1950 to 1980	Percent Change
Baltimore	949,708	939,024	905,759	786,775	–162,933	–17.2
Boston	801,444	697,197	641,071	562,994	–238,450	–29.8
Chicago	3,620,962	3,550,404	3,366,957	3,005,072	–615,890	–17.0
Cincinnati	503,998	502,550	452,524	385,457	–118,541	–23.5
Cleveland	914,808	876,050	750,903	573,822	–340,986	–37.3
Detroit	1,849,568	1,670,144	1,511,482	1,203,339	–646,229	–34.9
Indianapolis	427,173	476,258	744,624	700,807	–43,817[a]	–5.9
Kansas City	456,622	475,539	507,087	448,159	–8,463	–1.9
New York	7,891,957	7,781,984	7,894,862	7,071,639	–820,318	–10.4
St. Louis	856,796	750,026	622,236	453,085	–403,711	–47.1

[a] Indianapolis consolidated with Marion County and that accounts for the large population increase from 1960 to 1970. However, even the consolidation could not stem the outflow of residents to surrounding counties from 1970 to 1980.
Source: U.S. Bureau of the Census, various years.

create unique retail experiences in historical buildings, classical meeting places, or any other unique or unusual facilities that remained in downtown areas. Why use retail centers to reclaim past glory? Central cities, after all, had always been the location of glamorous shopping experiences. Rouse and others were attracted to the potential for remodeling historical buildings that were unique civic assets that still dominated the physical space of downtown areas. These buildings and railway stations often had intriguing architectural charms that could not be recreated and were in many instances the antithesis of sterile big box and block designs used for the suburban malls of the 1970s and 1980s. Those retail centers could boast little more than oceans of parking surrounding their bland buildings as few shopping centers paid any attention to the grand designs and architecture of America's legendary downtown department stores and arcades.

B. Rise, Decline, and Lessons Learned from Festival Marketplaces

It was hoped the new festival marketplaces with their unique charms and architecture would create an unusual retail experience and wrestle shoppers away from the cookie-cutter suburban malls and asphalt surroundings. Indeed, many of the redesigned grand buildings did recreate a special or different feeling akin to what may have existed in downtown areas in the 1940s and 1950s.

The Quincy Market at Faneuil Hall in Boston opened in the 1970s and its success at attracting crowds made it a model for cities like Indianapolis and St. Louis. Those cities lacked a meeting place as historic as Faneuil Hall, but they did have grand railroad stations, long underutilized and often abandoned. Those architectural treasures were remodeled into retail centers with unusual hotels (using railway cars or other assets from the train stations). Some festival marketplaces were successful, but numerous ones failed. Many central cities learned that merely packaging the same retail opportunities found in suburban malls in "new look" centers with unique historical and architectural features could not stop the movement of people to suburban areas or alter their preference to shop near where they lived. Suburbanites clearly indicated that their preference was for retail shopping located close to where they lived and where they could easily park their car. The attractiveness of festival marketplaces, simply put, did not create sufficient excitement (or offer unique experiences or stores). Suburban residents preferred easier access and convenient parking when shopping for clothes, furniture, appliances, art, and jewelry. Suburban malls may have been nothing more than a series of boxes linked together, but they had ample parking and were located close to where people lived.

The history of festival marketplaces taught civic leaders harsh, but important lessons. First, if there were to be any return of retail or consumer-based activities to downtown areas, truly unique experiences (and stores) that were unavailable in suburban locations would have to be offered. Second, that uniqueness would have to be accompanied by convenient parking options or close access to reliable mass transportation to get suburbanites to return to the downtown area. Uniqueness was the first priority; transportation ease was second. Third, retail experiences by themselves could not bolster people's interest in visiting, working, and possibly living in central cities.[16] What were needed were unique activities that did not exist anywhere else in a region. The search was on for that uniqueness or silver bullet. Sports and culture quickly assumed new positions of prominence.

C. *Indianapolis and a Civic Image Strategy*

Indianapolis was probably the first central city to blaze a new trail, learning some of its lessons from a failed festival marketplace. In the late 1970s, to save its downtown, Indianapolis' leadership launched an effort to become the "amateur sports capital" of the United States, while also including professional sports and cultural centers in their plans. Its National Basketball Association (NBA) team, the Pacers, was relocated from a midtown location to a new downtown arena, and a domed stadium was built to help attract an NFL team. Its grand theater was resurrected and became the permanent home of the Indianapolis Symphony, which also returned to downtown from a midtown location.[17] Indianapolis' apparent success in bringing hundreds of thousands of visitors to its new downtown through a policy focused on sports and entertainment attracted the interest and attention of several other cities with deteriorating core areas. Overnight, the festival marketplace had been replaced by sports and unique entertainment as the centerpiece of efforts to revitalize a city and its downtown area.

Why could sports, cultural, and entertainment centers succeed where festival marketplaces could not? Sports—and by this was meant facilities for large-scale events and games played by teams from the four major sports leagues or minor league teams—could not exist simultaneously in the suburbs and a downtown area. The same could be said for hosting live performance and concerts and for major cultural centers. Most regions had but one team from each sport and where they chose to play created a unique opportunity for development, as did theaters for the performing arts.

By the early 1980s, building new facilities for a region's professional sports teams emerged as the most popular policy tool to redevelop deteriorating downtown areas. Many cities that did not have a Major League Baseball (MLB), NFL, NBA, or National Hockey League (NHL) team set their sights on getting an expansion franchise or luring a team from another region. Those who could not get a team in one of the four major sports leagues frequently turned their attention to minor league teams and the performing arts in efforts to create unique downtown experiences. Again, a region that attracted touring theatrical companies or that had a resident orchestra could have those events take place only in one area or part of the region. The "home" venue for these events created unique experiences that attracted a region's residents. Many cities decided to pursue both strategies—use spectator sports and other unique performing arts opportunities to rebuild and restore downtown areas. Hosting unique regional entertainment venues became the policy rage in the 1980s, and the trend has yet to end.

D. Rise of Sports and Culture for Revitalization

Believing sports, entertainment, and culture were the "keys" to changing downtown areas, cities across North America raised taxes and spent billions of dollars to build facilities. While the vast majority of these efforts, like the festival marketplaces before them, failed to produce direct economic benefits for the investor-cities, this book focuses on the success some cities had that created real economic and community development opportunities. The lessons learned from this success can help other community leaders achieve positive outcomes from the investment of their tax dollars in sports, cultural, and entertainment venues. The book provides communities with a blueprint that ensures that the taxes spent on sports and entertainment facilities do far more than enhance the wealth of team owners, athletes, or entrepreneurs, and create better venues for fans. The analysis of outcomes in Indianapolis, San Diego, Los Angeles, Columbus, Ohio, Cleveland, and Reading, Pennsylvania, offer important lessons for large and small metropolitan areas across the world where sports, entertainment, and culture are being linked to revitalization efforts. Each of these case studies examines public/private partnerships, their accomplishments, and the important lessons for other cities.

It might seem that Los Angeles has little in common with Indianapolis and Cleveland and that lessons from San Diego would add little to the work underway in smaller regions or regions struggling with declining economic fortunes. Yet, as the analyses of the challenges faced and goals established will show, the lessons learned in each public/private partnership can help communities elsewhere that are focused on revitalization. The goal of this book is not to provide communities with a single blueprint, but with options and ideas for turning sports and other large-scale investments in entertainment and the arts into assets for development and growth.

Some policy analysts have criticized redevelopment anchored by public subsidies for sports, entertainment, convention centers, and museums.[18] These analysts are concerned that these projects deflect cities from pursuing other policies that are more likely to generate larger economic development returns.[19] There is also substantial concern that business leaders in concert with elected officials slant the use of public investments to ensure their corporations or wealthier residents of a region enjoy the benefits from the tax money used to build these facilities. There is no disagreement that tax dollars used for amenities that do not produce a broad range of benefits and redevelop downtown are indeed inappropriate subsidies.[20] The goal of this book is to identify the tactics and policies different cities used to ensure that their use of tax money for different amenities produced a broad set of benefits, including redeveloped downtown areas.

Attention is also directed at the community and citywide development activities pursued by each city. These elements are reviewed to illustrate that even when there was a focus by business and political leaders on downtown redevelopment there was often a simultaneous focus on job creation, community development activities, the rebuilding of neighborhoods, and, in one case, the advancement of an inner city school district. Despite what some critics have suggested, a focus on sports did not eliminate a more comprehensive approach to redevelopment activities. The presentation of information on downtown and other activities is designed to respond to those who argue that a focus on entertainment and other amenities for redevelopment simply panders to business interests concerned with elevating downtown property values and ensuring that tax money benefits corporate interests and the interests of higher income residents of a region.

IV. Why Should Cities Care about Sports, Entertainment, and Culture?

Critics of the focus on sports and entertainment to redevelop cities have correctly observed that such a perspective fundamentally realigns the purpose of local government. Initially, local governments' primary responsibilities for economic development included making sure that clean water and other necessary utilities were readily available. In time, local governments were also expected to help protect the public's health, build and operate quality schools, build and maintain local roads and other forms of transportation, protect the public from crime and improperly built and maintained buildings, and enhance the quality of life through the construction and support of public parks and libraries. Professional sports and larger performing arts centers were not on this initial list of priorities or responsibilities; the building of ballparks, stadiums, arenas, and concert halls was left to the private sector or philanthropic organizations. The public sector's focus was on guaranteeing an inherently democratic and equitable framework in fulfilling responsibilities that provided quality urban services, assets, and amenities to all residents regardless of their income and race.[21] In several instances, cities were found to provide different levels of services in different communities, and that sometimes led to the lawsuits and charges of discrimination.

Several cities, however, did make early efforts to attract sports teams. For example, in the 1950s, Baltimore convinced the St. Louis Browns to become the Orioles, the Boston Braves moved to Milwaukee, and the Dodgers and Giants were lured to Los Angeles and San Francisco. For most cities, however, a focus on sports teams or the building of large performing arts centers were not part of their public policy agenda in the post-World War II era. When central cities were growing markets, professional sports teams and entrepreneurs were eager to build new facilities to attract fans to sporting events and other forms of entertainment.[22] With downtown areas as the regional hub for recreation, arts organizations were also eager to build facilities at the center of a region's growing market. Cities were able to focus on ensuring an appropriate physical infrastructure existed while the private sector invested in the sports and entertainment industry and built its needed facilities.

This situation, of course, changed dramatically in the 1960s and 1970s with the explosive growth of the suburbs, the movement of people and jobs to the Far West, Southwest, and the South, and the beginning of the end of the Midwest's overwhelmingly large and growing supply of manufacturing jobs. With large-scale changes underway, issues involving the quality of life in central cities and in numerous eastern and midwestern regions began to dominate discussions of economic development. Many central cities were suddenly eager to consider larger and expanded roles in building a quality of life that encouraged people and businesses to stay.[23] Faced with the loss of wealthier residents to the suburbs and, in some instances, to other parts of the nation, many central cities, especially those in the Midwest, feared that if existing trends continued they would be unable to generate the taxes they needed to provide services to their residents and businesses and the growing concentrations of lower income households. As a result, to the classical agenda of a city's responsibilities were now added the building and maintenance of a high quality of life that would help to retain and attract middle and upper income households. These households not only had the taxpayers that the cities needed, but they constituted the intellectual or human capital that businesses required for their future growth. If a city no longer attracted residents, corporations were forced to relocate to areas where their future employees wanted to live.[24] The millennium of business location being dictated by geography was rapidly coming to a close as transportation and communication costs declined. The new millennium of environments for creative people was emerging, and cities that were not attractive to educated workers faced a declining economic future.[25]

A. *Human Capital and Amenities*

The changing structure of the United States and world economy—and the breakthroughs in communication and transportation—meant that companies could now locate where the best and brightest workers wanted to live. As people's income rose, they also wanted to live in areas that offered a greater number of varied and interesting tourism experiences that could be enjoyed on weekends. Thus, the new middle and upper classes wanted high-quality urban services and a high quality of life in what Pine and Gilmore (1999)[26] described as the "experience economy." It was not only that work and presentations had become wedded to experiences; it was that consumers had shifted their preferences to include a desire to be able to enjoy experiences through the unique entertainment produced by sports, arts, culture, and other amenities. Cities that offered the full range of these experiences were more desirable and businesses worried about being able to attract and retain the best talent sought locations that had the highest quality of life, the best mix of amenities, and a set of large-scale and neighborhood-based entertainment experiences that seemed to describe what America's "creative class" (Florida, 2002) or "idea generators" wanted when they chose places to live. People still lived where the jobs are, but companies that created those jobs wanted to locate where they were confident there would be the right mix of amenities that would appeal to the idea generators they needed to advance their business. Economic development is driven by human capital and corporations choose to locate in areas where they are most confident present and future employees want to live.

Professional sports remain an integral part of this mix and ignoring them was not a viable option. Communities do need to make public safety and education their highest priorities and can have a very high quality of life without being home to a professional sports team or a major collegiate sports program. Yet, virtually all of the towns and cities on the myriad "best places to live" lists are located in close proximity to facilities that are home to one or more professional sports teams, entertainment and performing arts centers, or universities and colleges with major sports programs.[27] The real opportunity for a city's leadership is not to choose between sports and public safety or education, but to understand how some community leaders in places like Indianapolis, Columbus, Ohio, San Diego, and Los Angeles were able to use sports, entertainment, and cultural facilities to advance the quality of life while producing tax revenue that could be used for public safety or any other needed service. As Eisinger observed,

> Few people would argue with the proposition that facilities that bring
> high or even mass culture, sports, and recreational opportunities to
> a city may enhance the quality of life. Stadiums and performing arts
> centers and festival malls help to transform places that would otherwise
> simply be markets or dormitories. ... The issue, then, is not whether to
> spend public money [for sports or entertainment facilities]; rather the
> issue is a matter of balance and proportionality.[28]

This book is about the balance achieved by successful leadership in several different cities and the positive economic development outcomes that took place. In each of the case studies, the risks taken by the cities, the commitment by the private sector, and the specific plans developed will be discussed. The outcomes in each situation for the downtown areas, for the cities and their financial capabilities, and other impacts will also be identified. Through these analyses, the opportunities available to other cities will be identified.

B. Are Sports, Entertainment, and Culture a City's Fool's Gold?

If numerous festival marketplaces failed, why should anyone have any faith that the outcomes for a San Diego or Columbus—if indeed successful and positive—were nothing more than unique cases? What is it that makes sports or entertainment different from retail (or other assets) that enables those venues to become special anchors for a development strategy that can help advance a city's economic development or public policy agenda? The ability of sports, entertainment, or culture to anchor urban development strategies lies in its timeless importance in virtually every society. While some disdain the importance of sports or simply ignore it, sports, for example, have been and remain an integral part of most, if not all, societies. Its history as a central part of societies and civilizations spans thousands of years. Some might think the mass popularity of sports is a product of the modern media age, ESPN, and fantasy leagues. Sports, however, had a similar level of importance for past civilizations that probably matches the zeal among those with fantasy teams and those willing to pay premium prices for the best seats to important games or championship contests. To be sure, at no other time in history have athletes earned the financial rewards now available, and never before have prices for tickets to some events been so expensive as demand for experiences continues to exceed supply. Some professional sports teams have become so popular that their market value exceeds a billion dollars. That, too, is a new phenomenon, but what is not new is people's focus on and interest in sports.

For example, ancient Rome used sports to showcase its technological achievements as well as its wealth through the building of a facility replete with luxury seating, the ability to host both aquatic and land-based spectacles, and room for 50,000 spectators. The Colosseum, built more than 1,900 years ago, was larger in terms of spectator capacity than the home fields of every MLB team except the New

York Yankees and the Los Angeles Dodgers.[29] Its incorporation of luxury seating with colorful cloth coverings to protect the elite from the sweltering sun was said to be part of the inspiration for the building of America's first indoor stadium, Houston's Astrodome and luxury seating.

For Western societies, written records from as early as 776 BCE document the importance placed on sport; those records are the earliest reports of the competition known as the Olympics. Some believe, however, that the Olympic competitions might have been held even earlier. Regardless, the games continued for more than six centuries before being abolished by the Romans in 393 CE. The Roman contribution to sport—some credit the Empire with the creation of professional sports or, at least, making sports a profession—begins in 310 BCE with the onset of gladiatorial games and the establishment of training centers for combatants. By 183 BCE, major gladiatorial contests involved as many as 60 pairs of fighters with far larger spectacles to follow in later years. The apex of sports in the Roman Empire involved the building of the Colosseum and the staging of events involving boats, animals, and gladiators. Beyond the brutality of gladiatorial games and the construction of facilities throughout the empire to underscore the Empire's prowess, the Romans also used sport facilities as a central component of the design of cities from Rome through the Decapolis (the 10 cities on the Eastern edge of the empire) to Pula (Croatia). Roman cities had sports facilities or performing arts venues at their center, a pattern American cities would follow in the 1980s and 1990s when many tried to rebuild deteriorating downtown areas abandoned by residents and businesses that preferred more suburban locations.

The Romans' credit for professionalizing sports is a result of their establishment of training centers (schools) for gladiators and a system where "rookies" or gladiators with lower or untested skills were sent to contests in smaller cities (or markets). As gladiators won matches in these "minor league" markets, they were promoted to matches in larger cities. Those who eventually made it to Rome could actually win their freedom if they survived. The technological mastery of flooding the lowest levels of the Colosseum to permit water games established the prowess of the Empire's engineering skills and was an early forerunner of the design of facilities to handle many different types of events. In the modern era, arenas are designed for basketball and other platform-type events, ice hockey and shows, and events involving dirt racing and "monster trucks."

Sport events also have a long history of being part of religious or holiday celebrations. The Great Ball Court at Mexico's Chichen-Itza is more than 1,000 years old and was the site of games tied to religious rites including human sacrifices that took place at the conclusion of the matches. The Hippodrome of Constantinople was the sporting and social center built in the second century (CE) and then expanded by Constantine in 324. The races held at this location began at least 1,700 years ago making sport a central part of urban life in the Byzantine period and extending through the years of the Ottoman Empire. The city's largest religious center faces the Hippodrome.[30]

Sports' cross-cultural significance or role is also underscored by the game of lacrosse. Invented by Native Americans, it received its modern name from French missionaries, and became adopted by many settlers in the New World. When the playing of lacrosse began is unclear, but what is apparent is that the native population of North, Central, and South America played sports long before the Europeans arrived. Sports have been part of numerous societies and assuming central religious, political, and social roles for at least 2,500 years. Today, sports remain an integral part of holiday celebrations with featured games on Christmas Day and the celebration of the New Year dominated by college football's bowl games.

The long-standing role of culture and entertainment in society is easily underscored by the role of the performing arts and plays in ancient Greece. The emergence and importance of the English theater dates back at least 500 years. Music's role in defining a city's identity and its cultural standing shares a similar if not a longer history. The continuing and long-standing nature of these assets suggests the prudence of their incorporation in revitalization strategies.

While some might dislike sports, their enduring importance and the physical value placed on the facilities used for games is what makes sports part of the social capital of a society. Social capital has been defined as institutions that facilitate "the development of relationships of mutual reciprocity embedded in social networks that enable action ... generate trust, establish expectations, and create norms. Social capital's value centres upon the fact that it identifies certain important aspects of a community's social structure and the significance of social organization."[31] Sports also become part of the social capital of a society through their role as socializing institutions that increase stability and as tools to underscore the political values and strength of a society.[32] Lefebrve has concluded that places within a city that encourage identification with a group facilitate the ability of individuals to build relationships that enhance identities and reduce the stress of isolation that can be endemic in large urban societies.[33]

How do sports and the facilities they use create this type of social capital? Any community can point to celebrations when teams win major games or championships and the "electricity" that seems to change daily life.[34] The power or strength of a society is underscored by the facilities built for sports, a point familiar to students of Roman history as when the gladiatorial games were held in the large structures built by the engineering expertise of the Roman Empire or when different governments and regimes seek to stage major athletic events to underscore the superiority and accomplishments of their society. The Greeks staging of the original Olympics to proclaim the virtues of their civilization underscored their achievements. In the modern era, international events in Berlin (1936) and Beijing (2008) were designed to emphasize the advancements and success of different political regimes. America's return to some level of normalcy after the 9/11 attacks was inexorably tied to the resumption of MLB games and the staging of the World Series.[35] The outpouring of emotion at these sporting events is probably the most poignant example of the role of sports as social capital. Social scientists have noted baseball's role in socializing immigrants to

American life in the early parts of the twentieth century and soccer's role in relieving the drudgery of industrial life in England and maintaining stability.[36]

Some might still note that there were ancient retail centers that attracted large crowds, and these, too, dominated in the center parts of cities across numerous empires. Are downtown sports facilities destined to fail, as have many downtown retail centers? Here the issue of an unique activity within a region and its availability at only one central location is critical. Professional sports teams, and to a similar extent live performances by leading entertainers and museums, cannot be replicated in multiple neighborhoods. While retail was able to decentralize to suburban areas, the vast majority of metropolitan regions will only have one team in each of the four major sports leagues, one set of museums, and a major arena for first-run concerts.[37] Where these teams play creates unique experiences for that region. The nation's largest metropolitan regions—New York, Chicago, and Los Angeles—have more than one team in some leagues, but the large population bases or unique historical circumstances explain these anomalies. Today, as will be explained in the next section, each of the four major sports leagues jealously protect the market interests of each owner by attempting to make certain that no new teams are created that could reduce the earnings of any other owner.

V. Sports, Entertainment, and Culture: The Trinity for Redevelopment

While sports facilities have received the most attention in assessments of redevelopment efforts, in virtually every instance, entertainment, arts, and cultural centers were integral parts of the overall development plan. Baltimore's Harborfront included a new ballpark and stadium, but it is also home to the National Aquarium. Indianapolis wanted to become the amateur sports capital, but its extensive downtown redevelopment plan included refurbished performance halls for the Indianapolis Symphony and the Indiana Repertory Theatre and several museums. Cleveland's redevelopment effort included five theaters for the performing arts and two museums. Reading, Little Rock, and Louisville each also included the performing arts as anchors in their redevelopment, and L.A. LIVE may well establish a new standard for a downtown entertainment zone with several theaters for movies and the performing arts joined to residential space, a museum, and a hotel. In essence, then, when the analysis is done of how cities successfully used sports for redevelopment, the formula also is laden with examples of the use of performing arts centers.

A. Cities, Sports Facilities, and Subsidies

The mania to revitalize cities and enhance their images through sports, entertainment centers, and the arts and culture begins with Indianapolis' declared policy to be the amateur sports capital of America in the 1970s. In the 1980s and 1990s, redevelopment focusing on sports and entertainment became a cross-continental mania. During three decades, taxpayers across North America paid all or most of the cost for building dozens of sports facilities.[38] Why did they do this? They and their elected officials were driven by a fear that if they failed to give a team or a sports league what they demanded some other city would "pay the piper" and an integral part of the losing city's image and quality of life would decline. That decline was seen as a threat to the ability to attract and retain corporations, which were afraid that many "losing" cities would be seen as less desirable by the human capital they needed for their own development.

Team owners were quick to capitalize on these fears and bidding wars ensued where the city that often paid what was demanded got to keep a beloved team or became a new home to the franchise. The fear that the city that failed to meet a team's demand would lose the franchise was not irrational. In the 1980s and 1990s, the Baltimore Colts, Los Angeles Rams, Cleveland Browns, and Houston Oilers moved to other cities, each in response to a better offer for a new stadium from, respectively, Indianapolis, St. Louis, Baltimore, and Nashville. The Chicago White Sox and Cleveland Indians announced they too would move if a tax-supported facility was not built, and rather than calling their bluff both communities raised taxes. New facilities with tax subsidies were also provided by several cities to secure expansion franchises. Cleveland (Browns), Denver (Rockies), Houston (Texans), and Phoenix (Diamondbacks) promised MLB and the NFL they would build new stadiums or ballparks if awarded a new franchise and each was successful in getting the team it wanted.

What has been the result of this tax-and-build frenzy for cities and regions? From an economic development standpoint, independent researchers have reached six sets of conclusions.

1. At the regional level, facilities and teams have only marginal effects, at best, on economic development.
2. Facilities developed for large-scale events that attract a large number of tourists can have very positive short-term effects, but there is scant evidence of any longer-term positive effects. Indeed some work suggests that, after the Olympics or World Cup, tourism levels drop substantially leaving regions with underutilized facilities or an excess of hotel rooms and other amenities that may be financially draining to support.[39]
3. If a set of amenities can continue on an annual basis to attract a large number of events that bring tourists to an area, some positive outcomes can be sustained.[40]
4. It does matter where facilities are built, in that downtown locations are able to (1) concentrate other amenities into a package that enhances local spending in the area of a facility and (2) it is indeed possible to move recreational spending through a facility's placement that does change local revenue streams.[41]

HELPING OWNERS AND PLAYERS AMASS FORTUNES

Taxpayer-supported subsidies are just one of the factors that can lead to increases in the values of teams and higher salaries for players. Television contracts and ticket revenues can be equally or more important in terms of increasing a team's value or the salaries paid to players. When teams do not have to pay the full cost for building facilities, that also improves everyone's bottom line. How well did the owners and players do?

Figure 1.1 shows the value of numerous NFL franchises in 1995 and 2007 as estimated by *Forbes*. Each of these teams moved into a new or substantially renovated facility that benefited from a large tax subsidy. The values for the Houston Texans (1999) and Cleveland Browns (1998) are based on the fees paid by their owners when the franchises were created. All values are in 2007 dollars, and the average gain in the value of the franchises was 227 percent. Many other factors contributed to this impressive change including a new television contract and higher ticket fees, but a subsidized facility also helped each team's bottom line.

The players have also done very well. Using salary figures for the 2000 and 2006 seasons (and for 2002 for the first year of play for the Houston Texans), the players enjoyed a 53.1 percent real increase in salaries and the increment was 65.2 percent if the Texans were excluded from the analysis (Figure 1.2). Camden Yards in Baltimore was the first of the new ballparks and, by 2010, 24 of MLB's teams will be playing in new or substantially remodeled facilities. Across the time period when each of the teams in Figure 1.3 moved into new ballparks, players' salaries have increased 220 percent (constant dollars) without including the extraordinary salaries paid by the New York Yankees or the Boston Red Sox, teams that did not play in new facilities.

5. It is possible to use sports facilities to anchor redevelopment efforts if plans immediately include financial commitments from the private or nonprofit sectors. When this takes place development patterns do change.[42]
6. While there is scant evidence of any regional effects, where development occurs within a region may well be as important as if it occurs. Sports facilities can and do change that pattern when that development is concentrated in downtown areas with other amenities and with commitments of private and nonprofit investments.[43]

Team owners and players have also benefited from the decision by cities to compete for franchises through the provision of subsidies for the building of new facilities. The tax money raised to reduce the owners' costs of building and maintaining new facilities lowers a team's operating costs. In an era when fans crave experiences and are willing to pay premium prices to attend games in beautiful facilities, this

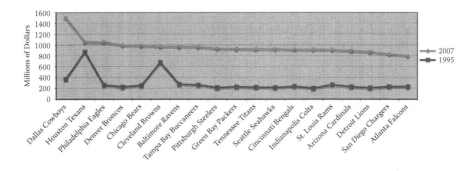

Figure 1.1   The changes in NFL team values after moving to a new facility: 1995, pre-new stadium value, 2007 post-new stadium value (in 2007 dollars). Created with data from *Forbes* magazine.

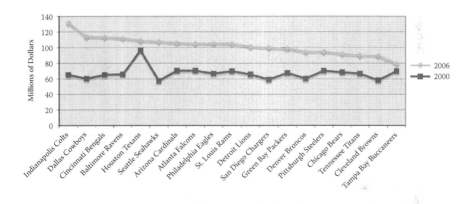

Figure 1.2   Real increases in NFL player salaries (in 2006 dollars). Created with data from *USA Today*.

has meant huge new revenue streams generating the potential for higher profits and players' salaries that have reached unprecedented levels. Simply put, the hundreds of millions of dollars borrowed by state and local governments to pay for new facilities have allowed team owners and athletes to realize new, previously unheard of levels of financial success that seemed unimaginable when Indianapolis and Baltimore launched this building spree. These two cities—focused on rebuilding their downtown areas—were then joined by a score of communities fearing being left with crumbling center cities or tarnished images if they were not home to major league teams. An "arms race" to provide team owners with new venues replete with new and lucrative revenue sources ensued. With a substantial portion of the construction or maintenance costs for these revenue streams supported by tax dollars, revenue levels exploded. This helped increase the value of teams to stratospheric levels and gave players the opportunity to demand a larger share of the revenue

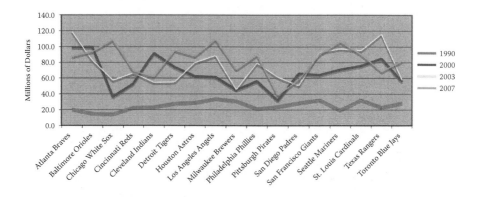

Figure 1.3   Real changes in MLB player salaries, 1990 to 2007 (in 2007 dollars). Created with data from *USA Today*.

from the luxury suites, club seats, enormous retail centers (team shops), numerous restaurants, and other attractions that were built into these sports palaces.

The new facilities also offered prominent opportunities for advertisers to paste their names across North America's urban landscape. Airlines, banks, high tech firms, health delivery organizations, energy companies, and insurance companies showered money on team owners to secure naming rights to entire facilities or to have an entrance way, plaza, or gate named for their company. Advertising on scoreboards and across walls—a time-honored practice in older facilities—continued as advertising messages adorned prominent walls and facades inside and outside the new facilities. A new technological innovation, ribbon boards, were installed around arenas and underneath the upper decks in ballparks and stadiums to provide constant advertisements and entertainment during every stoppage of play. In most instances, all of the profits from luxury seats, food, beverage, and souvenir sales, and, of course, the income from the naming rights and abundant advertising deals belonged to the teams.

If paying for all or a substantial part of a facility's construction cost while teams retained all or most of the revenue from suites and club seats, ticket sales, the sales of food, beverages, and souvenirs, and advertising was not enough to attract a team, some deals were even more generous. Some communities agreed to lease arrangements that minimized the franchise's responsibilities for rent and maintenance expenses.

B. Franchise Values and Changing the System

By 2007, *Forbes* magazine estimated that six franchises were worth more than $1 billion, with the Dallas Cowboys topping the list at $1.5 billion after receiving a $325 million subsidy for a new stadium. Twenty-two of the 32 teams in the NFL were estimated to be worth at least $900 million and more than 40 percent of all

MLB franchises were valued at $400 million or more. How did the players fare? They, too, were made substantially well off by taxpayers. Looking only at baseball teams that played in new or substantially remodeled ballparks in the 2007 season, players now earn—in real or inflation adjusted dollars—more than twice what they earned before the building spree began. How did the fans make out? Even after paying higher sales, parking, property, and car rental taxes to subsidize the new sports palaces, fans bought tens of millions of higher priced tickets. In 2007, 79.4 million tickets were sold to MLB games with fans undiscouraged by $50 ticket prices for some seats. In the NFL where tickets to regular season games are even more expensive, the league set its sixth straight attendance record in 2007 selling 22.2 million tickets even with individual game tickets in excess of $75. The NBA sold 43.6 million tickets to its games in the 2006–2007 season and prices for the best seats at many venues exceed $350. If these sports fans were frustrated by higher taxes for improved sports facilities, they did not show their frustration by boycotting games.

With fans buying tickets, it might seem there would be little interest from or benefit to owners from changing the system. There is, however, substantial dissatisfaction with the current system, and that festering resentment could be minimized, if not eliminated, with a different approach to facility development. For example, in many communities, large proportions of voters were against proposed tax increases even when a team threatened to move. MLB's commissioner, Fay Vincent, told Clevelanders he would support the team's relocation if they did not approve a tax hike to build a new ballpark, but 48 percent of the voters and a majority of those who lived and voted in Cleveland cast their ballots against a new ballpark.[44] The suburban residents who would pay more than two-thirds of the taxes to build the new facility were the margin of victory. Columbus, Ohio's voters rejected a subsidy for a new arena to secure an expansion franchise in the NHL and had the facility not been privately financed, the Blue Jackets would not have been created.

Jeffrey A. Timmons[45] found that slightly more than half, 54 percent of 35 referenda for tax-subsidized sports facilities over the past 27 years were passed; with 46 percent failing, there is clearly substantial discontent with the structure of many sports facility development proposals. While some proposals did enjoy very strong support (81 percent of the voters supported the building of a new ballpark and stadium in Detroit for the Tigers and Lions) in Arlington, Texas, even after an extensive and well-financed campaign by the Dallas Cowboys, the plan for $325 million in taxpayer support for a new stadium was supported by only 55 percent of the voters. There was virtually no financial support behind the antistadium forces, but a small group of opponents were able to convince 45 percent of the voters to oppose the use of tax dollars for a sports facility. In Houston, a proposal for a new ballpark received support from just 51.1 percent of the voters and a referendum placed before Milwaukee's voters for a new home for the Brewers was rejected. The ballpark was eventually built when the state legislature approved a substantial subsidy. The Minnesota Vikings and the Minnesota Twins saw several of their proposals for new facilities fail to receive legislative support and the Florida Marlins' proposals for a new ballpark was also initially rejected by the Florida legislature. The Tampa Bay Rays have also been seeking a new ballpark. By late 2008, progress had been made in Minneapolis (for the Vikings' new home) and in Miami (Florida Marlins) for new facilities after years of debate, but in St. Petersburg plans have yet to secure the needed public support even after the Tampa Bay Rays' unexpected American League pennant victory in 2008.

Electoral discontent is not the only measure of the resentment over the subsidies provided to teams. When the Colts left Baltimore for Indianapolis, they narrowly avoided seizure through an eminent domain action. The effort failed as the legal process took a few days and, when the Colts' owner heard about the threat, he arranged to move the team in the middle of the night. While Baltimore's effort was unsuccessful, in a resulting court action the right of a city to seize the tangible and intangible assets represented by a team was upheld. Baltimore's claim was only denied because the team had left a few hours before the papers could be legally served. As a result, while the Colts could not be seized, teams were declared assets that could be taken under eminent domain principles. Years later, Indiana's legislature held hearings on the issue of eminent domain and sports franchises when there was fear the Colts might leave. The city attorney of San Diego has ensnared the Chargers in numerous legal battles while also considering the use of eminent domain to prohibit a move. When the Browns moved from Cleveland to Baltimore, Ohio's Congressional delegation threatened to hold hearings regarding antitrust issues and the NFL's power to control the number of franchises that existed. Building partnerships that avoid these legal confrontations is in everyone's interests.

If teams were not important to communities, this conflict could just be shrugged off and classified as being far less critical than many of the other issues that mayors, county leaders, and communities must address. But sports and teams enjoy a level of importance and the ability to capitalize on that importance to secure subsidies calls for a very different approach to the building of sports facilities. Teams and the facilities they use generate a great deal of economic activity and attract a great deal of attention. These assets create the opportunity for cities and teams to fashion new approaches to the development of facilities that substantially enhance the financial benefits received by cities. If that can be achieved, citizens' dissatisfaction with many of the deals that led to the building of new ballparks, stadiums, and arenas can be minimized. Excessive tax increases could be substantially reduced or eliminated giving communities the opportunity to spend those scarce funds for education, safety, and community development.

VI. Misplaced Revenues, Misplaced Values

Any assessment of the role of sports, entertainment, and cultural facilities in urban revitalization occurs against the backdrop of the supposed, anticipated, or actual linkage between amenities and economic development. There are many social scientists and policy experts whose work has sustained the observation that there is, at best, a very weak, and possibly no causal connection between sports or any other set of amenities and economic development. These scholars caution that money spent on amenities—sports or otherwise—will not change regional economic development.[46] In that regard, public investments in sports facilities represent poorly focused tax dollars if redevelopment is the goal. It could also be suggested that policies that focus on sports, entertainment, and culture emphasize experiential values instead of a concentration on education for economic development. From their perspective, this book might appear to be unnecessary and that its emphasis on amenities for redevelopment will supplant other more important policies. Nothing could be further from the truth and such a perspective obscures the contributions or help this book can provide to community leaders in the formulation of public policies to revitalize downtown areas.

As will be more fully explored in Chapter 2, there should be little doubt in anyone's mind or debate over the importance of human capital and, therefore, education in and for economic development. Skilled labor, whether identified or called creative class workers, idea generators, or productive employees, is what drives an economy. The failure to produce and attract the educated workers that firms need will lead to economic decline. Areas that grow are those with higher concentrations of educated workers. In that regard, then, there should be no confusion that what is discussed in this book does not contradict the central view of the dominant and determining role of human capital in economic development and for any revitalization or rebuilding strategy. No one should doubt that any amenity is as important as programs to educate workers and ensure that skilled labor pools exist. It would be foolhardy to build sports or entertainment facilities while ignoring or underfunding human capital development activities.

Yet, the twenty-first century is increasingly being defined as the era when corporations and people became less bound to specific geographic areas by assets, such as waterways, as the costs of transportation and communication declined. As other needed resources (energy, capital, etc.) also become available regardless of a corporation's geographic location, a key question becomes: "Where do or would skilled workers prefer to live?" People no longer have to live where corporations must locate, as transportation options, the availability of other resources, and the declining cost of communication have broadened the locational choices. If labor becomes or is the driving force in a corporation's profitability, it follows that firms will seek to locate where they are assured of a steady flow of productive workers. Businesses will then try to locate where people want to live instead of luring them to the locations that are most convenient for the firm.

A collateral question on the minds of many communities' leaders is that with America's colleges and universities producing high numbers of trained workers, how does a city like Indianapolis, Cleveland, or Reading convince those individuals to live in its region? For these communities, the issue is not necessarily should investments be made in human capital. These investments are being made though the use of the state tax dollars generated by their residents. They face the challenge of convincing educated workers to choose to live in their regions instead of moving elsewhere. Climatic variables, to be sure, assume a role in attracting and retaining people and public leaders cannot remake a cold weather venue into a Sunbelt city. But some cold weather areas, such as Chicago or Minneapolis/St. Paul, are growing as fast as some warmer regions. What amenities or assets do they possess? Can Indianapolis or Cleveland—given their states' investment in human capital—attract and retain the graduates of leading public universities, such as The Ohio State University, Indiana University, Ohio University, Miami (Ohio) University, and Purdue University (not to mention private ones, such as Case Western Reserve University or the University of Notre Dame) and emulate the growth rates in the Chicago or Boston regions?

Social capital is also important in attracting people, as the number, scale, and diversity of nonprofit organizations advance the quality of life and offer opportunities for people to bond with others and create personal networks.[47] Yet areas such as Indianapolis or Cleveland have nationally recognized philanthropic communities and ethnic neighborhoods and have declined.[48] It is also possible that amenities, such as sports teams, entertainment, and culture may also be among the factors considered when people choose a place to live.[49] Could enhanced amenities add to the impressive assets that exist in Indiana, Ohio, or Pennsylvania (as well as those states' investments in human capital) and advance economic development in Cleveland, Indianapolis, or Reading? That possibility, also sustained by important empirical research, is what has focused some community leaders on ensuring that there is a vibrant set of amenities in their community. At the outset, then, this book is based on the understanding that human capital does indeed drive economic development.[50] What is also relevant, however, and will be more fully discussed in Chapter 2 is that as comparative geographical advantages decline in importance (as a result of lower transportation and communication costs) and as workers and firms have more locational choices, areas with higher levels of amenities will be more likely to be attractive to highly skilled labor. As a result all businesses that must strive to be as efficient and profitable as possible will also be attracted to these areas.[51]

In noting that amenities assume a role, recognition must also be made that there are community- or neighborhood-level amenities that may be far more important than "big ticket" items, such as sports facilities, museums, and cultural centers.[52] That issue will also be explored. The recognition that amenities are an asset or tool in the attraction and retention of skilled labor for economic development underscores the importance of strategies that leverage private sector resources for neighborhood level as well as big-ticket amenities.

VII. Goal and Organization of This Book

This book is about how cities can ensure that their economic and community development goals are part of any plan for a sports, cultural, entertainment, or arts facility and that sufficient economic returns exist to offset any tax increases. How can this be accomplished? It is accomplished by recognizing sports as well as other forms of entertainment, the arts, and culture have always been an important part of a society's social capital and that importance allows each of these assets to be an anchor for development plans and strategies. The resulting new buildings can generate sufficient revenues to ensure cities also accomplish their financial goals. The analysis in each chapter focuses on the unique politics, but the common theme of public and private investments. The assessments look at the fiscal risks each sector took, and the returns earned. Indianapolis, San Diego, Los Angeles, Columbus, and Reading each took important steps to change how cities can benefit when sports and cultural facilities are built. It now remains to extend their path, learn from their success and the ideas other cities have tried, and develop a model that turns cities from simply contributing to the wealth of teams and athletes into partners sharing in the economic benefits that result from the enduring importance of sports to societies and fans.

The path to this strategy begins with a review of several different ideas that have been at the center of the discussion and debates over the role of sports, entertainment, the arts, and cultural amenities in the redevelopment of downtown areas. Understanding how the relationship between cities and teams became unbalanced highlights the need for civic leaders to find nonconfrontational strategies to ensure that when tax dollars are used for sports facilities these dollars are turned from subsidies into investments. It is also important to understand that there is indeed a linkage between a focus on sports, entertainment, and cultural amenities and a region's economic development. The focus on redeveloped downtowns with sports, entertainment, and cultural amenities is tied to the idea that these assets attract and retain the human capital necessary to build a twenty-first century economy. Advocates for public investments in a wide-ranging set of amenities argue that these assets attract "the creative class" or idea generators that drive the twenty-first century economy. Does such a relationship really exist? Others suggest that entertainment, arts, culture, and sports follow wealth and the idea that building amenities will lead to economic development is nothing more than the latest elixir from different types of music men or members of "Brother Love's Traveling Salvation Show."[53] Finally, some have argued that the focus on sports, the arts, and entertainment to redevelop downtown areas is led by business and political elites who are able to control the benefits from these sort of revitalization efforts while eschewing policies and programs that might produce benefits for a wider segment of the community. Each of these issues form the theoretical material or framework for this book as it charts pathways for cities to redevelop downtown areas while minimizing subsidies and creating opportunities for real economic and community development.

Chapter 3 looks at the lessons learned from Indianapolis' history of using sports and the arts as an anchor for a development strategy that successfully rebuilt a desolate downtown area into an entertainment and retail center while also building a new downtown residential neighborhood. However, some of Indianapolis' missed goals and future tasks also need to be addressed. Chapter 4 studies the San Diego Padres' quest for a new ballpark, Petco Park, and the unprecedented public/private partnership where the team's owner "guaranteed" $311 million in new real estate development in exchange for the public sector's investment in a new ballpark. Los Angeles' investment in the STAPLES Center, home to the Lakers, Clippers, and Kings, and L.A. LIVE, as an anchor for the redevelopment of part of its downtown area, is analyzed in Chapter 5. Chapter 6 examines Columbus' (Ohio) Arena District and the partnership established with Nationwide Insurance that included the company's commitment to pay for the full cost of the arena that became the home of the NHL's Blue Jackets. This is followed (in Chapter 7) by an assessment of the success and limitations from the efforts in Cleveland to use sports, cultural, and entertainment facilities to anchor a recovery of declining downtown areas in a region plagued by persistent population losses and the shrinking of its manufacturing sector. The redevelopment effort led by Cleveland's business and political leadership also involved a set of distinctive community development efforts and those are also explored in the context of the region's ongoing stagnation. Chapter 8 looks at the success of efforts led by private sector leaders in the smaller market area of Reading, Pennsylvania, and Chapter 9 focuses on the lessons learned and the blueprint for making cities "Major League winners" from their dealings with professional sports teams, the entertainment business, and through the building of new sports, entertainment, and cultural facilities.

Endnotes

1. Rosentraub, M.S. 1997a. *Major league losers: the real cost of sports and who's paying for it.* New York: Basic Books.
2. See, for example, Baade, R. A. 1996. Professional sports as catalysts for metropolitan economic development. *Journal of Urban Affairs* 18 (1): 1–17. Also, Humphrey, B. and D. R. Howard, eds. 2008. *The business of sports: Economic perspectives.* New York: Praeger Publishers.
3. Sandy, R., P. J. Sloane, and M. S. Rosentraub, 2004. *The economics of sports: An international perspective.* New York: Palgrave McMillan.
4. Judd, D. R. and S. S. Fainstein, eds. 1999. *The tourist city.* New Haven: Yale University Press.
5. See, for example, Rosentraub, M. S. 1997b. Stadiums and urban space. In *Sports, jobs, and taxes: The economic impact of sports teams and stadiums,* ed. R. G. Noll and A. Zimbalist, 178–207. Washington, D. C.: The Brookings Institution. Also see Nelson, A. C. 2002. Locating major league stadiums where they can make a difference. *Public Works Management and Policy,* 7 (2): 98–114. Both works illustrate the impact the movement of economic activity can have relative to public policy goals. Within metropolitan areas, ensuring that levels of recreational spending takes place in central cities can relocate tax dollars that enhance the fiscal capacity of central cities that have large concentrations of lower-income households.

6. Zimbalist, A. 2006. *The bottom line: Observations and arguments on the sports business.* Philadelphia: Temple University Press.

7. See, for example, Baade, R. A. and R. Dye. 1988. *Sports stadiums and area development: Assessing the reality. Heartland Policy Study*, Number 68. Chicago: The Heartland Institute. Also: Danielson, M. N. 1997. *Home team: Professional sports and the American metropolis.* Princeton, NJ: Princeton University Press. Both works illustrate the hopes cities have for their investment in the facilities used by professional sports teams. My earlier book highlights the lack of planning by cities to capitalize on these investments (Rosentraub, M. S. 1997a. *Major league losers: The real cost of sports and who's paying for it.* New York: Basic Books.)

8. Some might also note that tax dollars that produce new levels of social capital would be another valid return or use of public money. The goal of all of the investments in sport, cultural, and entertainment centers in downtown areas was revitalization. The lessons learned by cities that were successful in creating a renewed downtown or attracting highly skilled human capital is the focus of this book.

9. Pierce, N. R. 2000. Ohio looks hard at what's lost through business subsidies. In *Readings in urban economic issues and public policy*, ed. R. W. Wassner, 151–153, Malden, MA: Blackwell Publishers.

10. See, for example, Euchner, C. C. 1994. *Playing the field: Why sports teams move and cities fight to keep them.* Baltimore: Johns Hopkins University Press. Also see Noll, R. G. and A. Zimbalist. 1997. Build the stadium—create the jobs! In *Sports, jobs, and taxes: The economic impact of sports teams and stadiums*, ed. R. G. Noll and A. Zimbalist, 1–54. Washington, D.C.: The Brookings Institution.

11. In some of the case studies done for my earlier book, public leaders repeatedly underscored the need for a team to produce a major league image. Leaders in Columbus, Ohio, as will be discussed in Chapter 6, also wanted a professional team to enhance its image despite the presence of The Ohio State University and its prominent sports teams. See Rosentraub, *Major league losers.*

12. Johnson, A. 2000. Minor league baseball: Risks and potential benefits for communities large and small. In *The economics and politics of sports facilities*, ed. W. C. Rich, 141–151. Westport, CT: Quorum Books.

13. Kennedy, S. and M. S. Rosentraub. 2000. Public–private partnerships, professional sports teams, and the protection of the public's interests. *The American Review of Public Administration* 30 (4): 436–459.

14. Hobbs, F. and N. Stoops. 2002. *Demographic trends in the 20th century: Census 2000 special reports.* Washington, D.C.: U.S. Department of Commerce, Bureau of the Census.

15. Ibid.

16. Rubenstein, H. M. 1992. *Pedestrian malls, streetscapes, and spaces.* New York: John Wiley & Sons.

17. The Hilbert family's financial contribution to improve and maintain the facility led to the hall's naming as the Hilbert Circle Theatre.

18. See, for example, Sanders, H. 2002. Convention myths and markets: A critical review of convent center feasibility studies. *Economic Development Quarterly* 16 (3): 195–210. Also see Sanders, H. 2005. Also see Sanders, H. 2005. Space available: The realities of convention centers as economic development strategy. Washington, D.C.: The Brookings Institution. Both of these publications deal with the possibility that downtown business leaders pursue economic development policies that are most likely to benefit their

land holdings or their corporations. David Imbroscio has also raised the possibility that the focus on downtown development by elites could crowd out other policy options. Imbroscio, D. L. 1998. Reformulating urban regime theory: The division of labor between state and market reconsidered. *Journal of Urban Affairs* 20 (3): 233–248.

19. Logan, J. R. and H. L. Molotch. 1987. *Urban fortunes: The political economy of place.* Berkeley: University of California Press.

20. In my earlier book, *Major League Losers*, the perverse welfare system that benefitted team owners and players and the limited economic gains produced by sports facilities was carefully documented. What is different about this book is its focus on the cities that through different strategies and policies were able to turn subsidies into investments. (Rosentraub, *Major league losers.*)

21. Eisinger, P. 2000. The politics of bread and circuses. *Urban Affairs Review* 35 (3): 316–333.

22. See, for example, Gottdiener, M. 2001. *The theming of America: American dreams, media fantasies, and themed environments.* Boulder, CO: Westview Press. Also, an earlier book also focused on these issues: Hannigan, J. 1998. *Fantasy city: Pleasure and profit in the postmodern metropolis.* London: Routledge Press.

23. Clark, T. N. 2004. ed. *The city as an entertainment machine.* Amsterdam: Elsevier–JAI Press.

24. Florida, R. 2002. *The rise of the creative class.* New York: Basic Books.

25. Rosentraub, M. S. and M. Joo. 2009. Tourism and economic development: Which investments produce gains for regions? *Tourism Management* (in press). http://www.elsevier.com/wps/find/journaldescription.cws_home/30472/description#description/d01:10.1016/j.tourism.2008.11.014.

26. Pine, J. and J. H. Gilmore. 1999. *The experience economy: Work is theatre and every business a stage.* Cambridge, MA: Harvard Business Press.

27. *Money Magazine*, 2008. 100 best places to live and launch. http://money.cnn.com/galleries/2008/fsb/0803/gallery.best_places_to_launch.fsb/index.html (accessed September 9, 2008).

28. Eisinger, *The politics of bread and circuses*, 330–331.

29. While Shea Stadium, home to the New York Mets from 1964 to 2008, had more seats than Rome's Colosseum, their new home, Citi Field, has a planned seating capacity of 42,000.

30. Wilson, J. 1994. *Playing by the rules: Sport, society, and the state.* Detroit: Wayne State University Press.

31. Misener, L. and D. S. Mason. 2006. Creating community networks: Can sporting events offer meaningful sources of social capital. *Managing Leisure* 11: 39–56.

32. Andrews, D. 2004. Sports in the late capitalist movement. In *The commercialization of sport*, ed. Trevor Slack, 3–28. London: Routledge.

33. See Lefebvre, H. 1996. *Writings on cities.* Malden, MA: Blackwell Publishers. Earlier assessments by Lefebvre are also important amplifications of this relationship: Lefebvre, H. 1991. *The production of space.* Malden, MA: Blackwell Publishers.

34. See Chema, T. 1996. When professional sports justify the subsidy: A reply to Robert A. Baade. *Journal of Urban Affairs* 18 (1): 19–22, for a practicing professional's perspective. Chema was a leader in the development of Cleveland's new ballpark and arena. Another professional (and an academic) has important insights into this point as well: Euchner, *Playing the field.*

35. Home Box Office (HBO) 2008. *Nine innings from ground zero: The healing of a nation began with the swing of a bat.* http://www.hbo.com/sports/nineinnings/ (accessed October 8, 2008).

36. See, for example, Levine, P. 1993. *From Ellis Island to Ebbets Field: Sport and the American Jewish experience.* Cary, NC: Oxford University Press. Also placing this point in an international perspective: Duke, V. and L. Crolley. 1996. *Football, nationality, and the state.* London: Addison Wesley Longman.

37. It has become increasingly common for metropolitan areas to have one large arena (seating for approximately 20,000 people) and a second smaller one for acts that attract 15,000 or fewer fans. In the largest markets it is possible for a region to have more than one large-scale arena. In addition, in cities that are also home to major universities, a second large arena could exist to serve the needs of the university. Some markets, such as Phoenix and the Minneapolis/St. Paul areas have two large-scale arenas. Whether or not these areas can attract enough events to financially sustain both facilities remains unclear.

38. Zimbalist, A. and J. G. Long. 2006. Facility finance: Measurement, trends and analysis. *International Journal of Sport Finance* 1: 201–211.

39. See, for example, Searle, G. 2002. Uncertain legacy: Sydney's Olympic stadiums. *European Planning Studies* 10 (7): 845–860. Also see Kang, Y. S. and R. Perdue. 1994. Long-term impact of a mega-event on international tourism to the host country: A conceptual model and the case of the 1988 Seoul Olympics. In *Global tourist behavior,* ed. M. Uysal, 205–226. New York: Haworth Press; Kurtzman, J. 2005. Economic impact: Sport tourism and the city. *Journal of Sport Tourism* 10 (1): 47–71; Chalip, L. 2002. *Using the Olympics to optimise tourism benefits: University lecture on the Olympics.* Barcelona: Centre d'Estudis Olympics. http://olympicstudies.uab.es/lectures/web/pdf/chalip.pdf (accessed December 21, 2008).

40. Austrian, Z. and M. S. Rosentraub. 2002. Cities, sports and economic change: A retrospective assessment. *Journal of Urban Affairs* 24 (5): 549–565.

41. Nelson, Locating major league stadiums, 98–114.

42. Rosentraub, M. S. 2000. Sports facilities, redevelopment, and the centrality of downtown areas: Observations and lessons from experiences in a rustbelt and sunbelt city. *Marquette University Sports Law Journal* 10 (2): 219–236.

43. Rosentraub, M. S. 2006. The local context of a sports strategy for economic development. *Economic Development Quarterly* 20 (3): 278–291.

44. Rosentraub, *Major league losers.*

45. Timmons, J. A. 2006. *Winning on the field and at the ballot box: The effect of the fan base on stadium subsidies.* Unpublished public policy thesis. Stanford University: Department of Economics.

46. See, for example, Coates, D. and B. R. Humphreys. 1999. The growth effects of sports franchises, stadia, and arenas. *Journal of Policy Analysis and Management* 14 (4): 601–624.

47. Hoyman, M. and C. Faricy. 2009. It takes a village: A test of the creative class, social capital, and human capital theories. *Urban Affairs Review* 44 (3): 311–333.

48. See, for example, Gronbjerg, K. A. and R. Clerkin. 2003. *Indianapolis nonprofit sector: Management capacities and challenges.* (Unpublished paper.) Indianapolis: Center on Philanthropy and the School of Public and Environmental Affairs, Indiana University.

49. Rosentraub and Joo, *Tourism and economic development,* (forthcoming).

50. See, for example, Garmise, S. 2006. *People and the competitive advantage of place: Building a workplace for the 21st century.* Armonk, NY: M. E. Sharpe.

51. Rosentraub and Joo, *Tourism and economic development*, (forthcoming).
52. See, for example, Clark, *The city as an entertainment machine*. Also, Professor H. Sanders has consistently documented the persistent overestimation of the positive effects of some big-ticket amenities and their ability to actually operate at levels sufficient to produce jobs and generate substantial economic returns (Sanders, H. 2005. *Space available: The realities of convention centers as economic development strategy*. Washington, D.C.: The Brookings Institution).
53. Reference is made here to a popular song written and performed by Neil Diamond.

Chapter 2

Teams, Cities, Elites, and the Real Value of "Big-Ticket" Amenities

I. A General Framework for Investments in Big-Ticket Items

The decision to spend tax money for big-ticket items, such as sports facilities, museums, or entertainment and cultural centers to anchor redevelopment efforts can be linked to five separate sets of ideas. Together these ideas form a conceptual framework that explains the use of these assets to create an identity and advance a region's economy. Within this framework lie the theories that explain and identify the expectations that guide the decisions made by governments to invest in big-ticket items. The case studies provide insight into the best ways to ensure that subsidies become investments while also expanding the empirical work available to sustain or refute various components of the conceptual framework.

Each of the five components of this general framework is involved in the decisions made in each city to invest in big-ticket items. The case studies focus on what was done and how each community tried to secure gains rather than merely provide subsidies. Each case then assesses outcomes and changes from the public sector's expenditures while also producing insight that can help guide future policy choices for revitalization efforts in cities around the world.

The first of these five elements deals with the very decision to focus on big-ticket items as opposed to other strategies for building an image and ensuring a high quality of life in a city. The second involves the role of sports, entertainment, and arts and cultural centers in the attraction and retention of the human capital that drives economic development in the twenty-first century. This issue also involves a focus on the image of the city and the role of all forms of recreation and community life in attracting and retaining residents.

The third issue involves the decision to concentrate resources for redevelopment in specifically targeted areas. That perspective is in sharp contrast to one that would rely instead on evolutionary change or a natural process of regeneration through the initiation of new businesses and economic activity produced by undirected economic actions. Jane Jacobs urged cities to focus on evolutionary change and urged planners to understand the role for land and buildings in underdeveloped parts of the city.[1] Jacobs' ideas are contrasted with those who fear "growth poles" within a region will divert development and leave some areas either in perpetual decline or in decline for a protracted number of years. Los Angeles and San Diego—cities in growing regions with many successful and vibrant neighborhoods and business districts—both feared the long-term consequences of a deteriorating downtown or inner city neighborhoods. Both created public/private partnerships to concentrate development in a specific area. The outcomes in both cities permit an assessment of the effects of large concentrated investments to change development patterns.

The fourth issue, the control of the decision to anchor redevelopment efforts to big-ticket items, is drawn from the work of Clarence Stone. In documenting the leading roles assumed by corporations in charting public policies related to economic development, the possibility existed that chosen tactics were designed to advance the narrow interests of businesses located in the downtown area. The inherent fear among researchers focused on the role played by corporate leaders is that policies and programs chosen by economic elites ignore other options, other parts of a city, and more fundamental factors that could actually advance revitalization efforts and economic development.[2] Any assessment of the role of big-ticket items in revitalization efforts must (1) look at the activities of business leaders to advance a region and its downtown area and (2) measure the effect of a focus on downtown development on new development in other parts of a city. A failure to address both of these points could ignore an important criticism of the focus on downtown amenities for revitalization and make it appear that the research produced is designed to support an agenda pursued by business leaders and often questioned by neighborhood advocates.

Critics of public subsidies for sports, entertainment, and arts and cultural facilities have suggested that business leaders attempt to control policymaking to advance their narrow corporate or personal self-interests and steer tax incentives toward projects that increase their wealth and reduce their costs.[3] Yet, other studies of decision making in urban areas have found that businesses are engaged in numerous civic initiatives, many of which help build inner city neighborhoods and create jobs.[4] The role of business leaders in decision making and the benefits created from the projects they supported is discussed in each chapter, but a more in-depth assessment is provided in the case of Cleveland's effort to rebuild its downtown area and other parts of the city. The role of private business leaders is also assessed in Reading, Pennsylvania, to provide two cases of the activities of business leaders to advance revitalization efforts in small- and medium-sized cities. These analyses show that, while there was indeed great interest in big-ticket items to change economic patterns and images, substantial attention was also focused on neighborhood-level projects and community development. The role of business leaders in redevelopment may be more complex and part of a far more varied political mosaic than critics of big-ticket investments have argued or feared. Further, as will be discussed, the focus on big-ticket items in each city was based on the perceived value of ensuring that large numbers of people returned to downtown areas. The effects or changes that resulted from the attraction of crowds to downtown areas are also examined in terms of the outcomes for Cleveland and Reading.

Lastly, the "unleveled playing field" perspective deals with the effects on cities of the elimination of market forces in determining the supply of sports teams. With supply constrained by the leagues' policies, a bidding environment is created whereby cities provide excessive subsidies to guarantee a team's presence. In smaller markets, larger subsidies are often provided to help smaller market teams earn sufficient profits to compete with franchises in larger market areas. In larger market areas, the control that the four major sports leagues have over the supply of teams leads to excessive profits resulting from too few teams existing given the number of fans that live in those regions.

Some communities have tried to challenge the cartel structure of sports through lawsuits designed to eliminate subsidies. Virtually all of these initiatives have been unsuccessful.[5] As a result, linking real estate development and revitalization efforts to the building of big-ticket amenities has the potential to eliminate the negative impact of subsidies and avoid conflict-based approaches to negotiations with team owners. It will be argued that the best strategy for a community when dealing with the absence of market forces in the supply of teams is to link the building of facilities to revitalization efforts. Cities that used that approach as opposed to the threat of lawsuits or the use of eminent domain to seize a team have found a better way to avoid inappropriate subsidies.

The perspectives that form this conceptual framework, which guides the decisions to use sports, culture, and entertainment for revitalization, are summarized in Table 2.1. Leaders looking at this summary would respond that all of the options have been pursued sometimes simultaneously by cities. What is important is that each of the cities studied invested in big-ticket assets, but also created public/private partnerships that included substantial private sector investment for development turning subsidies into strategic investments.

Table 2.1 Components of a Framework Linking Sports, Culture, and New Facilities to Revitalization

Component/Options	Examples	Where Used
Big Ticket Items, Iconic Architecture for Civic Image		
Iconic architecture	Ballparks, concert halls	Indianapolis, Los Angeles, Chicago
Neighborhood focus	Parks, paths, livable areas	Portland, Chicago
Amenity Theory to Attract and Retain Human Capital		
Sports, entertainment	Ballparks, concert halls, theaters	Nashville, Indianapolis, Columbus
Education	College tuition, workforce training	Kalamazoo, Georgia
Redevelopment Orientation		
Evolutionary change	Code enforcement, small grants and projects to retard deterioration and encourage small business development. Live/work space	Cleveland, Chicago, Columbus, Indianapolis
Large-scale plans	Master planned neighborhood, district, or downtown	San Diego, Indianapolis, Columbus
Participation Modes Used for Planning Redevelopment		
Elite (regime)	Led by downtown interests, chambers of commerce, city and corporate leaders only	Indianapolis, Los Angeles, Columbus, Cleveland, San Diego
Public engagement/ community benefit agreements	Widespread public hearings WITH plans developed or redrafted as a result of meetings	Cleveland, Los Angeles, Baltimore
Unbalanced Negotiations		
Legal actions	Lawsuits, eminent domain	San Diego, Baltimore, Oakland,
Development	Private investment	San Diego, Columbus, Indianapolis

II. The Value and Appropriateness of Big-Ticket Items

Sports facilities, museums, and entertainment and cultural centers are often referred to as big-ticket items because of their cost. While these large-scale projects are costly, the anticipated value produced comes from designs that can create an iconic image that forges an identity for a city or a region, and the role of the facilities as anchors for redevelopment strategies. At one extreme, the mere depiction of the Eiffel Tower, Fenway Park, the Washington Monument, the Roman Colosseum, Wrigley Field, the Statue of Liberty, or Carnegie Hall creates an identity for a city and their depiction immediately conveys the city's name. When images of these structures appear, a series of impressions are generated that gives that community an identity different from any other. Larger cities have several iconic structures that are often shown in a fast-moving montage designed to create an image of vitality, distinctiveness, and of a city that is a center of economic development and wealth.

A. A City's Image

This desire to create an iconic structure or set of amenities to enhance or change a city's image and improve the quality of life is often behind the desire to build a sports facility, a new museum, a park, or an entertainment center. The hope is that a facility or several will not only create an image, but also convince the most productive human capital that a particular city is "cool" and offers the amenities that will enhance their quality of life. Scholars, architects, and pundits have long discussed the importance of iconic architecture. Kotler, Haider, and Rein (1993) translated these concepts into marketing strategies for cities in their classic, *Marketing Places*. Its subtitle helped to explain the allure for big-ticket items: Attracting Investment, Industry, and Tourism to Cities, States, and Nations. It focused the attention of countless leaders on what they could or should do to advance the image of their city through the building of physical facilities that made a statement.

In the post-*Marketing Places* years, even large cities or those classified as "world cities" have built new iconic structures. For example, Chicago built Millennium Park to add to its long list of iconic structures and downtown Los Angeles was reimaged with Frank Gehry's design of the home of the Los Angeles Philharmonic Orchestra, Disney Hall, and the new entertainment center, L.A. LIVE. Smaller cities have followed the lead of larger communities in an effort to put themselves on the economic radar screens of companies. These cities also want to provide the amenities that are seen as capable of attracting and retaining the human capital needed by expanding businesses. Indianapolis boasts new museums, the Conseco Fieldhouse, and Lucas Oil Stadium (home to the 2012 Super Bowl) as part of its new image and skyline. Cleveland opened designer I. M. Pei's Rock and Roll Hall of Fame and Museum, and new downtown sports facilities were built to reconstruct its Rust Belt image. Nashville's Sommet Center was designed to extend and enhance the city's music-based image (the home of broadcasted country music, if not country music itself) and Arlington (Texas) has made investments in sports facilities to give it a Texas-sized image through the Ballpark in Arlington (now Rangers Ballpark in Arlington) and the megastadium that will be home to the Dallas Cowboys and the first Super Bowl to be held in North Texas in 2011.

There does not have to be anything inherently contradictory between a focus on an iconic big-ticket item and development of the kind of neighborhoods some believe are more likely to attract and retain highly talented workers. The residential areas surrounding Fenway Park and Wrigley Field, as well as the growing residential character of downtown Chicago, illustrate the value and possibilities for building and restoring neighborhoods around iconic structures or new entertainment and cultural amenities. The possibility for new neighborhoods is what has driven some of the big-ticket construction in several of the case study cities.

B. Amenities and the "Creative Class"

An alternative framework regarding the value of these large architectural images for economic development is summarized in the work of Richard Florida and Terry Clark.[6] They argue there are other (and smaller scale) amenities that are more important in the effort to attract and retain the human capital needed by today's businesses. Florida begins his description of what attracts human capital to particular cities with the story of a counter-culture computer genius leaving Pittsburgh for the concentration of young people and neighborhood-level entertainment venues in Austin, Texas. Florida's interviews in focus groups underscored for him that "lifestyle frequently trumps employment when they're (respondents) choosing where to live."[7] That lifestyle is defined by "the music scene, art scene, technology scene, outdoor sports scene, and so on … and, of course, nightlife is an important part of the mix. The people I talked to desire a nightlife with a wide mix of options. The most highly valued options were experiential ones—interesting music venues, neighborhood art galleries, performance spaces, and theatres."[8] His observations lead to the conclusion that big-ticket items have lost some of their luster and value as assets capable of attracting human capital.

Web sites detailing the music scene in Indianapolis and Austin highlight the point. There were 98 venues found in Austin, on AustinSinger.Com indicating live music was available at bars and restaurants. There were 35 similar nightspots listed for Indianapolis on Indianapolis.Com, but only nine offered the combination of food, drink, and live music. Austin is home to the University of Texas and its 50,000 students might create a different market. However, Columbus, Ohio, home to The Ohio State University and its more than 55,000 students had less than half the number of restaurants and bars offering live music boasted by Austin. Franklin (Columbus) County and Travis (Austin) County have about the same number of residents and both cities are their state's capital. These similarities in characteristics suggest the differences in the number of locations providing music with food and beverages is far larger in Austin. As Richard Florida reported, the counter-culture computer wizard off to the Sunbelt would indeed find more amenities catering to his taste in Austin than in Pittsburgh or other Midwest cities. There is indeed a greater set of live music entertainment options in Austin and a noticeable lack of major league sports teams and museums to rival Cleveland's Rock and Roll Hall of Fame or Museum of Art. Austin's symphony is excellent, but does not rate as highly as the Cleveland Orchestra. Relative to live theater, however, Indianapolis' eight venues compares quite favorably to the nine listed for Austin. There is an implied inference that big-ticket items more prevalent in Rust Belt cities cannot compete with the "hip neighborhood-level" entertainment amenities supplied by Austin.

Despite the impressive differences noted for Austin and the seemingly obvious conclusion that this sort of entertainment is associated with or even steers economic development, many statistical studies have not found the connections or linkages suggested by Florida's focus groups and publications. For example, the people who drive his "super creative class" account for merely 12 percent of the labor force and Steve Malanga concluded, "the basic economics behind his ideas just don't work. Far from being economic powerhouses, a number of cities the professor identifies as creative-age winners have chronically underperformed the American economy … since 1993, cities that score the best on Florida's analysis have actually grown no faster than the overall U.S. jobs economy, increasing their employment base by only slightly more than 17 percent. Florida's indexes, in fact, are such poor predictors of economic performance that his top cities haven't even outperformed bottom ones."[9] It also might be noted that while Austin has far more venues for music, live theater would seem to be more available in Indianapolis given its smaller population base and the absence of a large residential university. Did Indianapolis' focus on sports offset the difference in music venues, and was Indianapolis' inability to attract more creative class workers simply a function of the low number of venues with music?

The strident nature of some of the criticisms of Richard Florida's work could well be the product of its inherent indictment of development strategies that have long favored sports facilities, iconic architecture, and other big-ticket items. The business community and other elite groups have supported these strategies. Setting aside the potential for political bias, Peck notes that the real limitation in Florida's work may be in understanding exactly what the creative class wants in terms of lifestyle and amenities.[10] As many have observed, creativity, innovation, and patents do indeed drive an economy and attracting and retaining the best and most agile minds is important for businesses and locations. "Notwithstanding the presentational benefits of linking contemporary art and culture to economic development efforts, the awkward question is what is meaningful from a public policy standpoint (and) … Whether or not this will stimulate creative economic growth, however, is quite another matter."[11] One is left to wonder if neighborhood cultures can be created by investments directed by a so-called creative class policy or if one could ever find a city that has truly ignored building neighborhoods and fostering associations, etc. While Indianapolis has fewer clubs than Austin, it does boast far more neighborhood associations and was the first city to have such organizations that help to advance the very culture that Florida links to creativity.[12] Can and do neighborhood associations build a neighborhood culture similar to or different from clubs with music?

Hoyman and Faricy compared economic development outcomes using measures of human capital, social capital, and the creative class. They noted that human capital theory was a more powerful predictor of desired outcomes than either Richard Florida's creative class or the presence of social capital assets. Amenities were not expressly evaluated. Some elements defined as part of the human capital theory encompassed parts or overlapped with measures of Richard Florida's creative class leaving one to question if the two concepts—creative class and human capital—overlapped or were mutually independent of each other. Regardless, their work continued to underscore that human capital is indeed the most important factor relative to advancing economic development.[13] What may be essential for local community and city leaders, however, is an understanding of the assets that attract and retain human capital in a specific geographic area. That critical concern is what has convinced many community leaders that they need both big-ticket items and a focus on revitalized neighborhoods. The effort to separate human capital theory, social capital assets, and Richard Florida's ideas about a creative class might have less relevance to community leaders than understandings of the role of civic assets, sports, culture, entertainment, and lively neighborhoods in attracting and retaining highly skilled workers.

Few if any elected or community leaders doubt that education and training must be at the forefront of spending for economic development. But, many community leaders would point to the substantial investments made by their respective states in education to develop human capital. For example, Ohio, Indiana, and Pennsylvania are each home to exceptional colleges and universities that graduate thousands of well-trained workers each year.[14] Even with those investments, Cleveland, Reading, and Indianapolis still struggle to attract and retain highly skilled workers. Stagnating population and growth levels in those cities have convinced leaders in each to seek a mix of amenities that can either match or compete with the attractions available in Boston, Chicago, and Minneapolis. With each state making major investments in their higher education systems, and with workers able to locate anywhere, cities strive to have a mix of assets and amenities that appeal to a wide spectrum of workers. With millions of tickets sold each year to sporting events, it is clear that major league teams are valued amenities. Thus, too, are theaters for the performing arts and museums. To be sure, big-ticket assets alone are insufficient to create a desirable city. Yet, their absence also denotes for many a lower quality of life. The case studies illustrate the outcomes from investments in big-ticket items while also looking at community and neighborhood development activities.

C. Amenities or Neighborhood Development?

Every city that has been attracted to the idea of iconic architecture for its image or the building of sports facilities, museums, or cultural centers could simultaneously point to myriad projects designed to enhance the culture and quality of life in numerous neighborhoods. Columbus' leaders would point to its Germantown, and Indianapolis would point to the Fountain Square neighborhood and its local theater as well as the Bohemian area known as Broad Ripple. Cleveland, too, has many successful urban neighborhoods and could show interested people its Bohemian West Side and the racially mixed area around Shaker Square. There is no disagreement that highly skilled workers or members of the creative class are important for economic development. Indeed, all of the case studies will underscore that leaders in these cities believed the big-ticket projects would help attract and retain human capital and no city ignored neighborhood development projects. In summary, even when big-ticket items are developed, they cannot be allowed to supplant a simultaneous focus on neighborhoods. While public resources were involved with all of the big-ticket projects, there is also evidence of substantial efforts to advance neighborhood development.

What is needed is a "common ground" approach that recognizes the importance of both neighborhoods and iconic structures to create both recognizable images for a city and unique opportunities for its residents. Mason refers to this as a need for policies that underscore the synecdochic aspects of both neighborhoods and big-ticket items—images that represent the entirety of a city.[15] Through unique images created by big-ticket items and neighborhood representations, distinct and lasting impressions of a city are created. Instead of choosing one approach or another, perhaps the evidence is that a balance between big-ticket images and neighborhood scenes is the key to human capital attraction. Paris, Chicago, New York, and Barcelona each possess international images created by iconic architecture and neighborhood street scenes. Perhaps that is what attracts human capital, and that possibility is addressed in the next section. Indianapolis' balanced approach is illustrated with its new Culture Trail being built in downtown amid several big-ticket assets (Figure 2.1).

III. Amenities, Human Capital, and Economic Development

There is little disagreement with the idea that businesses in the twenty-first century locate where they have the greatest confidence people with the needed skills and talent want to live.[16] Where there is disagreement is with the importance of large-scale amenities, such as a sports facility or a museum or a theater district, in attracting talented workers.[17] This disagreement is different from arguments involving Richard Florida's work. Some suggest that regardless of the type of amenity—clubs with live entertainment or sports facilities—it is the presence of wealth that creates a demand and market that attracts investors interested in providing entertainment and cultural opportunities. Facilities are then built in these areas as entrepreneurs

Figure 2.1 Uniting big-ticket items and neighborhood amenities: Indianapolis' downtown bike path. (Photo by Mark S. Rosentraub.)

seek to profit from the discretionary income that can be spent as a result of a region's growing wealth.[18] Advocates of this position question or wonder if the reverse relationship is true. If subsidies are used to ensure the presence of sports teams and arts and cultural amenities, will their existence attract human capital and businesses? Will the economic development that results from rising levels of human capital and new business expansion produce the wealth needed to guarantee that a sports team, entertainment center, or arts and cultural amenity continues to exist without ongoing subsidies?

The critics who challenge or question whether sports or any other amenity can or will attract human capital suggest that policy focuses on education and training should assume a paramount position in any regional economic development strategy. Advocates of the position that cities can change their images and create an attractive environment for entrepreneurs argue that entertainment centers do not minimize the need for education and training systems. They underscore that while all regions are focused on improving and enhancing education and training through investments in primary, secondary, and higher education, amenities must also be present to ensure the presence of desired images and development levels. The human capital or economic development argument that underpins the policies followed in Indianapolis, Columbus, Cleveland, and Reading was based on the idea that cities can attract the "idea generators" or "creative class" that drives development through the building of amenities and a new civic image.

When mass manufacturing offered millions of jobs and industries were dependent on the specific physical locations (frequently with access to water) to minimize production costs, people moved to where these businesses needed to locate. Success in the twenty-first century economy, as Garmise notes, is increasingly a function of the competitive advantage of places relative to their ability to attract and retain human capital.[19] With ideas increasingly becoming the currency of innovation and the inputs that drive an economy and business' future, corporations now locate where people want to live. The age-old axiom that people move to where the jobs are is changing and the new reality is that corporations locate where they believe (1) people want to live and (2) in areas where they have the greatest confidence that they can attract and retain the human capital required to foster innovation. Communities, cities, and regions that attract idea generators or the people likely to foster innovation are now as important for a corporation's location as a river was in the nineteenth century. As more and more manufacturing is outsourced to foreign countries and that which remains in the United States becomes computerized and less labor intensive, job growth for most regions is dependent on being a location where innovations are developed, ideas formulated, new discoveries made, and new processes and procedures created. Perhaps innovation and ideas—best enumerated by patents filed—have always driven the economy.[20] But, at a time when America was home to both innovation and manufacturing, the focus for many companies was on physical location where manufacturing could be the most profitable. With ideas, centers of innovations, and research increasingly separated from mass manufacturing locations, businesses now choose idea centers for their homes. Idea centers are the places that people choose to live based on what is important to them in terms of valued amenities: climate, entertainment, recreation, sports, culture, and neighborhoods.

Building on the themes of competitive advantage explained by Porter,[21] Garmise directs community leaders to focus on policies and programs that ensure that their communities are the ones that produce, attract, and retain the "creative classes" or idea generators needed by firms. This focus means that regions have to build urban environments that include the resources needed for human capital development and the amenities that define the quality of life. What this means for economic development is that leaders must build communities in which people want to live instead of focusing on ways to reduce costs to encourage businesses to locate in their region. It also means that a region must have educational or training programs to produce the human capital needed or continuously attract that capital. In practice, a human capital approach to economic development requires a focus on establishing exceptional education and training programs, but it also means making sure that the right mix of amenities is also available to give cities and regions the image and quality of life demanded by high-value human capital.[22]

With the migration to the southern and western states, some might think that climate is an overpowering factor in the locations chosen by highly educated workers. Growth rates in the Boston, Chicago, and Minneapolis/St. Paul regions, however, suggest that other factors can overcome weather and make an area a favored location for idea generators. The reality that northern regions and areas with snow and cold temperatures can also grow and prosper suggests that other factors also influence the location decisions of highly skilled workers. This reality is what has focused cities across the nation on amenities, such as sports, entertainment, arts, and culture. The idea, which is not at all far-fetched, is that with a sufficient amenity base, even 50 inches of annual snowfall and a ranking as the sixth coldest city in America (Minneapolis/St. Paul), could be overcome to make a region a magnet for human capital.

Florida and Clark sustain this line of reasoning, placing their emphasis on neighborhood-level amenities.[23] Neither Florida nor Clark minimizes the role of education in producing the social climate or amenity package that will attract highly skilled workers, but both underscore that cultural amenities that can range from neighborhood-based entertainment to bicycle paths are far more important than previously acknowledged. While this understanding might lead to a potentially excessive focus on consumption and entertainment, as Stacy Warren fears, in this race to retain human capital and establish the appropriate civic image, cities that do not have the right mix of amenities run the risk of becoming tied to an image of decline.[24] Communities without the appropriate and popular mix of amenities also risk having an image of being "minor league" or not being as exciting or as "fun a place to live" in comparison to cities with those amenities.

With rising income levels in such places as New York, Toronto, Chicago, and Boston, one would expect to find numerous amenities as there is a large and growing market demanding and willing to pay for upscale entertainment. For cities similar to Indianapolis or Cleveland, producing a range of big-ticket or neighborhood-level amenities, or a set of unique venues in a downtown area, requires establishing public/private partnerships to attract investors. Ensuring amenities are placed in downtown areas could even mean unique partnerships are required in faster growing areas like Los Angeles or San Diego where more attractive opportunities exist in other parts of the city.

A. Supply of Amenities

An investor's decision to be involved in providing an amenity is related to his/her interest in securing a profit and in being associated with a particular asset's presence in a region. Sloane described these two sets of aspirations or attributes as profit maximization and welfare maximization.[25] Profit maximization involves the actions of an owner of any amenity interested only in securing the greatest return from his/her investment. Welfare maximization refers to the intangible benefits or gains an owner receives as a result of ensuring an amenity's presence in a community (e.g., a team, orchestra, opera, etc.). Many supporters of the Cleveland Orchestra take great satisfaction from its national ranking and international prestige and their donations are made not to secure any financial return, but to guarantee the orchestra's success and presence in Cleveland.[26]

In communities where a welfare-maximizing benefactor is not present and when private entrepreneurs perceive the risks of earning a profit from the building of sports, entertainment, or arts and cultural facilities are too great, a new asset will only be built if the public sector also makes an investment. The public sector's investment reduces the risks to the private sector partner and helps to guarantee the profitability of the project. In some instances, the public and nonprofit sector partners are asked to finance the capital costs associated with both the tourist amenity and needed support facilities (hotels, restaurants, etc.). The public sector is also frequently responsible for any improvements needed in transportation, water, or environmental systems.[27]

B. Importance of Amenities

Rosentraub and Joo looked at amenities and the distribution of human capital in more than 300 metropolitan areas across the United States and concluded that "while it may be unclear if amenities attract human capital, the absence of amenities does reduce a region's attractiveness to workers, (and) investments in amusements and sports attractions were associated with higher levels of employment in the tourist sector, increasing household income levels, (and) the number of businesses in an area. Further, sports have a positive effect on the regional economy in both fast- and slow-growth cities."[28] These findings illustrate the importance of amenities for regional economic development through the association or concentration of a higher proportion of skilled human capital in regions with more amenities. Rosentraub and Joo also remind policy makers that an association between amenities and development does not imply causality. If the subsidies provided were too large, alternative investments could have been more productive or had larger impacts on regional development levels. Relative to image and identity, sports and amusements have an important influence and impact on household income levels and the number of businesses in an area, and those outcomes are linked to larger concentrations of human capital workers.

For some it may still be unclear if the "chicken or egg came first." In other words, did the concentration of highly skilled human capital workers, universities, or businesses create the demand for amenities? Or did the presence of amenities, including universities, lead to the concentration of highly skilled workers? For many public officials, the relationship appears simultaneous or dynamic.[29] For example, a city like Indianapolis could argue that it has leading colleges and universities and it is home to one of the world's most dynamic and innovative pharmaceutical corporations employing hundreds of scientists or "idea generators." In addition, the city is also home to Indiana University's Medical Center and several hospitals whose doctors have been pioneers in the advancement of important new procedures and therapies. Yet, it found itself languishing with too few amenities to attract more workers and businesses. It had a base of innovative businesses and a number of Florida's "creative class" workers. What it needed was more amenities.

Indeed, those critics of the relationship between amenities and development (amenity theory) who champion policies that emphasize education and worker training argue that every region has assets. In the same vein, it could be argued that many regions have excellent schools and education systems, worker training programs, and universities, yet they lag in development levels compared to other regions with more amenities. That would leave those regions to wonder if more amenities would attract more human capital. In this sense, then, the process is probably dynamic with causality hard if not impossible to identify. The real issue relative to theory validation is whether or not the investments in amenities change the distribution of human capital. That issue is directly addressed in the analysis of outcomes in both Indianapolis and Cleveland.

IV. Organic Urban Change versus Planned Redevelopment

Jane Jacobs championed the view that cities, as the home to complex economic and social processes and organizations, have a need for areas in decline with low rents at the same time that other neighborhoods boom. What is the positive value of areas with lower land values? These lower cost or inexpensive areas become favored locations where start-up businesses can find the space they need at an affordable price. These areas also serve as places where young talent can live as they try to develop new technologies, new processes, new companies and art. If all neighborhoods in a city were redeveloped, the cost of land and space would thwart the creation of new businesses as there would be no place for those start-up operations to exist.[30] Projects like those initiated by San Diego and Los Angeles, if not those of every city studied, would be prime examples of the destructive tendencies of planners against which Jane Jacobs campaigned her entire life. Large-scale planned developments that remade downtown areas—or any parts of an urban region—did not in her view evolve from the interactions and needs of the people and businesses that live in and help cities grow.

Jacobs also emphasized the value of ideas exchanged among people in urban areas and the contributions of these conversations to a somewhat serendipitous process by which new ideas are galvanized into economic enterprises and then new businesses. Marshall may have been the first to suggest that innovation emanates from the ideas exchanged by people through their interaction with each other.[31] He spoke of innovation coming from ideas in the air (a reference to conversations and exchanges between members of the creative class) and in that way established a foundation from which Jacobs would argue for lower priced land and neighborhoods to attract people experimenting with innovations. The focus on industry clusters and the creation of competitive advantage—ideas and theories explored by Porter[32]—can also be seen to draw inspiration from or linked to Marshall's ideas. These clusters employ large numbers of people with similar interests. When they meet and interact, ideas are exchanged and enhanced. Those interactions reinforce a competitive cluster and the existence of amenities attracts other potential workers and creates venues in which ideas are exchanged.

In this vein, then, large-scale projects are artificial efforts to create spaces for idea-generators to meet or efforts to create a sort of "bohemian" environment from which it is hoped economic development will emerge. Rather than disagreeing with Jacobs basic concepts, the planners behind projects like San Diego's Ballpark District, Columbus' Arena District, and Los Angeles' STAPLES Center and L.A. LIVE would argue that they just accelerated or advanced the natural process. Where Jacobs preferred an evolutionary approach and a natural evolution of ideas, innovation, clusters, and development, the political and economic elites pushing for redevelopment of aging neighborhoods and downtown areas want to accelerate change. Can they succeed by following some of the ideas and perspectives advanced by Florida, Clark, and Stolarick to establish clusters of creative class workers and idea-generators?[33] Or, is Jacobs' view valid that new development and clusters for idea-generators only occurs through a natural evolution? Some examples of success and failure from these large-scale planned development efforts are identified in Table 2.2.

A. Delayed Development or Stagnation?

Public leaders in each of the cities studied in this book decided sufficient time had passed and, with development and change not taking place as quickly as needed, they implicitly asked, "How long does one wait before interceding to change the location of economic activity and improve conditions in a declining part of a city?" Beyond the issues of the creation and attraction of clusters of highly skilled human capital and firms, such a question is particularly relevant for cities trying to ensure that the collected property and income taxes are sufficient to pay for needed public services. When a declining area improves, or when businesses that grew in that area expand, more tax money is realized. However, there is also risk that growing businesses or people, as their incomes rise, choose to live in other areas beyond the taxing boundaries of a city. If that occurs, a city that decides to follow Jacobs' perspective and rely on a more natural process where declining or slow-growth areas are the fertile ground for new business development could find itself fueling the economy of other cities while its own tax base stagnates or declines. Hence, ensuring that sufficient levels of amenities exist to attract and retain developing and expanding businesses is indeed a critical policy option that could be a necessary component

Table 2.2 Examples of Failure and Success from Planned Redevelopment

City	Facility/Date Opened	Measure of Success or Failure
Expectations Not Met		
Columbus, Ohio	City Center Mall/1988	Anchor stores lost, vacant space; no residential development or meeting areas opened for the "creative class"
Los Angeles	Convention Center/1971	Few bookings through 1998, tax support needed for capital and operating expenses; no development and no meeting places for "creative class"
Arlington, Texas	Ballpark in Arlington/1994	Little real estate development surrounding the facility and no meeting places
Charlotte	Coliseum (Arena)/1986	Little real estate development; replaced by downtown facility integrated into a large-scale revitalization effort
Expectations Met		
Indianapolis	Several facilities built 1974 through 2008	New image; city investment of $2.5 billion attracts more than $5 billion in additional investment; numerous restaurants, theaters, expansion of Lilly Corporation
San Diego	Ballpark (Petco Park)/2004	Public investment of $200+ million led to more than $1 billion in private redevelopment investment, thousands of residences, new neighborhood with access to mass transit and the coast
Los Angeles	STAPLES Center/1999; L.A. LIVE/2007–2010	Public investment of less than $200 million leads to $2.8 billion in private investment; surrounded by residences and includes many entertainment venues

complementing Jacobs' perspectives. Simply put, a city without a desired amenity base could face the flight of new firms and highly skilled human capital.

Within regions there is also a possibility that certain areas are preferred by successful start-up businesses and they relocate to these higher profile neighborhoods to become part of clusters of activities beyond the boundaries of the central city that fostered their existence. If that takes place, a city that chooses not to intercede to bring development to a stagnating area could lose out on future development activities. The movement of successful businesses to preferred areas is related to the theory of growth poles discussed by Perroux and Hirschman.[34]

B. Growth Poles

There is disagreement as to what actually constitutes a growth pole. There is also concern that there is insufficient empirical evidence to sustain the observation that successful areas (often labeled growth poles) can absorb all investment and, therefore, deflect economic activity away from other parts of a region. Yet, in the case of San Diego and Los Angeles, both cities had waited for years and perhaps decades for development to occur in parts of their downtown areas. Los Angeles did not see any redevelopment after the building of a convention center and feared accelerating decline in that area as well as in several other parts of downtown.[35] At the same time, other sections of Los Angeles were experiencing substantial growth and rising land values while attracting more investment and business activity. A large portion of Los Angeles' downtown area was deteriorating and leaders were concerned that the recently expanded convention center would continue to fail. Los Angeles' leadership saw no benefit from having a downtown area with an expanding core of deteriorating and derelict properties. In San Diego, an area immediately adjacent to downtown had also languished even after the development of a new transportation system and renovations in other parts of the downtown area. There was concern that if deteriorating conditions continued or even spread the advances in other parts of downtown would be threatened. Neither city chose to wait for a natural process to bring redevelopment or to incorporate a declining area into a long-term plan to serve as a fertile area for new businesses to form and begin their work. Each fearing its downtown core could continue to deteriorate and the implications of that decline decided on aggressive action to force new development into designated areas.

All cities have to evaluate whether or not Jane Jacobs' views of death and life through urban regeneration is likely to occur in a timely manner to protect a city's fiscal health. As the cases of Los Angeles and San Diego will show, leaders there chose not to wait. The evidence provided in those case studies can help assess whether concerted public policy actions to divert economic activity was successful or not. Indianapolis, Cleveland, and Reading—fearing widespread deterioration and not just a declining part of their cities—moved more aggressively and their experiences tell the tale of amenities and redevelopment in the declining Rust Belt parts of the United States. The measurement of success in each of these cases is the extent to which additional private capital was attracted to invest in residences and other amenities. If that took place, then it would be argued that a new center of activity had been created that diverted capital from other growth poles or faster growing parts of the region or country. As noted, all cities would point out that they emphasize both

Figure 2.2 Two faces of revitalization. (a) A downtown bed and breakfast; (b) the Indianapolis Arts Garden spanning Illinois Avenue. (Photos courtesy of Mark S. Rosentraub.)

neighborhood revitalization and large-scale activities, but there often are far more public funds committed toward big-ticket items. Figure 2.2 depicts one example of neighborhood and big-ticket redevelopment in Indianapolis. The restored Bed and Breakfast Inn is part of the Massachusetts Avenue revitalization effort and the downtown Arts Garden links a retail mall to hotels and office buildings.

In an era of mobile capital, a critique of Jacobs' views could be offered in noting that urban revitalization of transitional areas might occur only when real estate prices rise sufficiently in one part of a city making another part that was unattractive suddenly valuable. It is possible if alternatives to those areas exist or if there is no expansion of the economy that the normal process of regeneration she championed does not occur. Fort Greene Place in Brooklyn was a deteriorating area for decades and its revitalization is linked the rising value of real estate in Manhattan. To avoid longer commutes, Brooklyn became a desirable location and a gentrification process ensued. One can find similar neighborhoods in many growing cities as well as examples of areas that have yet to benefit. That would seem to sustain aspects of Jacobs' theory, but in cities similar to Indianapolis and Cleveland locked into the throes of a severe restructuring of the economy there was no economic expansion in other parts of the city that increased the attractiveness of other inner city

Figure 2.2   (continued).

neighborhoods. Waiting for growth that occurs naturally did not appear to be a viable option. Those cities. just like downtown Los Angeles or parts of San Diego, may well benefit from large-scaled and planned redevelopment efforts.

V. Business Leaders and Urban Redevelopment

Clarence Stone in his study of Atlanta's political power structure furthered a line of research and reasoning initiated by Hunter assessing the roles played by corporate, community, and elected leaders in shaping a region's economic development strategies, policies, and public investments.[36] An intellectual debate ensued between those who found decision making to be shaped by competing groups—the pluralistic approach to understanding power in American cities[37]—and those who found that small groups of corporate, community, and political leaders controlled economic development decisions.[38] To describe the associations or linkages between leaders, two terms are repeatedly used. The first, *a growth coalition*, refers to business and other community leaders that unify to support public policies that will facilitate building, expansion, and growth in an area.[39] If this coalition sustains itself across long periods of time and strives to control the use of tax money, then some use the term *regime* to describe these nonelected groups that then direct economic development strategies. There is a degree of vagueness or flexibility in the application of these terms. For example, Rosentraub and Helmke found that business leaders in a small city unified when there was a need for concerted action, but did not have the degree of control over decisions nor the permanence conveyed by the use of the word regime and as used by Stone, Elkin, and others.[40] The key point for any study of the role of big-ticket items is to acknowledge that business leaders might well assume a lead role in seeking support for a ballpark, museum, or another amenity. But, at the same time, these same groups might also be supporting myriad other economic development initiatives designed to revitalize a downtown area and a city. The focus on big-ticket items might well enhance the interests of some corporations, but changing a city's image and making the city a more attractive place to live, will also be shown to be integral to the actions of business leaders that frequently seek to have amenities built in downtown areas.

Some have also argued that some decision processes involving big-ticket items have limited opportunities for widespread public debate and participation. Yet, voters in Cleveland twice rejected proposals for a new ballpark. Voters in Columbus, Ohio, also rejected a tax increase for a new arena supported by the business community. San Diego's voters approved the ballpark district plan. If the voters had rejected the proposal, a new ballpark for the Padres would not have been built. The public's participation may be limited to votes on a specific referendum to support public money for a facility, but that is not unusual. Planning efforts in most cities involve extensive public hearings, but in the end it is elected city or county officials that have the final vote on citywide and neighborhood plans, the design of facilities, and their fit into neighborhoods and overall development strategies. As will be demonstrated, business leaders had far less control than some critics of big-ticket items have argued.

Noting that voters and elected officials have control over public investment decisions there is still an antidemocratic nature to the empowerment of any small group to lead revitalization efforts. Yet, what also must be acknowledged is that in communities where business and elected leaders are not working together there is a frequent complaint that there is a lack of concerted leadership to either advance a region's economic development or lead new initiatives.[41] The provision of excessive subsidies for economic development identified and studied in Squires' collection points to the possibility of unbalanced power that can be exerted by corporate leaders. This imbalance may have led to excessive subsidies to sustain the development desired by elite groups.[42] Other factors, however, also assume large roles in explaining why subsidies persist when it comes to the building of sports facilities and local elites may have assumed a far smaller role in the provision of subsidies than earlier researchers concluded.[43] (This point is discussed in the next section.) What needs to be acknowledged is that concerted action by business leaders has the potential for advancing a city's interests. The ways in which different cities accomplished that objective is detailed in each of the case studies as sports facilities, entertainment complexes, and arts and cultural centers were built to revitalize downtown areas.[44] There is also legitimate concern that a focus on big-ticket amenities has diverted communities from exploring and implementing alternative economic development strategies.[45] What will be shown, however, is that no community or region ignores neighborhood or community interests when building sports facilities, entertainment complexes, or other amenities.

In each of the cities, business and elected leaders formed partnerships to lead the redevelopment efforts. In Los Angeles, a new mayor's staff built a partnership with the owners of two professional sports teams. In San Diego, the owner of the Padres reached out to the city and other leaders to create a new plan and initiative. In Cleveland and Indianapolis, the entire redevelopment effort was led by business and community leaders that could well fit Stone's definition of a regime. In Columbus, when business leaders saw their proposal for a tax increase to build a new arena defeated by voters, they quickly put forward a new plan that protected the public's interest. Even those in Columbus critical of the original plan for a new arena applauded the creation of the Arena District, the building of the new arena for a professional hockey team paid for by private investors, and the new development projects that followed. In Cleveland and Indianapolis, support for and focus upon a big-ticket redevelopment strategy did not preclude active participation in other community development efforts and extensive redevelopment in other parts of the cities.

VI. The Unbalanced Playing Field between Teams and Cities

The essential problem for the public sector in its negotiation with franchise owners is the leagues' control of the number of teams that exist and where they play. A free market does not exist; the supply of teams—valued assets for the social capital of communities—is controlled by small groups of owners making each league a cartel. When challenged with regard to their status, team owners and the league respond that, while there are defined market areas for each team and the league controls the total number of teams that exist, power is needed given the competition that exists for fans' attention and their discretionary dollars from other forms of entertainment. That argument is best resolved by a look at the value of teams and some very simple examples.

A. What Are Teams Worth?

Each year *Forbes* estimates the value of professional sports teams in North America. Nineteen NFL franchises and the New York Yankees are worth more than $1 billion and the Dallas Cowboys top the list with an estimated value of $1.6 billion. More than half of the 62 franchises, 54.8 percent, are worth at least $500 million (Table 2.3). These values were sustained at the same time that consumers spent

Table 2.3 *Forbes Magazine's* **Estimate of the Value of MLB and NFL Franchises (2008)**

Team	Value ($)	Team	Value ($)
Dallas Cowboys	1,612,000,000	Oakland Raiders	861,000,000
Washington Redskins	1,538,000,000	Minnesota Vikings	839,000,000
New England Patriots	1,324,000,000	New York Mets	824,000,000
New York Yankees	1,306,000,000	Boston Red Sox	816,000,000
New York Giants	1,178,000,000	Los Angeles Dodgers	694,000,000
New York Jets	1,170,000,000	Chicago Cubs	642,000,000
Houston Texans	1,125,000,000	Los Angeles Angels	500,000,000
Philadelphia Eagles	1,116,000,000	Atlanta Braves	497,000,000
Indianapolis Colts	1,076,000,000	San Francisco Giants	494,000,000
Chicago Bears	1,064,000,000	St. Louis Cardinals	484,000,000
Baltimore Ravens	1,062,000,000	Philadelphia Phillies	481,000,000
Denver Broncos	1,061,000,000	Seattle Mariners	466,000,000
Tampa Bay Buccaneers	1,053,000,000	Houston Astros	463,000,000
Miami Dolphins	1,044,000,000	Washington Nationals	460,000,000
Carolina Panthers	1,040,000,000	Chicago White Sox	443,000,000
Cleveland Browns	1,035,000,000	Cleveland Indians	417,000,000
Green Bay Packers	1,023,000,000	Texas Rangers	412,000,000
Kansas City Chiefs	1,016,000,000	Detroit Tigers	407,000,000
Pittsburgh Steelers	1,015,000,000	Baltimore Orioles	398,000,000
Seattle Seahawks	1,010,000,000	San Diego Padres	385,000,000
Tennessee Titans	994,000,000	Arizona Diamondbacks	379,000,000
Cincinnati Bengals	941,000,000	Colorado Rockies	371,000,000
New Orleans Saints	937,000,000	Toronto Blue Jays	352,000,000
St. Louis Rams	929,000,000	Cincinnati Reds	337,000,000
Detroit Lions	917,000,000	Milwaukee Brewers	331,000,000
Arizona Cardinals	914,000,000	Minnesota Twins	328,000,000

Table 2.3 *Forbes Magazine's* **Estimate of the Value of MLB and NFL Franchises (2008)**

Team	Value ($)	Team	Value ($)
San Diego Chargers	888,000,000	Oakland Athletics	323,000,000
Buffalo Bills	885,000,000	Kansas City Royals	301,000,000
Jacksonville Jaguars	876,000,000	Pittsburgh Pirates	292,000,000
Atlanta Falcons	872,000,000	Tampa Bay Rays	290,000,000
San Francisco 49ers	865,000,000	Florida Marlins	256,000,000

$9.7 billion for movie tickets in 2007[46] and a whopping $23.4 billion for DVDs.[47] It might be hard to argue that the leagues need market controls when they achieved this level of economic success despite more than $30 billion in sales related to motion picture entertainment. In addition, 11 of the 20 most watched television shows of all time were sports events.[48] The importance of sports in American society is clearly evident by its enduring popularity and the leagues need no market protections to ensure their financial success.

Further, while sports do compete with other forms of entertainment for consumers' discretionary dollars, long-standing scholarship has analyzed and noted the social significance of sports to societies and the social capital it creates.[49] That importance suggests that even when or if sports were engaged in more direct competition for revenue with other forms of entertainment, its special place in the life of virtually all societies would allow it to continue to assume its domination.

A simple example to show the effect of this control is to note that the Cleveland Indians, playing in a market area of approximately 2.1 million people, has an estimated market value of $417 million. In 1999, Larry Dolan purchased the team for $320 million producing an absolute gain of almost $100 million, a 30.3 percent return on his investment in less than 10 years. In constant (2007) dollars the investment of $320 million would be equal to $394.2 million. In real terms, then, the return on the investment was 7.1 percent. While other investments could generate larger returns, the Dolan family also enjoys the intangible benefits of owning a storied franchise. Regardless, these numbers suggest that a population base of 2.1 million people is sufficient to produce the financial returns required to attract investors.

The New York metropolitan area with 18.8 million residents has but two MLB teams. If all that is needed to build a market value of $417 million and attract investments is a regional population of 2.1 million (as in the case of the Cleveland Indians), how many teams should exist in the metropolitan New York region? While nine would certainly be absurd, so is two, given the demand for baseball in the region. Being able to limit the number of teams in the market to two has helped the Yankees secure a market value in excess of $1 billion while the

THE NEGOTIATING GAME IN PRACTICE: HOW CITIES
SOMETIMES MISS THEIR VALUE TO TEAMS

In the late 1980s, the Chicago White Sox threatened to move to Florida and that prompted major concessions from the Illinois legislature for the building of a new ballpark. The public sector agreed to pay almost 100 percent of the cost of the new facility. And where did the White Sox threaten they would move? They were prepared to move to the Tampa/St. Petersburg area where the Tampa Bay Devil Rays now struggle to attract fans. The Chicago metropolitan region had a June 2006 population of 7.9 million; Tampa/St. Petersburg area had 2.7 million people. Even if one divides the Chicago market in half because of the presence of the Cubs, the White Sox were threatening to leave a larger market for a smaller one. In addition, in 2005 the Chicago metropolitan area had a median income level of $68,550 while the comparable figure for the Tampa Bay/St. Petersburg area was $52,150. Would the White Sox have been better off in a smaller market with a lower median income figure, or did Illinois misread the value of their market?

Chicago also decided to assume responsibility for a majority of the cost to renovate Soldier Field. That project cost $587 million and the public sector paid $387 million even though there were no realistic relocation options available to the NFL's Bears. The team had looked for a better deal throughout the region considering, first, a short move across the border into Indiana and, when that was not feasible, examined the possibilities in Chicago's western suburbs. Despite the realization that the Bears could not find a better location in the NFL's second largest market area, the team was still able to

Mets are valued at more than $800 million. If there were more teams in the New York region, the revenues earned by the existing franchises would decline. If the Yankees earned less, they would have fewer dollars to spend for players and then the Indians could compete with them for the best athletes without a subsidy from taxpayers in Greater Cleveland. Similar observations could be made regarding the NFL's power over market forces, especially when the Pittsburgh region with approximately 2.7 million people allows the Steelers to be worth more than a billion dollars. The Dallas/Fort Worth region, with more than twice the number of residents, also hosts but one NFL team. If free market forces existed, more teams would exist in that region.

B. Implications of the Leagues' Control of the Supply of Teams

With no free market dictating how many teams exist, cities that want a local franchise are forced into bidding against other communities. To be sure there are markets secure a substantial public investment to one of the nation's most historic athletic facilities, Soldier Field.

When MLB, which had purchased the Montreal Expos, decided to relocate the franchise, Washington, D.C. was competing with one of its western suburbs as well as locations in southeastern Virginia and Portland, Oregon. In short order, the choices were narrowed to Portland or Washington, D.C. Again, from a statistical standpoint, there did not seem to be much real competition. The Washington, D.C. region had a 2006 population of 5.1 million people, more than twice that of Greater Portland (2.1 million). Median household income in Greater Portland in 2005 was a robust $65,900, but this was $20,000 lower than the $86,200 figure for Washington, D.C. and its suburbs. Despite these advantages, Washington, D.C. agreed to spend $611 million for a new ballpark to secure the team. The team committed $20 million toward construction and accepted an amusement tax on tickets sold and the sale of memorabilia.[52] The team is also responsible for all routine maintenance across the term of the lease with its rental payments starting at $3.5 million and then escalating to $5.5 million in the seventh year. In future years the rent increases by 2 percent (less $110,000) and there is an additional rental fee of $1 for every ticket sold in excess of 2.5 million. Rent increments can only be negated if the Nationals' attendance falls below the median of all MLB teams across any three-year period. Lastly, necessary capital improvements are the responsibility of the public sector. If the public sector and the team cannot agree on what constitutes a necessary capital improvement, an outside arbitrator reviews the claim and decides whether the team or the public sector must bear the cost.

in which the leagues want teams to advance their image and exposure, yet even in Chicago and New York, MLB and NFL teams have secured, in some instances, public investments to pay for facilities and in other instances other incentives. Given the market value of teams in Chicago and New York, any public support is hard to justify. Yet, those incentives are sometimes provided to avoid the possible relocation of a team to another part of the metropolitan region outside of the city's limits. In the Dallas/Fort Worth region, Arlington has consistently provided public support for teams and has been successful in convincing the Texas Rangers to remain in the city and the Dallas Cowboys to move to their community. Dallas, in turn, provided subsidies for a new home for its NBA and NHL teams to minimize the risk of their relocation to other parts of the metropolitan region. Smaller regions are forced to provide subsidies or risk a team being lured to another area.[50] Zimbalist and Long estimated the public investment in new sports facilities built from 2000 to 2006 to be almost $5 billion (2006 dollars).[51] Many other facilities were built in the 1990s, and the public sector's investment for the new home of the Indianapolis Colts that opened in 2008 was in excess of $700 million.

C. How Did the Leagues Amass Their Economic Power?

Sports teams and leagues emerged in the United States in the post-Civil War period and at a time when commercial entertainment became a major industry. Propelled both by the growth of the U.S. economy and the number of cities with large population bases, a demand for entertainment was produced. In 1870, the United States had 14 cities with 100,000 or more residents and 8 with as many as 200,000. Twenty years later, three cities had at least one million residents and 16 urban centers had populations of 200,000 or more. By the turn of the twentieth century, America had 19 cities with 200,000 or more residents and 11 with at least 300,000. The expanding economy gave these urban residents extra money and the demand for entertainment created commercial opportunities. Burlesque, live theater, P. T. Barnum's circus, the forerunner of the modern movie, and the founding of the National Baseball League (today's National League) each occurred in the 1870s. Through the next decades, the movie industry would expand, and a second professional baseball league would be established.

These new businesses were not subject to any oversight from the public sector. No one envisioned that teams would become valued community assets, and there was no appreciation of the social capital produced by sports teams. Sports were regarded as just another form of entertainment, and entrepreneurs were free to respond (or not) to the demand for teams. Regulation of sports or protection of the public interest beyond limited issues of building safety were not part of any public or social agenda.

In the earliest years of professional sports, entrepreneurs experimented with two different forms for professional sports games and the attracting of paying customers. Teams of paid players would sometimes "tour" and play against people or teams in a variety of local communities. This process was referred to as *barnstorming*, with the word affectionately recalling the use of barns and pastures as part of the improvised playing fields for baseball. Owners learned that while these forays into the outlying parts of cities or rural areas could be profitable, far more money could be earned by playing games in the midst of the larger urban centers between teams of paid professional athletes following a well-publicized schedule and an agreed upon set of rules. Impartial umpires were added so fans could be assured that rules were followed and not manipulated to benefit one team.

Commercial sport was initially a risky business, but probably no more volatile than other entertainment enterprises.[53] Many teams failed, some owners then relocated and started new teams in other cities, and some owners moved their existing teams to other cities. From the original teams in the National League, only the Braves, Cubs, and Reds remain with the Boston Braves having made two moves (to Milwaukee and then to Atlanta). The New York Giants joined the league in 1883 along with the Philadelphia Phillies, followed by the Pittsburgh Pirates in 1887, the St. Louis Cardinals in 1892, and the Brooklyn (Trolley) Dodgers in 1890.

The Phillies, Pirates, and Cardinals still play in their original home cities and the Dodgers and Giants moved to Los Angeles and San Francisco.

As the country continued to grow, and the National League was a bit lax in expanding to other cities, a competing league emerged. The American League was founded in 1901 with teams in Baltimore, Boston, Chicago, Cleveland, Detroit, Milwaukee, Philadelphia, and Washington, D.C. The new American League placed teams in Boston, Chicago, and Philadelphia to compete with the older league and after two years the owners of the Baltimore Highlanders decided to challenge the Giants and Dodgers in New York and renamed the team the Yankees. The Milwaukee franchise would move to St. Louis (to become the Browns) in 1902 giving that city a team in each league. After World War II, the St. Louis Browns would move to Baltimore (1954) replacing the team that moved to New York in 1903. The forerunners of the modern NFL and NBA followed this model of establishing leagues of teams in different towns and cities and then gradually relocating all franchises to the largest urban centers. For example, today's NBA was founded in Fort Wayne, Indiana, where the Zollner (team owner's name) Pistons played for 16 years (9 years in the NBA) before relocating to Detroit.

The central business principle for each league was that each owner respected the market area of other teams. This meant they would not move into market areas served by other teams and would play games only with teams that were league members. Eventually, all competing leagues in each sport merged to minimize competition for players (thereby lowering salaries) and maximize the ability to receive support from local governments. The American and National Leagues formed Major League Baseball and then bought out the fledgling Federal League. The American Football League, founded in 1961, merged with the NFL after less than six years of direct competition, representing the second wave of mergers that created the current NFL. Mergers also led to the formation of today's NBA.

As noted, to underscore their power, teams did move even when fans and cities objected. The Brooklyn Dodgers, New York Giants, St. Louis Browns, Boston Braves, Milwaukee Braves, Washington Senators (first and second franchises), Montreal Expos, Houston Oilers, Oakland Raiders (to Los Angeles and then back to Oakland), Los Angeles Rams (to Anaheim and then St. Louis), Cleveland Rams, Cleveland Browns, Syracuse Nationals, and Kansas City Kings each relocated. Every move is tied to an owner's desire to serve a market where there is excess consumer demand for professional sports and to make sure that every community understands the implicit control enjoyed by the leagues. Communities understand the costs of failing to provide subsidies.

The key to being able to attract public sector support is to create and maintain an artificial scarcity of franchises and require a four-phase program for success. First, to thwart the possibility that entrepreneurs who wanted franchises, but did not get them, start a new league anchored in underserved areas, a slow process of expansion is required to place teams in new and emerging markets. Second, if a new league emerges, the more established one will let it try to operate for a few years to see if its owners can actually compete for players and absorb the inevitable start-up costs. If the new league is able to survive, absorption of the most successful franchises might be the best strategy to ensure that player costs do not escalate to the point that profitability is reduced. Third, all leagues pursue strategies designed to ensure that the most lucrative broadcast revenue deals are available only to its members. Fourth, the leagues have also tried to secure the necessary legal protections to sustain control over the supply of franchises independent of market forces. Each of the leagues has pursued these policies and the histories of their success are documented.[54] This success ensures the continued existence of the environment in which subsidies can be secured. How does a city survive and prosper in such a setting?

VII. Challenging the Leagues in Court, at the Statehouse, or in Congress

Some have suggested that to protect themselves cities should include damage clauses in the leases between a team and a city for use of a facility. There are two limitations with this line of argument. First, any specification of damages must be part of a lease that is negotiated with the team. As already noted, the negotiating table is slanted toward the teams. With that bargaining power, no team's legal representatives are going to accept penalty clauses or damage specifications that are excessive or onerous. Second, damage clauses provide no protection for a community if a lease is expiring and the owner decides to accept a more lucrative offer from another city.

Another example of the relatively worthless nature of liquidation clauses to protect the public interest is the recent battle between Seattle and its NBA franchise, the Sonics. The team's owner, in November 2007, announced his interest in moving the team to Oklahoma City while continuing to make the required rental payments for the remaining few years of the lease. The NBA supported the team's decision, in part because of Seattle's inability or unwillingness to build a new arena. The NBA's commissioner noted that if the team left Seattle, the city would never get another team. As reported by the Associated Press on November 8, 2007, David Stern, commissioner of the NBA, said:

> I'd love to find a way to keep the team there because if the team moves, there's not going to be another team there (Seattle), not in any conceivable future plan that I could envision, and that would be too bad.[55]

This recent battle—and the owner's success in getting approval to move his team—highlights the limitations with liquidated damages and illustrates the power of the leagues to control supply.

The lessons from Baltimore's experience when the Colts decided to move to Indianapolis provides one example of a legal tool that can be used to thwart a team's relocation plans. Baltimore tried to seize the team under its eminent domain powers drawing from the experience gained when Oakland tried to use this tool. Oakland tried to seize the Raiders when the team relocated to Los Angeles years earlier and while a lower court ruled California's eminent domain laws pertain only to real estate, the state's Supreme Court held that, because intangible property could be valued just like real estate, it too was subject to eminent domain. The case was then remanded for trial to the original lower court, but Oakland could not successfully demonstrate the public purpose served by seizing the team.[56]

To avoid a legal debate over the issue of whether or not a team's presence contributes to a public purpose, Maryland passed a law including professional sports teams among the assets in a state that could be seized under its eminent domain laws. Empowered with this new legal protection, Baltimore filed to seize the team, but delivered the papers a few hours after the famous midnight move of the team's assets from their headquarters in Maryland to Indiana. Baltimore continued with its lawsuit and its right to seize the team as valuable intangible property under Maryland's new law was sustained. The court concluded that the law only applied to businesses in Maryland and, by the time Baltimore had served the proper legal documents, the Colts were domiciled (in a legal sense) in Indiana.

The Maryland case identifies one legal tool that a community could use if appropriate state laws existed. It certainly would be in the public interest for each state that is home to a professional sports team to ensure that its eminent domain laws permit a taking of intangible property such as a professional sports team. However, one must recognize that the four sports leagues will oppose such legislation. When Indiana briefly considered amending its laws to guarantee that teams could be seized, substantial opposition from the professional sports leagues and their allies ensured that the bill was never brought forward from its committee. Such opposition and political pressure can be anticipated if any state pursues a change in its eminent domain laws. This is not to suggest that eminent domain is not valuable as a tool to protect the public's interest. The political process can be a very difficult arena in which to ensure that the public's investment in a facility for a professional sports team generates economic benefits.

The ability to change the negotiating table between cities and teams through new federal laws has been equally unsuccessful. In 2001, the U.S. Senate's Committee on the Judiciary did not support the Fairness in Antitrust in National Sports Act (FANS). Various Congressional hearings called when teams have moved, most recently when the Browns moved to Baltimore, also failed to result in the passage of any law that would have changed the protections offered to cities if a team attempted to leave. Indeed, looking across myriad times there have been hearings and discussions at state legislatures or at the Congress one is reminded of the Supreme Court's words in *Toolson v. New York Yankees*, "Congress has had the ruling under consideration, but has not seen fit to bring such business under these laws."[57] States and the federal government have known that teams valued by communities have been moving to other cities since the 1950s. In more than a half-century only one state has passed just one law and Congress has failed to take any action to protect the social capital value of teams. Recognizing that legislative activity is unlikely to occur, perhaps the best and only way to protect a city's financial interests is to focus on real estate development instead of legal and political processes to change the outcome for cities when they spend tax dollars to build sports facilities.

VIII. Revitalization and Development as an Alternative to Subsidies

So what is the value of this history and the control the leagues have over the supply of teams for this book? The importance lies in the reality that the negotiation table when dealing with a team regarding a sports facility is tilted in their favor. Therefore, cities will be more often in the position of having to make concessions or providing subsidies. The best and probably only way to turn those subsidies into investments is to anchor each and every amenity to a development plan that has a very real potential to produce economic and community development for a city. If such a strategy is not followed, cities are far less likely to see any tangible economic returns from their commitment of tax money. Past research clearly shows there are extremely limited or nonexistent economic benefits from a team's presence or a facility (or any other amenity) that is not part of a comprehensive redevelopment effort. This book is designed to provide community leaders with the potential for economic benefit if amenities are part of a comprehensive revitalization strategy.

Each of the case studies focus on how cities built the amenities they wanted and then tried to guarantee that subsidies became investments in a comprehensive redevelopment strategy. Some might argue that focusing on real estate development to ensure benefits exist from payments for amenities is either avoiding a confrontation on the excessive market control engineered by the sports leagues or biasing the desired strategy toward a single response. The criticism that excessive reliance on real estate development could have negative consequences for a city's development will be addressed in many of the case studies.

IX. Summary

The focus on big-ticket amenities for revitalization is rooted in understandings of the need to attract and retain human capital. Each expenditure has been made in response to the view that amenities are inexorably linked to human capital and the regions that will prosper in the future are those that attract and retain more of these idea-generators or members of Richard Florida's super creative class. The big-ticket investments are complemented by neighborhood-level development even though elites are inexorably involved in the decisions made. The cities that have turned subsidies into investments have not directly confronted the cartel status of sports, but have chosen paths that linked owners or others to development strategies that turned subsidies into profitable or valuable investments. Did every city succeed? The results and the lessons learned unfold in the chapters ahead.

Endnotes

1. Jacobs, J. 1993. *The death and life of great American cities.* New York: Modern Library.
2. Stone, C. 1989. *Regime politics: Governing Atlanta, 1946-1988.* Lawrence: University of Kansas Press.
3. Squires, G., ed. 1989. *Unequal partnerships: Political economy of urban redevelopment in post-war America.* New Brunswick, NJ: Rutgers University Press. Squires and his colleagues initially raised the issue of the motives and goals of public/private partnerships in *Unequal Partnerships.* Subsequently, numerous others have questioned the motives of business leaders in advocating for the building of amenities, sport facilities, and convention centers that involve large investments of tax dollars. See, for example: Cagan. J. and N. deMause. 1998. *Field of schemes: How the great stadium swindle turns public money into private profit.* Monroe, ME: Common Courage Press. Also: Sanders, H. 2002. Convention myths and markets: A critical review of convention center feasibility studies. *Economic Development Quarterly.* 16 (3): 195–210.
4. Moret, S., M. Fleming, and P. O. Hovey. 2008. Effective chambers of commerce: A key to regional economic prosperity. In *Retooling for growth: Building a 21st century economy in America's older industrial areas,* ed. McGahey, R. M. and J. S. Vey, 119–148, Washington, D.C.: Brookings Institution.
5. Kennedy, S. and M. S. Rosentraub. 2000. Public-private partnerships, professional sports teams, and the protection of the public's interests. *The American Review of Public Administration* 30 (4): 436–459.
6. The idea that a creative class of workers—something that is an interesting elaboration of the importance of human capital—drives economic development has initiated a flurry of discussions and analyses. Clark's work has helped focus attention on the role of amenities in attracting and retaining valued human capital. See: Florida, R. 2002. *The rise of the creative class.* New York: Basic Books; and: Clark, T. N., ed. 2004. *The city as an entertainment machine.* Amsterdam: Elsevier-JAI Press.
7. Florida, *The rise of the creative class,* 224–225.
8. Ibid., 224–225.
9. Malanga, S. 2004. The curse of the creative class. *City Journal,* Winter, 36 (40): 36–45.
10. Peck, J. 2005. Struggling with the creative class. *International Journal of Urban and Regional Research* 29 (4): 74–770.
11. Ibid., 749.
12. Swindell, D. 2000. Issue representation in neighborhood organizations: Questing for democracy at the grassroots. *Journal of Urban Affairs* 22 (2): 123–137.
13. Hoyman, M. and C. Faricy. 2009. It takes a village: A test of the creative class, social capital, and human capital theories. *Urban Affairs Review* 44 (3): 311–333.

14. Longworth, R. C. 2007. *Caught in the middle: America's heartland in the age of globalism.* New York: Bloomsbury USA. In this book, the point is underscored that the Midwest is home to some of the nation's greatest universities producing thousands of graduates each year. Many of these well-trained engineers, managers, etc., leave the Midwest for cities that have assumed a larger role in a variety of global networks. This underscores the point that in Pennsylvania, Ohio, Indiana, and Michigan substantial investments are being made to develop human capital. A focus on building amenities has not displaced this commitment. There are also substantial amounts of money spent on primary and secondary education. Despite these investments, cities like Cincinnati, Cleveland, Columbus, Detroit, and Indianapolis have not become as popular destinations for people with advanced education and job skills. This has encouraged leaders in several cities to pursue policies designed to enhance amenities. The leaders of one national real estate development firm headquartered in Cleveland reported that they have substantial trouble convincing some staff to locate in their main office. These people are very willing to be assigned to offices in Washington, D.C., New York, and Denver.

15. Mason, D. S. 2008. Synecdochic images and city branding. Unpublished paper presented at The Role of Sports and Entertainment Facilities in Urban Development Conference, Edmonton, Alberta, February 12, Faculty of Physical Education and Recreation, University of Alberta (and the Edmonton Chamber of Commerce).

16. McGahey, R. and J. S Vey, eds. 2008. *Retooling for growth: Building a 21st Century economy in America's older industrial areas.* Washington, D.C.: The Brookings Institution.

17. Wojan, T. R., D. M. Lambert, and A. McGranahan. 2007. Emoting with their feet: Bohemian attraction to creative milieu. *Journal of Economic Geography* 31: 711–736.

18. See, for example, Hannigan, J. 1998. *Fantasy city: Pleasure and profit in the postmodern metropolis.* London: Routledge Press. Also see Hoffman, L., S. S. Fainstein, and D. R. Judd, eds. 2003. *Cities and visitors: Regulating people, markets, and city space.* New York: John Wiley & Sons.

19. Garmise, S. 2006. *People and the competitive advantage of place: Building a workplace for the 21st century.* Armonk, NY: M. E. Sharpe.

20. Fogarty, M.S., G. S. Garofalo, and D. C. Hammack, C. 2002. *Cleveland from startup to the present: Innovation and entrepreneurship in the 19th and early 20th centuries.* Cleveland: Center for Regional Economic Issues, Weatherhead School of Business, Case Western Reserve University, http://generationfoundation.org/pubs/ClevelandFromStartupToPresent.pdf.

21. Porter, M. E. 1985. *Competitive advantage: Creating and sustaining superior performance.* New York: The Free Press.

22. Hannigan, *Fantasy city.*

23. Florida, *The rise of the creative class*; Clark, *The city as an entertainment machine.*

24. Warren, S. 1994. Disneyfication of the metropolis: Popular resistance in Seattle. *Journal of Urban Affairs* 16 (2): 89–108.

25. Sloane, P. J. 1971. The economics of professional football: The football club as a utility maximiser. *Scottish Journal of Political Economy.* 18 (2): 121–146.

26. Observations based on interviews with philanthropists in Cleveland in 2007; the identity of the benefactor and the exact date of the interview are withheld on their request.

27. Rosentraub, M. S. 1997a. *Major league losers: The real cost of sports and who's paying for it.* New York: Basic Books.

28. Rosentraub, M. S. and M. Joo. 2009. Tourism and economic development: Which investments produce gains for regions? *Tourism Management* (forthcoming).
29. Chema, T. 1996. When professional sports justify the subsidy: A reply to Robert A. Baade. *Journal of Urban Affairs* 18: (1) 19–22.
30. Jacobs, J. 1969. *The economy of cities*. New York: Penguin Books; Jacobs, *The death and life of great American cities*.
31. Marshall, A. 1920. *Principles of economics*, 8th ed., London: Macmillan and Company.
32. Porter, M. E. 1990. *The competitive advantage of nations*. New York: Free Press.
33. Florida, *The rise of the creative class*; Clark, *The city as an entertainment machine*; Stolarick, K. and R. Florida. 2006. Creativity, connections and innovation: A study of linkages in the Montreal region. *Environment and Planning A* 38: 1799–1817.
34. Perroux, F. 1955. Note sur la notion de pole de croissance. *Economique Appliquée* 1–2: 307–322; Hirschman, A. O. 1958. *The strategy of economic development*. New Haven: Yale University Press.
35. Based on interviews with Dr. Charles Isgar and Steve Soboroff, March 2008.
36. Stone, *Regime politics*; Hunter, F. 1953. *Community power structure: A study of decision makers*. Chapel Hill: University of North Carolina Press.
37. See, for example, Dahl, R. A. 1961. *Who governs? Democracy and power in an American city*. New Haven: Yale University Press; Jennings, M. K. 1964. *Community influentials: The elites of Atlanta*. New York: Free Press.
38. See, for example, Molotch, H. 1979. Capital and neighborhood in the United States: Some conceptual links. *Urban Affairs Quarterly* 14: 289–312; Molotch, H. 1993. The political economy of growth machines. *Journal of Urban Affairs* 15 (1): 29–53; Logan, J. R. and H. L. Molotch. 1987. *Urban fortunes: The political economy of place*. Berkeley: University of California Press; Elkins, D. R. 1995. The structure and context of the urban growth coalition: The view from the chamber of commerce. *Policy Studies Journal* 23 (4): 583–601; Davies, J. S. 2002. Urban regime theory: A normative-empirical critique. *Journal of Urban Affairs* 24 (1): 1–17. Each of these excellent works provides insight into the definition of regimes and growth coalitions. While differences exist, a concern is reflected that groups of business leaders might organize to advance their economic interests and to ensure that public subsidies are provided to support their economic agenda. The material in Chapters 7 and 8 is designed to offer additional insights by illustrating the extensive set of economic development initiatives pursued by business organizations.
39. Elkins, The structure and context of the urban growth coalition, 583.
40. Rosentraub, M. S. and P. Helmke. 1996. Location theory, a growth coalition, and a regime in a medium-sized city. *Urban Affairs Review* 31 (4): 482–507.
41. Ibid.
42. Squires, G., ed. 1989. *Unequal partnerships: Political economy of urban redevelopment in postwar America*. New Brunswick, NJ: Rutgers University Press.
43. See, for example, Swindell, D. and M. S. Rosentraub. 2009. Doing better: Sports, economic impact analysis, and schools of public policy and administration. *Journal of Public Administration Education* 15(2) (forthcoming).
44. See, for example, Delaney, K. J. and R. Eckstein. 2003. *Public dollars, private stadiums: The battle over building sports stadiums*. New Brunswick, NJ: Rutgers University Press. Also see Sanders, Convention myths and markets, 195–210; Sanders, H. 2005. *Space available: The realities of convention centers as economic development strategy*. Washington, D.C.: The Brookings Institution.

45. See, for example, Imbroscio, D. L. 1998. Reformulating urban regime theory: The division of labor between state and market reconsidered. *Journal of Urban Affairs* 20 (3): 233–248. Also see Levine, M. 2000. A third world city in the first world: Social exclusion, racial inequality, and sustainable development in Baltimore, Maryland. In *The social sustainability of cities*. ed. M. Polese and R. Stren, 123–156. Toronto: University of Toronto Press; and Reese, L. A. and D. Fasenfest. 2004. *Critical evaluations of economic development policies*. Detroit: Wayne State University Press. These works highlight that amenities have not been successful in substantially changing the economic plight of inner city neighborhoods.
46. Barnes, B. 2008. A film year full of escapism, flat in attendance. *New York Times,* January 2. http://www.nytimes.com/2008/01/02/movies/02year.html (accessed July 6, 2008).
47. Snider, M. 2008. DVD feels first sting of slipping sales. *USA Today,* January 7. http://www.usatoday.com/life/movies/news/2008-01-07-dvd-sales-slippage_N.htm (accessed January 5, 2008).
48. Brown, G. and M. Morrison, eds. 2008. *ESPN sports almanac 2008*. Lake Worth, Florida: Sports Almanac.
49. See, for example, Nicholson, M. and R. Hoye, ed. 2008. *Sport and social capital*. London: Elsevier. Also see Wilson, J. 1994. *Playing by the rules: Sport, society, and the state*. Detroit: Wayne State University Press.
50. Rosentraub, M., S. D. Swindell, and S. Tsvetkova. 2009. Justifying public investments in sports: Measuring the intangibles. *Journal of Tourism* (forthcoming).
51. Zimbalist, A. and J. G. Long. 2006. Facility finance: Measurement, trends and analysis. *International Journal of Sport Finance* 1: 201–211.
52. Those revenues do constitute payments from the team. In the absence of the extra tax, there would be no reduction in prices and the team would realize more income.
53. Scully, G. 1995. *The market structure of sports*. Chicago: The University of Chicago Press.
54. Rosentraub, M. S. 1999. *Major league losers: The real cost of sports and who's paying for it,* revised ed. New York: Basic Books.
55. http://sports.espn.go.com/nba/news/story?id=3100691. A year later David Stern tried to mollify NBA critics in Seattle, saying the city might be a destination for a smaller market team that confronts problems and would yearn for the larger population numbers of metropolitan Seattle. http://seattletimes.nwsource.com/html/nba/2008498903_soni12.html
56. Kennedy and Rosentraub, Public-private partnerships, professional sports teams, and the protection of the public's interests, 439–459.
57. *Toolson v. New York Yankees* 346 U. S. 356,1953: 347.

Chapter 3

Indianapolis as
the Broker City

When the history is written of the efforts of declining central cities that aggressively focused on sports, tourism, culture, or entertainment to revitalize downtown areas, special attention will be accorded to Indianapolis. Beginning in the 1970s and then sustained by the administrations of four different mayors (three Republicans and one Democrat) across four decades, Indianapolis' leadership rebuilt a moribund downtown center and kept it vital and expanding with a second wave of capital projects to replace facilities built to initiate the rebuilding process. Few, if any, communities that used sports, culture, entertainment, or tourism for revitalization have been as focused as Indianapolis. No other region has initiated the building of a second wave of facilities to replace the original cornerstones of the policy as the older assets became economically obsolete. There are numerous lessons and guidance to be learned from Indianapolis' plan and its sustained effort to turn subsidies into investments.

I. The Indianapolis Plan: Goals, Objectives, and History

In the late 1960s and early 1970s, Indianapolis' leadership thought a consolidated form of local government joining suburban areas with the central city would create a new vitality that would convince people and businesses to redevelop the city. UniGov (the popular term given to this particular consolidation and the name still used today) established a blueprint for other communities that would consider

A GROWTH COALITION FOR INDIANAPOLIS

A growth coalition is a term used by social scientists to refer to elites in a community joining together to advance regional development. Some social scientists have observed or suggested that the profit motives or self-interest of the individuals or institutions that dominate these groups bias the selection of strategies and projects supported. Some have also worried that the selection of notoriously "big-ticket" items, such as ballparks, arenas, museums, entertainment complexes, retail centers, office buildings, and convention centers preclude other strategies or an emphasis on other assets that might create more jobs. Critics have pointed to the projects selected by growth coalitions as favoring older views and strategies for economic development.

In response to this criticism, it should also be noted that growth regimes get things done. The projects implemented create jobs and a wide range of benefits. In addition, the idea that these groups of elites only support projects and programs that directly enhance real estate values or business prospects for its members is contradicted by the investments made by some of these coalitions. For example, the Lilly Endowment—a clear member of Indianapolis' coalition for sports and downtown development—has, at the same time that it supported building big-ticket sport facilities and a convention center, made commitments of hundreds of millions of dollars for community development. Its extensive support of public education and programs to reward public school teachers have helped to substantially improve Central Indiana and it has been a major contributor to the building of the region's arts and cultural assets. Cleveland's Greater Cleveland Partnership (another growth coalition comprised of the region's leading corporate leaders) has long supported housing and community development for inner city neighborhoods and made a substantial financial commitment to the Cleveland Public Schools. The performance record of urban growth coalitions remains a complex web of different sets of activities that includes substantial support for big-ticket items while also emphasizing activities designed to advance communities across different regions.

city–county mergers as the path to reducing suburbanization and revitalizing inner city areas. As recently as 2003, Louisville and Jefferson County, Kentucky, created a new consolidated government. Far earlier variations on consolidation were used in Jacksonville, Miami, and Charlotte. Scores of communities have looked at UniGov to see if a consolidated form of local government could help advance redevelopment efforts.[1]

City–county consolidation did not change population trends for Indianapolis. Prior to consolidation, the area that would become the merged city was home to 66.3 percent of the region's residents. By 1980, consolidated Indianapolis was home

Noting that the performance of coalitions, even if skewed toward support for sports facilities, convention centers, and other downtown projects, has led to important improvements, does not obscure issues related to representation and participation in these organizations. The groups could not be described as democratic. Only leaders or others who are thought of as elites participate and invitations to join are quite restricted. The meetings of these organizations are neither open to the public nor a matter of public record. Membership is frequently limited to directors from the largest corporations and foundations in a community. Local university presidents are sometimes involved, and from time to time elected leaders are included if their presence does not create a requirement for meetings to be open to the public.

Molotch illustrated how elites or leaders met in social or business settings to discuss issues of mutual benefit that led to certain projects for redevelopment (while other options were usually not considered).[4] There is also evidence that growth coalitions skew the allocation of public funds to meet their agenda often without any public dialogue. Growth coalitions or their members are also involved in financing political campaigns.

At the same time that these limitations and problems are recognized, in other communities one can also find evidence of frustration when there is no leadership group to advance a region's economic future.[5] There is a fine line between ensuring that the public, private, and nonprofit sectors cooperate for regional economic development and also ensuring that the public's interest is represented. In some instances, these growth coalitions or machines, which become regimes when they have extended longevity and membership from the same organizations, have pursued narrow agendas that concentrate benefits. Indianapolis' original growth machine, which indeed became a regime as it led the downtown and sports development effort across three decades, did not become more inclusive until later years, and even then some in the community resented what was still seen as elite leadership. At the same time, few questioned the success in rebuilding downtown and changing the city's image.[6]

to slightly more than half, 53.7 percent, of the metropolitan area's population.[2] In the years after formation of the consolidated government, city leaders were quick to recognize that something besides a new form of local government would be required to rebuild the downtown area and help Indianapolis hold onto residents and businesses. It did not take waiting for the results of the 1980 U.S. Census to develop a new strategy.

One might think the continuing loss of residents to the suburbs and the on-going deterioration of downtown were sufficient to encourage elected and community leaders to think about innovative approaches to revive Indianapolis. The catalyst that launched the sports and downtown development plan was neither population losses nor declining residential property values. In the aftermath of the consolidation that made Indianapolis the 11th largest city in the United States in 1970—an improvement from its 26th place ranking in 1960 prior to consolidation—local leadership commissioned a national survey to understand the perception of the city's image. The study's results indicated the city suffered from a "nonimage." It was simply unknown to too many Americans. Indianapolis was virtually a nondescript part of the Midwest, located somewhere southeast of Chicago and known to exist at least one day a year—a result of the international publicity surrounding the annual Indianapolis 500 auto race. Beyond that, the city was relatively unknown.[3]

What could give Indianapolis a new image? Lore and different views of history agree that a growth coalition of local leaders with financial support from the Lilly Endowment chose sports with a special focus on amateur sports as the route to Indianapolis' new image. At the same time, the coalition agreed to try to concentrate development in the downtown area. While the selection of sports may have been influenced by demography (all or most of the members of the growth coalition were men), what was undeniably unique was the agreement that the facilities would be built downtown. This decision was made at the time of the "suburbanization" of sport facilities with teams following their wealthier fans to the areas beyond the city limits of older areas. Some notable examples were the Cleveland Cavaliers moving to Richfield, the Washington Senators relocating to suburban Arlington (Texas), the Dallas Cowboys moving to Irving, the Detroit Pistons and Lions moving to Pontiac and Auburn Hills, and new facilities for the Kansas City Royals and Chiefs located in suburban Kansas City. Some may have thought Indianapolis' leadership was completely wrong-headed. But they were more than a decade ahead of the trend of building downtown sports facilities to anchor revitalization strategies. In this regard, the growth coalition did forge a new policy direction and take some risks that probably left many scratching their heads.

The rebuilding of downtown Indianapolis and the implementation of the "amateur sports strategy" began with an arena. The anchor tenant was to be the Indiana Pacers who were playing their home games at a facility approximately four miles north of downtown. While the theme for Indianapolis' new image and the social glue that united the growth coalition was amateur sports, professional teams were an integral part of the strategy. After the arena, attention was focused on the expansion of the convention center through the incorporation of a domed stadium. The new stadium provided needed exhibition space, but was designed to lure an NFL team to the city. The notion that an NFL team would want to play in a city nicknamed "India-No-Place" was seen by many as also unrealistic and as impractical as building sport facilities in downtown areas. If Indianapolis could attract an NFL team, then the sports strategy would have three professional crowns: NBA and NFL franchises and the most famous event in automobile racing (the Indianapolis 500). These assets would not only hold together the growth coalition for the continued rebuilding effort, but give the city an image that dwarfed its status as a modest-sized Midwestern city and help launch a new phase of economic development.

The dome as part of the Indiana Convention Center was completed in 1983 and dedicated on September 8, 1984. In less than a year, the NFL's Colts would move from suburban Baltimore to downtown Indianapolis giving the city a third asset for its sports identity. Suddenly Indianapolis had two major league-level sports teams and the largest event in automobile racing. Maybe Indianapolis could really have a vibrant downtown that changed not only its image, but development patterns as well. Everything seemed possible in the wake of the Colts' move from Baltimore.

To entice amateur sports organizations to locate their championship events in Indianapolis—and to consider moving their headquarters to the self-proclaimed capital of amateur sports—several new facilities were needed. A new track and field stadium, tennis center, and state-of-the-art natatorium were built on the Indiana University–Purdue University Indianapolis (IUPUI) campus on the northwest edge of the downtown area. On several occasions, Olympic team trials were held at some of the new facilities. In 1982, a bicycle racing facility was opened 6.1 miles northwest of the downtown area. When Chile and Ecuador had to withdraw as hosts for the 1987 Pan American games, Indianapolis agreed to hold the games and with the help of thousands of volunteers turned the games into a great success enhancing the city's image. Then, in 1997, Indianapolis succeeded in convincing the NCAA to relocate from suburban Kansas City to the new White River State Park in downtown Indianapolis. Dreams were becoming a reality in the midst of the former cornfields and declining downtown area of Indianapolis.

II. Indianapolis, Sports, and Redevelopment: What Was Built, How Much Was Invested, and Whose Dollars Were Spent?

Indianapolis' growth coalition always described the sports and real estate revitalization strategy as a public/private partnership. This tag line or slogan was also quite in vogue during the 1980s, but its very mention created concern that government-assisted development was nothing more than subsidies for the rich and their corporate interest. This perspective was reviewed in several case studies included in Squires' *Unequal Partnerships*. In sharp contrast to the praise offered by such groups, the Committee for Economic Development for public/private partnerships cautioned that:

> What has frequently been overlooked, however, is the inherently unequal nature of most [public/private] partnerships. Frequently they

exclude altogether the neighborhood residents most affected by development decisions. Public goals often go unmet and democratic processes are undermined. ... The principal beneficiaries are often the large corporations, developers, and institutions because the tax burden and other costs are shifted to consumers. And perhaps the most important public benefits—jobs—are either temporary or low paying or, in the case of good jobs, go to suburbanites or other out-of-towners recruited by local businesses.[7]

Porter and Sweet warned that "the linchpins of public–private partnerships are negotiation and cooperation ... (and) almost by definition require equitable commitments of capacity and investment."[8] Unfortunately, these preconditions were rarely met as the public sector invested far more than did their private sector partners, and the public sector seemed to be overmatched in negotiations as a result of the ability of private capital to move to the regions providing the largest subsidies.

Eisinger writing more than a decade later, and looking back over two decades of tourist and sports development projects in downtown areas, many of which were public/private partnerships, noted a skewing of the civic agenda toward the economic interests of downtown elites.[9] He also focused attention on the distribution of benefits from these public–private partnerships for big-ticket items. Inevitably there were substantial increases in the value of teams and higher salaries for players.[10] These questions and observations make it crucial to understand exactly what was accomplished by Indianapolis' strategy to rebuild its downtown area and image through sports and myriad related public/private real estate development deals. If Indianapolis is the benchmark relative to the use of sports and cultural facilities for redevelopment, then what happened there, how much money was spent and by whom, and who benefited must be addressed. The analysis that follows is designed to understand if the public/private partnerships changed the trajectory of development in Indianapolis or merely enhanced the wealth of team owners, developers, and other land owners.[11] The analysis helps to understand if the growth coalition diverted public resources from community uses as Harrison and Bluestone[12] argued to public/private partnerships or if Indianapolis achieved a balance between big-ticket projects and neighborhood development.[13]

A. What Was Built?

Nine major sports facilities were built between 1974 and 2008 with the last, Lucas Oil Stadium, the new home for the Indianapolis Colts, opening prior to the NFL's 2008 season (Table 3.1). Two years after the 1999 opening of Conseco Fieldhouse, Market Square Arena was demolished, but the anticipated development of residential housing on that site had not been initiated by 2008. When Lucas Oil Stadium

Table 3.1 The Sports Facilities in Downtown Indianapolis

Facility	Description	Opened	Replaced
Market Square Arena	Indoor arena for Indiana Pacers; capacity 16,530	1974	1999
Tennis Center	Seating capacity 10,000	1979	
Track and Field	Seating capacity 12,111	1982	
Natatorium	Championship pools, capacity 5,000	1982	
Hoosier Dome	Indoor stadium for Colts, other events, conventions, capacity 57,980	1984	2008
Fitness Center	Training and fitness center for all athletes, public	1988	
Victory Field	Minor League Baseball Park, capacity 15,000 for Indianapolis Indians	1997	
Conseco Fieldhouse	Home for Indiana Pacers, other events, capacity 18,345	1999	
Lucas Oil Stadium	Domed stadium for Indianapolis Colts, NCAA Championships, other amateur sports events; conventions, events; capacity 63,000 (expandable to 70,000)	2009	

opened, the planned conversion of the RCA Dome into additional space for the Indiana Convention Center was initiated.

While publicly embracing amateur and professional sports, the redevelopment effort was broadened to include cultural centers in an effort to make downtown a year-round destination for all forms of live entertainment. The Indiana Theatre was renovated in 1980 as the home of the Indiana Repertory Company, the region's largest live performance troupe. In 1984, the Circle Theatre reopened as the home of the Indianapolis Symphony. A turn-of-the-century grand showplace that first opened in 1916, it was abandoned in the 1970s. The Indianapolis Symphony Orchestra was playing at a midtown location (much like the Indiana Pacers), but after the facility was restored to its original grandeur, the orchestra made the theater its home. The new downtown home of the Indianapolis Zoo and Botanical Gardens opened in 1988, and the Eiteljorg Museum of American Indian and Western Art opened in 1989. An IMAX theater opened in 1996 followed by the new home for the Indiana Historical Society in 1999, and the Indiana State Museum in 2002. A spectacular renovation of the Indianapolis-Marion County Public Library also was completed in 2006. These facilities made downtown Indianapolis the cultural capital of the state and region, adding crowds and expanding the definition of recreation and tourism activities far beyond sports. The museums, zoo, park, and theaters helped to also remake downtown Indianapolis into a residential neighborhood.

B. Who Paid How Much for the New Downtown?

Three separate sets of concerns are raised when growth coalitions or regimes steer revitalization strategies. As Squires and the other contributors to *Unequal Partnerships* noted, there was fear that the public sector would be expected to invest far more than either private businesses or the nonprofit sector. Others were concerned that a regime focused on downtown would ignore other development possibilities and focus private sector development on the downtown area to the exclusion of other communities. Finally, there also was a concern that the outcomes from a downtown redevelopment and sports strategy would fail to generate any real economic, demographic, or social changes for the city or region.

Before addressing each of these elements in turn, a scorecard of sorts is presented to identify the money invested in downtown Indianapolis from 1974 through 2006. Information for Lucas Oil Stadium is included (even though it did not open until 2008), but Table 3.2 does not include proposed future developments that may well result from the building of the new stadium. Those planned developments are identified in Table 3.3 to amplify the analysis.

Table 3.2 The Investments Made in Rebuilding Downtown Indianapolis, 1974–2007 (in millions of 2007 dollars)

Project Type	Public Sector		Nongovernmental		
	Local	Nonlocal	Private	Nonprofit	Total
Sports	998.2	188.8	329.6	191.9	1,708.5
Culture/entertainment	166.7	51.5	355.1	296.9	870.2
Commercial	1,323.3	977	2,224.9	8.8	4,534.0
Residential	49.2	112.6	380.4	3.7	545.9
Education		663.9			663.9
Total	2,537.4	1,993.8	3,290.0	501.3	8,322.5

Source: Department of Metropolitan Development, Indianapolis; Indianapolis Downtown, Incorporated; *Indianapolis Star.*

Table 3.3 Approved and Funded Future Projects for Downtown Indianapolis by Type and Year of Completion

	Project Year Completion		
Project Type	2007	2008	2009
Residential	85.0	129.0	64.1
Commercial	50.0	34.6	326.4
Entertainment	20.9	10.3	68.7
Total	155.9	173.9	459.2

Note: In millions of dollars, present value, discount rate used, 10 percent.

Source: Indianapolis Downtown, Incorporated.

Indianapolis was able to use its resources to leverage substantial investments from the private sector, other governments, and nonprofit organizations to rebuild its downtown area. At the high end, and with one notable caveat, Indianapolis' commitment was less than $2.52 billion. The reason that this is the "high-end estimate" is that it includes all of the local funding for the new domed stadium, Lucas Oil Stadium, the home of the Indianapolis Colts. Other local governments (from the counties that surround Indianapolis) paid part of the public sector's investment in the $720 million facility. The investment in the new library, $142.7 million, is also included. This facility is located in the northern part of the downtown area and is a substantial asset for residential development and establishing the identity of downtown and adjacent areas as vibrant residential neighborhoods. The library is also an extremely valuable resource for all of Indianapolis' inner city neighborhoods providing computer resources as well as books and videos. The Indianapolis-Marion County Public Library Board is an independent unit of government collecting taxes from the consolidated city/county area. The new building was needed even if a revitalization effort had not been underway.

The total investment in downtown Indianapolis from 1974 through 2006 was $8.3 billion (constant dollars). For a (high-end) total commitment of $2.52 billion in public money, Indianapolis was able to leverage $5.79 billion from other sources. For every dollar that Indianapolis invested in its downtown area, an additional $2.30 was committed. Using data from the Indianapolis Downtown Incorporated, the present value of the residential, commercial, and entertainment projects that will be completed over the next few years is $789 million (Table 3.3). Including those projects in the total amount invested in downtown Indianapolis would mean that for every $1 invested by the city it was able to leverage $2.92.

INDIANAPOLIS DOWNTOWN INCORPORATED

To advance downtown's development, and to lead the effort to broker deals that would bring new companies to the downtown area and then ensure that their interests and needs had advocates, Indianapolis Downtown Incorporated (IDI) was created. Over the years, its actions and membership would lead it to be described as another growth coalition or machine. IDI also has to be given credit for helping to protect and enhance the tax base of the downtown area. Its success attracted the attention of other cities and many created similar organizations that assisted businesses that decided to relocate to redeveloping downtown areas.

The mission of the IDI clearly suggests that while its focus is on the downtown area it is concerned with the advancement of the entire region.

Because central Indiana needs a strong and vibrant core, IDI exists to continually improve downtown Indianapolis. IDI is action-oriented and empowered to address, in partnership with the public and private sectors, critical issues that affect the growth, well being, and user-friendliness of downtown. IDI focuses on three areas: development, management, and marketing.

The Board of Directors as listed on its Web site include representatives from the consolidated city/county government and members of the city/county council, representatives of the state government, one union leader, and numerous representatives of leading corporations and educational institutions located in the downtown area. Some other committees do have community representatives, but for the most part the organization is clearly a regime comprised of the institutions in downtown Indianapolis.

While some might object to the organization's membership structure, few can raise any complaints with its performance, effectiveness, and the impact it has had in terms of the redevelopment of downtown Indianapolis. That redevelopment, in 2006 dollars, has already surpassed $8.3 billion, and there is probably no mayor or city council member in the United States who is not envious of the success. While the IDI cannot take credit for that level of investment, its stewardship and assistance should not be underestimated in terms of the services it provides to institutions that have made large investments in downtown and the confidence it exudes and maintains in the future for downtown Indianapolis. IDI also assures that all institutions in the downtown area cooperate to enhance the value of the investments made. IDI also coordinates initiatives and activities to facilitate the attraction of visitors, businesses, and residents to the area.

III. Has Indianapolis Been Changed by the Sports and Downtown Redevelopment Strategy?

The inevitable question when more than $8 billion is spent becomes, "What did you get for the money?" The information in Table 3.2 and Table 3.3 allows people to assess whether or not the public/private partnerships were true partnerships and if what was leveraged was worth the commitment. Later in this chapter the specifics of the financing of Conseco Fieldhouse for the Pacers and Lucas Oil Field for the Colts will be examined to provide additional insight into the challenges small market areas face when dealing with professional sports teams. Before that discussion, however, the most important question must be addressed. Did the sports strategy for the revitalization of the downtown area change or improve Indianapolis?

There is no single answer to this question. Some people wanted Indianapolis to have an image far different from what it had in the early 1970s. Some wanted to ensure that downtown Indianapolis would remain a vital part of the region. For others, the strategy and investments were linked to expanding the regional economy, ensuring that the region's largest employers remained in Central Indiana and Indianapolis, and that the region attracted and retained a highly skilled and educated workforce. It is also important to understand whether the investment in downtown Indianapolis negatively impacted other neighborhoods.

A. Maintaining Downtown Indianapolis

Guaranteeing that a certain level of development took place in downtown Indianapolis does not generate growth for the region if facilities would have been built elsewhere in the area. While there may well be an aesthetic gain from a rebuilt downtown and important local tax base shifts, unless Indianapolis' overall growth rates changed from those of other Midwest cities, then there may have been no overall economic gain from the downtown focus. In terms of the dollar investment, it has already been demonstrated that there was a substantial amount of spending in the downtown area. How did that level of spending compare to what was invested in other parts of the consolidated city? To address that question, building permit data for residential and commercial properties was analyzed. The results are displayed in Figure 3.1 and Figure 3.2.

There has been a pronounced increase in the number of residential units built in the downtown area, but the overwhelming number of new homes and apartments were constructed in Indianapolis' suburban townships. Only in 2006 did the number of units built in Center Township (the location of the downtown area and the surrounding neighborhoods) exceed 10 percent of the total construction in the consolidated city/county. There was another slight surge in 1996 followed by a decline before there was a steady increment beginning in 1999. While these results

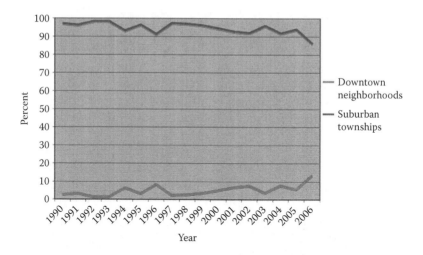

Figure 3.1 The percentage of residential units built in the consolidated city/county of Indianapolis located in downtown neighborhoods and suburban townships, 1990–2006. (From Department of Metropolitan Development, Consolidated City/County of Indianapolis and Marion.)

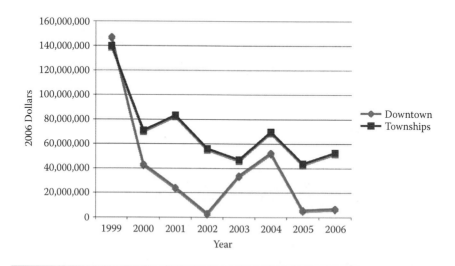

Figure 3.2 Commercial investment in downtown Indianapolis and throughout the consolidated city (in 2006 dollars). (From Department of Metropolitan Development, Consolidated City/County of Indianapolis and Marion.)

might be disappointing, it is also important to note that the development of the downtown and surrounding areas as competitive neighborhoods with appropriate amenities beyond the recreation and tourism assets in the downtown area took time to create. The mortgage and credit issues of 2007 and 2008 had a slightly chilling effect, but the increment and the proposed new projects suggest downtown Indianapolis has become a viable neighborhood. Furthermore, while these numbers are small, for a city where there were very few people living downtown, the building of new units on a consistent basis across the late 1990s and through 2006 is an important change. These data also illustrate that the focus on downtown did not retard residential development in other parts of the city.

The dollar value of commercial development in the downtown area and throughout the consolidated city from 1999 through 2006 is described in Figure 3.2. There was a substantial increment in commercial real estate investments in the downtown area from 2002 through 2004 following a decline from the end of the century. There was also a decline after 2004 in the dollar level of investments, but with the projects now planned there will be another increment if those facilities are built. The pattern of investments in the downtown area and the other townships is similar, but there have been years where there was a clear concentration of activity in downtown (1999, 2003, and 2004). There has been a substantial level of private investment in the downtown area and several large projects should be completed before 2010 (see Figure 3.2). There was substantial development in other parts of the city as well.

In 1990, there were 14,894 residents living in downtown Indianapolis and this increased to 17,907 in 2000.[14] Birch, relying on U.S. Bureau of the Census information, also reported that there were 7,141 housing units in the downtown area in 2000. This means that average occupancy was 2.51 people per unit. Between 2000 and 2006, a total of 3,775 units were built in the downtown area based on information from Indianapolis' Department of Metropolitan Development. Assuming that 95 percent of these units were occupied and using the average number of people per unit that existed in 2000, downtown Indianapolis had 21,682 residents in 2006. This represents an increase of 6,788 people in 16 years. While the numbers are small, this would mean a 45.6 percent increase.

Overall, Indianapolis is enjoying a very modest population growth. In 2000, the Census counted 781,864 people living in the consolidated city/county. The 2007 estimate is that Indianapolis had 795,458. The 13,594 new residents represent an increase of less than 2 percent. The largest population growth in the region is concentrated in the suburban counties surrounding Indianapolis. From 1990 through 2006, the nine-county Indianapolis MSA (metropolitan statistical area) region grew 37.1 percent, increasing from 1,294,217 residents to 1,774,665. This growth is largely centered in the counties surrounding Indianapolis. While it could be suggested that in the absence of the downtown redevelopment and sports strategy, there would have been no residential growth in the downtown area, the causal connection between the investments and a slowing of suburban growth cannot be established.

B. Regional Economic Changes and the Centrality of Downtown Indianapolis

While enhancing the city's image and rebuilding the downtown area were the often-discussed goals for the sports strategy, an improved regional economy that produced higher incomes for residents was also a critical goal. Central Indiana and Indianapolis, like many other Midwest centers, were seeking solutions to recover from the decline of the manufacturing sector. The new image, it was hoped, would attract the creative class.

One of the initial assessments of the economic impact of Indianapolis' sports strategy looked at initial changes from the 1970s through 1989.[15] While there was a clear increment in the number of jobs in sport organizations and those related to sports, the city's share of the jobs in the Indianapolis region had actually declined as had the region's ranking with regard to average family incomes compared with other Midwest areas. In the short run, then, Indianapolis' sport and downtown development strategy had neither reversed the outflow of jobs to suburban areas nor raised income levels for families.

In an analysis of downtown employment in Midwest cities that had emphasized sports and entertainment and that looked at outcomes through 2000, Austrian and Rosentraub concluded:

> The experiences of Cleveland and Indianapolis indicate that a down-town sports strategy can help to sustain the centrality of an urban center's core area, but not as a result of tangible outcomes related to the sports investment itself. In other words, the presence of the teams and their facilities did not spawn the creation of a large number of new jobs. However, the focus on a tourism-based set of facilities and experiences did lead to the creation of higher paying service sector jobs in tourism-related industries. The focus on sports and tourism-related industries did appear to create a set of connections or excitement within downtown areas that stemmed the outflow of jobs to more suburban locations. ... If sports and the tourism-related industries contribute to the retention of firms, and if progressive financing tools can be used to secure this end, then an important tool can exist for downtown redevelopment. If, however, regressive financing schemes and excessive subsidies are involved, the opportunity cost of the programs has to be assessed and it is likely that more productive uses for public resources could be found.[16]

Austrian and Rosentraub, while finding positive outcomes from enhancements to employment in the hospitality sector and a relative stabilization in the location

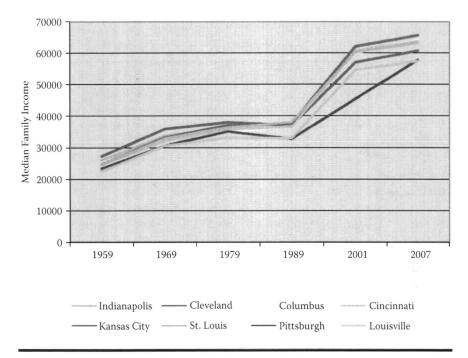

Figure 3.3 Median family income levels in selected Midwestern metropolitan areas, 1959 to 2007. Source: U.S. Bureau of the Census.

of jobs, could not find evidence of higher income levels in cities that had invested in their downtown area. While reducing or slowing the loss of jobs to suburban areas reduces the stress on the central city's tax base, evidence through 2000 did not illustrate a growth in concentration of higher paying jobs. Would a longer-term analysis illustrate more positive outcomes?

Figure 3.3 illustrates median family income levels for eight Midwest MSAs across almost 40 years. Two observations are immediately apparent. First, there was little change in the Indianapolis region's relative position from 1959 through 2007. Indianapolis had the second highest median family income in 1959 and the third highest in 2008. Second, while the median income levels of all of MSAs were more tightly clustered or similar in 1959, there was a slightly larger spread or variability in 2007. Indianapolis was able to remain at the top end despite this increasing variance. Average variance—the measure of the difference between median family income in any one MSA and the average of median incomes across the eight regions—increased for Indianapolis from $995 in 1959 to $3,909 in 2001 before slipping a bit to $2,541 in 2007. (This indicates that Indianapolis was in a better position relative to the other cities in this regional grouping.) In the years when the variance was greatest, 2001 and 2007, Indianapolis' median family income was second and third highest.

Median family income in the Indianapolis MSA was $1,713 higher than the average of all eight areas (and Indianapolis' mean was included in the determination of the mean for all regions) in 2007 and $3,088 higher in 2001. Indianapolis' low point was actually in 1979 when the difference was just $511. If that time period is accepted as an approximate point where the sports and downtown development strategy is in place, then the gains relative to median family income in future years were fairly impressive. This outcome does not mean the sports and downtown redevelopment strategy caused the income gains. It cannot be said that the investment in downtown led to higher salaries, as the growth in some other cities that followed other strategies was larger. Indianapolis' revitalization strategy was associated with a level of growth, but over time, the rate of growth was reduced.

All regions are constantly engaged in efforts to advance their economies. Cleveland also focused on a downtown revitalization strategy that included the building of three new sports facilities, a new museum, and refurbishing the largest theater district outside New York City. St. Louis built the Arch in an effort to advance tourism in its region. Indeed, it is safe to say that every region launched several initiatives in response to declines in the manufacturing sector. Each community benefited from the expansion of certain lead businesses while each also lost several others to faster growing parts of the country. There was some evidence that of all the regions that invested in sport facilities only Indianapolis exhibited any statistical evidence of a positive outcome related to its overall sports strategy.[17] As important as that finding was, Indianapolis was able to sustain its position relative to median family income over almost 50 years despite a substantial restructuring of its regional economy (Figure 3.3). From 1990 to 2009, the Indianapolis MSA lost 23,200 manufacturing jobs, but the number of people employed in the leisure and hospitality sector jumped from 56,900 to 86,500, an increase of 29,600 jobs.

Figure 3.4 describes the changing employment structure of the Indianapolis MSA and several trends are critical. There was only a modest increment or slight decrease in employment in the information, services, and financial sectors. The growth of the health sector related to investments by the Indiana University Medical School and the Lilly Pharmaceutical Corporation are also evident. Both of these institutions are located in the downtown area, and in the case of the Lilly Corporation, the enhancement of downtown was pursued to ensure its long-term commitment. The large increase in the number of jobs in the transportation and utilities area was a function of expansion at the airport and the location of "mini hubs" for FedEx and the U.S. Postal Service. Those increments, at best, would have been tangentially related to what was taking place in the downtown area. This category of employment also includes jobs related to the wholesale and retail trade, and in those sectors of the Indianapolis MSA's economy there was an increment of 47,900 jobs between 1990 and 2009. Many of these jobs were tied to the improvements in the hospitality sector.

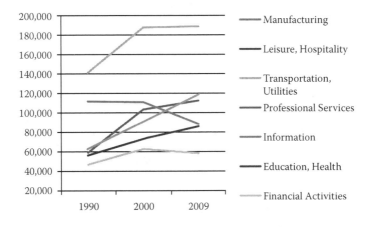

Figure 3.4   The changing concentrations of employment in the Indianapolis MSA, 1995–2007. (Data compilations by Mark S. Rosentraub from Bureau of Economic Analysis, U.S. Department of Commerce.)

The downtown development strategy appears to have encouraged private sector firms to remain. There were 81,412 private sector workers in the downtown area in 1990. By 1995, there were 92,666 and this number has remained relatively constant through 2005. Private sector payrolls in the downtown area have declined slightly from a high of $4.7 billion in 1995 to $4.5 billion in 2005 (constant dollars). The number of firms has remained about the same (Table 3.4). Despite the decentralization of the economy across this time period and the substantial population growth that has taken place in Indianapolis' suburban areas, private sector employment levels in downtown have remained relatively stable. The slight decline in private sector payrolls (3 percent) is a matter of concern. At the same time, with the expansion in the size of the health sector with its concentration of workers in the nonprofit sector, it is likely that payrolls have remained relatively stable or increased.

Indianapolis' success in retaining payroll dollars in its downtown area is compared to changes in other Midwest central cities in Figure 3.5. The percentage of the private sector payroll that is concentrated in the downtown areas is charted from 1994 through 2005. While there was a modest increase in the location of payroll dollars concentrated in downtown Indianapolis, an increase of 2.7 percent from 1994 to 2005, the pattern was not substantially different from the experiences in other Midwest centers. For example, Chicago enjoyed the largest increase, 4.4 percent, and Columbus (Ohio) the sharpest decline, 5.2 percent. Kansas City had the most change involving an increase and then a decrease, but at the end of the period was at the same point. Again, nonprofit and government payrolls were not included and for Indianapolis, with the location of the state capitol and

Table 3.4 Private Sector Employment in Downtown Indianapolis, 1990 to 2005

Employment Characteristic	Year		
	1990	1995	2005
Number of employees	81,412	92,666	91,246
Payroll[a]	$3,788	$4,659	$4,522
Number of firms	2,559	2,708	2,580

Note: Data compilations by author from Bureau of Economic Analysis, U.S. Department of Commerce.

[a] In millions of (2005) dollars.

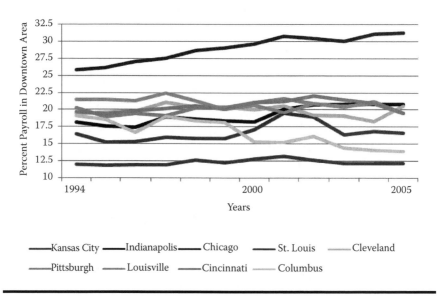

Figure 3.5 The percent of countywide private payroll dollars in each city's downtown area, 1994 to 2005. (Data compilations by Mark S. Rosentraub from Bureau of Economic Analysis, U.S. Department of Commerce.)

Indiana University's hospitals in the downtown area, there was an increase in payrolls matching the growth in the health sector. Relative to private sector employment, the downtown redevelopment strategy with its emphasis on sports had a modest effect on the concentration of private sector employment as measured by payroll dollars (see Figure 3.5).

The next measure of centrality shifted the focus to Marion County and the jobs located within 20 miles of the central business district. A view of the location of

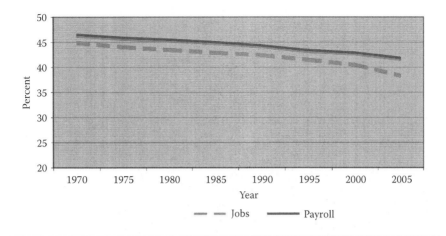

Figure 3.6 The proportion of the Indianapolis MSA's public and private sector jobs and payroll dollars located in Marion County, 1970 through 2005. (Data compilations by Mark S. Rosentraub from Bureau of Economic Analysis, U.S. Department of Commerce.)

public and private sector payroll dollars in the region that are concentrated in the consolidated city/county of Indianapolis is provided in Figure 3.6. There has been a gradual, but continuing decline in the proportion of jobs and payroll dollars in both the private and public sectors concentrated in Marion County. This gradual downward trend extends from 1970 to 2005. In 1970, 46.5 percent of all public and private sector payroll dollars were concentrated in what largely constitutes the consolidated city/county of Indianapolis; this declined to 41.8 percent in 2005. The number of public and private sector jobs in the county accounted for 38.4 percent of the MSA's employment in 2005, a decrease of 6.6 percent from 1970. Some might note that Indianapolis' ability to retain a substantial number of jobs and payroll dollars in its downtown area over almost four decades, characterized nationally by a decentralization of economic activity, constitutes an impressive level of success for the revitalization strategy.

Figure 3.7a/b compares job concentration in nine Midwest MSAs. Indianapolis was not as successful at retaining jobs as was Cleveland, but was able to retain a larger proportion of jobs than Chicago (Cook County) or Cincinnati (Hamilton County) and the same proportion as St. Louis City and County (Figure 3.8a). When the comparisons are made with Pittsburgh, Louisville, Kansas City, and Columbus, Indianapolis' success is far less evident. Among these cities, Indianapolis (by 2005) had the second lowest job concentration level.

Figure 3.8a/b looks at the changing concentration of private sector payrolls as opposed to the number of jobs. While Indianapolis had the greatest concentration of private sector payroll dollars in its core county in 1970 and it did very well at retaining private sector payrolls, other areas did slightly better. Cleveland, a community

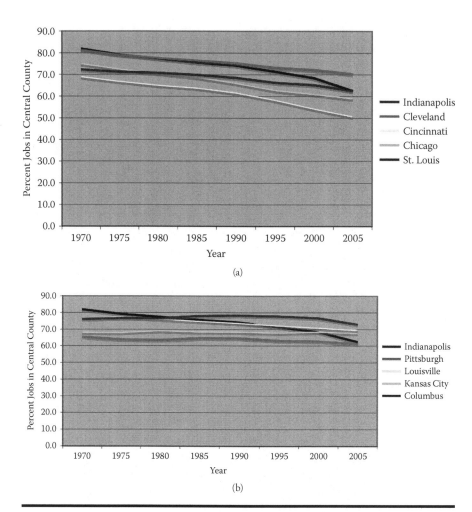

Figure 3.7   The concentration of jobs in the central counties in selected Midwest MSAs, 1970–2005. (From U.S. Department of Labor.)

that also had a pronounced downtown redevelopment strategy, actually fared best at retention of private sector payrolls, while Cincinnati and Chicago had the largest proportional declines. In the second group of communities, Indianapolis' decline was the largest with Louisville, Pittsburgh, and Kansas City maintaining more of the private sector payrolls in the central counties.

A final, if somewhat more complicated, view of changes is presented in Figure 3.9 illustrating the growth in private sector payrolls in each of the main or central city counties in the nine metropolitan regions as well as the total private sector payroll in 2005. Indianapolis/Marion County enjoyed a 917.9 percent increase

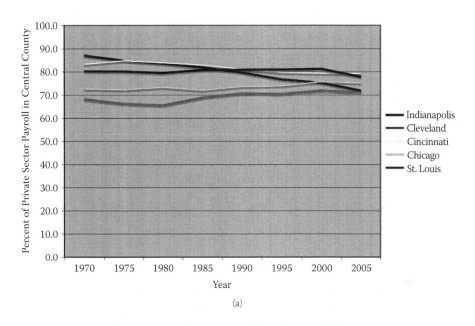

(a)

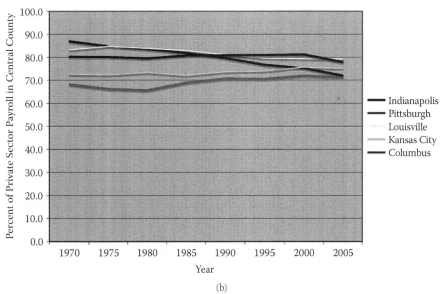

(b)

Figure 3.8   The concentration of private sector payrolls in central counties in selected Midwest MSAs, 1970–2005. (From U.S. Department of Labor.)

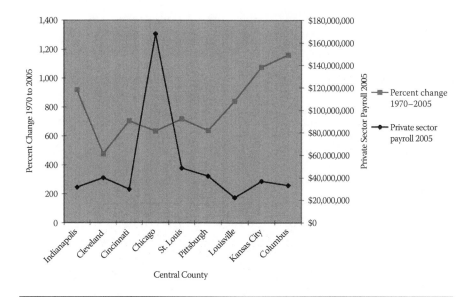

Figure 3.9 Percent change in private sector payroll dollars in central counties, 1970–2005 (in 2005 dollars) and 2005 private sector payroll levels. (From U.S. Department of Labor.)

in private sector payrolls across the 35-year period; only two areas, Kansas City and Columbus, had greater growth rates. In 1970, the private sector's payroll in Indianapolis exceeded those of two other central counties: Louisville and Columbus. In 2005, Indianapolis' rank was unchanged with a private sector payroll exceeding that of Cincinnati and Louisville. While the sports and downtown development effort was associated with a very large growth rate, the consolidated city/county will need to sustain that rate of expansion through the end of the decade and into the next to change its ranking relative to the other Midwest regions in terms of total private sector payroll dollars or salaries available to residents.

Finally, as a residential neighborhood, there have been impressive gains, but the number of individuals living downtown remains relatively small compared to other neighborhoods. With approximately 20,000 residents, less than two-tenths of 1 percent of the region's population lives in the downtown area. The downtown area's population accounts for approximately 3 percent of the residents of the consolidated city of Indianapolis.

In summary, the downtown focus did not mean that development did not also take place in other parts of Indianapolis, and median family income rose allowing Indianapolis to maintain its ranking among nine other Midwest regions. There were important increments in the number of jobs related to tourism, transportation, professional services, finance, and those offset the losses in the manufacturing sector. There was little change in information technology jobs. Downtown employment has increased. Unfortunately, there has been steady decline in the concentration of jobs and private payrolls in the downtown areas relative to the region and these declines were more pronounced than in other Midwest regions. While Indianapolis' downtown area is a showplace attracting crowds, it has not led to a more pronounced concentration of jobs and payrolls when compared to outcomes in other areas.

C. Image of Indianapolis: Intangible Benefits and the Journey from "Indiana-No-Place" to Super Bowl Host City

Changing Indianapolis' image was a main goal for the redevelopment effort. Not only was there the national survey that found Indianapolis didn't have an image, but many also point to favorite son Kurt Vonnegut's remark as a reason for the sports strategy. Appearing on *The Tonight Show,* the author described Indianapolis as a cemetery with lights that came to life one day a year for the Indianapolis 500.[18] Others recall with disdain John Gunther's post-World War II description of the city in his 1947 classic, *Inside U.S.A,* as dirty and a hotbed of racism.[19] Few would have believed in the early 1970s that Indianapolis could become a favored location for NCAA championships and a city that would host a Super Bowl (2012). Figure 3.10 pictures downtown Indianapolis in the 1970s; the photos in Figure 3.11a-c show a far different downtown today.

Figure 3.10   Downtown Indianapolis in the early 1970s. (Photo courtesy of the Indiana Sports Corporation; photographer unknown.)

(a)

(b)

Figure 3.11 (a) Downtown Indianapolis today. (Photo courtesy of the Indiana Sports Corporation.) (b) The Conseco Fieldhouse, home of the Indiana Pacers. (Photo courtesy of the Indiana Sports Corporation.)

Figure 3.11   (c) Indiana Repertory Theatre. (Photo courtesy of Mark S. Rosentraub.)

In numerous surveys of residents and visitors, Indianapolis is repeatedly described as a city with a downtown area with "lots to do" and an abundance of recreation, entertainment, and cultural facilities. The professional sports teams and physical and visual appeal of downtown are similarly described and ranked as important assets for the region and the state. In rankings of the state's leading assets and things that make residents proud to live in Central Indiana, the professional sports teams and downtown events generally are regarded as important as any other asset.[20] When asked to place a value on the intangible benefits of hosting the Indianapolis Colts, respondents to a survey—if projected across the population of Central Indiana—reported benefits that are worth in excess of $25 million per year.[21] The Colts were attracted to Indianapolis because of a new stadium in the 1980s and the new look of the downtown area. The team recommitted to Indianapolis for an additional 30 years when the counties in the metropolitan area and the state agreed to build another new home for the Colts that will also host the NCAA men's and women's basketball championships twice each decade.

For 2006, Indianapolis Downtown Incorporated reported that 17.1 million visitors attended events or attractions in the downtown area, with 85 percent of the residents of Marion County reporting at least one trip to the core area for recreation or entertainment. A decline in visits among residents of the metropolitan area was observed for the first time since 2002, but three-quarters of those who did visit rate the downtown area as "very safe." Almost 800,000 people attended conventions in the downtown area, and the hotel occupancy rate for the year was 63.3 percent. A total of 85 percent of the downtown office space was leased even though adjusted average rental rates have decreased 13 percent since 2000. Housing prices continued to increase through 2007 led by strong demand for condominiums that had an average sale price in excess of $270,000. The residential vacancy rate stood at 8.3 percent and has declined for three consecutive years, but rental rates have increased, in real terms, by just 1 percent since 2000.[22]

IV. Challenges on the Horizon: Subsidies and Revenues

While downtown Indianapolis has numerous entertainment and cultural amenities, a large university, growing health delivery centers, and planned expansions by the Eli Lilly Pharmaceutical Corporation, the importance of the two major sports teams to the future has not changed. Each needed a new facility and despite the increased attractiveness of downtown Indianapolis, large subsidies were provided in response to the teams' arguments regarding their ability to compete with other clubs.

Central Indiana is one of the nation's smallest markets for sports whether one uses population, the number of large firms, or the wealth of residents as a measure of size. The NFL provides extensive protection for small market teams through the sharing of revenue from its national television and Internet contracts and from the sales of most souvenirs and clothes. The ability to raise additional revenues through luxury seating and advertising does give some teams more funds to spend on players and greater levels of profitability. There are salary caps with penalties for offending clubs, but teams in larger markets with more revenue potential are more profitable. As a result of similar issues in the NBA, both the Pacers and Colts have insisted on lease arrangements that provide them with financial protection and the potential to increase their revenues and earn profits.

The Colts' effort to secure revenue protection from Indianapolis began in the 1990s as the RCA Dome, with fewer than 60,000 seats, sparse luxury seating, and too little space for concessions offered the team few of the revenue options existing elsewhere. Indianapolis eventually agreed to make a series of modifications to the Dome to create more luxury seating, but also had to agree to guarantee that the Colts' gross revenues would be at the average of all of the NFL's teams. Shortfalls would require payments from the city. That subsidy grew to tens of millions of dollars each year in the early part of the twenty-first century. The Colts needed a new facility that could give the team the potential to generate needed revenues while also giving Indianapolis an asset it could use for other events.

The Colts' lease for Lucas Oil Stadium provides no guaranteed revenue levels. In addition, the team agreed to stay in Indianapolis for 30 years and there is no "escape clause." The team also accepted the provision that any legal dispute regarding the team's location or adherence to the terms of the lease would be adjudicated in an Indianapolis court (which would likely be quite sympathetic to arguments put forward by the city). Further, the revenue guarantees provided by the public sector to the team during their tenure at the RCA Dome were not extended.

What did the Colts get in exchange for these concessions?

The public sector paid $620 million or 86 percent of the cost of the $720 million facility. The team's investment was $100 million and the forfeiture of guaranteed revenue from the public sector. Had the new facility not been built, the public sector would have been making payments of approximately $20 million each year to subsidize the Colts' operations. The Colts retain all revenue from naming rights, advertising, and the sale of luxury seating. These seats and suites now offer amenities similar to what is available in many other facilities. The risk is that this luxury seating must still be sold in the league's smallest market and one characterized by slow growth. While the revenue is not guaranteed, the revenue potential elevated the team's value on Forbes' list making the team the eighth most valuable at $1.076 billion.[23] Indianapolis does have the right to use the facility for numerous other events and signed a contract to host the NCAA men's and women's Final Four basketball tournaments twice each decade for the next 30 years. During conventions, the facility can also be used for additional exhibition space. All events previously held in the RCA Dome, including scores of amateur sports contests, will be held at Lucas Oil Stadium. The old dome was razed in 2008 and the space was incorporated into the convention center. Yet, the public subsidy exceeds $600 million and without another round of substantial private sector investment, the investment is full of risks for both the team and the public sector. For the team, it must now try to generate sufficient revenues in a very small market. For the public sector, it must continue to attract private investments and host myriad events to ensure that its investment does not become a major subsidy producing marginal economic returns.

By the early 1990s, Market Square Arena, which was built for the Indiana Pacers in 1974, was economically obsolete. Its design would not easily accommodate modifications. Further, its elevation (Market Street actually passed under the arena at ground level) made the logistics of staging concerts and other entertainment events impractical and costly as all equipment had to travel through the two available freight elevators to the floor level that was 20 feet above the street. Conseco Fieldhouse opened in 2000 replete with luxury seating, large concourses, numerous advertising and naming opportunities, and street level access for spectators and equipment. The public sector was also responsible for the financing of most of the facility and maintenance for any repairs in excess of $50,000. The team handled all other maintenance that was identified as "minor," but also retained all revenue from events held at the facility. Its $3.4 million payment for parking and rental fees was tied to a maximum operating loss of $2 million. If in any year the cost of operating the team after all revenue received produced a loss of more than $2 million, the team could move unless the public sector provided a subsidy to reduce the operating deficit. In essence, the lease requires the public sector to ensure that the team's losses do not exceed $2 million even after (1) paying for most of the cost of building the new facility, (2) agreeing to be responsible for all major maintenance costs, and (3) assigning virtually all of the revenues generated by the facility to the team's holding company.

Indianapolis is not only home to two professional sports teams, but the Central Indiana market is called upon to support the sports programs of two Big 10 universities (Indiana and Purdue), one independent university (Notre Dame), and the athletic programs of several smaller but highly successful colleges. In addition, the ability of the teams to draw from a statewide market is hampered by the popularity of the Chicago Bears and Chicago Bulls in Northwest Indiana. The Cincinnati Bengals also have fans living in Southern Indiana. As a result, the Central Indiana market is indeed "stressed" when it comes to supporting sports teams and both the Colts and Pacers were concerned that even with new facilities their abilities to earn revenues were constrained.

One example of this stress or strain surfaced for the Pacers in 2009 as the team's fortunes on the court slumped. Fans were "turned off" by the team's losing ways and outrageous attacks of fans in the stands. For the 2007–2008 season, the team had the lowest attendance level in the league and the city had to face the very real possibility that it would have to begin paying a subsidy to make sure that the Pacers would not leave. By 2009, the fear became a reality.

In February 2009, the team announced that it was anticipating a loss of $15 million and that it had been losing money for years. The team informed the Capital Improvements Board that it would need financial help in 2010 asserting that it had actually lost money in 25 of the past 27 years. Because of these losses, the team might be preparing to ask to renegotiate its entire lease or an additional annual investment from the public sector, or both. While it might seem implausible that the team lost money on the arena in some years past, by 2009 financial problems had developed for several teams in smaller markets. For example, the Cleveland Indians began offering "2 for the price of 1" season tickets for the 2009 season and the Phoenix Coyotes, who filed for bankruptcy protection in 2009, regularly offered "2 for the price of 1" tickets for many games in the 2008–2009 season. These actions by teams in larger markets made it entirely plausible to understand that the Pacers were indeed confronting substantial financial losses in the midst of the economic recession.[24]

The inclusion of subsidy provisions in the leases and the assumption of responsibility for most or all of the costs of the facilities used by the teams (while they received most if not all of the revenues) begs an important question: Would Indianapolis really risk losing either franchise if subsidies were not provided? While many markets clamor for a new NBA franchise, in terms of regions with larger populations and without an NBA team, the Los Angeles regions eastern suburbs have grown to the point where they have enough residents to support a team. It is highly unlikely, however that the owners of the Lakers and Clippers would support a third NBA team in their region. The San Diego metropolitan region is also much larger than Indianapolis. The Clippers decided to move to Los Angeles rather than continue in San Diego. With the Padres (MLB) and Chargers (NFL), San Diego may not be able to support three teams. The Seattle region is also larger and, after losing the Sonics, that area is a likely relocation candidate. That option did not exist in 2000. St. Louis, which lost the Hawks in 1968, does not have an NBA franchise, and neither does Pittsburgh, but with three franchises in both of those cities, there would seem to be too few people to support a fourth. Cincinnati is slightly larger, but there are already two professional sports franchises in that market and adding a third would create problems. In short, the options related to relocation for the Pacers remain quite limited, and Indianapolis is probably the best option. This suggests that moving the franchise is not a viable option.

The relocation options for the Colts were also limited. There was concern the Colts might move to Los Angeles. After the Rams left Anaheim for St. Louis and the Raiders returned to Oakland, the Los Angeles metropolitan area represented a lucrative alternative. The politics of locating and building a new, football-only facility in Southern California are difficult and a local business leader had already agreed to pay for a new stadium if awarded a franchise. These politics made relocation for the Colts only possible if the team was to be sold to that individual and that was not a consideration. This effectively removed Los Angeles as a relocation option for the Colts.

There are some markets larger than Indianapolis without an NFL franchise. Portland, Oregon, is larger, but that community would have to build a facility and the issue has never been seriously debated. In the absence of a facility, it seems Indianapolis is a better location. The San Antonio MSA is also larger, but with NFL teams in the Dallas/Fort Worth area and in Houston, support from other NFL owners for relocation there could be problematic. Realistically, there was also no relocation option for the Colts.

What lessons emerge from Indianapolis' experience with the Pacers and Colts? Despite a revived downtown and a total investment of more than $8 billion in a wide-ranging set of entertainment, commercial, residential, and retail facilities, Indianapolis' market size still places it in a precarious position when negotiating with teams and owners. Further, the investment has not led to a level of population growth and corporate relocations that have propelled the market to a level where extreme confidence can exist with regard to its ability to support two professional sports teams, the events at the Indianapolis Motor Speedway, and the teams fielded by leading universities. As the Colts were able to point out, the intangible benefits of the team's presence were substantial and indeed larger than the public's investment in the new stadium.[25] To host two teams in a small market, however, continues to demand large investments by the public sector.

To be sure, a prudent assessment would conclude that the relocation options for the Colts and Pacers were and remain realistically small and, therefore, public and community leaders could take more strident stands in the negotiations with both teams. Such a stance might well have placed far more risk with the teams if the public investment in Lucas Oil Stadium was smaller and if Indianapolis did not agree to reimburse the Pacers for excessive losses. If the teams did not move, but the owners were sufficiently alienated by an aggressive negotiating stance on the part of the public sector, then they could have decided to follow a strategy to minimize players' salaries. Indianapolis needs the ownership of both teams to be committed to winning and, to that end, favorable revenue situations in a very small market need to be protected. But the possibility remains that both deals could have provided for more protection for the public sector.

V. Indianapolis: The Broker City to Be a Major League Winner

Indianapolis wrote the textbook on using sports and cultural facilities to revital- ize its downtown area. Three substantial accomplishments stand out as lessons for other cities. First, Indianapolis' leadership put forward a plan that was both an intangible vision of what could be built and a physical blueprint of what was needed and where, for the rebuilding of a deteriorating core area. Partners in the private and nonprofit sectors, as well as state government officials and residents, could understand the goals and direction. The focus was initially on sports, but was then broadened to include culture and the arts. This three-pronged reliance on sports, the arts, and culture to build a downtown that underscored entertainment and destinations for visitors and residents generated confidence because it created a single vision for a city that for too long seemed to wander from initiative to initia- tive to improve its image.

The plan was not the product of a review process that incorporated public input or which encouraged reviews and comment. The strategy was championed by a regime that got things done, but opportunities for public participation—created in later years—existed long after the policy focus was chosen. There were extraordi- nary levels of discussion, debate, and analysis among community leaders, but the conversations were restricted to leadership.

Second, Indianapolis succeeded in leveraging substantial financial investments for the revitalization effort from the private and nonprofit sector as well as the state government. Rebuilding downtown Indianapolis was an effort led by the city's investment, but its success was a function of the billions of dollars invested by other institutions and governments. For every dollar Indianapolis committed to the revitalization effort, $2.92 came from other sources. That level of success is not only a model for other cities to emulate, but underscores the point that no rebuilding effort can succeed without private capital. Few would oppose leveraging ratio in excess of $2.90 for every $1 invested by the city. A measure of the success of the planning effort and vision is the confidence leaders from other sectors of the economy expressed through their investment of funds.

Third, Indianapolis overhauled its image among its own residents and in the eyes of national leaders and institutions. In 1974, it would have been hard to imagine that Indianapolis would be a favored location for national or international events. Today, a very different reality exists and relative to the goal of changing its image, the revitalization effort was an impressive success. Downtown Indianapolis attracts people and events at a level unimaginable relative to the city's image in the 1970s. That success has helped to create new employment and economic development opportunities related to tourism and the hospitality sector.

What also cannot be overlooked, however, is that a local investment of $2.5 billion has meant that the civic leadership of Indianapolis must constantly lead efforts to advance real estate investment. It is, in essence, the broker for the deals needed to complement the public funds committed to rebuilding the downtown area. No guarantee of any private sector investment accompanied the commitments made by Indianapolis. San Diego, Los Angeles, and Columbus (as will be described) had guaranteed levels of real estate investments made by private sector interests tied to the building of sport facilities. Indianapolis, more similar to Cleveland, had to secure development deals after it made commitments to build big-ticket items. If the commitment of public money for sports, cultural, and entertainment amenities was to reap dividends, Indianapolis had to become a broker attracting events and other investors. The city then also had to be sure that an organizational structure was in place to assist in making events successful and to continue to attract other games and meetings. The city also had to have an agency focused on downtown—from addressing the needs of potential investors—to advocating for needed improvements that maintain the downtown area's attractiveness.

Three organizations were created to perform the needed broker roles that steers the development of downtown Indianapolis. Indianapolis Downtown Incorporated exists to build partnerships between the private sector and the city to advance the growth, well being, and user-friendliness of the core area. The Indiana Sports Corporation was created to be the catalyst to attract sporting events to the city and then to oversee the services the event organizers need to achieve their results. The Sports Corporation coordinates the activities and services needed from the public sector with and for event organizers. The Corporation has also recruited, when needed, thousands of volunteers to help with an event. Lastly, the Department of Metropolitan Development as well as deputy mayors (depending on the mayor) work with corporations and others to focus development in the downtown area. These three organizations excel at making deals and cultivating the necessary public, private, and nonprofit partners to facilitate development.

Noting that three strong organizations—two of them nonprofit corporations— exist in a city to coordinate economic development would be seen by many as evidence of the exact sort of leadership expected or needed for Rust Belt cities. In many other cities, there are often calls for more executive leadership to coordinate economic development, especially when different parts of the public sector appear to fail at cooperating to achieve a common goal.[26] While coordinated leadership is not a problem for Indianapolis, the city must constantly create new partnerships to leverage returns from its big-ticket items. For example, immediately after closing the deal to build the new stadium for the Colts and expand the convention center, Indianapolis had to guarantee that a new hotel would be built. The 34-story JW Marriott Hotel, with 1,005 rooms and three smaller hotels on the same site, involves a private sector investment of $377 million and $48 million from Indianapolis.[27] It is likely that several more deals will have to be "brokered" to be sure the public investment in the stadium is successful. Indianapolis will have to assist in attracting scheduled events and expand efforts to ensure that downtown Indianapolis remains inviting and user friendly.

The emphasis on downtown did lead to an increase in employment in the core area from 1990 to 1995, and Indianapolis was able to maintain the level of employment from 1995 to 2005. Across these 10 years, the number of private sector jobs declined by almost 1,500, but with the growth of the Indiana University hospitals and IUPUI, it is likely that the number of downtown workers in 2005 was quite similar to the number in 1995. However, the regional concentration of jobs in the downtown area declined. In addition, Indianapolis' ability to retain private sector jobs and payroll dollars in its downtown area was not as successful as similar efforts in other Midwest regions. While a concentration of jobs was maintained downtown, there was more regional decentralization in the Indianapolis MSA than elsewhere in the Midwest.

From the perspective of revitalizing and rebuilding a downtown area, leveraging funds from the private sector, maintaining a downtown area's centrality, and creating an entirely new image, Indianapolis' sports strategy made it a Major League Winner. That gain, though, must be tempered by the reality that the sports and downtown redevelopment did not lead an economic transformation of the region or translate into higher family incomes. There was no loss of wealth, just less gained. Further, the hoped-for overall economic and population growth did not occur. The area still fails to attract large numbers of migrants. Indianapolis was able to use sports and an emphasis on culture to rebuild its downtown area, dramatically change its image, and create a management structure to coordinate the revitalization of the core area. The city attracted billions of dollars in new investment and, with a leveraging ratio of almost 3:1, Indianapolis produced a set of benefits that turned large sports subsidies into strategic investments and positive cash flows. And yet, it may be called upon to provide more subsidies to its sports teams to keep them profitable.

Endnotes

1. Leland, S. and M. S. Rosentraub. 2009. Consolidated and fragmented governments and regional cooperation: Surprising lessons from Charlotte, Cleveland, Indianapolis, and Kansas City. In *Who will govern metropolitan regions in the 21st Century?* ed. D. Phares, Armonk, NY: M. E. Sharpe (forthcoming).
2. Rosentraub, M. S. 1997a. *Major league losers: The real cost of sports and who's paying for it*. New York: Basic Books.

3. Hudnut, W. 1995. *The Hudnut years in Indianapolis, 1976-1991*. Indianapolis: Indiana University Press.
4. Molotch, H. 1993. The political economy of growth machines. *Journal of Urban Affairs* 15 (1): 29–53.
5. Rosentraub, M. S. and P. Helmke. 1996. Location theory, a growth coalition, and a regime in a medium-sized city. *Urban Affairs Review* 31 (4): 482–507.
6. See, for example, McGovern, S. J. 2003. Ideology, consciousness, and inner city redevelopment: The case of Stephen Goldsmith's Indianapolis. *Journal of Urban Affairs*. 25 (1): 1–26. Also see Vogelsang-Coombs, V. 2007. Mayoral leadership and facilitative governance. *American Review of Public Administration*. 37 (2): 198–225; and Wilson, D. 1996. Metaphors, growth coalition discourses, and black poverty neighborhoods in a U.S. city. *Antipode* 28 (1): 72–96.
7. Squires, G. 1989. ed. *Unequal partnerships: Political economy of urban redevelopment in postwar America*. New Brunswick, NJ: Rutgers University Press, p. 3.
8. Porter, P. R. and D. Sweet. 1984. *Rebuilding America's cities: Roads to recovery*. New Brunswick, NJ: Rutgers University, Center for Urban Policy Research, p. 214.
9. Eisinger, P. 2000. The politics of bread and circuses. *Urban Affairs Review* 35 (3): 316–333.
10. Rosentraub, M. S. 2006. The local context of a sports strategy for economic development. *Economic Development Quarterly* 20 (3): 278–291.
11. Logan, J. R. and H. L. Molotch. 1987. *Urban fortunes: The political economy of place*. Berkeley: University of California Press.
12. Harrison, B. and B. Bluestone. 1988. *The great u-turn: Corporate restructuring and the polarizing of America*. New York: Basic Books.
13. Eisinger, The politics of bread and circuses, 316–333.
14. Birch, E. 2005. *Who lives downtown?* Washington, D.C.: The Brookings Institution, Metropolitan Policy Program.
15. Rosentraub, M. S., D. Swindell, M. Przybylski, and D. Mullins. 1994. Sports and a downtown development strategy: If you build it will jobs come? *Journal of Urban Affairs* 16 (3): 221–239.
16. Austrian, Z. and M. S. Rosentraub. 2002. Cities, sports and economic change: A retrospective assessment. *Journal of Urban Affairs* 24 (5) 549–565, 561–562.
17. Baade, R. A. 1996. Professional sports as catalysts for metropolitan economic development. *Journal of Urban Affairs* 18 (1): 1–17.
18. Hudnut, *The Hudnut years in Indianapolis, 1976-1991*.
19. Rosentraub, *Major league losers*.
20. Children's Museum of Indianapolis. 2005. *The economic impact and value of The Children's Museum to the central Indiana economy*. Indianapolis: The Children's Museum.
21. Rosentraub, M. S. D. Swindell, and S. Tsvetkova. 2009. Justifying public investments in sports: measuring the intangibles. *Journal of Tourism* (forthcoming).
22. Indianapolis Downtown, Incorporated. 2006. *Annual report*. Indianapolis: Indianapolis Downtown, Incorporated.
23. *Forbes*. 2008. NFL team valuations. http://www.forbes.com/lists/2008/30/sports-money_nfl08_NFL-Team-Valuations_Rank.html (accessed December 1, 2008); http://www.forbes.com/lists/2008/32/nba08_NBA-Team-Valuations_MetroArea.html (accessed December 4, 2008).

24. Schoettle, A. 2009. Fieldhouse flop? Pacers: We've lost money 9 of last 10 years. *Indianapolis Business Journal*, February 7; https://www.ibj.com (accessed February 7 2009).
25. Rosentraub, Swindell, and Tsvetkova, Justifying public investments in sports.
26. Larkin, B. 2008. How Cleveland fumbled away Eaton corporation. *The Plain Dealer*, October 5, D1, 3.
27. Swiatek, J. 2008. A work in progress: Even before designs are finalized, massive JW Marriott project is forging ahead. *The Indianapolis Star,* October 5, D1, 4.

Chapter 4

Shared Risk, Shared Returns: San Diego's Unique Partnership for a Ballpark, Convention Center Hotel, and a New Downtown Neighborhood

I. Introduction

The 1980s and 1990s was an era of unprecedented subsidies for sports facilities. Arlington (Texas), Baltimore, Chicago, Cincinnati, Cleveland, Dallas, Detroit, Green Bay, Jacksonville, Milwaukee, Phoenix, Seattle, St. Louis, St. Petersburg, Tampa, and Toronto raised taxes to ensure teams would call their communities home. These tax increases repaid the bonds sold to pay for the public sector's share of the cost of building the new facilities. With the teams given control of all of the new revenue generated from luxury seating, naming and sponsorship rights, and the expanded retail venues included in these new facilities, they had the revenue needed to repay any debt they incurred. As *Forbes* would report each year, the additional revenue also substantially increased the value of each team creating an opportunity for owners to realize a substantial return on the money they invested to buy the team. In no instance did a public sector partner receive a commitment or assurance that new private investments would be made to produce additional tax dollars. Each city could follow in Indianapolis' footsteps and put forward a plan and then actively broker additional deals for new development that might generate new tax revenues to offset their investment. While each city assured residents they would try to enhance development and secure new taxes, in essence taxpayers were left to "hope" something positive in terms of real estate development and new tax revenues would occur. Deals like that would not work in San Diego.

The San Diego Padres wanted a new ballpark to produce the revenues needed to guarantee the team could compete for players with franchises in larger markets and remain profitable. Owner John Moores was not willing to sustain losses or be a "welfare maximizer" securing benefits from having provided San Diego with a winning baseball team.

A. Fiscal Challenges for the Padres

Earning profits or sufficient revenues to remain competitive had been a long-term challenge for every owner of the Padres. While San Diego probably has America's best climate, few large corporations have their headquarters in the region, and while residential property prices soared in the latter half of the 1990s and into the first part of the twenty-first century, the region had a relatively small base of high-income residents. The Padres also played their home games in a facility where the NFL's Chargers were given control over important revenue streams.

The team's fiscal position was further constrained by its location. To the north was wealthy and populous Orange County—as well as the growing "Inland Empire"—but, so too was the American League team, the Los Angeles Angels of Anaheim. If residents of Orange County or the Riverside area wanted to see a National League team, the Dodgers were formidable competitors for the Padres in their effort to attract these fans, as they had been entrenched in the Southern California market since the 1958 season. To San Diego's south is Mexico and the income levels in the Tijuana area offered few customers for luxury seating or high priced tickets.

B. "Poisoned Environment" for Sports Subsidies

Regardless of the validity of these market issues, a typical tax-supported subsidy for a new ballpark was not feasible. Years of contentious relations between San Diego and the Chargers had created a large and vocal opposition to tax increases for professional sports. In the absence of an innovative approach and the creation of a public/private partnership with risks and benefits equally shared, there would be no new ballpark. The plan developed by the Padres' owner and San Diego guaranteed the building of a new hotel and other development to produce the new tax dollars needed to repay the city's investment in the ballpark. This was a unique public/private partnership for the revitalization of a downtown area and the building of a ballpark. An assessment of the Ballpark District's successes and failures provides civic leaders everywhere with an opportunity to consider whether a strategy with risk and new revenue streams for the public sector and the team creates a new way to revitalize a downtown area and ensure a new facility is politically acceptable and built. The testing of this approach in a relatively small market also means that the lessons learned might create a model that could be used anywhere.

II. The Padres and the "Need" for a New Ballpark

The Padres began play in 1969 and the challenges of the local market almost led to their quick demise. By 1974, the team's owners were threatening to move the team to Washington, D.C. Ray Kroc (founder of the McDonald's chain) purchased the team to assure its continued presence in the city. His wife, Joan, assumed sole ownership of the team in 1984 after his death and continued to underscore their family's commitment to keeping the Padres' franchise in San Diego. More concerned with San Diego having a team than with profits, the Padres' future seemed assured. In 1984, the team won its first National League pennant. In 1990, Joan Kroc decided to sell the team to a group of 15 local business leaders; local ownership met her goal of assuring the team's continued presence in San Diego.[1] Operational losses led this group to sell controlling interest to John Moores in December 1994. Moores, a Houston native, made his fortune in software, but was unable to buy his hometown Astros. Wanting to own a team, he jumped at the chance to purchase controlling interest in the Padres. With Moores at the helm, the Padres won four division titles as well as the 1998 National League pennant.

The Padres played their home games in the San Diego Stadium renamed for legendary sports writer Jack Murphy and later known as Qualcomm Stadium. The facility opened in 1967 as the home for the NFL's Chargers. When the Padres' franchise was created, they became tenants in a facility controlled by the Chargers. The Chargers' lease gave them control of all revenues leaving the Padres as the financial stepchild or the Cinderella of San Diego's teams. John Moores understood that a baseball team in a relatively small market that did not have access to and control of all the revenue-generating amenities in newer facilities would never be profitable. He wanted his team to win, but he did not want to lose money.

Baseball teams are located in 26 different metropolitan areas. The San Diego market, by population, is the 17th largest although the 13th (the San Francisco/Oakland metropolitan area) is home to two teams. That region is adjacent to the San Jose–Sunnyvale–Santa Clara area with its 1.74 million residents providing the Giants and Athletics with lucrative marketing opportunities in an adjacent metropolitan area not served by another baseball team. In terms of the wealth in the Padres' market area, as measured by personal income in 2006, the San Diego metropolitan area also ranked 17th (if Toronto was included). Using each metropolitan area's gross domestic product as a measure of the corporate wealth available as a market for luxury seating, the San Diego area also ranked 17th. These rankings created enough important challenges, but without exclusive control of the revenue streams provided by a new ballpark, the Padres seemed destined to either lose money or become noncompetitive (Table 4.1).

When the Padres began to discuss a new ballpark with the city, the team compared its revenue earning potential to that of the Cleveland Indians who had recently moved into a new, baseball-only facility. In 1997, the Indians, playing in what would become a market area smaller than metropolitan San Diego, was able to generate $134.2 million. The Padres earned $20 million less from the sale of tickets. The Padres also received only 29 percent of the revenue from the rental of luxury suites at Qualcomm Stadium, the balance accruing to the primary tenant, the San Diego Chargers.[2]

To more fully explain the revenue limitations that confronted the Padres, the team circulated a 1998 report of estimated earnings of selected MLB teams (Table 4.2) to elected officials and the community to illustrate the revenues earned by the Arizona Diamondbacks, Atlanta Braves, Baltimore Orioles, Cleveland Indians, Colorado Rockies, Texas Rangers, and New York Yankees in that year. Every team except the Yankees had a new facility, and the Yankees were included to illustrate the challenges faced by small market teams relative to the franchises in larger and wealthier regions. Each of these teams had total gross revenues that were at least $30 to $40 million greater than the amount of money earned by the San Diego Padres.

In 1996, San Diego's Mayor Susan Goldberg created a committee to explore the financial challenges facing the Padres and, in 1997, the Task Force on Padres Planning—comprised of community and citizen leaders, many of whom were connected to leading local institutions and businesses—concluded that (1) the team was losing money and (2) any hope for an improved fiscal position rested with a new ballpark. The Task Force agreed with the Padres' owner that there was no short-term fix or longer term improvement that could be made at Qualcomm Stadium that would address the team's financial position.

III. Politics of San Diego's Sports World

The economic arguments regarding the team's viability in San Diego and the threat to move elsewhere were not going to convince elected officials or the public to invest in a new ballpark. San Diego had (and continues to have) a tumultuous relationship with the owner of the San Diego Chargers who had long demanded a series

Table 4.1 Population, Income, and Gross Domestic Product (GDP) of Metropolitan Areas with MLB Teams (income and GDP in billions of dollars)

Metropolitan Area	2007 Population	2006 Personal Income	2005 GDP
New York	18,815,988	910.8	1,056.4
Los Angeles	12,875,587	505.2	632.4
Chicago	9,524,673	391.3	461.4
Dallas/Fort Worth	6,145,037	235.3	315.5
Philadelphia	5,827,962	250.5	295.2
Houston	5,628,101	229.5	316.3
Toronto	5,555,912[a]	166.1	209.2[b]
Miami	5,413,212	216.5	231.8
Washington	5,306,565	270.9	347.6
Atlanta	5,278,904	184.1	242.4
Boston	4,482,857	223.1	261.1
Detroit	4,467,592	170.6	198.6
San Francisco/Oakland	4,203,898	233.3	268.3
Phoenix	4,179,427	137.0	160.0
Seattle	3,309,347	144.3	182.2
Minneapolis/St. Paul	3,208,212	138.8	171.4
San Diego	2,974,859	125.9	146.3
St. Louis	2,803,707	104.2	116.2
Tampa/St. Petersburg	2,723,949	94.3	101.0
Baltimore	2,663,286	115.8	118.1
Denver	2,464,866	106.7	131.6
Pittsburgh	2,355,712	91.8	102.1
Cincinnati	2,133,678	76.5	91.0
Cleveland	2,096,471	78.4	99.3

(continued on next page)

**Table 4.1 (continued) Population, Income, and Gross Domestic
Product (GDP) of Metropolitan Areas with MLB Teams (income
and GDP in billions of dollars)**

Metropolitan Area	2007 Population	2006 Personal Income	2005 GDP
Kansas City	1,985,429	74.3	91.2
Milwaukee	1,544,398	60.9	73.3

ᵃ 2003 estimate.
ᵇ Estimate from *Financial Times,* Canadian dollars.
Source: U.S. Bureau of the Census; Bureau of Economic Analysis,
  StatsCanada.

of improvements to Qualcomm Stadium. The Chargers' lease for Jack Murphy/
Qualcomm Stadium included a "trigger clause," which became a lightning rod for
public opposition to sports teams and their demands. Years of debates between the
team and different community groups, individuals (who filed law suits), and the
city of San Diego created a hostile and volatile political environment. The Padres
could not ignore this environment and the resentments that existed even though
their fiscal situation was substantially different from that which confronted the
Chargers. In essence, San Diego became a battleground where advocates and some
city officials were opposed to anything that resembled a subsidy for a professional
sports team. A bit of background is required to understand why the Padres eventually proposed what was at the time one of the most unique public/private partnership for a new sports facility.³

In 1995, the City of San Diego and the Chargers reached an agreement to
remodel Jack Murphy Stadium and the team's lease was extended through 2020.
The public perception was that San Diego's investment in the redesign secured
the team's presence for 25 years. The Chargers' leadership made public statements
declaring their relief in having matters resolved and looked forward to another generation in San Diego. In 1996 and 1997, the Chargers released a letter to the public
underscoring their commitment to the city, but noting that if the team was under
"severe financial hardship" it would have the right to renegotiate the terms of the
lease. The team also underscored that the renovations being made, while of extreme
value to the team, were undertaken to assure that San Diego could host the 2004
Super Bowl. The tone of the letter started the public's distrust of "stadium deals,"
but more disclosures would make matters worse.

The 1995 lease actually included two components that generated inflamed public resentment. First, the city guaranteed that the Chargers would be able to sell
60,000 nonluxury seats to every home game for at least 10 years (regardless of the
team's performance). If 60,000 seats were not sold, then the city was responsible
for buying any unsold tickets regardless of their price. The so-called "ticket guarantee" was not only unique in the relationship between cities and teams, but the

Table 4.2 The 1998 Estimated Earnings of Selected MLB Teams (in $000s; some estimates projected from 1997 figures)

| Team | Tickets Sold | Revenue From | | | | MLB Shared Funds | All Other Sales, Advertising | Total Estimated Income |
		Local Media	Luxury Suites	Club Seats				
AZ Diamondbacks	53,071	6,000	7,245	4,872	15,510	27,316	$114,014
Atlanta Braves	57,740	7,000	10,075	10,427	15,510	27,316	$128,068
Baltimore Orioles	72,846	14,000	5,940	11,134	15,510	27,316	$146,746
Cleveland Indians	60,158	17,865	11,144	35,005	15,510	30,000	$169,682
Colorado Rockies	60,152	7,600	4,531	9,979	15,510	27,316	$125,088
New York Yankees	60,611	50,000	2,900	16,335	15,510	27,316	$172,672
Texas Rangers	48,273	12,000	12,000	10,099	15,510	27,316	$125,198

Sources: Street and Smith's Sports Business Journal various issues; 1998 Inside the Ownership of Professional Sports Teams, Team Marketing Report, Inc., Chicago; U.S. Security Exchange Commission.

city's obligation was unconditional. In other words, the team could perform poorly or the Chargers could set unrealistic ticket prices for seats with poor sight lines and neither of these actions reduced or eliminated the city's liability to buy unsold tickets.[4] The guarantee was seen as a blank check for long-term access to tax dollars regardless of the team's performance and pricing policies.

The second element that ruffled political feathers across the city was the "triggering clause" tied to the issue of "severe economic hardship." Severe financial hardship was defined to mean that the team's player costs would exceed 75 percent of a designated set of revenues. If the team exceeded this threshold—the triggering point—the lease would have to be renegotiated or the team could leave for another venue. With the team suggesting two years into the lease that the "trigger" point was already being reached, the public lost faith in any deal with a professional sports team. Voters and numerous community groups did not trust the city to protect taxpayers or its interests. Proposing a new ballpark for the Padres in this environment required a deal or partnership that was quite different and even unique. Otherwise, a new ballpark was the proverbial "nonstarter" given local politics.

This was the political or social environment in which the Padres found themselves as they explored the options for a new ballpark. Ironically, while the public referendum on the Padres proposal would pass in 1998, a series of legal challenges and political situations and a crisis would delay construction and the ballpark's opening until 2004. During that time, the Chargers' debate would continue and dominate local news. For example, information surfaced that in 2001 the Chargers' ownership had preliminary conversations with the Anschutz Entertainment Group (AEG) that was interested in building a new football-only facility in downtown Los Angeles. The implication for the public was clear. After receiving tax money to improve Jack Murphy Stadium and a ticket guarantee, the team's owner was still interested in moving the team to Los Angeles. Then in April 2002 the Chargers' owner announced he wanted to renegotiate the lease as the triggering point had been reached. The team would be unable to provide the financial data to sustain that position at public hearings. Later in that same year, the team decided to relocate its preseason training facility to Los Angeles County, which further exacerbated the public's confidence and patience with sports teams and their owners.

While the drama with the Chargers unfolded, a federal corruption investigation linked Padres' owner John Moores to the substantial financial gains a San Diego council member had made from the public offering of the stock of a company he owned. There were also charges that some gifts were made to the council member during the time she was fighting cancer. The gifts involved help provided by the Moores Family to facilitate treatments. However, those details were slow to emerge creating other problems for the project as investigations progressed.

A total of 17 lawsuits were also filed. Once all of those cases were resolved—none were successful in challenging the legality of the procedures followed—and the stock and the ethics issues resolved (no crimes were found to have occurred), construction continued. There was, however, one brief additional "hiccup." In April

2003, the city found that the team had changed the agreed-to design so that fewer seats might be built. The city ordered that the ballpark be built as specified and the Padres immediately complied. Petco Park (the naming rights to the facility were sold before the facility opened) hosted its first game in March 2004 (the first game was between two college teams) and was ready for the Padres' 2004 season.

IV. Task Force II and the Generation of Substantial Public Benefits

If a new ballpark for the Padres were built with any tax dollars, it would have to create important benefits for San Diego. The city's leadership established three requirements:

1. The ballpark would have to be located where the people of San Diego wanted it.
2. There would have to be assurances provided that sufficient levels of new construction would take place to generate new tax revenues to offset the public's investment.
3. The team owner would also have to guarantee that a new headquarter hotel near the San Diego Convention Center would be built.

In the earliest negotiations, three sites were discussed. The Padres preferred a Mission Valley location near Qualcomm Stadium. Any site in the suburban Mission Valley area offered excellent access to the region's major east/west and two north/south freeways. The popularity of the Mission Valley area would have made it relatively easy to assure new development to generate property taxes, but that development would have occurred even if a ballpark was not built. As a result, it would be difficult to claim the property taxes from new residences or commercial offices in the Mission Valley area represented new income for San Diego (Figure 4.1).

The other two sites were downtown. One location on the waterfront near the convention center had strong appeal to the team. The city, however, favored the aging East Village district (the current site of Petco Park) north and east of the convention center on the landward side of East Harbor Drive (Figure 4.2). The Gaslamp district north and west of the ballpark had seen the opening of numerous restaurants and pubs. The nearby Horton Plaza retail center was also successful, but no redevelopment had occurred in the East Village. San Diego was willing to invest in a ballpark located in the East Village, but wanted two other "public benefits."

V. Public Benefits and the Stigma of Subsidies

San Diego wanted a headquarter hotel for the convention center in the East Village and a revitalization plan that would generate sufficient new tax revenues to offset its

Figure 4.1   Shown are Qualcomm Stadium, oceans of parking, and the freeway convenience of Mission Valley. (Taken from Google Maps.)

investment in the ballpark. John Moores wanted to limit his investment in a new ballpark to approximately $150 million. A debt of that magnitude would permit the team to pay competitive salaries to players and ensure that he did not lose money. It was initially anticipated that the ballpark would cost $411 million.[5] The City of San Diego agreed to spend $186.5 million for the ballpark; the Padres committed $81 million to the ballpark's construction and $34 million for land acquisition and the building of needed infrastructure. The team also agreed to be responsible for any cost overruns. San Diego, through its Redevelopment Agency, pledged $88.5 million for land acquisition and the Unified Port of San Diego agreed to invest $21 million. Of the anticipated $411 million investment, the public sector planned to spend $296 million. The public share was equal to 72 percent of the anticipated total cost.

In the end, the ballpark cost $483.1 million (the distribution of responsibilities is illustrated in Figure 4.3), and the team assumed responsibility for 38.8 percent of the project. San Diego paid 42.6 percent of the project's cost and the Redevelopment Agency supported 17.2 percent of the bill. The Unified Port of San Diego supported 4.3 percent as its commitment of $21 million never increased. The public sector paid 64.2 percent of the cost of the ballpark project (including needed land and infrastructure) if the Port's contribution is included. If that is excluded, then San

Figure 4.2 Pictured are Petco Park, the Convention Center, and East Village. (Taken from Google Maps.)

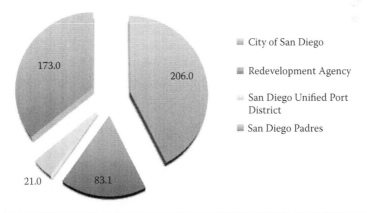

173.0

206.0

21.0   83.1

- ▦ City of San Diego
- ▦ Redevelopment Agency
- ◢ San Diego Unified Port District
- ▦ San Diego Padres

Figure 4.3 The shares (approximate) of the $454 million cost for the new ballpark for the Padres (in millions of dollars). (From the author's analysis and calculations, City of San Diego's Centre City Redevelopment Commission Corporation (2007) and Public Facilities Financing Authority (2002).)

Diego's cost was the share supported by the city itself and its redevelopment agency, which amounted to $289.1 million or 59.8 percent of the project's costs.

The proposal that was approved by 59.6 percent of the voters authorized San Diego to enter into a Memorandum of Understanding (MOU) with the Padres, the city's Redevelopment Agency, and the city's Centre City Development Corporation (CCDC) to:

1. Create a ballpark redevelopment district
2. Construct a baseball park
3. Redevelop the East Village area

The redevelopment area was designated as the *Ballpark District*. The city's investment in the project was capped at $225 million. What made the deal unique, and how it was presented to voters was that the Padres—through their owner—was committed to a redevelopment strategy that (1) would generate enough new tax dollars to pay for the public sector's investment and (2) ensure development of a convention center headquarter hotel. The most important public benefit, and the one that was the centerpiece of the campaign to secure voter approval for the financing plan and creation of the ballpark district, was that sufficient levels of new real estate development had to occur before and immediately after the opening of the ballpark. That new real estate development would then generate the new taxes required to repay San Diego's investment in the ballpark. Further, if the opening of the hotel were delayed past the opening of the ballpark, then the Padres would be responsible for paying a share of the lost hotel taxes. San Diego planned to use the new hotel taxes to pay its share of the maintenance costs associated with the operation of the ballpark.

All parties agreed to the MOU on July 14, 1998. San Diego and the Padres also agreed to complete a set of tasks by April 1, 1999. If those tasks were completed, then the land would be purchased and construction would begin. San Diego required the Padres, or John Moores, to have in place by April 1, 1999, the financing for the headquarter hotel (which would have at least 1,000 rooms). The Padres or their owner also had to provide assurances that sufficient commercial, residential, and/or retail development would take place prior to and just after the ballpark opened to generate the taxes needed to pay for the bonds used by the Redevelopment Agency.

The public sector's investment in the ballpark had two components. First, San Diego committed to an investment not to exceed $225 million. Second, the Redevelopment Agency, created in 1958 and comprised of the mayor and the entire city council—pledged $83.1 million. To repay the bonds for the city's investment, San Diego would rely on an increment in the taxes paid by hotel guests (transient occupant tax or TOT), the incremental property taxes generated by the new development in the Ballpark District, and new sales taxes. The city also planned to rely on the increase in the TOT to pay its share of the annual maintenance expenses for

Petco Park. The investment made through the Redevelopment Agency, which is, of course, part of the city of San Diego but a separate legal entity, was to be repaid by increased property taxes resulting from the residential, commercial, and retail development that would take place in the Ballpark District. The related development was then looked to as the source of revenue to repay the vast majority of the city's investment through its two "legal hats."

At first blush, the deal certainly looks like a familiar set of sports subsidies cleverly disguised by the participation of two public entities that are essentially the same since the city council and mayor constitute the governing bodies for San Diego and its Redevelopment Agency. The unique aspects of this deal or partnership were the commitments made to build the desired hotel and secure the new development needed to retire the debt created to pay San Diego's share of the ballpark's expenses. Before San Diego would make its substantial investment—through the city or through the Redevelopment Agency—the financing for the hotel and the promised level of new development had to be in place. On March 30, 1999, San Diego's city manager reported to the city council that the assurances were in place to meet John Moores' commitments. The council accepted the city manager's recommendation and committed to acquiring the land and building the required infrastructure. The ballpark district was officially created on March 31, 1999.[6] San Diego had guaranteed ticket sales for the Chargers, but the Padres' owner was required to provide assurances that the tax revenues needed to avoid a subsidy would be generated. This was a substantial reversal from the Chargers' deals and negotiations.

Relative to the public benefits secured, many could object to a convention center hotel being described as a public need. While San Diego's climate and amenities, as well as the coastal location of its convention center, made the city a meeting planner's delight, city leaders believed a headquarters or flagship hotel would mean more meetings (that would, in turn, generate more jobs and taxes). The city did not want any responsibility for building the hotel and had been frustrated that private developers had not come forward with plans for a new hotel. The Ballpark District created an opportunity get a hotel built that could meet the needs of convention attendees and out-of-town visitors to the ballpark. But to get that hotel built, the city had to invest in a ballpark. For its investment, San Diego received a commitment to have a baseball team in the city for at least 22 years, a new ballpark, a convention center hotel, and real estate development assurances that would lead to a redevelopment of the East Village area and generate the taxes needed to pay for their investment in the ballpark.

This plan represented the first time that a team or team owner had assured a city that a sufficient level of real estate development would take place to generate the tax revenues needed to pay for the public sector's investment in a ballpark. The team was also agreeing to meet revitalization goals established by a city and to locate the new ballpark where the city wanted. These were unprecedented commitments. Yet, prudent perspectives on growth and development require acknowledgment of the possibility that the tax dollars generated by a new hotel and new development might not be new revenues for San Diego. The development in the downtown area could have replaced projects that would have taken place in other parts of the city. The public sector perceived great value in ensuring that the development took place in the East Village area, and the movement of economic activity to conform to public plans can be as important as the occurrence of the economic activity itself. Because the city council had declared it a matter of public importance to redevelop the East Village, having a new headquarter hotel built and an assurance that new taxes supported the public's investment in the ballpark, the issue to evaluate or assess is the extent to which these goals were realized. The city and sports fans would have to rely on the public statements by John Moores that if the ballpark were built he would spend the money necessary to keep the team competitive. There was no protection for the city or guarantee that the team would spend a certain proportion of its revenues for players.

VI. Scorecard on the Ballpark District: What Was Built

While the large conference hotel with 1,000 rooms was not built, two hotels did open in the Ballpark District. That change was accepted by San Diego reflecting market changes after 9/11. By 2008, a total of 747 new hotel rooms were built. The Hotel Indigo with 210 rooms has a Summer 2009 scheduled opening and completion date. When that hotel is finished, JMI Realty would have exceeded the minimum number of guaranteed rooms, and come close to meeting the hoped-for 1,000 room headquarter hotel. A fourth hotel, The Spinnaker was in the planning stages in 2008 and could have as many as 250 rooms. If that hotel opens as scheduled, JMI Realty would have developed 1,200 new hotel rooms. The total number of new hotel rooms near the convention center would then have been extended.

The 2007 year-end report by the Centre City Development Corporation (CCDC) noted that more than 3,000 market-rate residential units had been built in the Ballpark District and 594 price-restricted units had also been occupied. In addition, 546,670 square feet of commercial space had been built. The value of this new construction was $1.13 billion, 360 percent more than what was specified in the MOU for Phase I. The Padres committed to a total of $487 million of new development in the Ballpark District across *two development phases*.[7] The level of construction activity was not only surpassed during Phase I, but the anticipated or promised development was actually more than double the amount included in the campaign literature urging people to vote for the creation of the Ballpark District and the building of a new home for the Padres. If all currently planned projects are built, by the end of the planned Phase II (2010), a grand total of more than $2.87 billion of new development completely financed by the private sector will have occurred in the Ballpark District (Table 4.3 and Table 4.4). If all of the planned development occurs, the amount

Table 4.3   New Construction in the Ballpark District through 2007

Project	Units/ Rooms	Square Feet	Cost ($ in millions)
6th and K (offices, parking)		15,000	1.5
Diamond Terrace (condominiums)	113		29.0
Diamond View Tower (offices)		325,000	81.0
Element (condominiums and offices)	65	9,670	23.0
Entrada	172/40		17.0
Fahrenheit Lofts	77		27.0
Hotel Solamar	235	7,000	50.0
ICON	327	16,000	115.0
Island Village (price controlled)	280	5,000	16.0
Lillian Place (price controlled)	74		14.5
M2i	230	12,000	82.0
Market Street Village I	225	43,000	38.0
Metrome	184		51.0
Nexus	68	3,000	24.3
Omni Hotel	512		110.0
Padres Parkade (1,000 parking spaces)		3,000	23.0
Palm Restaurant		7,000	1.0
Park Boulevard East	107		30.0
Park Boulevard West	120	6,000	30.0
Parkloft	120		83.2
Park Terrace	233	25,000	81.0
Potiker Family Senior Residences	200		16.6
Lofts At 677 7th Street	153	5,000	23.7
The Mark	260	8,000	105.0
The Metropolitan	32		62.0
TR Produce		42,000	12.0

Note: Where a slash (/) is used, the number to the right indicates units that are price controlled for affordability.

Source: Centre City Development Corporation, 2007.

Table 4.4 Projects in the Ballpark District with 2008 to 2010 Completion Dates

Project	Units/Rooms	Square Feet	Estimated Cost (in million $)
14th and K	222	9,000	$ 79.5
15th and Island	617	20,000	188.1
15th and Market	274	25,000	100.9
Alta	179	11,000	64.9
Axiom	205/41		72.0
Ballpark Village	1,600	517,000	1,400.0
Cosmopolitan Square	290	29,000	107.3
Echelon	183		64.0
Hotel Indigo	210		47.3
Laundry Lofts	208	2,000	73.0
Library Tower	174/16	12,000	69.0
Market Street Village II	244/24	14,000	88.2
Parkside	77/76	10,000	17.0
Seventh and Market	418/84/220[a]	14,000	300.0
Strata (hotel)	236	12,000	84.0
The Legend	183	30,000	80.0
The Lofts at 655 6th Avenue	183	12,000	18.0
Triangle	57	4,000	17.0

[a] This project will have 418 market-rate units, 84 price-controlled units, and 220 hotel rooms.

Note: Where a slash (/) is used, the number to the right indicates units that are price controlled for affordability.

Source: Centre City Development Corporation, 2007.

built would be more than five times (in real dollars) what was included in the MOU for Phase I and II. It is also important to note relative to design issues that many of the residential projects included a substantial amount of first-floor retail space. This created the neighborhood retail services that residents needed as well as opportunities for fans walking to Petco Park, the new home of the

San Diego Padres, to spend more time in the area, adding to the vitality of neighborhood life in the district.

VII. The Scorecard: Taxes Generated

San Diego was depending on increases in hotel taxes (TOT), new property taxes, and sales tax growth to pay for the bonds it issued to develop the ballpark and the district. The Redevelopment Agency turned to the CCDC to manage the projects in the Ballpark District and planned to use the new property taxes generated to make the payments that supported the bonds it issued to cover its investment as well as San Diego's commitment. While it is possible to trace the location of new property tax dollars, attributing TOT revenues to specific areas is far more difficult. It is also difficult to trace the location of sales tax dollars. Before turning to the growth in property tax revenues in the Ballpark District, changes in TOT and sales tax revenues are analyzed.

The increments in the TOT from 2002 and 2003 appear in Table 4.5. The data are presented using both 2002 and 2003 as base years, as the early year was clearly an aberration given the reactions in the aftermath of the 9/11 attacks. If 2002 is used as the base year against which to determine the growth, the total increment in TOT revenues through 2007 was $146 million. With 2003 as the base, the total increment was $96.2 million (see Table 4.5).

How much of this TOT increase could be or should be attributed to the new hotels in the ballpark district? The CCDC has estimated that $6.9 million in new taxes are generated each year by the hotel properties built in the Ballpark District (through 2007). This will increase after the new hotel's scheduled opening in 2008

Table 4.5 Transient Occupancy Taxes (TOT) and the City of San Diego, 2002–2007

Year	TOT Collections ($)	Increments from 2002 ($)	Increments from 2003 ($)
2002	95,175,000		
2003	105,263,000	10,088,000	
2004	113,209,000	17,494,000	7,946,000
2005	120,792,000	25,617,000	15,529,000
2006	136,803,000	41,628,000	31,540,000
2007	146,379,000	51,204,000	41,116,000

Source: City of San Diego, Comprehensive Annual Financial Report, City of San Diego, 2006, 2007.

and will rise further if another planned facility opens in 2009 or 2010. It is also possible that the increased popularity of the team and the building of the Ballpark District increased traffic at the convention center and attracted more visitors. A conservative estimate of the new TOT revenues directly attributable to the Ballpark District would be $6.9 million.

Sales tax revenues earned by San Diego and reported in their financial statements have been quite inconsistent. For example, in 2004 the city listed $238.4 million in revenue only to see it decline to $197.2 million in 2005. There was a robust increment to $227 million in 2006, but then in 2007 the city forecast revenues of $234.9 million, but received only $225.8 million. As a result, it seems more prudent to suggest that any sales tax revenues generated by activity in the Ballpark District helped to restore revenue to the city's budget in line with what was produced for 2004.

The TOT revenue was designed to cover San Diego's maintenance responsibilities at the ballpark and contribute to the city's cost for building the facility. Complete repayment of the capital cost of the facility was to come from new real estate taxes. By 2007, $1.147 billion in new construction had taken place in the Ballpark District. The CCDC estimated that the annual TIF value (new taxes produced) is $12.84 million. As detailed in Table 4.4, the construction in progress and planned would produce an additional $2.87 billion in new development. If all of the projects represented by that construction cost are completed, the annual TIF value for the CCDC would be $32.2 million. For this analysis, it was assumed that there would be a slowdown in residential construction as a result of the credit crisis and the stabilization of residential property values. Only half of the projects were included in the tax revenue projection meaning that the credit crisis and decline in property values would be equal to the loss of half of the planned projects. If only $1.47 billion in development is completed, the annual increment in taxes to the CCDC would be $16.5 million. When this is added to the current TIF value of $12.84 million, it is reasonable to anticipate that by 2010 the annual increments in property tax revenue would be approximately $29.3 million. If the TOT increment of $6.9 million is added to this total, annual revenues climb to $36.2 ($12.84 + $16.5 + $6.9) million. This provides a complete view of the tax revenues generated by the Ballpark District.

Considering an overall assessment involves several important assumptions. The cost of the ballpark is recorded as are the amounts invested by the team and the public sector. Maintenance costs are more difficult to estimate. Agreements also are often modified across decades of operations. For example, the team decided to make some improvements in 2006 and paid the full cost of those enhancements to the ballpark. This raised their investment in the facility, but was neither included in the original MOU nor in Table 4.6. San Diego's commitment to maintain the facility could increase across the years if there are structural problems that are not anticipated. Unforeseen expenses can and do arise.

There are also assumptions underlying any revenue estimation especially given the volatile conditions that existed in late 2008 and into 2009. As a result, all of the development completed through 2007 is included in Table 4.6, but the development anticipated by 2010 was reduced by 50 percent. This is a very arbitrary decision reflecting declining real estate trends, but a conservative approach was deemed more realistic. In addition, very small increments in value after 2010 were applied and in each instance the increase was projected to occur once every five years to adjust for the possibility of longer lasting effects from the credit crisis.

A similar approach also was taken in calculating future TOT revenues with increments also occurring only once in every five years. With these conservative assumptions, the public sector's investment would become cash positive in 2028 and produce $1.4 billion in total returns by 2032. When a 5 percent discount rate is used, the present value of San Diego's net position is –$324 million (see Table 4.6). This means that using the conservative revenue estimates and a discount rate of 5 percent, through 2032 (the year in which the city will repay all its debt), San Diego's net position in 2009 dollars would yield a **loss of $324 million** (in constant dollars).

The outcome, of course, changes substantially if the conservative assumptions are somewhat relaxed. For example, in Table 4.7, it is assumed that the developments planned for 2008, 2009, and 2010 are built and that after that the TIF revenues grow at 5 percent each year. It could also be assumed that the TOT revenues grow at 5 percent per year beginning in 2009 and continue to grow at that rate every year. With these assumptions in place, revenues exceed costs in 2024 and the present value (2009) of San Diego's revenue position is **+$1.38 billion** using the same 5 percent discount rate (see Table 4.7).

VIII. The Ballpark District: Development, Land Use, and the Best Use of Urban Land

Those opposed to the Ballpark District and the building of the Padres' new home included those who feared San Diego would again be subsidizing sports owners and those who thought the East Village should continue as a location for artists, start-up businesses, and some residents. Before any conclusions are reached with regard to the fiscal merits of the project, the issue of the development strategy adopted by San Diego should be addressed.

San Diego lacked a large residential base in its downtown area and city officials were intent on anchoring a new residential flavor to the Ballpark District. Still others impressed with Jane Jacobs' philosophy suggest that the best course of action is to let regeneration occur through the reuse of properties by start-up businesses. To encourage regeneration these advocates prefer transitional areas with live/work space. By the 1990s, the East Village was an area with some artists' studios, shops,

Table 4.6 San Diego's Investment in the Ballpark District and Tax Gains: Conservative Assumptions (in $000s)

Year	City of San Diego Responsibilities				Total Cumulative Expense	Revenue Increments			Net Position
	Equity Payment	Bond Payments	Facility Maintenance	Agency Bond Payments		Hotel TOT	TIF Revenue	Cumulative Increment	
2002	40,715				40,715				-40,715
2003		15,000		7,500	63,215				-103,930
2004		15,000	3,500	7,500	89,215				-193,145
2005		15,000	3,500	7,500	115,215				-308,360
2006		15,000	3,500	7,500	141,215		12,840	12,840	-436,735
2007		11,000	3,500	6,000	161,715	6,900	12,840	32,580	-565,870
2008		11,000	3,500	6,000	182,215	6,900	12,840	52,320	-695,765
2009		11,000	3,850	6,000	203,065	6,900	12,840	72,060	-826,770
2010		11,000	3,850	6,000	223,915	6,900	29,340	108,300	-942,385
2011		11,000	3,850	6,000	244,765	6,900	29,340	144,540	-1,042,610
2012		11,000	3,850	6,000	265,615	7,245	29,340	181,125	-1,127,100
2013		11,000	3,850	6,000	286,465	7,245	29,340	217,710	-1,195,855
2014		11,000	4,235	6,000	307,700	7,245	29,340	254,295	-1,249,260
2015		11,000	4,235	6,000	328,935	7,245	32,274	293,814	-1,284,381

Year								
2016	11,000	4,235	6,000	350,170	7,245	32,274	333,333	-1,301,218
2017	11,000	4,235	6,000	371,405	7,607	32,274	373,214	-1,299,409
2018	11,000	4,235	6,000	392,640	7,607	32,274	413,095	-1,278,954
2019	11,000	4,659	6,000	414,299	7,607	32,274	452,976	-1,240,277
2020	11,000	4,659	6,000	435,958	7,607	35,501	496,084	-1,180,151
2021	11,000	4,659	6,000	457,617	7,607	35,501	539,192	-1,098,576
2022	11,000	4,659	6,000	479,276	7,987	35,501	582,680	-995,172
2023	11,000	4,659	6,000	500,935	7,987	35,501	626,168	-869,939
2024	11,000	5,124	6,000	523,059	7,987	35,501	669,656	-723,342
2025	11,000	5,124	6,000	545,183	7,987	39,052	716,695	-551,830
2026	11,000	5,124	6,000	567,307	7,987	39,052	763,734	-355,403
2027	11,000	5,124	6,000	589,431	8,386	39,052	811,172	-133,662
2028	11,000	5,124	6,000	611,555	8,386	39,052	858,610	113,393
2029	11,000	5,124	6,000	633,679	8,386	42,957	909,953	389,667
2030	11,000	5,637	6,000	656,316	8,386	42,957	961,296	694,647
2031	11,000	5,637	6,000	673,322	8,386	42,957	1,012,639	1,033,964
2032	11,000	5,637	6,000	695,959	8,386	42,957	1,063,982	1,401,988

Net present value with a 5 percent discount rate   **-$324,000**

Table 4.7 San Diego's Investment in the Ballpark District and Tax Gains: Less Conservative Assumptions (in $000s)

Year	City of San Diego Responsibilities					Revenue Increments			Net Position
	Equity Payment	Bond Payments	Facility Maintenance	Agency Bond Payments	Total Cumulative Expense	Hotel TOT	TIF Revenue	Cumulative Tax Increment	
2002	40,715				40,715				−40,715
2003		15,000		7,500	63,215				−103,930
2004		15,000	3,500	7,500	89,215				−193,145
2005		15,000	3,500	7,500	115,215				−308,360
2006		15,000	3,500	7,500	141,215		12,840	12,840	−436,735
2007		11,000	3,500	6,000	161,715	6,900	12,840	32,580	−565,870
2008		11,000	3,500	6,000	182,215	6,900	12,840	52,320	−695,765
2009		11,000	3,850	6,000	203,065	7,245	12,840	72,405	−826,425
2010		11,000	3,850	6,000	223,915	7,607	32,274	112,286	−938,054
2011		11,000	3,850	6,000	244,765	7,987	32,274	152,548	−1,030,271
2012		11,000	3,850	6,000	265,615	8,387	32,274	193,208	−1,102,678
2013		11,000	3,850	6,000	286,465	8,806	32,274	234,288	−1,154,854
2014		11,000	4,235	6,000	307,700	9,246	32,274	275,809	−1,186,746
2015		11,000	4,235	6,000	328,935	9,709	32,274	317,791	−1,197,889

Year								
2016	11,000	4,235	6,000	350,170	10,194	33,888	361,873	-1,186,186
2017	11,000	4,235	6,000	371,405	10,704	35,582	408,159	-1,149,432
2018	11,000	4,235	6,000	392,640	11,239	37,361	456,759	-1,085,313
2019	11,000	4,659	6,000	414,299	11,801	39,229	507,790	-991,822
2020	11,000	4,659	6,000	435,958	12,391	41,191	561,371	-866,409
2021	11,000	4,659	6,000	457,617	13,011	43,250	617,632	-706,394
2022	11,000	4,659	6,000	479,276	13,661	45,413	676,706	-508,964
2023	11,000	4,659	6,000	500,935	14,344	47,683	738,733	-271,166
2024	11,000	5,124	6,000	523,059	15,061	50,068	803,862	9,638
2025	11,000	5,124	6,000	545,183	15,814	52,571	872,248	336,702
2026	11,000	5,124	6,000	567,307	16,605	55,199	944,052	713,447
2027	11,000	5,124	6,000	589,431	17,435	57,959	1,019,447	1,143,464
2028	11,000	5,124	6,000	611,555	18,307	60,857	1,098,612	1,630,520
2029	11,000	5,124	6,000	633,679	19,223	63,900	1,181,735	2,178,576
2030	11,000	5,637	6,000	656,316	20,184	67,095	1,269,013	2,791,273
2031	11,000	5,637	6,000	673,322	21,193	70,450	1,360,656	3,478,608
2032	11,000	5,637	6,000	695,959	22,252	73,973	1,456,881	4,239,531

Net present value with a 5 percent discount rate $1,380,270

and coffee houses. There were also some fledgling business start-ups in the area. Some of the aging warehouses had been converted into live/work lofts giving the area a small residential profile. The ballpark and the Ballpark District dramatically altered the development process. The East Village was an area where these perspectives on regeneration collided. San Diego's political leadership wanted a large-scale development—a sort of new downtown area—replete with new hotels for its convention center and an accelerated timetable for commercial and residential development. Others led by Wayne Buss, an architect, focused on environmentally appropriate development, fought to sustain an alternate vision for the area as a Bohemian neighborhood, a sort of Greenwich Village for San Diego.[8] The city's leadership from both the public and private sectors had another vision. The city wanted a downtown neighborhood anchored by hotels and the ballpark to provide a large number of market-rate homes with an appropriate concentration of houses for families with modest incomes. The city's plan did substantially increase the number of residents in the area and leadership did not believe there was a shortage of space for business start-ups or for artists. Their concern was with ensuring that the downtown area would become a neighborhood with thousands of residents, new hotels, and new commercial space that might also provide employment opportunities. In their view, development had languished and the battle between a Bohemian culture and a modern mixed-use downtown neighborhood ended with billions of dollars in new private development, a ballpark, and several new hotels.

Figure 4.4 and Figure 4.5 show the development that has taken place beyond the left field and right field walls; in the center lies the community park (a minibaseball field), one where families and children play baseball all year. Figure 4.6 looks through the Ballpark District neighborhood to the convention center. Figure 4.7 shows the minipark and surrounding development, and Figure 4.8 identifies one of the new hotels now managed by the Marriott Corporation that helped the convention center to advance its competitive position.

While any assessment of the Ballpark District has to look at the public's investment and taxes generated, it is also important to consider, in a qualitative sense, what was built. "Tens of thousands of condos, townhomes, and apartments have been built as part of hundreds of housing projects. Retail and entertainment projects have injected vitality into downtown. This effort has transformed downtown from its gritty past into the hottest neighborhood around," wrote the *San Diego Union Tribune*.[9] It is now a realistic goal that as many as 50,000 people may live in the downtown area before 2020 and a new large-scale supermarket has even opened. It is also important to note that the Ballpark District has helped to preserve some older facilities. For example, the TR Produce building, built in 1934, has been refitted with two stories of office space and new condominiums:

> Completed in 1934, the TR Produce building is one of about a dozen surviving structures from around 1870 to the early 1930s in the East Village. The old produce building and the new commercial

Figure 4.4 Development beyond Petco Park's left field wall. (Photo courtesy of Mark S. Rosentraub.)

condominium complex within its walls are a novel combination of historic preservation and new construction. Under an agreement struck with a local preservationist group, the old and new buildings barely touch each other. The new structure was built within the walls of the produce building. Standing on a stilt-like structure of steel columns, the new metal-and-glass commercial condominium complex rises above the old brick walls to peer into the ballpark.[10]

There were approximately 12 older industrial buildings that remained in the area. Bruce Coons, executive director of the nonprofit Save Our Heritage Organization, "led the negotiations that set standards for the reuse of 11 historic buildings in the ballpark area with both the developer and city officials."[11] This led to the incorporation of the Western Metal Supply Company building as part of the left field wall in the ballpark. Chris Wahl, vice president and partner of San Diego–based Southwest Strategies LLC, and spokesman for the Downtown Residential Marketing Affiance, probably summarized things most accurately when he noted, "What the ballpark has done is opened up an entirely different part of downtown that didn't previously exist from a residential standpoint. East Village has completely

Figure 4.5 Development beyond Petco Park's right field wall. (Photo courtesy of Mark S. Rosentraub.)

taken off."[12] In 2006, *The New York Times* reviewed the project and noted that the goal of an extraordinary level of development had indeed taken place.[13] At the same time these accomplishments are noted, it is important to note the destruction of the Bohemian character of the East Village and the implementation of a development strategy that dramatically changed its character and image.

IX. The Ballpark District and San Diego: Mutual Risk in a New Model for Public/Private Partnerships

While many cities had made very extensive commitments to build sports facilities, there were never assurances or commitments from a team's owner to ensure private sector investment. Indianapolis' sports strategy was tied to a large-scale revitalization effort, but there the city essentially was responsible for facilitating additional private sector investments. Neither the Colts' nor the Pacers' ownership made any assurances for any real estate investments. The Pacers' owners, who are developers, did participate in the building and management of Circle Centre Mall, but that

Figure 4.6 The Ballpark District neighborhood and the Convention Center. (Photo courtesy of Mark S. Rosentraub.)

effort was not specifically associated with the city's investment in Market Square Arena or the Conseco Fieldhouse. In scores of other cities, even with large public sector investments in facilities, team owners were unwilling to make any commitments or assurances that real estate development would take place.

San Diego, the Padres, and JMI Realty created a new framework for a public/private partnership. Each took risks, but the potential for mutual success also existed. San Diego could realize substantial property tax revenue growth. The credit crisis of 2008/2009 could also lead to the city losing money on its investment. JMI Realty also assumed substantial risk and it too could lose money. While the bargaining position between cities and teams is uneven, the establishment of development goals and linking them to the provision of public subsidies as was done in San Diego can ensure that the public sector's development goals are a priority and, in this instance, achieved. For the first time, a city's participation in the financing and maintaining of a sports facility was directly linked to assurances provided by a team's owner that new real estate development would take place where the public sector deemed it necessary and appropriate. This accomplishment cannot be minimized.

Figure 4.7 The park, a minibaseball field and residential and commercial development. (Photo courtesy of Mark S. Rosentraub.)

It is also important to note that JMI Real Estate continues to assume a lead role in developing the Ballpark District, as does the CCDC. In that regard, while San Diego must continue to play a development broker role similar to the work Indianapolis must do to ensure its sports investments pay off, San Diego has a specific private sector partner that continues to lead efforts to expand and enhance the District. That work could help ensure that San Diego does indeed realize the revenues needed to repay its debt and secure a positive return on the total investment. The tax revenues earned for the development in the Ballpark District may have been new growth for San Diego, but it must be conceded that had the ballpark not been built in the East Village area, some of the development might have taken place elsewhere in the city. It is also possible that the development could have occurred beyond the city's borders. San Diego's goal was to concentrate development in the East Village area. Undeniably that goal was achieved even though it meant changing the character of the neighborhood.

The analysis of gains and losses for San Diego from the Ballpark District did not focus on other expenses, such as public safety and traffic control. Those costs would not have been any different regardless of the ballpark's location, so it does not seem to be especially relevant to include those costs. Similarly, regardless of where in the

Figure 4.8   A new hotel and the view from Petco Field to the Gaslamp District. (Photo courtesy of Mark S. Rosentraub.)

region the Padres played their home games, the team would still generate intangible benefits. Those gains might offset the costs of traffic control and public safety.

Finally, it must be recognized that the development of the Ballpark District was a decisive policy choice by San Diego to forego strategies related to Jane Jacobs' ideas and to transform the neighborhood in a relatively short period of time to a largely upscale downtown area. San Diego's leadership chose to infuse public and private money to substantially alter redevelopment patterns. The leadership wanted a new residential and commercial area to create a very different image for the downtown area. Leadership also wanted new hotels for the convention center. San Diego's leadership not only created a new model for other cities to follow when dealing with professional sports teams, but it is also secured its development goals. While it is clear some community organizations would have preferred a different strategy, with more than $1 billion in private sector investment, and more than another $1 billion poised to occur, the Ballpark District would be a welcome addition to the revitalization effort of most cities. Indeed, few mayors or city council members anywhere would not agree with an assessment that San Diego has indeed become a Major League Winner.

Endnotes

1. Joan Kroc's decision to sell the team was associated with ongoing stresses with MLB and her fellow owners as described in a 1997 interview with the author. She also described her firm desire that the team had to remain in San Diego and stressed that to the new ownership group.
2. Rosentraub, M. S. 1998. *The San Diego Padres and the proposed ballpark and redevelopment plan: An assessment of business, economic, and spatial issues.* San Diego: San Diego Padres Baseball Club.
3. Some teams have paid all of the capital costs for a new facility in exchange for public support for needed infrastructure. The Washington Redskins (1997), Miami Dolphins (1987), and Carolina Panthers (1996) privately financed their new stadiums, but the economics of football create possibilities that did not exist for the Padres. In 2000, the Giants built a privately financed ballpark in downtown San Francisco, but that market offered options that were not viable in San Diego. The Padres had to come up with a different approach.
4. Rother, C. 2002. Chargers offered to explore dropping ticket guarantee. *San Diego Union Tribune,* www.sandiego.gov/chargerissues/documents/explore.shtml (accessed March 30, 2008).
5. See, Chapin, T. 2002. Beyond the entrepreneurial city: Municipal capitalism in San Diego. *Journal of Urban Affairs* 24 (5): 565–581; and San Diego. 1998. Memorandum of understanding between the city of San Diego, the Redevelopment Agency of the city of San Diego, the Centre City Development Corporation, and the Padres, L. P. concerning a ballpark district, construction of a baseball park, and a redevelopment project. City of San Diego: Resolution R-291450, Attachment A.
6. San Diego, 1999. Manager's report. City of San Diego, Report No. 99-64.
7. Rosentraub, *The San Diego Padres and the proposed ballpark and redevelopment plan.*
8. Williams, J. 2004. Warehouse rejuvenation transformed East Village. *San Diego Union-Tribune,* December 12, http://www.signonsandiego.com/uniontrib/20041212/news_mz1j12buss.html (accessed March 28, 2008).
9. *San Diego Union-Tribune.* 2004. Change the mix: A vibrant downtown now needs more offices. March 31, B8.
10. Newman, M. 2006. The neighborhood that the ballpark built. *The New York Times,* April 26, 10.
11. Ibid.
12. Broderick, P. 2006. It takes a baseball park to raise a village. *San Diego Business Journal,* October 9, 27 (43): 40.
13. Newman, The neighborhood that the ballpark built.w

Chapter 5

A White Elephant, an Arena, and Revitalization: Using Location and the Glitz of *L.A. LIVE* to Rebuild a Downtown Area

I. Introduction

Los Angeles in the early 1990s was rocked by riots after police officers were acquitted in the videotaped beating of Rodney King and recurring gang violence. Amid a fear of cascading crime and increasing numbers of homeless people, the actions of Los Angeles police officers made it seem that life in Los Angeles was defined by conflicts and violence. The popular 1991 movie *Grand Canyon* seemed to capture the essence of Los Angeles' image. After rescuing a white motorist being taunted by gun-wielding gang members, a lead character laments that things were not supposed to be this way. Another character wrestled with the moral issues raised by the homeless. The bleak future predicted for Los Angeles in an earlier movie, *Blade Runner*, seemed to be an emerging reality.

In 1993, Richard Riordan was elected as the city's first Republican mayor in three decades, promising voters that as a successful businessman he was "tough enough" to handle Los Angeles' violence and its other problems. Spending several million dollars from his personal fortune, Mr. Riordan defeated a city council member, Michael Woo, in a city where a majority of the voters were nonwhite. Historians will debate and describe Riordan's legacy that included the hiring of 3,000 additional police officers and other changes he made to fight crime, reduce violence, and change the city's image. Few would have imagined that when he asked a staff member to think about ways to improve the fate of downtown Los Angeles' $500 million convention center that a new era in public/private partnerships for sports facilities and revitalizing downtown areas would emerge.

The Los Angeles Convention Center opened in 1971 in the southern part of the downtown area with more than 200,000 square feet of exhibition space. When the facility failed to attract conventions, public leaders ignored the deteriorating neighborhood surrounding the center and decided instead to support a dramatic expansion of its exhibition space. It was hoped that if the center had 500,000 square feet available for meetings and exhibitions it could succeed while a smaller complex would fail. While it is possible that a smaller facility discouraged some meeting planners from selecting Los Angeles, crime levels, the lack of adjacent hotels, the deterioration of the downtown area, and the lack of other amenities close to the center were likely contributing factors convincing convention planners to choose other Southern California destinations.

Regardless of the reasons, the convention center had become an expensive "white elephant" with public money being drained to cover the capital and operating costs of the mammoth structure. Mayor Riordan wanted to reduce the hemorrhaging of tax money and to improve the area around the facility. Perhaps a "new look for downtown" would mean more conventions. From those hopes emerged a new arena (the STAPLES Center), the Nokia Theatre and L.A. LIVE, and a new residential and commercial building boom in downtown Los Angeles. Advertising and real estate development opportunities at the juncture of two of America's busiest freeways led the revitalization effort. Now, a decade after the STAPLES Center opened and with the Nokia Theatre and parts of L.A. LIVE completed, the lessons learned from this effort and its impact can be assessed. Los Angeles, using its power of eminent domain and its willingness to transfer land to a private developer was able to achieve a set of goals charted by a mayor who wanted change and revitalization "fast tracked." Los Angeles is a Major League Winner and the lessons learned can help other cities change subsidies for sports, entertainment, and cultural centers into investments for revitalization.

II. Thinking Outside the Box: Bringing the Lakers and Kings Downtown

When the new convention center expansion was dedicated, Dr. Charles Isgar, a member of Mayor Riordan's staff, attended the event. Looking at the deteriorating area surrounding the expanded center he wondered why anyone would hold their annual meeting in the midst of an area with so little to offer visitors. San Diego's convention center was set against the Pacific Ocean with easy access to a growing downtown area with restaurants. Orange County's convention center was near Disneyland and a host of other attractions in suburban Anaheim. Los Angeles had a convention center amid a deteriorating downtown area and in a city thought to be crime-ridden, riddled by gang violence, and prone to race riots as a result of rampant discrimination by the police. A 500,000-square-foot facility could not succeed in that environment.

Isgar began to wonder what a new arena might mean for changing the area and creating an entirely new image for downtown Los Angeles. Why a new arena? The Lakers (NBA) and Kings (NHL) played their home games in suburban Inglewood at a 30-year-old economically obsolete facility located in a suburban city. Teams across the NBA and NHL were building or would soon build facilities with luxury suites, club seats, and numerous other revenue streams. The Lakers and Kings needed a new facility and Isgar recruited a respected developer, Steve Soboroff, to help convince the teams that downtown Los Angeles was the exact place for a state-of-the-art sports palace.[1]

If convincing the teams to relocate to downtown Los Angeles was not a sufficient challenge, there was one other political element that had to be addressed. The new facility would have to be built without any public subsidies. A majority of the members of the Los Angeles City Council were Democrats and would be eager to attack any plan from a Republican mayor that subsidized another big-ticket investment. A subsidy request by a mayor who himself was a wealthy real estate developer would be portrayed as one "good ol' boy" Republican helping his buddies or Los Angeles' regime get expanded access to public money. On the other hand, if the arena could be built without a subsidy, Mayor Riordan would be champion of a market-based approach that helped revitalize downtown Los Angeles. Such an outcome could be a springboard for his reelection campaign. The challenge was to identify the peculiar and profitable assets that downtown could offer to the teams' owners that would make them willing to pay for 100 percent of the costs of a new arena.

A. The Lakers, the Kings, and the "Fabulous Forum"

The Lakers' began play in Minneapolis in 1947 as part of the National Basketball League (NBL). The team, led by one of the first "big man" superstars, George Mikan, moved from the NBL to the Basketball Association of America in 1948 joining franchises from New York, Boston, Chicago and Philadelphia. The NBL and the Basketball Association of American merged, creating the NBA for the 1949–1950 season. The Minneapolis Lakers continued to be one of the league's dominant teams attracting large crowds wherever they played. By 1960, the NBA had become a stable entity, but the Lakers' owner sought a more profitable location. Aware of the success of Walter O'Malley, who had moved the Dodgers to Los Angeles for the 1958 baseball season, the Lakers moved to Los Angeles in 1960. The team decided to retain its nickname—"Lakers" referred to the large vessels that traveled the Great Lakes, but could also be associated with the thousand lakes of Minnesota—despite the absence of lakes or Great Lakes ships in the Los Angeles region.

The team initially played their home games in the Los Angeles Memorial Sports Arena. Opened in 1959, the arena is adjacent to the Los Angeles Memorial Coliseum and both facilities are in Exposition Park, which is located directly across a large boulevard from the University of Southern California (USC). USC has played its home football games at the Coliseum for decades (and in 2008 signed a 25-year lease extension) and also used the Los Angeles Memorial Arena for basketball games before opening a new facility, the Galen Center, closer to campus in 2006.

In 1965, the political and social geography of the Exposition Park area and downtown Los Angeles was severely impacted by the riots in the nearby Watts neighborhood. While the Watts area is more than five miles from the sports facilities in Exposition Park, the devastation from the riots and the impression of lawlessness had a substantial impact on perceptions and the image of the city. The Lakers, like so many other teams during that time period, thought a more suburban location would be more profitable since it would be perceived as being removed from unsafe inner city areas. In addition, teams wanted facilities surrounded by acres of parking. A location in suburban Inglewood put the Lakers closer to their fan base that was concentrated on the wealthier west side of the metropolitan area while still providing convenient freeway access. Inglewood was a developer-friendly city willing to provide what was necessary to help build a new arena. The city was seen by many as being far easier to deal with than either Los Angeles or the commissioners who oversaw the facilities in Exposition Park.[2]

The Lakers were sold in 1965 to Jack Kent Cooke, a Canadian-born entrepreneur, who also wanted to bring an NHL team to Los Angeles. Building a new suburban arena would make more sense and have a greater likelihood of being profitable if there were two tenants. In 1967, Cooke paid the NHL's $2 million fee to acquire the franchise rights for the region and the Los Angeles Kings were created. Cooke now had two teams for the new arena (called *The Forum*) meaning there would be at least 78 events (more if they qualified for the playoffs) held in his arena. If he were successful in attracting entertainers, the circus, and other events, the arena would be very profitable.

B. The "Fabulous Forum" and Its Limitations

The Forum was designed to be a showplace. Drawing inspiration from Rome's ancient forum, the round shape also permitted it to be surrounded by open parking lots creating the familiar look of a saucer-like building sitting amid an asphalt ocean of space for cars. Convenient freeway access put the facility within easy reach of the overwhelming majority of the fans and the wealthiest parts of the region. While the Forum had no suites or club seats, its courtside seating became known as "Jack's seats" in honor of Jack Nicholson. These 2,400 folding chairs surrounding the court quickly became the most expensive seats for professional sports anywhere in the world. But the absence of suites and club seats created an opportunity for Isgar and Soboroff to see if a new arena with expanded revenue streams in downtown Los Angeles might be of interest to the current owners of the Lakers and Kings.

Luxury seating at sport facilities was a product that in the 1990s did not exist in the Los Angeles market. The Coliseum where USC and UCLA, as well as the Rams and Raiders, played their home games had no club seats or suites.[3] The Rose Bowl also had no luxury seating. The Forum and Los Angeles Memorial Sports Arena were built long before the advent of suite and club seats. A new arena, regardless of its location, would have the potential to offer businesses and sports fans a new product.

C. Arena Economics and the Appeal of Downtown Los Angeles

The people who would make the new arena a reality were the owners of the Kings and Lakers. The ownership odyssey that brought the right combination of entertainment and real estate entrepreneurs into place began in 1979 when Jack Kent Cooke sold the Lakers and Kings to Jerry Buss for $67.4 million ($208.3 million in 2008 dollars). At that time the transaction was the largest sports deal ever. Buss' main interest, however, was basketball and in 1987 he sold the Kings to Bruce McNall. After selling part of the team, McNall would eventually sell controlling interest in the Kings to Philip Anshutz and Edward Roski. Then, in 1998, Buss would sell part of the Lakers to Anschutz for $268 million. Unlike Buss, who was focused on basketball, Anshutz was the head of an entertainment mega-corporation (Anshutz Entertainment Group or AEG) and Roski was chairman of the board and chief executive officer of Majestic Realty Co., one of the largest privately held real estate companies in the United States. Their expertise and interests would attract them to the possibility of an arena as part of a larger entertainment district and real estate development project in which the teams would be the centerpieces or anchor attractions. Their main concern involved assembly of the land required for an arena and a large mixed-use entertainment complex.

As it turned out the owners were already focused on building a new arena replete with luxury seating and able to generate other revenue streams for the teams. There were three available options. The Forum could be extensively remodeled or a new arena could be built adjacent to the Forum on the existing parking lots. Remodeling presented a problem regarding the teams' location while work was underway. Building a new facility adjacent to the Forum would allow the teams to continue to play in the Forum, which would be razed when the new building opened, restoring

THE "DISNEYFICATION" OF SPORTS

A story that may or may not be an urban myth is that when Walt Disney looked at all of the development surrounding his Disneyland and the revenues others were realizing from locating near his park, he said, "If I do another park, I would own all of the hotels and other activities that people enjoy when they visit Disneyland." Disney World was the result of that observation and contained several different amusement parks, numerous hotels and restaurants, and a host of other entertainment options and retail outlets to serve visitors. Disney World established the concept of "tourism planning for the entire visitor's experience." Disneyfication refers to the inclusion of all consumption and related entertainment options being built within a lead entity or prime entertainment center. Transferred to sports, this meant expanding the footprint of an arena or ballpark to include space for retail operations or associated entertainment options for fans.

As a result, if a visitor is coming to an attraction like Disney World or a ball game, it means providing to these people the full range of activities for their day or visit within the facility or park. For Disney World, this meant not just hotels for overnight stays, but a mix of hotels to provide higher end luxury to those who want that product and more modest and moderately priced facilities for other families. It also meant the creation of other parks and other events and attractions to keep a family occupied for an entire week. Walt Disney World also offered a full range of restaurant choices, expanded retail outlets with expensive and moderately priced items, and even a cruise line with a day camp to provide parents with a vacation for them after several days of chasing children around Disney World.

For sports, Disneyfication means first and foremost a focus on the total experience and providing for fans the luxury they want when attending a game. This leads to a wide range of "price points" with more expensive seating providing the expected amenities. It also means providing improved sight lines for all fans to ensure that teams can meet the price points fans are willing to pay. Because fans usually enjoy food and beverages before and after events, it means building facilities with wide concourses that permit people to be served high-quality food and beverages in a relatively short amount of time. It means providing meeting spaces for people to network before and during the

the ample parking provided at the site. Parking for fans would be a problem while construction was taking place. The third option involved assembling sufficient land elsewhere for a new arena and a large-scale entertainment center with additional opportunities for both commercial and residential development. As negotiations began and the team owners mentioned other locations for the project (in an effort game. Every new arena also had expanded retail outlets for team merchandise. Lastly, it also meant designing facilities to maximize the opportunities for advertising and for naming options. If an arena attracts a million or more visits in a given year, these attendees offer to advertisers the chance to deliver a sustained message about their products to an exclusive group of consumers who would be spending several hours in a set location watching an event.

The goal of the Disneyfication process is to offer to fans a complete, first-class experience regardless of where they sit, in as perfect, clean, and comfortable a setting as possible. Dark and dank restrooms were artifacts of a bygone age, as were low-quality food and drink. In addition, the arenas and other sport facilities are designed to maximize the opportunity to use games and events as convenient and comfortable meeting places where sporting events and entertainment are enjoyed while engaging in extensive social networking. Facilities built in the 1960s were not designed with these assets or additional revenue sources.

Los Angeles' new arena was designed with 160 luxury suites that could be leased to clients for all Lakers and Kings games, and when the Clippers decided to play their home games at the new arena, the suites could also be leased for those games. The STAPLES Center also has 32 party suites that can be leased for any individual game and event. The facility also has 2,500 "premier" or club seats (which offer food and beverage service at the seats and various other amenities). STAPLES Center seats 18,997 for basketball, 18,118 for hockey, and 20,000 for concerts. The facility itself contains 900,000 square feet with broad concourses and meeting places for people to network and watch the events at the same time. By comparison, the "Fabulous Forum" had seating for 17,505 fans for basketball, 16,005 for hockey, and 18,000 for concerts. It had no luxury suites, but it did have 2,400 club seats, nor did it have the broad concourses to support expanded sales and create meeting places. Without a new arena, the team owners were leaving quite a bit of money on the table that fans were eager to spend.

But the teams' owners wanted to take Disneyfication to a new level. If they could build an entertainment and mixed-use project adjacent to the arena, they could offer visitors multiple pre- and postgame activities and activities for fans who did not have a ticket to the game. All that they needed was enough land close to the region's freeway system.

to convince Los Angeles to offer more incentives), it became clear that a new arena was seen as a necessity and that there were few if any sites where sufficient land existed to build both an arena and a large-scale entertainment center. It also became clear that Anshutz and Roski were both interested in a large-scale development complementing the arena, and that was not possible at the Inglewood site.

III. Downtown Los Angeles: Liabilities and Assets

A new arena had to be part of a much larger project and vision to respond to downtown Los Angeles' limitations as a development site. First, the riots in 1992 after the verdict in the Rodney King case lasted six days and 53 people died. There was more than $1 billion in property losses and the damage to the city's image was incalculable. The beating of a white truck driver (Reginald Denny) hauled from his truck by African Americans was broadcast and then replayed countless times. Denny was not rescued by the police, but by black residents of the area who also saw the beating on television. All of North America saw rioters out of control, people being murdered, the wanton destruction of property, and a police department unable or unwilling to protect people and respond to massive unrest. Indeed, minutes after Denny was rescued, television cameras photographed the beating of Fidel Lopez by another mob. With both whites and Hispanics being singled out and violently attacked, Los Angeles appeared to millions to be a city locked into endless racial violence and lawlessness.

Second, the entire Rodney King incident—from his arrest and beating to the acquittal of the police officers charged in the attack on King to the rioting where the police withdrew instead of rescuing those innocent people being attacked—created an image that violence in Los Angeles was out of control. While the events did not take place in the downtown area, it was impossible to separate images of civil unrest and wanton attacks from another part of the city. The announcement that the police were withdrawn while a white truck driver and Hispanic worker were singled out for attack further underscored that Los Angeles was a dangerous place for residents, visitors, and workers. Something spectacular was needed to create a new image. Third, the downtown area itself had other limitations. In 1993, office occupancy rates had declined by 30 percent[4] and hotel occupancy rates were also falling.[5] Only a truly extraordinary project could help to reverse these trends and images.

Ironically, while the downtown area had an image of being unsafe, crime rates declined in 1993 and 1994. Property and violent crimes had been reduced by more than one-third since 1992 and the number of reported thefts declined 44 percent. Regardless, business owners reported that the perception of a lack of safety and gang violence was the reality they had to address regardless of the actual crime numbers released by the Los Angeles Police Departments.[6]

Despite these problems or issues, downtown Los Angeles also offered some uniquely valuable assets. Some of these were linked to the limitations of the Inglewood location. First, building a new facility in the parking lots adjacent to the Forum would have created severe parking problems for two years. There were no other convenient locations available to replace the lost parking spots. In contrast, building a facility in downtown Los Angeles would mean operations could continue at The Forum. Second, while it might have been possible to build a new

Figure 5.1 The Forum (arrow), Hollywood Park Raceway, and the possible location for a new arena. (Taken from Google Maps.)

arena in Inglewood across from the existing facility, that location would not offer any other development opportunities. An entertainment complex would not have been possible. The land surrounding the site to the west and east was residential and it was unrealistic to think it could have been acquired or taken in an eminent domain action. To the north was a cemetery and unless the racetrack would be razed, there were really no possibilities for any additional development (Figure 5.1). On the other hand, downtown Los Angeles had sufficient land for an arena and a large entertainment complex.

Third, Los Angeles was committed to assisting in the assembly of needed acreage. Land with convenient access to the region's freeway system is in short supply.

Los Angeles County has more residents than any other county in the United States and the large number of single-family homes produces a population density rate below that of San Francisco, Denver, and even neighboring Orange County. There are few, if any, large tracts of unencumbered land with convenient freeway access. The downtown Los Angeles site was adjacent to north–south and east–west freeways and the city was willing to use its eminent domain powers to ensure that the land needed for an arena and an entertainment complex would be assembled and sold to the teams' owners.

The development opportunities available at the downtown Los Angeles site are vividly illustrated in Figure 5.2. Depicted is the convention center; the original building is the structure bounded by Pico Boulevard and Figueroa Street. The expansion that created the full-scale $500 million white elephant includes the

Figure 5.2 Land and location: The convention center, STAPLES Center, adjacent properties, and freeway access (Taken from Google Maps.)

addition that is east of the STAPLES Center. The development opportunity was the surface parking lots on the other side of Chick Hearn Court and facing the STAPLES Center. Today that area is the location of the Nokia Theatre, the soon-to-be-opened convention center hotel, a movie complex, and a set of restaurant and retail outlets and commercial space all packaged as *L.A. LIVE*. The land Los Angeles was willing to assemble through eminent domain and then provide for development was the parcels on which the STAPLES Center currently sits, the adjacent lots, and what is the parking lot in Figure 5.2. Notice also that the land offers excellent freeway access. The Pasadena–Harbor Freeway (I-110) provides north–south access to the region. At the bottom left of Figure 5.3 is the intersection of the I-110 with the Santa Monica Freeway (I-10) providing the site with excellent east–west access.

Figure 5.3 Location, location, location: The intersection of the Harbor/Pasadena and Santa Monica Freeways and STAPLES Center. (Taken from Google Maps.)

IV. Sealing and Selling the Deal

Los Angeles had three goals in the negotiations with the teams:

1. It wanted extraordinary facilities built as close as possible to the convention center to change the identity and image of the downtown area.
2. The city also wanted all of the deteriorating buildings near the convention center replaced.
3. The new arena had to be built without any public subsidies.

The assets of land, location near the freeway system, and a willingness to assemble the parcels were obviously important bargaining chips to offer in exchange for the owners' commitment to meet the city's goals. Given the risks associated with building a downtown arena in the 1990s, these assets might not have been enough to get a new arena built without any tax dollars. Los Angeles had one additional jewel, however, and that one made building a facility without a subsidy possible. Los Angeles had a "deal maker."

The proposed site for the arena is adjacent to one of the busiest freeway interchanges in the world. The Santa Monica and Harbor Freeways have an average daily vehicle count of 325,000 (California Department of Transportation). This made the location extremely valuable in terms of the placement of advertising messages if Los Angeles was willing to allow the team owners to strategically build advertising towers. Those pylons towering over the freeways would create a unique and extremely valuable revenue stream complement to a naming rights deal for the arena. These incentives or assets that would give the team owners revenue streams no other city or location could offer. If the team owners were permitted to erect their advertising towers and if Los Angeles assisted in assembling the land, each of the city's goals could be achieved (see Figure 5.3).

The teams' owners created the L.A. Arena Company and agreed to build the arena and a large-scale entertainment complex directly across the street. The arena would be placed on land adjacent to the convention center and the new headquarter hotel would be part of the entertainment complex. The L.A. Arena Company also had to sign 25-year lease commitments guaranteeing that the Kings and Lakers would play at least 90 percent of their home games at the new arena. If for any reason the L.A. Arena Company went into bankruptcy and the Kings and Lakers were free to terminate their leases, Los Angeles would own the arena and the land on which it stood. It was also agreed that Los Angeles would not have any responsibility for debts created by the L.A. Arena Company if it did default. The team owners would be financially responsible for ensuring that the city was not liable for any financial obligations of the L.A. Arena Company.

The keys to the deal for the teams' owners were Los Angeles' guarantee to assemble the land and the granting of the right to build the advertising towers. To protect the public's interest in outdoor advertising, the city's attorneys inserted several clauses. Los Angeles insisted that the arena not be named after any alcohol, beer, tobacco, or firearms, company.

> and no exterior signage will be placed on any convention center property, which will contain alcohol (including beer), tobacco, or firearms advertisements. The Venture [L. A. Arena Company, LLC] would be allowed to place beer advertisements on a pylon on Venture property, but would not be allowed to place tobacco, firearms, or other alcohol advertisements on the pylon. The Venture proposes a marquee and/or temporary display at the entrance to the Arena, which would announce events being held at the Arena. If the name of the event sponsor is an alcohol, tobacco, or firearms company, the name may appear on the marquee or temporary display.[7]

The L.A. Arena Company wanted two locations for its advertising pylons that would be built on convention center land adjacent to the I-10 and I-110 freeways. The locations selected had to be mutually acceptable to Los Angeles and the Venture, but the pylons at both sites had to be "viewed from the 10 Freeway and the 110 Freeway."[8] The Venture was given seven years to develop a convention center hotel and a complex of restaurant and entertainment facilities. The Venture, before initiating construction of the entertainment complex and convention center hotel, had to submit a master plan for the proposed project. Los Angeles also had the authority to approve or request modifications to the plan and its approval was required before construction on the project could begin.[9] One of the two advertising towers at the heart of the public/private partnership for the arena and the entertainment complex is shown in Figure 5.4.

V. Los Angeles' Investment and Returns

To assemble the land and build the needed infrastructure for the arena, the public sector had to invest $71.1 million. The cost of the arena has been estimated at between $375 and $400 million. With this much spent for the facility (in 1999 dollars), Los Angeles did receive a Taj Mahal of arenas. This was an important objective for Mayor Riordan's administration that was actively engaged with several partners in numerous projects to rebuild the entire downtown area. Los Angeles' goal was for the construction of a first-class arena. When the final cost was realized and announced, Los Angeles knew it had an extraordinary asset for its downtown redevelopment effort.

The breakdown of the investments made by each partner is detailed in Figure 5.5a and Figure 5.5b. The private sector paid for 81 percent of the total cost if the final construction cost was $375 million and 82 percent if the final cost was $400 million. Los Angeles borrowed $38.5 million equal to 10 percent of the project's cost. The Los Angeles Convention Center committed $20 million (5 percent of the project's costs) drawn from the interest it earns on its reserve fund to pay its bonds.

Figure 5.4 The advertising pylon that made an arena and entertainment complex possible (with the convention center hotel's construction). (Photo courtesy of Mark S. Rosentraub.)

PROTECTING THE PUBLIC'S INTEREST

The public sector's share of the costs for the STAPLES Center under either scenario would be considered somewhat larger than was typical or expected at the time for a market as large as Los Angeles. However, the city's loan and the Convention Center Debt Service Fund replacement was to be supported by revenues generated by the arena (AEG guaranteed that, if those revenues did not materialize, the company would be responsible for providing the needed revenues to Los Angeles). Thus, if it is assumed just for the sake of argument at the moment that the $12.6 million from the Community Redevelopment Agency was never repaid, the public investment declines to a maximum of 4 percent. That would have made the STAPLES Center deal the most favorable among any negotiated at the time by any city.[10]

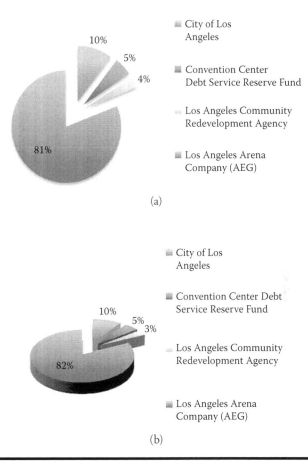

(a)

(b)

Figure 5.5   The investments made to build the STAPLES Center. by each partner by percentage. (a) If the facility cost $375 million; (b) if the facility cost $400 million.

The Los Angeles Community Redevelopment Agency invested $12.6 million or paid for between 3 and 4 percent of the project's costs. The L.A. Arena Company is a subsidiary of AEG (see Figure 5.5a and Figure 5.5b). AEG (one of the leading sports and entertainment presenters in the world) owns STAPLES Center and met its commitment to build one of the finest and most lavish arenas, thereby aiding in the redevelopment of downtown Los Angeles.

To ensure repayment of its investment of $71.1 million, the public sector received a portion of the parking fees collected and the proceeds from a ticket tax. Given projected attendance levels, the anticipated fund should have been more than sufficient to meet these obligations. When the contract was presented to the city council, there was concern that taxpayers might still not be completely protected from any potential losses. While partisan politics might have played a role in the emerging opposition, the matter was quickly resolved when AEG agreed to be responsible for any financial shortfalls in Los Angeles' ability to retire the debt on the bonds or replace the lost interest from the convention center's bond repayment fund. As the $12.6 million investment by the Community Redevelopment Authority occurred later, the public sector received no guarantees on its repayment. Those funds would have to be generated by new taxes or other revenue.

A. Were the Taxpayers Protected?

Los Angeles sold bonds to finance its investment and the annual payment was $3,872,694. The public sector had other costs. There was the lost interest by using money from the Convention Center's repayment fund ($900,000). The arena company was also responsible for paying $451,830 for use of city-owned property (Los Angles 1998: Annex B, Annex C).[11] This means that each year Los Angeles needed to receive $5,232,099 in extra revenue to offset its investment. The revenues received from each source are identified in Table 5.1 and the Annual Balance refers to the cash remaining after the $5,232,099 is repaid. The credits refer to Los Angeles' Jobs Incentive Credit program. Firms that create jobs in Los Angeles receive tax credits and the arena company was entitled to this benefit as well. The value or credit given for each job created was specified in the Gap Funding Agreement.[12] At the end of fiscal year 2008, it is estimated that the entire debt will have been completely repaid. After the loans are repaid, the account will still have a surplus of $6.2 million (see Table 5.1). That surplus will continue to grow as Los Angeles continues to receive income from the dedicated revenues. The ticket tax remains in effect and the city continues to receive a share of all parking revenues.

In 2003, Los Angeles and AEG agreed that, for a single, one-time payment of $14,700,000 and a payment of $1,800,000 to cover related city administrative costs, the developers and teams would be released from any obligations to offset future revenue shortfalls. Given that a shortfall was encountered just once and that the revenue streams were performing to expectations, tapping the prepayment fund for approximately $1 million per year for the remaining years of the bond yielded a very favorable outcome for Los Angeles.

The column labeled Credits also involves expenses that AEG paid with the city's permission that were related to the arena and the development of the area. In 1998, the city and AEG agreed that a set of expenses for development that were Los Angeles' responsibility—if paid for by AEG—could be submitted for approval as a credit toward the company's responsibilities to provide revenues to pay for the bonds and any other expenses associated with the city's investment in the arena.

Only in 2005 was there an actual shortfall, but with the accrued surpluses from previous years, Los Angeles had more than enough revenue in its Arena account to make its required bond payment. While there was no subsidy from the city to have the arena built—and Los Angeles continues to receive revenues from the dedicated streams and through the rental payments made by the Arena Corporation—there is still the matter of the $12.6 million from the Community Reinvestment Agency. That

Table 5.1 Payments to Los Angeles to Sustain Its Investment in the STAPLES Center

	Admission Tax	Prepayment	Parking	Interest	Credits	Total	Annual Balance
2001	$3,248,429		$96,433	$585,931	$3,989,577	$7,920,370	$2,695,846
2002	4,474,167		172,658	4,674	1,330,872	5,982,371	757,847
2003	4,013,673	405,088	168,955	744,667	780,272	6,112,655	888,131
2004	4,005,049	828,277	348,859	110,250	479,418	5,771,853	547,329
2005	3,197,584	1,075,751	186,027	70,938	0	4,530,300	-694,224
2006	5,250,282	1,031,652	482,968	20,044	0	6,784,946	1,560,422
2007	3,984,224	987,909	1,289,167	124,430	0	6,385,730	1,161,206
2008	4,000,000	949,000	800,000	100,000	0	5,849,000	624,476
Estimated cumulative balance on 6/30/2008							**$6,184,034**

Source: City of Los Angeles year end financial reports and 2008 budget.

expenditure represents less than 2 percent of the money spent by AEG for STAPLES Center, the Nokia Theatre, and L.A. LIVE. Before moving on to the question of the level of development in downtown Los Angeles, it is important to determine if the growth in property taxes or other revenue streams repays that commitment too.

In a report prepared in 2003 for Los Angeles' controller, Professor Robert A. Baade found that new developments near the arena generated $3,399,034 annually in new property taxes. If it is assumed that the new buildings were only built because of the presence of the arena, these tax dollars represent new revenue. Since the area was languishing for years prior to the building of the arena, it is reasonable to expect that these taxes represent new income.[13]

Using a 7 percent discount rate, on the full increment of $3,399,034 and assuming no additional development, the investment of $12.6 million was completely repaid by mid-2006. If it is assumed that just half of the development was a result of the presence of the new arena ($1,667,952)—or that other development would have taken place generating 50 percent of the property taxes even if the arena was not built in the downtown area or elsewhere in Los Angeles—the loan from the Community Reinvestment Agency will be repaid by mid-2012. Under either assumption, it can be concluded that the revenues to repay the Community Reinvestment Agency's investment were realized in an accelerated period of time (Table 5.2). As a result, the entire public sector investment in the arena was repaid and the public sector continues to receive new income each year.

There are other taxes that are paid by AEG and the teams that were not included in this tabulation that yield returns for Los Angeles. For example, AEG pays $4 million each year in possessory interest charges based on its use of public land that is exempt from property taxes.[14] There is also a gross receipts tax paid by AEG for the arena's operations (about $300,000 each year) and the Lakers and Kings also pay taxes. These were not included in Table 5.1 or Table 5.2 as an argument could be made that all of these taxes would have been paid as long as the new arena was built somewhere in Los Angeles County.

B. Rebuilding Downtown: Housing

The arena's development coincided with the building of a substantial number of new residences in downtown Los Angeles. From the date of the announcement of the agreement to build the arena, through the fourth quarter of 2007 a total of 10,748 residential units were built in downtown Los Angeles. This effectively doubled the number of units in the area and the number of market rate units available in the area increased by almost 300 percent (Table 5.3). While 2008 brought with it a slower housing market across the United States, 8,224 units were under construction with 7,395 classified as "market rate." While it is prudent to expect a slowdown in the absorption of these units in the current market, when occupied there will be a total of 30,000 units in downtown Los Angeles, an almost 300 percent increase over the pre-STAPLES Center period. In 2007, three-bedroom condos in downtown Los

Table 5.2 Repaying the $12.6 Million Investment by Los Angeles's Community Reinvestment Agency (7 percent discount rate applied)

Year	Tax Growth 100 Percent	Repayment at 100 Percent	Tax Growth at 50 Percent	Repayment at 50 Percent
2002	$3,399,034	$3,399,034	$1,667,952	$1,667,952
2003	3,161,102	6,560,136	1,551,195	3,219,147
2004	2,939,825	9,499,961	1,442,612	4,661,759
2005	2,734,037	12,233,998	1,341,629	6,003,388
2006	2,542,654	14,776,652	1,247,715	7,251,103
2007			1,160,375	8,411,478
2008			1,079,149	9,490,627
2009			1,003,608	10,494,235
2010			933,356	11,427,591
2011			868,021	12,295,612
2012			807,259	13,102,871

Sources: Baade, R.A. 2003. *Los Angeles city controller's report on economic impact: STAPLES Center.* City of Los Angeles Office of the Controller; Office of the Assessor, City of Los Angeles.

Table 5.3 Downtown Housing: Units Built through 2007

Time Period	Affordable	Market Rate Rentals	Market Rate Condos	Market Rate Total	Grand Total
Prior to 1999	8,445	2,532	829	3,181	11,626
1999 to 2007	1,312	5,338	4,048	9,436	10,748
Total	9,757	7,740	4,877	12,617	22,374

Source: The Downtown Los Angeles Mark Report and 2006 Demographic Survey of New Downtown Residents, Los Angeles Downtown Center Business Improvement District, February, 2007.

Angeles had an average sale price of $794,250. In 2000, the average sales price was $282,641 (constant dollars). This represented a real increase of 281 percent in the market value of housing in downtown Los Angeles. While sales prices were rising across Los Angeles during this time, an increase of this magnitude in housing prices in *downtown* Los Angeles was a notable achievement.

VI. Rebuilding Downtown Los Angeles: L.A. LIVE

Within seven years, development was to have been initiated on the entertainment complex that was to include a headquarter hotel for the convention center. AEG began to purchase the land across from the arena soon after its construction began. The redevelopment agency acquired a few parcels through its power of eminent domain and then sold the land to AEG for the price it paid ensuring that taxpayers did not subsidize the land acquisition costs for the promised hotel or the new entertainment complex. The use of eminent domain to transfer property from one private owner to another—which the U.S. Supreme Court would uphold in 2005—does remain as a policy issue raising important equity issues. After the Supreme Court's decision, several states passed laws making the use of eminent domain to transfer property from one private sector owner to another more difficult. Relative to the issue of developing downtown Los Angeles, or remaking it, the Development Authority purchased land and then transferred it at cost to AEG. The use of the public sector's power can be considered a subsidy or an incentive to ensure a type of development chosen by the city council. To the extent that eminent domain reduces the costs to the developer, one could argue that a subsidy exists. However, there was no fiscal subsidy by taxpayers in terms of the costs of land and its assembly for the proposed development.

Though construction of the entire L.A. Live complex was still underway in 2009, the Nokia Theatre at L.A. LIVE opened in October 2007 with seating for 7,100. AEG envisions 125 or more events per year and offers performers a venue where no seat is more than 220 feet from the stage. The theater is set at one end of an open square designed to be Los Angeles' Times Square. The entire project may involve as much as four million square feet of commercial space, residences, and a year-round entertainment center. ESPN opened one of its Sport Zone entertainment centers and restaurant in the complex and has located the West Coast production and headquarters facilities for its ESPN Network at L.A. Live. L.A. LIVE is also home to a 14-screen multiplex movie theater with seating for a total of 3,800 patrons. A more private theater with 880 seats was also built for private screenings of movies. A bowling alley is also part of the complex as will be a smaller live entertainment venue with 2,200 seats (Club Nokia). When completed, there will be several restaurants and a substantial amount of commercial office space.

The L.A. LIVE complex also includes the promised headquarter hotel, but when AEG was unable to attract a partner to share in that facility's construction cost, it asked to reopen negotiations with Los Angeles. The company wanted the city to make an investment to offset the additional capital it would need because no partner was interested in building a hotel in downtown Los Angeles. This represented a material change in the original contract.

AEG proposed that Los Angeles invest all of the hotel tax revenue it would be receiving from guests for a period of 25 years by transferring those funds to the company. It was estimated that this would represent an investment of $246 million by Los Angeles. AEG also asked the city for a $16 million interest-free loan to be repaid across four years and that $4 million in development fees be waived.[15] Lastly, AEG also asked the Community Redevelopment Agency to invest $10 million to pay for needed infrastructure costs. In 2006, the Redevelopment Agency also approved a transfer of $5 million in extra revenue from another downtown tax increment financing district to be used for infrastructure at L.A. LIVE. The Los Angeles City Council agreed to each of these requests.

To calculate the total public sector investment in the L.A. LIVE project (including the convention center hotel), a present value calculation was performed using a 5 percent discount rate.[16] The present value of the public sector's investment in L.A. LIVE was $167.6 million. The present value of the transfer of $246 million of hotel taxes across 25 years is $145.6 million. The present value of the foregone interest for the four-year loan was estimated at $2.98 million. (The loan has already been repaid.) The waiving of development fees ($4 million) and the investment by the Community Redevelopment Agency ($15 million) were included at full value and not discounted.

What is Los Angeles getting in return for this investment? The convention center hotel will stand 49 stories tall, adding to Los Angeles skyline. Eighteen floors will house a Marriott Hotel with 878 rooms. A Ritz-Carlton Hotel will use five floors and contain 123 rooms. A total of 26 floors will be Ritz Residences with 224 condominium units. While there were hopes for a larger hotel, at 1,001 rooms, the Los Angeles Convention Center will have an extraordinary convention headquarter hotel within a very short walk of its main entrance. While there is indeed disappointment that the promised hotel linked to the arena required a substantial investment by the city, it is equally true that the anticipated entertainment complex is far more elaborate then originally anticipated and beyond the scope of the original agreement. In exchange for the material adjustment to the original agreement, AEG was proposing to build a far more extensive complex than initially discussed and its investment in the project would be at least $2.5 billion. ESPN's agreement to relocate some of its production and management facilities from Connecticut to L.A. LIVE also created image, visibility, and marketing benefits for Los Angeles.

Many communities might conclude that a public investment of $167.6 million that leverages $2.5 billion in private funds is worth the change to the original agreement, which did not involve any additional public money for the entertainment complex or hotel (the leveraging ratio is $15 private sector dollars for every public sector dollar invested). It could also be argued that the hotel is being built as agreed to at the time of the arena's development and that the public money is a second investment in a far larger entertainment district. Regardless of the rationalization used, Los Angeles is investing $167.6 million to have the hotel built as part of a $2.5 billion entertainment, commercial offices, and residential development. Did Los Angeles need another entertainment center that warranted a $167.6 million subsidy?

Some critics suggested that the Nokia Theatre would just compete with the STAPLES Center, the Shrine Auditorium, the Gibson Auditorium at University City Walk, and the Forum in Inglewood. The Nokia Theatre, however, was designed to capture events from New York and other cities and award presentations that were not held at those facilities.[17] Some of the events held at the Nokia Theatre have included the Grammy Awards and the American Idol competition. These are important successes, but it is also true that many entertainment venues in Los Angeles were built without subsidies.

In the absence of the building of L.A. LIVE, it is possible that other forms of development might have taken place. Would it have been reasonable to expect $2.5 billion of activity within a few years? That seems highly unlikely, but just as in the case of The Ballpark District in San Diego, the public/private partnership established with AEG meant that the development would occur in a very short period of time. Los Angeles' elected leadership unanimously supported the idea of ensuring that the development took place in the shortest period of time. The STAPLES Center, the cornerstone of the development, is shown in Figure 5.6, and L.A. LIVE is shown in Figure 5.7a and Figure 5.7b.

Figure 5.6 Shown is the STAPLES Center. (Photo courtesy of Mark S. Rosentraub.)

(a)

(b)

Figure 5.7   (a) Schematic view of L.A. LIVE across Chick Hearn Drive from the Staples Center from WWW.LALIVE.Com. Reproduced with the permission of AEG. (b) On the left is the Nokia Center and on the right is ESPN's broadcast headquarters (Photo courtesy of Mark S. Rosentraub).

COMMUNITY DEVELOPMENT AND L.A. LIVE

The focus of several cities, elected officials, and growth regimes on sports facilities for redevelopment of downtown areas has been criticized for an emphasis on tourism and consumption that produces few if any benefits for lower and moderate income residents. This has prompted calls for programs that advance community development. Economic development has as its focus the increment in wealth generated by projects without respect to the distribution of those benefits. Community development emphasizes a balance in the distribution of benefits and ensuring that groups and neighborhoods traditionally ignored or made worse off by revitalization efforts have their interests protected. With their focus on tourism, recreation, and consumption, the STAPLES Center and L.A. LIVE could easily fall into the trap of displacing people and businesses that are a part of a lower income neighborhood in order to attract and entertain wealthier households and visitors.

Community benefits agreements have emerged as a tool by which neighborhoods or cities negotiate with developers to make sure that there is a set of direct benefits for lower income individuals and neighborhoods. Professor Saito at the University of Southern California had observed that redevelopment programs in Los Angeles had an almost time-honored tradition of adversely impacting low-income and minority neighborhoods.[18] In response, the Los Angeles City Council had passed legislation requiring the payment of living wages (1997) and created its first community benefits agreement in 1998.

To avoid any conflict, AEG agreed to a community benefits agreement that included several commitments. First, AEG agreed to fund a needs assessment to identify the need for parks, open space, and recreational facilities in an area south and west of L.A. LIVE and to provide at least $1 million to develop the recommended assets. Second, AEG also agreed to create and manage a residents' parking program to ensure sufficient on-the-street automobile parking for residents not displaced by the redevelopment effort or living in newly constructed condominiums and apartments. AEG's investment in the program was set at not less than $25,000 per year for the initial five years of the program's operation.

Third, AEG also agreed that at least 70 percent of the jobs associated with L.A. LIVE's development, building, and operation would offer living wages as defined by the Los Angeles City Council. The level established by the council in 2001, as "living wage," was $16,058 if health insurance benefits were also provided and $18,658 in the absence of that benefit. Fourth, training programs were established to ensure that people living within three miles of the STAPLES Center and L.A. LIVE would have an opportunity to gain the skills required for employment. Fifth, AEG also agreed to ensure that between 500 and 800 new affordable rental units be built in the immediate area. These units had to remain affordable for 30 years with minimum and maximum income levels established by the city council. These units had to be within a three-mile radius of the STAPLES Center and L.A. LIVE development. Sixth, AEG pledged to work with local community groups to develop more affordable rate housing units in the area. Seventh, AEG also agreed to provide $650,000 to one or to a combination of identified community organizations to assist in the building of affordable apartments. Lastly, AEG also agreed to be responsible for the relocation of families displaced by the building of the arena or of the L.A. LIVE complex.

VII. Rebuilding Downtown: Other Iconic Projects

The rebuilding of downtown Los Angeles included several other projects, two of which were undertaken without regard to or in connection with STAPLES Center and L.A. LIVE. Together, however, the completion of Disney Hall (Figure 5.8)—the new home of the Los Angeles Philharmonic Orchestra—and the new cathedral, Our

Figure 5.8   Pictured above is Disney Hall. (Photo courtesy of Mark S. Rosentraub.)

Figure 5.9 Our Lady of the Angeles Cathedral is shown above. (Photo courtesy of Mark S. Rosentraub.)

Lady of the Angels (see Figure 5.9), identified downtown Los Angeles as a home to iconic projects. The arena and L.A. LIVE at the southern end of downtown and a cultural amenity, Disney Hall on the north established the endpoints or bookends for the revitalization strategy. Los Angeles joined Indianapolis and Cleveland in using both sports and cultural amenities to anchor its redevelopment efforts.

Disney Hall, a project Lillian Disney helped launch with a $50 million gift to create a memorial for her husband Walt, would take more than 16 years to complete. The 1994 Northridge earthquake damaged the structure, which raised costs. Several other crises led to additional cost overruns. In addition, the original cost estimate failed to include the expense for a new garage. After every problem was addressed, the $274 million edifice opened in 2003. Our Lady of the Angels, which opened in 2002, cost $189.7 million.

VIII. Conclusions

What became STAPLES Center and L.A. LIVE—and the thousands of housing units that came after the arena was built—was a result of an effort to resuscitate a "dying convention center." As described by Los Angeles' chief legislative analyst, the housing and the other development was the "gravy" or "the very welcome and unexpected unintended consequences" of a project designed to save the convention center.[19] Even the fact that the arena and L.A. LIVE became bookends of the redeveloping area of downtown (paired with Disney Hall) was basically good fortune. To be sure, there were broad strokes of a plan for revitalizing downtown Los Angeles that spanned two different administrations, but there was no real strategic plan. Some community leaders reported that there was no vision or exciting ideas for revitalizing the downtown area. The money being lost by the convention center was just another example of the mismanagement of the entire downtown area. Many civic leaders concluded the convention center was placed in the worst part of downtown hoping something good would happen. Rarely if ever does hoping cause something good to happen.

The problems did not end with the lack of a strategic plan or vision. The city had failed for more than 20 years to find any investor interested in building a headquarter hotel for the convention center hotel. Have things improved for the convention center in the postarena era? With a larger number of events, the convention center generates enough revenue to cover its operating costs.

Leaving the convention center issue aside, the building of the arena was a fiscal success. By assembling land and permitting the construction of two advertising towers, Los Angeles was able to have an arena built at no public cost. In addition, the city's receipt of specific revenues from the operation of the arena ensures that it will receive a positive cash flow for decades. The public sector did have to make a large investment to have the entertainment complex and hotel built, but that ensured that L.A. LIVE would be an extraordinary entertainment and commercial center replete with residences. Leveraging $15 in investments from AEG for each dollar it committed, many would consider Los Angeles a Major League Winner when it comes to L.A. LIVE, too.

The arena deal was also a success for AEG and the Lakers. In December 2008, *Forbes* released its valuation estimates for all NBA franchises. The Lakers are the second most valuable NBA franchise with an estimated value of $584 million. The Knicks were valued at $613 million and the third most valuable franchise, the Chicago Bulls, was estimated to be worth $504 million. More importantly, the Lakers' debt was estimated to be equal to just 4 percent of the team's value. The debt figures provided by *Forbes* include the team's responsibilities for the cost of the arena. The operating income (revenue over expenses before taxes, interest, depreciation, and amortization) was $47.9 million for FY2007. AEG was able to make its substantial investment in the arena and still see the value of the team rise past the one-half billion level with a relatively low level of debt.[20]

Was the arena responsible for the revitalization of downtown Los Angeles? Local officials and community leaders believe that had the arena not been built, and if L.A. LIVE was never created, not only would the convention center have never seen a new hotel, but the housing and office boom that propelled the redevelopment would also have never taken place. Carol E. Schatz, president and CEO of the Central City Association of Los Angeles labels the STAPLES Center as the catalyst for downtown's resurgence. In her view, there was no real revitalization prior to the announcement that the arena would be built in the downtown area. Under her leadership and the support of the Center City Association, the adaptive reuse ordinance was also passed, which helped expedite the conversion of commercial properties into apartments and condominiums. The policy offers developers (1) expedited review and exemptions from commercial development regulations, (2) exemptions from updates in planning codes relative to floor area ratios, height, residential density, and parking, and (3) excluded mezzanines from floor area ratio calculations. This made conversions of commercial properties to residential condominiums and apartments easier to finance and with an anticipated demand as a result of the success of the STAPLES Center, new projects were undertaken. The ordinance was passed in December 2001.

Los Angeles got a state-of-the-art arena built where it wanted and needed one, and did so with no tax subsidy. The STAPLES Center continues to produce annual revenues for Los Angeles even if no other development takes place. In terms of the convention center hotel and the L.A. LIVE complex, Los Angeles did make an investment. Its returns there, however, are substantial. Some would take issue with Los Angeles extending the Jobs Credit Program to the arena corporation and allowing those funds to be counted toward repayment of the obligation to the city. Again the magnitude of the investment dwarfs the scale of the concession, and the program existed for all businesses, not just for the arena corporation. The jobs credit was another subsidy that raised Los Angeles' overall investment in the project.

Like San Diego, Los Angeles channeled development to a part of downtown that had languished for years. It chose not to follow Jane Jacobs' ideas. To many it seemed that without new investments channeled by the public sector to the area little improvement would occur. Critics of the L.A. LIVE project correctly noted that Los Angeles had many valuable and popular tourist and entertainment destinations. Did it really need another set of complexes, especially one that required a subsidy? The answer to that question lies in Los Angeles' leadership's, desire to change the location of entertainment and tourism. The investment of $500 million in the convention center had not produced any meaningful returns. Leadership feared that, without a substantial relocation of economic activity, the convention center would continue to lose money and the area would also continue to deteriorate. Indeed, to thwart that deterioration a far larger public investment might have been required. Instead, trading location, land assembly, and a small subsidy (compared to the private investment made), the area was rebuilt and transformed within a decade.

That transformation did lead to an entirely different neighborhood being built. Los Angeles did ensure that a large number of below-market-rate apartments were built and even required through the community benefits agreement that AEG provide a modest investment to permit community organizations to build additional housing to serve moderate- and low-income families. AEG's involvement with community organizations also creates an opportunity for these groups to benefit from the substantial expertise that the corporation has in developing communities. While the neighborhood has been changed and some families were relocated, the benefits substantially exceeded the costs. Given the number of new below-market apartments created, the benefits extend beyond the usual concentration of gains that accrue only to the upper and middle classes. The decision to use public resources to relocate a substantial amount of tourist and entertainment activity could also be criticized, but that policy decision was carefully weighed and on numerous occasions was unanimously reaffirmed by the city council and subsequent mayors.

Downtown real estate prices in Los Angeles are now in a period of decline—a result of the national contraction in the housing market—but the slide appears to be smaller than what is taking place in other parts of the region. As a result, some projects have been postponed or scaled down.[21] The price of real estate even in the depressed market of 2008 and 2009 is far above the $80/square foot paid by Los Angeles to assemble the land for the STAPLES Center and L.A. LIVE sites. In that regard, the project has been an important success and if prices recover, even the higher-end prices paid by some could be restored or surpassed in future years.

Given its size, do any of Los Angeles' decisions, options, or actions offer lessons for other cities? There are indeed some important lessons. Los Angeles used a willingness to assemble land with excellent access to the region's transportation system and the unique value of outdoor advertising along transportation networks to secure a large-scale private sector investment. Other communities might have similar locations that could be used to leverage private investments and all have the ability to assemble land. In the end, the ability to assemble land at a very desirable location that could leverage signage and advertising may well be the important lesson for all cities that Los Angeles offers. Los Angeles' leadership used those assets to attract private capital to what was regarded as a highly undesirable downtown area.[22] That lesson is something no city should overlook.

Endnotes

1. Interviews conducted with Dr. Charles Isgar and Steve Soboroff (former senior advisers to Mayor Riordan) on March 10, 2008.
2. Several individuals interviewed for this book observed that they had found the Coliseum to be a difficult board with members having important political differences that impacted different negotiations. It may well be that the Coliseum Commission is just shrewd in its negotiations. Farmer observed that some of the commission's proposals and their public disclosure may have created an unwarranted and unfounded reputation for a lack of flexibility, Farmer, S. 2007. SC, Coliseum Commission still trying to find solution. *Los Angeles Times*. December 14. Internet ed. http://articles.latimes.com/2007/dec/14/sports/sp-newswire14 (accessed March 10, 2008).

3. The Los Angeles Rams played their home games at the Coliseum from 1946 until 1979 and then moved to Anaheim where they played at Anaheim Stadium from 1980 through 1994. The Rams relocated to St. Louis in 1995. With no professional football team in Los Angeles, the Oakland Raiders relocated and played home games in Los Angeles at the Coliseum from 1982 to 1994. For the 1995 season, the Raiders returned to Oakland. UCLA played its home games at the Coliseum from 1928 through 1981 and then made the Rose Bowl its home field after the Raiders moved to Los Angeles. UCLA never enjoyed playing on a field adjacent to its archrival's (USC) campus and the presence of the Raiders made UCLA the third tenant. Those factors each contributed to the decision to relocate.

4. Hamashige, H. 1994. Downtown L.A. office rents tumble more than 30%: but high-rise towers ride out quake with little damage—Los Angeles, California—Special Report: Quarterly Real Estate. *Los Angeles Business Journal* (January 31), online ed., http://findarticles.com/p/articles/mi_m5072/is_n4_v16/ai_15125486 (accessed March 8, 2008).

5. Deady, T. 1994. L.A. County hotel room occupancy shows a significant increase in 1993. *Los Angeles Business Journal*, (March 7), as cited in *High-Beam Encyclopedia*, online ed., http://www.encyclopedia.com/doc/1G1-15277102.html (accessed April 1, 2008).

6. Turner, D. 1995. Police crackdown causes crime rate to plummet in downtown LA. *Los Angeles Business Journal* (April 3), online ed.: contained at BNET http://findarticles.com/p/articles/mi_m5072/is_n14_v17/ai_17015000 (accessed March 10, 2008).

7. Los Angeles, 1997a. *Proposed arena at the Los Angles Convention Center* — memorandum to the Ad Hoc Committee on the sports arena from Keith Comrie, city administrative officer, and Ronald Deaton, chief legislative analyst. Los Angeles: Office of the City Council, 4.

8. L. A. Arena Company, LLC. 1996. *Proposal for L. A. Arena Company LLC to Los Angeles City Council, Mayor Richard Riordan, Los Angeles Convention and Exhibition Center, and the Los Angeles Community Redevelopment Agency*. Los Angeles: Office of City Council, 10.

9. Los Angeles, 1997b. *Los Angeles Convention Center Arena: Proposal summary*. Internal Memorandum, City Council. Los Angeles: Office of the City Council.

10. Baade, R. A. 2003. *Los Angles City Controller's report on economic impact: STAPLES Center*. Los Angeles: City of Los Angeles, Office of the Controller.

11. Los Angeles 1998. *Gap funding agreement between city of Los Angeles and L. A. Arena Company, LLC (Los Angeles Arena Project)*. Los Angeles: Office of the City Council, Annex B, Annex C, March 26.

12. Ibid., Annex D.

13. It is possible that the development that took place near the arena would have been built in other parts of Los Angeles if no new facility were built near the convention center. If that took place, then the property taxes would not be new income, but would represent a transfer of funds from one part of the city to another. It cannot be determined if the new buildings near the arena displaced activity from another part of Los Angeles. What can be stated with a high degree of confidence is that in the absence of the arena it is extremely unlikely new development would have taken place near the convention center given that little if any construction had taken place for several years. The assumptions made in calculating the repayment of the $12.6 million in Table 5.2, however, effectively address the possibility that

development would have taken place in other parts of the city or even at the convention center site. Under the most strident restrictions, the $12.6 million is repaid by 2012 and Los Angeles continues to receive higher property tax revenues in every year beginning in 2013.

14. The $4 million figure is an approximate annual payment each year since the STAPLES Center opened and was confirmed by a telephone interview on June 17, 2008, with AEG's chief fiscal officer. In some years, the amount paid was slightly less than $4 million and in recent years has slightly exceeded $4 million.

15. Zahniser, D. 2005. L.A. LIVE promoters tout Times Square West. *Daily Breeze*, September 18, 2005, online edition, http://www.joelkotkin.com/Commentary/DB%20LA%20Live%20promoters%20tout%20Times%20Square%20West.htm (accessed December 5, 2008).

16. The use of a 5 percent discount rate that some might argue is too low actually increases the value of the public sector's investment in L.A. LIVE. Had a 7 or 10 percent discount rate been utilized, the present value or the public sector's investment would have been less. The 5 percent rate provides a conservative, but higher estimate of the public sector's investment.

17. Riley-Katz, A. 2007. Nokia Theatre ready for its close-up: Construction of AEG's $120 million project down-to-wire. *Los Angeles Business Journal*, October 15, Internet ed.: http://findarticles.com/p/articles/m1_m5072/is_42_29/ai_n21080011 (accessed March 9, 2008).

18. Saito, L. T. 2007. Economic revitalization and the community benefits program: A case study of the L.A. LIVE project, a Los Angeles sports and entertainment district. Los Angles: Department of Sociology, University of Southern California.

19. Interview with Gerry Miller, chief legislative analyst, City Council of Los Angeles, conducted March 14, 2008.

20. *Forbes*. 2008. NBA team valuations. http://www.forbes.com/lists/2008/32/nba08_NBA-Team-Valuations_MetroArea.html (accessed December 4, 2008).

21. Viles, Peter. 2008. L. A. land: Downtown blues. *Los Angeles Times*, online ed., https://latimesblogs.latimes.com/laland/2008/03/downtown-blues.html (accessed December 10, 2008).

22. The building of STAPLES Center and L.A. LIVE in downtown Los Angeles would not have occurred without the leadership of Mayor Riordan and the work of Dr. Charles Isgar and Steve Soboroff. When Isgar initially raised the idea of a downtown arena with the teams' owners, his concept was soundly rejected in favor of a suburban location. Isgar then recruited Soboroff to join him in his effort to bring the teams to downtown Los Angeles. Isgar and Soboroff became a "dynamic duo" of sorts and with the strong support of Riordan they were able to turn the interest of Philip Anshutz and Edward Roski from more suburban locations and other locations in Los Angeles to the downtown area adjacent to the dying convention center. Without the leadership and commitment of these three men—Riordan, Isgar, and Soboroff—downtown Los Angeles would look far different today than it does. Their work underscores the critical importance of committed and visionary leaders for the success of revitalization efforts and the rebuilding of downtown areas.

Chapter 6

Columbus, Major League Sports, and a New Downtown Neighborhood: A Failed Initiative and a Privately Built Arena

A decade ago, a 75-acre area along the Scioto River less than a mile west of this capital city's downtown was an industrial no man's land, consisting of barren rail yards, old warehouses, and a shuttered nineteenth-century penitentiary. But that was before Nationwide Realty Investors, an affiliate of Nationwide Mutual Insurance, turned the area into the Arena District.[1]

I. Introduction

In May 1997, voters in Franklin County—home to Ohio's capital city Columbus—rejected a referendum to increase the local sales tax to pay for a new arena and create the Downtown Family and Sports Entertainment District. The new arena, projected to cost $203.5 million, was touted as the linchpin for a public/private partnership to bring an NHL team to the city. The private sector partner was willing to pay the franchise fee to the league; the public sector was to be responsible for the full cost of the new arena. Had the sales tax increment been approved,

Columbus would have had a team from one of the four major leagues for the first time in its history. Columbus was home to the Crew soccer team, but some civic leaders had longed for a baseball, basketball, football, or hockey team. The voters' decision seemed to bring to an end Columbus' dream for a team from one of the major sports leagues.

Columbus is located in the middle of Ohio, 107 miles northeast of Cincinnati and 142 miles southwest of Cleveland, where Ohio's two larger metropolitan areas are home to the state's major league baseball and football teams. Despite rapid growth, the Columbus region is still smaller than its urban rivals. In 2007, the Columbus area's population of 1,754,337 made it Ohio's third largest behind the Cincinnati region (2,133,678 residents) and metropolitan Cleveland's population of 2,096,471. Columbus has been Ohio's fastest growing region and, from 1990 to 2007, the 349,169 new residents produced a growth rate of almost 20 percent. The Cleveland/ Akron region grew by 1.4 percent, adding 39,522 residents, while the Cincinnati tristate region added 288,761 people and grew 13.5 percent (Table 6.1).

The relatively small population bases of each of these Midwest cities (compared to other cites with professional teams) meant that Columbus needed to focus on hockey if it was to have a team from one of the four major leagues. With MLB teams in Cincinnati and Cleveland, both franchises need to attract fans from the greater Columbus region to meet their attendance goals. Both also broadcast games throughout central Ohio. Neither could afford to share the Greater Columbus market with a third MLB team. Similarly, the NBA's Pacers located in Indianapolis 170 miles to the west count on fans from Eastern Indiana and Western Ohio to fill their arena. They, too, would oppose the presence of an NBA expansion franchise for Columbus or a relocation request by an existing team.

NFL teams in Pittsburgh, Cleveland, Cincinnati, and Indianapolis also surround Columbus, and they would likely oppose an expansion in their midst. With so many teams in close proximity to Columbus, it also meant there was no incentive for the NFL to place another team in a saturated market area. The existing distribution of sports teams left hockey as the only possible option even though there was a competitor, the Pittsburgh Penguins, playing in an aging arena a mere

Table 6.1   Population Changes in Ohio's Largest Metropolitan Statistical Areas, 1990 to 2007

Metropolitan Region	Years		Percent Change		
	2007	2000	2000 to 2007	1990	1990 to 2007
Columbus	1,754,337	1,612,844	8.8	1,405,168	19.9
Cleveland	2,795,827	2,842,970	−0.02	2,756,305	1.4
Cincinnati	2,133,678	2,009,654	6.1	1,844,917	13.5

Source: U.S. Bureau of the Census.

167 miles to the northeast. While many would argue that the separation between these two markets was too little to sustain another franchise, there would clearly be less opposition, as there was no NHL team in Ohio, Indiana, or Kentucky. The path of least resistance to hosting a professional sports team from one of the four leagues led to the NHL.

Ironically, of course, Columbus never really needed professional sports to be considered "major league." First, and almost a sidebar in terms of Columbus' image as a major league city, the Columbus Crew of Major League Soccer (the MLS) had played in the city since 1996. Second—and first in the hearts of all Ohioans—Columbus is home to The Ohio State University (OSU) and its legendary football team and extraordinary set of NCAA Division I sports programs. As a result, the region did not suffer from a lack of passion, excitement, sporting events, or national championships. The success of the university's football team has led to the perennial selling of all 102,329 seats in its mammoth stadium to every game. There are few experiences in professional sports that can match the excitement generated by the Buckeyes and their fans and the spectacle of games in the fabled Horseshoe—the nickname for the cavernous on-campus stadium. Yet, civic leaders wanted a professional sports team so the city would enter the elite echelon of other communities that were home to major league teams. A new arena, to serve as a home for an NHL team, was also looked to as an anchor to revitalize a sagging and deteriorating downtown.

During the campaign for a sales tax increase to fund a new arena, proponents argued that the referendum was the last chance to bring a major league team to the city. Within 30 days of the rejection of the proposition (known as Issue 1), however, a new proposal emerged with the Nationwide Insurance Company agreeing to pay for the arena that would serve as an anchor for the redevelopment of a major portion of the downtown area. In addition, Columbus' Arena District as it would become known would create a model for making cities Major League Winners when it comes to avoiding subsidies and using a sports facility as an anchor for revitalization efforts. Columbus' Arena District illustrates how even midsized metropolitan regions can eliminate subsidies when dealing with professional sports franchises and at the same time use a sports facility to engender redevelopment.

How did it happen and what was accomplished? What were the characteristics of this unique public/private partnership that led to the rebuilding of a dilapidated and lethargic part of downtown Columbus? How did this Ohio city become the model for cities everywhere considering sports or entertainment facilities as anchors for revitalization? These questions are answered in this chapter.

II. Fighting for a Toe Hold in Professional Sports

The Arena District story begins and ends with Columbus' civic leadership—and probably thousands of sports fans—that wanted the growing region to be home to a major league professional sports team. That leadership would continue to find a way to make the presence of an NHL team a possibility even after the voters rejected the proposed increase in the local sales tax. As Ohio's third "C" (behind Cleveland and Cincinnati), Columbus was not a member of the club of cities with professional sports teams.

A. *Sports Leagues and Their Placement of Teams in Cincinnati and Cleveland*

Cincinnati was home to what may have been America's *first* professional sports team, MLB's Cincinnati Reds. Founded in 1869 as the Cincinnati Red Stockings, there may have been earlier professional baseball teams, but none survived to join any of the emerging leagues. The Red Stockings modernized their name to the Red Legs and then the Reds, but since beginning play with a 45 to 9 win on May 4, 1869, they have called Cincinnati home. Indeed, their beginning featured an 81-game winning streak and charter membership in the National League of Professional Baseball founded on February 2, 1876. The Red Stockings joined with teams in Boston, Chicago, Hartford, Louisville, New York, Philadelphia, and St. Louis to begin a new era in American sports: the creation of a professional league that would play a regular schedule of games to determine a champion each season. The new league also ensured that a common set of rules would be followed and the games would be presided over by impartial umpires. The Reds' uninterrupted tenure in Cincinnati made that city part of America's sports royalty and something to use in establishing bragging rights over Columbus. For years, baseball's National League would open its season with a game in Cincinnati denoting the privileged position of the Queen City in the pantheon of American sports.

Cleveland's Indians had an equally storied past as a founding member of the American League. Created in 1901, the American League was formed to challenge the monopoly over professional baseball and the status of the National League of Professional Baseball. The American League eventually placed teams in some of the same markets where National League teams played, and as owners began to compete for players, salaries rose. To avoid rising costs and minimize competition in the same markets, the leagues soon merged and formed Major League Baseball. Cincinnati and Cleveland had their teams and, when MLB turned its attention to expansion in the 1960s and later years, the focus was on the booming regions in the west and south. MLB had no interest in Columbus other than as a home for a minor league team.

Cleveland's Browns began play in 1946 as members of the All-American Football Conference (AAFC) and became part of the modern NFL in 1950. A dominant force in the AAFC, they continued to be a championship caliber team through the 1980s, reaching the playoffs in 22 of their initial 40 seasons. Their success made the team a mainstay of Ohio sports and was another example of an asset that Cleveland had and Columbus did not. Of course, Cleveland never had a collegiate football team with the prominence of Ohio State, but that did not add enough to Columbus' stature for some civic leaders. When the American Football League was formed to compete with the NFL, it placed an expansion franchise in Cincinnati for the 1968 season. The legendary Paul Brown (former coach of the Cleveland Browns) was the owner of the Bengals. Rather than compete head-on with The Ohio State Buckeyes, the American Football League and Paul Brown chose the larger market area of Cincinnati where far less competition for football fans existed. The University of Cincinnati had and continues to field a Division One NCAA football team. That team is neither as successful nor as popular as the Buckeyes.

Columbus was also not chosen by the upstart American Basketball Association (ABA) to host a franchise when it emerged to challenge the monopoly status of the NBA. ABA teams were placed in Louisville and Indianapolis to serve two states where basketball was a legendary high school and college sport. Cincinnati had an NBA franchise from 1957 through 1972 when the Royals moved there from Rochester, New York. That team would eventually move to Kansas City and then to Sacramento, and the ABA would not place a basketball franchise in Cincinnati. The Louisville franchise was disbanded when the ABA merged with the NBA, but the Indiana Pacers joined the NBA. A group of Columbus investors tried to buy the Pacers, but when local owners came forward in Indianapolis, Columbus was left to realize that in Ohio only Cleveland would have an NBA team. Attention focused on the NHL and crystallized with a proposed new arena, a call for downtown revitalization, and an investor willing to pay the $75 million franchise fee required by the NHL.

B. An Effort to Make Columbus Home to a Major League Team

A growth coalition that included a set of participants that would qualify it to be considered a regime formed to secure support for a new arena. The regime included local developers, the local newspaper's owner, the owner of the local minor league hockey team, leadership from the Chamber of Commerce, Lamar Hunt (owner of the Columbus Crew), and leadership from several corporations including Ameritech and Nationwide Insurance. A public/private partnership was created with the Franklin County Convention Facilities Authority (FCCFA). The linkage to the FCCFA was required to ensure that, if the needed land for the arena could not be secured through market transactions, the threat of eminent domain could be used to convince reluctant owners to sell needed parcels. The FCCFA's involvement also assured tax-exempt status for the new facility and access to reduced financing costs through the issuance of bonds likely to be classified as tax-exempt.

As already noted, the voters rejected the sales tax increment. The campaign brought forth the same sort of opposition that existed in San Diego and Los Angeles with regard to higher taxes to support subsidies for professional sports when no investment strategy existed. In those two areas, unique arrangements were created and presented in advance of any vote. As mentioned, the Padres dealt in advance with any opposition with guaranteed levels of private sector investments in a hotel and other properties before asking voters to approve the use of public money as part of the investment in a partnership to build a ballpark. In Los Angeles, AEG agreed to pay for a new arena while also building a hotel and extraordinary new entertainment facility before asking the City Council for its investment. Even though Los Angeles' investment grew by more than $150 million, by the time the city had to make that commitment AEG had already committed more than $2.8 billion to the projects (arena and entertainment district).

In Columbus/Franklin County, the more common tactic of first asking for a sales tax increase without any private sector investment for real estate development or a plan for redevelopment was put forth. The private sector investment at the time of the vote was limited to the payment of the franchise fee to the NHL to ensure the team would exist. The risk relative to the cost of building the arena was assumed by the public sector. Even if the project had collapsed, the team owner would have retained the franchise and been able to move the team to another city. The public sector would have the expense and responsibility for the arena. In this regard, the initial proposal was similar to those that had led to the creation of subsidies with dubious financial returns for the public sector.

Throughout the campaign, proponents argued that this was Columbus' last chance to be home to a major professional sports franchise. This threat rather than the promise of private sector investment was thought to be sufficient to secure voters' support. Proponents then also discussed (or threatened) that there was no "Plan B" or backup strategy if the voters rejected the sales tax increment. If the sales tax proposal failed, there would not be any other effort to secure an NHL franchise (or any other professional team for that matter). With the NHL interested in expansion on an existing schedule, all of the usual psychological factors were in play. Even with these implied threats, the referendum still lost.[2]

III. A Privately Built Arena, Real Estate Development, and a Unique Public/Private Partnership

After the defeat of the sales tax referendum—indeed within approximately 30 days—another plan was put forward, one that would not require voter approval and one that *would not*, in the end, require the substantial investment of tax dollars. While the public sector would be involved and its authority for development and eminent domain utilized, the only taxes expended would be those generated by new real estate development in the Arena District. The development needed to repay the public sector's investments would be guaranteed by Nationwide Insurance through its commitment to pay for any shortfall in the funds needed to repay the bonds sold by the public sector. The new plan, whether it existed prior to the election or not, addressed most if not all of the concerns of the project's opponents who led the "vote no" effort. The physical plan for redevelopment created far more than anyone envisioned—a new neighborhood and not just an arena—and the financial risk was assumed by the private sector. It cannot be underscored enough that this was a complete reversal of the original plan presented to voters that asked for a $200 million subsidy through a sales tax increase without a vision or plan for a new neighborhood and its redevelopment or a commitment for private investment.

The key participants in the growth coalition that argued for the sales tax increase created the new proposal. Its rapid development and presentation led some to suggest that perhaps this idea existed all along. What would have been the incentive to move forward with the vote on the sales tax increment instead of presenting what became known as the Arena District plan as the initial concept? Perhaps the idea for the Arena District did not exist. Or, it may have been that the lure of having access to public money for the arena itself without committing private money was too great a temptation to avoid. After all, had the tax referendum passed, the risks certainly would have been far less for Nationwide Insurance.[3] Had the sales tax passed, other commitments made by the public sector would not have been necessary. Whether or not a "Plan B" always existed or not, what is important is that a new proposal was put forward. This proposal, while requiring important public sector commitments, involved a substantial level of private investment and, in the end, would create a new model for the development of sports facilities while also redeveloping a downtown area.

A. The Arena District Plan

The key element in the plan for the Arena District was Nationwide Insurance Company's commitment to build the arena without any tax money. Nationwide agreed to pay for 90 percent of the cost of building a new arena; the balance of the cost was to be paid by the corporation that owns Columbus' daily newspaper. The public sector's contribution was limited to responsibilities for land assembly and financing the needed infrastructure improvements. Nationwide Insurance is the seventh largest employer in the Columbus metropolitan area, with more than 8,500 employees, and at the national level a "top 100" in terms of the size of corporations, with 36,000 employees. Annually, the corporation ranks among the largest insurance companies in the United States by policies sold. For 2007, the corporation reported $21 billion in annual revenues and $160 billion in assets.

The City of Columbus agreed to pay for the infrastructure improvements needed to build the arena and also agreed to a property tax exemption for the arena even though a private company would own the facility. The project, however, included more than just the arena. The property tax exemption applied to the arena, the garage built adjacent to the arena, and the restaurants and all other improvements at the site of the arena. "But various valuations and appeals placed the arena's value anywhere from $44 million to $156 million. …"[4] The local schools were not to be harmed by this property tax exemption and it was also agreed that Nationwide Insurance would make a payment "in-kind" to the school district equal to the property taxes that would have been paid. Those funds would come from a tax on tickets sold to every event held in the arena. The taxable value of the arena was contested with Nationwide Insurance placing its value at $44 million and the school district arguing that it was worth $156 million. After six years of negotiations, a compromise was reached and it was agreed the school district would receive revenue from a $1 ticket tax surcharge. Columbus would then also transfer to the school district 50 percent of the annual municipal income tax revenue received from players and employees of the NHL teams (the Blue Jackets [Columbus' new hockey team] and all visiting team members as well).

While this proposal or mechanism held the school district "harmless" relative to revenue flows, no income stream from the arena's operation was pledged to the City of Columbus. In addition, the city's transfer of municipal income tax revenue to the school district resulted in the City of Columbus receiving less money. Columbus' investment in the project then includes all of the foregone income tax revenues. Rather than Nationwide being responsible for payments to the school district to ensure that the community's schools were not fiscally harmed by the TIF (tax increment financing), Columbus is now responsible for honoring part of that guarantee.

B. Financing the Arena District

The Columbus Blue Jackets—the expansion NHL team—agreed to pay an annual rent of $3 million for the initial 10 years of the lease. After that, the rental rate would increase to $3.3 million per year. Nationwide Insurance looked to that income stream, parking revenues, and the advertising value of having its name on the arena as the return on its investment. The parking revenues were to come not only from attendance at arena events, but from the scores of visitors attracted to extensive new development in the Arena District. Nationwide Insurance was committed to real estate development in an effort to ensure that there would be a steady stream of visitors, workers, and residents to build the value of its investment and guarantee the return on its financial commitments. As Nationwide's headquarters building was located at the edge of the Arena District, the transformation of the area from one characterized by decline and an absence of vitality to a vibrant residential and entertainment district would also be of value to the firm.

As part of the public/private partnership for the development of the arena, Columbus agreed to give Nationwide Insurance a 10-year lease for an existing site it owned. Nationwide was also granted an option to purchase land in the seventh year at its "fair market value." The city council also agreed to declare the arena site itself a "blighted area" making it possible for the FCCFA to acquire it through its eminent domain powers (as a public entity). FCCFA would own the land and lease it to Nationwide for 99 years. The lease payments would be $150,000 for the initial 10 years. From year 11 to 25, the rental rate for the land was set at $165,000 per year. The rental rate in years 26 through 50 would be $165,000, adjusted upward each year by the consumer price index to account for inflation. The FCCFA paid $11.7 million for the land. Nationwide Insurance's plan was to make this payment from the funds it received from the Blue Jackets through its lease with the team.

Columbus also would be responsible for the environmental restoration of the sites and estimated that its total expense (when all infrastructure costs were included) would be $32.6 million. The final cost for Columbus was $36.6 million, meaning the original estimate was off by 12.3 percent, a rather small proportion for a project as large as the Arena District.[5] A bond was sold pledging the increment in property taxes from the redevelopment of the Arena District as the revenue to repay the debt. Similar to the strategies followed in San Diego and Los Angeles, a TIF district was created based on the anticipated development in the area. In this manner, Columbus would likely have no expense, but increments to its general revenue fund would result only if development levels produced more than enough revenues to repay the bonds. In other words, the property taxes collected from the new development first had to be used to make the payments on the bonds sold to raise the $36.6 million. If the new development resulted in more tax revenues than what was needed to make the bond payments, Columbus would enjoy an increment to its general revenue fund.

The total public investment then was $48.3 million (Columbus' costs plus the investment by the FCCFA) reduced by the annual lease payments to the FCCFA and the anticipated growth in property values in the Arena District. If the TIF produced enough revenue to repay the bonded debt, the public sector's investment would be substantially reduced, and under certain scenarios could actually decline to zero or generate a positive cash flow. The private sector investment was $150 million for the arena (construction cost) plus the $75 million franchise fee paid to the NHL. Nationwide Insurance spent $140 million and the *Columbus Dispatch,* the region's newspaper, invested $10 million. The shares of the public/private partnership are depicted in Figure 6.1 with regard to the arena construction. The total public sector investment amounted to less than one-quarter, 23 percent, and the private sector investment was equal to the rest. With the public sector investment guaranteed by Nationwide Insurance, the plan could be considered 100 percent funded by the private sector.[6]

When the franchise fee paid by the team owners is included in the calculation of the total costs for the partnership—without the team there might have been no interest in an arena and, thus, no reason for a public/private partnership—the public share declines to 17 percent (Figure 6.2). Regardless of which scenario is chosen as the more accurate depiction of the partnership, the public sector's investment, just like those of the private sector partners, was tied to revenue streams designed to cover the cost and perhaps even generate a return. Columbus was pledging increases in property tax revenues to not only repay the bonds it sold to raise the money needed, but was optimistically expecting a return to enhance its general revenue fund. The FCCFA would receive lease payments and while there was no

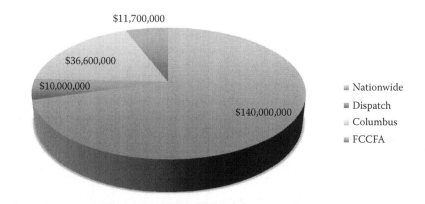

$11,700,000

$36,600,000

$10,000,000

$140,000,000

■ Nationwide
■ Dispatch
▩ Columbus
■ FCCFA

Figure 6.1   The financial commitments to the public/private partnership to build Nationwide Arena and provide the land for the Arena District by source.

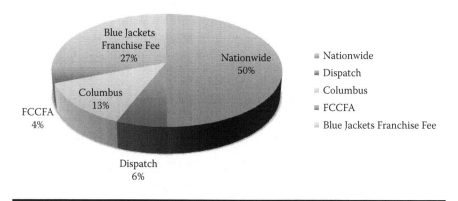

Blue Jackets
Franchise Fee
27%

Nationwide
50%

Columbus
13%

FCCFA
4%

Dispatch
6%

■ Nationwide
■ Dispatch
▩ Columbus
■ FCCFA
▩ Blue Jackets Franchise Fee

Figure 6.2   The percentage of public and private investments in the partnership by source: Franchise fee included.

expectation that the payments would repay the investment, the authority would now have access to more space and anticipated more conventions and other events to increase its overall revenue levels and contributions to the region's economy. Nationwide Insurance pegged its return to the lease with the team, the income from other events staged at the arena, and the parking revenues throughout the district. For the *Columbus Dispatch*, the added advertising revenue from having a major league team in the city was the source of its optimism. As noted by many, the great advantage to a newspaper from a team's presence is the advertising revenue generated as a result of increased readership.[7]

There are some cost estimates that place the total cost of the arena at $175 million. Some of these estimates may well include the infrastructure investments made by the public sector. Other reports reduce Nationwide's commitment by subtracting the payments made by advertisers or others to secure suites. These payments, however, simply transfer the construction cost of the arena from Nationwide to others while reducing the revenues to the team or arena operator that would normally accrue to them had the public sector paid for the facility.

The land for the facility was secured through condemnation and the use of the FCCFA's eminent domain powers. As in Los Angeles when the land was acquired, developers or Nationwide Insurance paid the full costs for acquisition. But this amounted to the transfer of land from one set of private parties to another to ensure that development endorsed by Columbus took place where the city wanted it to occur. Some project critics from each community suggested that allowing governments to steer land to chosen developers to meet the city's objectives can lead to an abuse of power and interference with an individual's rights. There is also the issue of disrupting economic development patterns that are more evolutionary, and the recognition that what was developed (an arena and a high-income neighborhood) was a project that caters to wealthier segments of society.

Proponents for the Arena District, just as those who would support the outcomes in Los Angeles and San Diego, would note that development levels had stagnated for so long that public action to move economic activity into Columbus was long overdue. For example, the number of people living in the downtown area had declined from 44,000 in 1960 to an estimated 3,500 in the late 1990s.[8] Waiting more than 40 years for development to take place was for others clear evidence that without substantial public intervention to redirect economic activity, improvements or enhancements would not occur. In the global competition in which cities now find themselves, Greater Columbus might be growing and expanding, but the downtown area was moribund. This was a real lost opportunity given the proximity of The Ohio State University and the extraordinary level of talent and number of younger people in the city each year. Columbus' leadership wanted to capture this talent, and to that end, wanted a lively downtown. Waiting for development in the downtown area to occur without a substantial stimulus seemed akin to letting another great opportunity pass the city by.

IV. Columbus' Arena District: An Early Assessment

Nationwide Arena opened in September 2000 and the Blue Jackets played their first home game a month later. The Arena was designed to be an anchor for development in and of the District. An important design feature relative to accomplishing the development goals was the building of the team's practice facility—the (*Columbus*) *Dispatch*[9] Ice Haus—as an adjacent component. The practice facility was designed so that many of the team's practices were open to the public. More importantly, when the team was not using the Ice Haus, community events including youth and amateur hockey or other activities could take place in the in the practice facility. In this way, the facility became an anchor for a wide-ranging number of events attracting thousands more people to the District. The practice facility added to the "neighborhood feel" of the area by creating public space where children and other residents of Columbus could use the facility as well as enjoy watching the team practice. This community element to a professional sports facility had never been tried on this scale before. Some new ballparks are designed with public viewing areas so that practices can be watched as people stroll by the outside of these facilities. No other facility, however, has a component that is also available for amateur use. The *Dispatch* Ice Haus creates an impression that Nationwide Arena is also a neighborhood center for youth and amateur hockey—or where residents can watch their professional team—at the same time that it also serves as a home for the Blue Jackets' practices and high-end entertainment events. San Diego's Ballpark District includes a miniature baseball field that is part of a public park and it too has a public viewing area where residents can watch the team practice and play games, but there is no full-scale field for amateur and youth baseball. In this regard, what was built or included in the Arena District was quite unique, and very successful in advancing its image of a new and unusual downtown neighborhood. Nationwide Arena hosts the usual array of entertainment events and hockey games, but is also home to scores of community events. M S I, a Columbus-based planning, urban design, and landscape architecture firm worked with the city to develop the master plan for the area. Figure 6.3 is the 2004 vision plan for the entire Arena District presented to the community.

The arena appears in the center of the figure to the immediate right of the parking/vacant lots. The proposed minor league baseball facility, to the left of the parking/vacant lots, opened in 2009. The district is relatively small at 75 acres, but it would be inappropriate to consider this 75-acre plot the entire Arena District or the area impacted by the arena project. Legally, of course, and from a planning standpoint, this 75-acre area was the Arena District created by Columbus and in which the TIF district was located to pay for the public's investment. Immediately north of the Arena District is the Short North community that has enjoyed a renaissance of development activity, which includes numerous restaurants and several hundred new residences. This area has enjoyed new development in the years immediately after the arena plan was presented to the city council.

Short North itself extends to the beginning of the area adjacent to the campus of The Ohio State University. The university initiated a development of its own at the intersection with Short North called *Gateway*. Gateway is anchored by the university's main bookstore (operated by a commercial firm). The store is among the largest in the United States and the development adjacent to it includes residences and numerous restaurants and pubs. When all of the development is complete, there will be a set of three linked neighborhoods from the university to the downtown area: Gateway, Short North, and the Arena District. This will create the Greenwich Village atmosphere that has escaped downtown redevelopment in

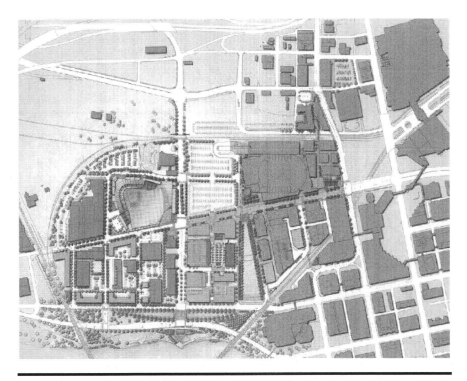

Figure 6.3   The master vision for Columbus' Arena District. (From M S I, Columbus, Ohio. With permission.)

Columbus. The Arena District is relatively small; its impact and linkages to other development efforts is substantial and it may well be the glue that has helped to finalize the building of a residential and mixed-use urban corridor from The Ohio State University to downtown Columbus.

From 1999 through January 2008, there has been a total of $374.6 million of private sector development in the Arena District. This figure excludes parking garages and the pedestrian walkways built as part of the infrastructure required or needed to facilitate development. The $374.6 million encompasses projects initiated as early as 1999 and as recently as 2006. When the construction budget figures are presented in 2006 dollars, the total private sector investment is $399.5 million (Table 6.2).

The importance and significance of this level of investment—relative to the success of the Arena District in changing development patterns—is best underscored by the failure of the retail mall built in the downtown area across from the State Capitol, a short distance from the activity taking place around the sport facility.[10] Given the continuing growth of Columbus' more distant suburban areas, it is likely development would have been concentrated in the suburban areas if the arena had not been built. For example, the fastest growing county in Ohio is Delaware

Table 6.2 Development in the Arena District through January 2008

Arena District Projects	Project Initiated	Construction Budget	In 2006 Dollars
West Street Office Building	2006	$10,500,000	$10,500,000
Condominiums at North Bank	2006	50,000,000	50,000,000
Marconi Blvd Office Bldg	2005	16,500,000	17,157,577
Burnham Square Condo	2004	25,000,000	26,768,359
Eye Center	2003	17,000,000	18,553,110
Jones Day Office Building	2003	25,000,000	27,283,985
Arena Crossing Apartments	2002	35,000,000	39,189,723
Schottenstein, Zox, Dunn Office Bldg.	2001	15,000,000	16,987,436
Lanman Building	2000	800,000	905,997
PromoWest Pavilion	2000	5,500,000	6,228,726
Arena Grand Theatre Complex	2000	125,000,000	141,561,965
URS Office Building	2000	13,300,000	905,997
191 West Nationwide Boulevard	1999	15,000,000	18,104,078
401 North Front Office Boulevard	1999	9,000,000	10,862,447
McFerson Commons Apartments	1999	5,000,000	6,034,693
Ohio Moline Plow Office Building	1999	7,000,000	8,448,570
Total		**$374,600,000**	**$399,492,660**

Source: City of Columbus, Downtown and Economic Development Department.

County that lies to Columbus' immediate north. Delaware County's growth from 1990 to 2006, as well as the growth outside of Columbus but in Franklin County, illustrates a familiar trend (Table 6.3). Growth is concentrating in areas outside of the downtown core area of central cities. This is a particularly important outcome for Columbus given its size. At 212.6 square miles, Columbus accounts for almost 40 percent of the land in Franklin County. With large suburban areas within its boundaries, people can still live in the city, but outside of any inner city areas. The shift of population away from the downtown area, as well as the collapse of the mall created in the late 1980s, could well sustain the argument that in the absence of the arena downtown property values would have declined.

Table 6.3   Population Changes in Central Ohio

Community	Population 1990	Population 2006	Increase	Percent Change
Columbus	632,270	757,117	124,827	19.7
Franklin County[a]	333,964	403,183	69,219	20.7
Delaware County	67,526	162,689	95,163	140.9

[a] Balance of Franklin County (excludes Columbus).
Source: Mid-Ohio Regional Planning Council.

Various sources indicate that the total private sector investment in the Short North and Arena District areas will exceed $500 million.[11] It is indeed possible that more development will take place. There has also been new development in the downtown area and other reports may well have included some of that new construction in the figures reported for the Arena District. It could be argued that new development throughout the downtown area is related to the success in the Arena District. However, to present a relatively conservative view, the investment dollars included are those for projects located completely within the area designated as the Arena District by Columbus.

Currently, the new property taxes generated in the Arena District are insufficient to meet the bond payments and Columbus' own projections do not indicate that the needed revenues will be collected until 2010. Through 2007, Nationwide Insurance had provided Columbus with $7,856,938 to offset the difference between the new property taxes generated by the development in the Arena District and the annual bond payments required for the city's investment in needed infrastructure and to purchase the needed land. Nationwide Insurance Company agreed to be responsible for 65 percent of the total cost of the bond payments if the new projects built in the Arena District did not generate sufficient new property taxes to repay the debt assumed by Columbus for the Arena District's creation and development.[12] This commitment guaranteed that Columbus' investment would not require the use of existing tax revenues. It is expected that after 2010 the development completed will generate sufficient levels of new property taxes to eliminate the need for Nationwide Insurance to provide supplemental payments. Further, since there have already been a number of projects completed, sufficient revenues exist to eliminate the possibility that Columbus would need to provide funds from other sources to meet its responsibility.[13] Had the TIF district produced no revenues at all, Columbus would have been responsible for 35 percent of the bond payments and if the projects produced less than 35 percent of the revenue, Columbus would have had to pay a small portion of the bond's cost. Columbus has never had to make a payment for the bond using any revenue from any other tax source.

It is still possible to suggest that the property tax increment to Columbus from the development that is taking place in the Arena District is a subsidy. After all, had that development taken place elsewhere in Columbus, it is likely the city would have been able to retain all of the tax revenues generated by new projects. Those funds could then have been used to deliver services or for other projects to advance the community or meet residents' demands for services. To the extent that the development would have taken place elsewhere in Columbus there is indeed an opportunity cost loss for Columbus taxpayers. If any or all of the development had taken place beyond the city's borders, then there is no subsidy at all, as the money is a direct result of the arena's presence and the transfer of economic activity to downtown Columbus. Further, given Nationwide's commitment to pay for a substantial portion of any revenue shortfalls in repaying the city's debt for the development taking place in the Arena District, few would argue that the benefits generated for Columbus were not worth some opportunity costs or foregone property taxes.

V. Columbus' Arena District: What Was Built

The Arena District is quite similar to San Diego's Ballpark District. It was designed to be a neighborhood and not just an entertainment area. Green space was maximized as were areas for people to live, work, and stroll in a park-like atmosphere. The STAPLES Center and L.A. LIVE, in contrast, are primary destinations that adjoin transportation linkages, two downtown neighborhoods, and a commercial center. San Diego's Ballpark District and Columbus' Arena District were designed as neighborhoods with an anchor attraction. Nationwide Arena had to be a "good neighbor" and fit within the confines of a neighborhood much like the vision for Petco Park in San Diego.

The anchor tenant is Nationwide Arena and its exterior used the brick, glass, and steel components that matched other buildings in the area. To be sure that the arena fit into the neighborhood, the building's external height was limited to 80 feet. The extensive use of glass allows pedestrians to look into the facility at all times and provides spectators with a view of Columbus' skyline. The arena can seat 18,500 fans for hockey games and up to 20,000 for basketball, concerts, and other events. The arena has 58 suites and 3,200 club seats (Figure 6.4).

Views of the Arena District and its movie theaters, green space, residential, and commercial space are provided in Figure 6.5. While the Arena District is home to important sporting and entertainment events, a 5,000-seat amphitheater for outdoor entertainment in the warmer months (and a 500-seat indoor cabaret theater) is also part of the neighborhood and were made an integral part of its design. Nationwide Arena enjoys a seamless fit into its own neighborhood and with the adjacent Short North area providing ease of access for pedestrians and a walking area for visitors. Since the arena's opening, more permits have been filed to build

Figure 6.4 Pictured is Nationwide Arena. (Photo courtesy of Mark S. Rosentraub.)

approximately 3,500 residential units in the downtown, Arena District, and Short North neighborhoods. The first residential units did not open until 2004, but four complexes of apartments and condominiums were completed by 2008. By 2009, there were also 13 restaurants and pubs operating in the Arena District and an 11-screen Arena Grand movie theater opened in 2006.

VI. Conclusions

Columbus, Ohio, achieved something that has eluded many similar-sized center cities and metropolitan areas. Columbus was able to avoid a tax increase and to have a private firm build the arena needed to attract a professional hockey team. The public sector's investment was limited to supplying the required infrastructure and land. The public sector's investment was $48.3 million and that commitment will be repaid by the new property taxes generated from the new building in the Arena District and adjacent neighborhoods. Columbus is also giving to the Columbus Public Schools 50 percent of the income tax it receives from the payrolls of players and other employees of the Blue Jackets and the visiting NHL teams. That investment will be between $1 million and $1.5 million each year. In addition,

Figure 6.5   Shown is the Arena District. (Photo courtesy of Mark S. Rosentraub.)

in any year that the new property taxes are insufficient to meet the city's debt payments, Nationwide Insurance agreed to provide up to 65 percent of the needed funds to ensure that Columbus' residents would not be responsible for any of the costs of developing the Arena District. Through 2007, Nationwide has provided more than $7.9 million to ensure that the bond payments were made. Projections indicate Nationwide will continue to need to make extra payments through 2010, thus raising their investment in the Arena District.

Even if it is argued that the property tax increment used to repay the $48.3 million bonds sold to finance the needed infrastructure and land assembly represents foregone income, the overall outcomes still make the city a Major League Winner. It is also unlikely that all of the development that has taken place in the Arena District would have occurred elsewhere in Columbus. Growth patterns in the region suggest that some of the new residences, restaurants, and entertainment venues may well have occurred in other parts of the county or in the growing county north of Columbus.

For its investment, Columbus also received far more than an arena. The lesson from Columbus and the secret to the city's success lies in the incentives for Nationwide Insurance to create the Arena District. To secure the highest possible return on its investment in the arena and its commitment to other real estate

Figure 6.5 (continued).

development, Nationwide has a vested interest in the Arena District's success. This led to the need or incentive to:

1. Create a vision for a new neighborhood
2. Present a unified plan integrating residences, entertainment, and commercial properties into this new neighborhood
3. Attract and encourage other entrepreneurs to invest in the area
4. Coordinate activities with the adjacent Short North neighborhood

These outcomes produced for Columbus a redevelopment effort in its downtown area that had previously eluded the city's leadership. Earlier downtown redevelopment efforts involved the building of a retail mall and hotels across from the state capital. The hope was that the return of retail to the downtown area would attract residences and slow the rapid outmigration to the northern parts of the city, county, and region. Columbus' City Center could not compete with Eaton—the new lifestyle center built on the northeast side of the region—nor with Polaris, a large retail mall and shopping district located near the Franklin and Delaware County borders.[14] The Arena District succeeded where the City Center retail mall failed because it offered an unusual urban neighborhood incorporating residences

Figure 6.5   (continued).

into an area with unique entertainment venues, businesses employing thousands of
people, a wide array of restaurants and pubs, pedestrian-friendly paths and areas,
and easy access to other vibrant urban neighborhoods. In short, the Arena District
was everything that could not exist in a suburban area that was built to accommodate cars, large-retail centers, and single-family homes with large lots. The Arena
District offered an entirely different lifestyle and residential product, and its success
creates a model for other cities to emulate.

As important as was the creation of a new urban neighborhood for the redevelopment of Columbus' downtown area was the city's achievement relative to negotiating with team owners and for professional sports. Columbus' Arena District
highlights how any city can avoid excessive subsidies through a focus on using a
sports facility to anchor the development of a unique neighborhood. That neighborhood then offers a lifestyle that is unavailable or impractical to build in suburban
areas. The neighborhood's special assets and amenities attract residents, employers,
and most importantly, other investors who then extend and enhance the assets and
amenities in the immediate and adjacent areas. In October 2008, the Columbus
City Council gave Nationwide permission to build an additional 450 residential
units, 300,000 more square feet of commercial space, an 80,000-square-foot supermarket, and an eight-level garage with space for 1,600 cars. Retail stores are planned

for the street level of the garage.[15] While Nationwide may need additional time to complete this last phase of the project in the midst of a recession, there seems to be little doubt that the last elements for the Arena District will be built.

For sports teams, the lesson of the Arena District is that integrated development of a facility with an urban neighborhood can create extraordinary opportunities for returns on an investment in an arena or ballpark and team. Making teams and their facilities good neighbors and part of a unique urban neighborhood is, simply put, good business. Columbus' design meant a commitment to the brick facades that characterized the area as well as the inclusion of green space to make the Arena District a neighborhood in which people lived, worked, and enjoyed professional sports and entertainment. San Diego's ballpark district and it success also underscores what can be accomplished when teams or other organizations link a sports facility to neighborhood development. That effort proves this point in a metropolitan area of almost 3 million people adjacent to the Pacific Ocean. Columbus' Arena District shows it is also possible to tie a sports facility to the building of a new urban neighborhood in a smaller metropolitan area of less than 2 million residents located in the center of a slow-growth region with far colder winters. Indeed, perhaps the Arena District identifies the redevelopment path that can help smaller and slower-growth regions build the images and reputations needed to attract and retain the human capital that has for the past decades decided to settle in other parts of the country.

The public sector's investment of approximately $50 million and the sharing of income tax money with the school district was a prudent investment given the returns. The public sector also had to acquire land and make it available for the development plan presented by Nationwide's planners. It is true that land was taken from one set of individuals and transferred to others to ensure that the neighborhood could be built. Few who walk the streets and pedestrian alleys of the Arena District, or sit in its green space, would disagree with the notion that the long-term public interest was indeed served by the building of the Arena District.

Columbus and Franklin County were also able to bring another sports venue to the Arena District, and again did so without large subsidies. Columbus has been the long-term home to AAA minor league baseball. A new ballpark was built and opened in 2009. The new ballpark and related infrastructure improvements cost $81 million. More than $40 million was secured from a naming rights agreement and prepaid corporate sponsorships, a grant from the state of Ohio, the sale of the old ballpark, and interest income earned on the project's finances. A $42.4 million revenue bond was sold to complete the financing and it will be repaid through use of the remaining naming rights payment, sponsorships, and a ticket tax. If the ticket tax and further corporate sponsorships are sufficient to retire the bond, the public investment will amount to $7 million from the state plus $3.3 million from the sale of the land on which the old minor league ballpark stood. This public investment would complete the Arena District and the city's financial returns will come from additional real estate development that will take place and the completion of the Arena District as Columbus' revitalized downtown neighborhood.

Despite these achievements, there is one other issue for Nationwide Arena and Columbus. While Columbus and Nationwide were focused on building a new arena for an NHL team, The Ohio State University also built a new arena for its basketball teams and other events. In 1998, the Schottenstein Center opened on the campus of the university. Nationwide Arena is located 4.2 miles to the south or a short 10-minute drive from the 19,500-seat facility. Early losses required The Ohio State University to restructure repayment of their arena's construction bonds. "It (the Schottenstein Center) netted $1.9 million over expenditures in fiscal 2004, its record year, and $1.2 million in 2006. But that amount has plunged in the past two years as higher fees for performers ate into profits: $367,000 in fiscal year 2007 and $175,000 in fiscal year 2008."[16] When the Schottenstein Center was conceived and built there was a commitment that it would not compete for regional events but concentrate on serving the university's requirement or needs for a venue to host indoor events. That commitment made it possible for Columbus to still pursue its dream of an area to anchor a revitalization program for the downtown area. Economic pressures may have led to the university's decision to host events that could also be held at Nationwide Arena. At the current time, there are about 125 events each year at Nationwide Arena.[17] Similar facilities in Cleveland and Indianapolis try to host more than 200 events each year underscoring the under-utilized capacity at the home of the Blue Jackets. The region is too small to support two facilities. In the future Columbus, Nationwide, and The Ohio State University may well have to figure out ways to ensure that both facilities realize their economic potential.

Endnotes

1. Schneider, K. 2008. A waterfront revival in Columbus, Ohio. *The New York Times*, December 3. B4.
2. A detailed history of the electoral battle, campaigns, and the defeat of the sales tax referendum for the new arena is provided by Curry, T. J., Schwirian, K., and Woldoff, R. A. 2004. *High stakes: Big time sports and downtown redevelopment*. Columbus: Ohio State University Press.
3. Curry, Schwirian, and Woldoff, *High stakes*.
4. Burns, M. 2007. Nationwide, schools settle arena valuation dispute. *Columbus Business First*, December 5. Online edition. http://columbus.bizjournals.com/columbus/stories/2007/12/03/daily22.html (accessed April 3, 2008).
5. Bach, A. 2007. *Arena District. Urban Land*. Case Number C037003, January–March, Washington, D.C.: The Urban Land Institute.
6. The possibility that some of the development would have taken place elsewhere in Columbus is considered later in the chapter. If the Arena District displaced development that would have been fully taxed, then Columbus' investment proportion increases as a result of the opportunity costs associated with projects that would have occurred elsewhere in the city.

7. Trumpbour, R. 2007. *The new cathedrals: Politics and the media in the history of stadium construction.* Syracuse, NY: Syracuse University Press; Rosentraub, M. S. 1997a. *Major league losers: The real cost of sports and who's paying for it.* New York: Basic Books.

8. Sheban, J. 2004. Rise in urban housing cheered. *The Columbus Dispatch*, June 3, 1E.

9. Naming rights for the practice facility was part of the participation agreement that included the $10 million investment by the newspaper.

10. Pramik, M. 2007. City Center might close once Macy's leaves. *Columbus Dispatch*, September 27. http://www.dispatch.com/live/content/local_news/stories/2007/09/27/city_center.html (accessed April 5, 2008); Rose, M. M. 2008. Forlorn downtown mall waits, *Columbus Dispatch*, August 1, A1.

11. Iarns, A., P. Kaplan, A. Bauerfeind, J. Huestis, and K. Quilliman. 2006. Economic development and smart growth: 8 case studies on the connections between smart growth development and jobs, wealth, and quality of life in communities. Washington, D.C.: International Economic Development Council; Bach, *Arena District. Urban Land.*

12. City of Columbus. 1998. *Capital improvements project development and reimbursement agreement for Nationwide Arena District, September 15.* City of Columbus: Office of the Mayor.

13. Nationwide Insurance Company and the City of Columbus agreed that new property taxes generated by development in the Arena District would be sufficient to retire the debt associated with the city's responsibilities for (1) assembling land and (2) building the needed infrastructure. The initial projects generated sufficient revenue to pay 35 percent of the annual bond payments. In any year that the new property taxes could not meet all of the required payments on the assumed debt, Nationwide Insurance is responsible for the difference in payments between the new property taxes generated and the bond payment due to creditors. The amount of Nationwide's payments through 2007 was confirmed through e-mail exchanges with Michael Stevens, deputy development director of Jobs and Economic Development, City of Columbus, August 26, 2008. Stevens also projects that payments from Nationwide will be needed through 2010. After that date, the projects completed should generate the needed revenue to repay the debt.

14. Rose, M. M. and M. Pramik, 2009. Goodbye, City Center. *The Columbus Dispatch,* February 4, 1. The City of Columbus in February 2009 decided to not only close the City Center Mall, but to demolish it. Demolition was scheduled for the summer of 2009 and the plan is to build a park area and prepare the land for future residential and commercial development. It is hoped that the Columbus Commons will become similar to the Arena District and perhaps even link to it.

15. Schneider, A waterfront revival in the Midwest.

16. Bush, B. 2008. Rivals to this day: As Ohio State's Schottenstein Center turns 10, its bumpy history with Nationwide Arena hasn't been forgotten. *Columbus Dispatch:* http://www.crainscleveland.com/apps/pbcs.dll/section?category=fram...es_2008_11_17_arena_anniv.ART_ART_11-17-08_A1_KOBTM3E.html_sid=101 (accessed November 17, 2008).

17. Ibid.

Chapter 7

Can a City Win When Losing? Cleveland and the Building of Sports, Cultural, and Entertainment Facilities in the Midst of Population Declines and Job Losses

I. Introduction

Cleveland followed in Indianapolis' footsteps using new entertainment, cultural, and sports facilities in an effort to (1) arrest downtown decline, (2) create a new image, and (3) slow or reverse regional economic contraction. Unlike Indianapolis, however, there was only a general strategy or a loose vision that guided the redevelopment effort rather than a detailed plan. In addition, Cleveland did not concentrate its new assets in one part of its downtown area. The restored theater district, Playhouse Square, is at the eastern end of the downtown area. Two of the new sports facilities are at the southern extent of the downtown area with the third and two new museums on downtown's northern edge, adjacent to Lake Erie (Figure 7.1).

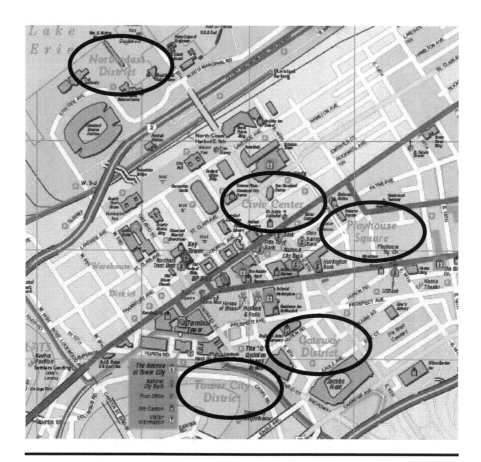

Figure 7.1 Downtown Cleveland and the dispersion of facilities. Note: Cleveland Browns Stadium, the Science Museum, and the Rock and Roll Hall of Fame are in the Northeast District on the shores of Lake Erie. The ballpark and the arena are in the Gateway District (southern edge of the downtown area) at the map's bottom (center), and Playhouse Square lies on the right-hand side of the map (the eastern edge of downtown). (From: www.positivelycleveland.com — the official Web site of the Convention and Visitors Bureau of Greater Cleveland.) (Courtesy of Rustbelt Cartography.)

Cleveland's reliance on sports, entertainment, and culture as the anchors for its redevelopment strategy was as pronounced as Indianapolis' focus, but the newly built or restored assets were dispersed across a far larger area.

Lodged between Cleveland's anchors for its revitalization strategy were various retail and commercial properties. Unfortunately numerous vacant buildings and storefronts were also interspersed between the new assets or amenities. The failure to concentrate the new facilities in a section of the downtown area and completely restore one part of a core was surprising given the city's rich planning history that emphasized carefully detailed plans and focused redevelopment. In the early years of the twentieth century, Cleveland commissioned urban visionary Daniel Burnham to produce a master plan for part of its downtown when a new city hall, county court house, public library, railway station, and convention center were to be built. That plan led to a unified design for a core area surrounding and adjacent to Public Square. A new master or focused plan for downtown's revival in the last decades of the twentieth century was not developed even though more than a billion dollars was spent by the public sector to build confidence in the city's future.

Dispersed revitalization efforts usually mean vacant and, in some cases, deteriorating properties will be mixed among newer assets creating an air of decay amid redevelopment. Concentrating assets in designated areas is more likely to lead to a more successful revitalization strategy encouraging entrepreneurs to seek opportunities within a defined entertainment district or in areas immediately adjacent to the revitalized section. The residential or commercial projects that surround the revitalized core area then permit the redevelopment effort to expand outward from a strong and successful center. In contrast, placing assets in diffused sections of a large downtown area, as was done in Cleveland, produces more challenges to ensure that abandoned or underutilized properties are quickly redeveloped. In addition, the presence of vacant or abandoned properties weakens an image of restoration and viability.

The success achieved by Indianapolis, Los Angeles, San Diego, and Columbus from a more concentrated approach makes Cleveland's inclusion in a book on cities that were successful in the use of amenities for a new image and downtown seem a bit odd. It would seem from a design standpoint that Cleveland's effort is a case study of how not to revitalize a downtown area in contrast to the successes elsewhere. In addition, the scale of the public subsidies for the three sports facilities and the Rock and Roll Hall of Fame and Museum further complicates classifying Cleveland's effort as a success. In later years, the leases for the ballpark and arena would be redone and the operating subsidies eliminated. But when the new ballpark and arena opened in 1994, the Indians and Cavaliers were recipients of some of the most generous subsidies given any teams. Finally, in Cleveland, the public sector's spending of tax dollars was not tied to any specific commitments for private investments to rebuild part of the downtown area. Cleveland and Cuyahoga County invested tax dollars in sports facilities and then in the Rock and Roll Hall of Fame hoping the private sector would recommit to the city's future. Why then should Cleveland be included in a book focused on cities that successfully used sports and culture for revitalization?

The private sector investments and revitalization efforts that took place *after* the building of the sports and cultural facilities in a city with long-term population losses makes Cleveland's experiences critical for this volume. The public sector's investments were made to bolster confidence in Cleveland's future at a time when population losses, racial conflicts and riots, the severe contraction of the manufacturing sector, and the relocation of several large corporations created an image of an urban area in the midst of a rapid decline. It is not an overexaggeration to note that a crisis of confidence dominated conversations about Cleveland. The public sector made a strategic and dramatic decision to make very large investments in big-ticket items to create an image of confidence and present a vision for a far better future anchored to new, first-class amenities. The goal of these investments was to convince residents, visitors, people across America, and private investors that Cleveland and Northeast Ohio's future was as bright in the 1980s and 1990s as it was that day in 1902 when Daniel Burnham was hired to present the city with a new plan for its downtown area.

Many cities and regions that were former manufacturing centers around the world find themselves in situations similar to Cleveland. Population and job losses abound amid calls for concentrated public efforts coordinated with private sector partners to reverse the trend across North America and in several European centers (Belfast, Bilbao, Manchester, etc.). What happened in Cleveland following these large investments to inspire confidence therefore is important to understand, as many older manufacturing centers continue to reinvent themselves through a focus on sports, entertainment, and the arts. Was Cleveland's effort successful? This chapter looks at the success from a revitalization effort in a former manufacturing capital that took place amid substantial global economic change.

At the abyss of the loss of confidence and at the height of outmigration, George Voinovich agreed to run for mayor if the private sector would reengage with the city. After becoming mayor, he empowered business leaders who then dedicated substantial corporate resources to community development projects while also championing the use of sports and cultural amenities to rebuild downtown Cleveland and its image. Could Cleveland's public/private partnership change the city's fate? This chapter addresses this difficult question by looking at private investments in the downtown area, the city, and the country in the longer term compared to what was taking place in the years before the big-ticket strategy and a billion dollars of public subsides. This assessment will help community leaders in other areas experiencing severe economic contractions to better understand what is possible from a confidence-building strategy focused on big-ticket items and neighborhoods when a region's economy and population levels decline. A study of Cleveland's longer-term success from the public sector's investments also adds to the understanding of the options for formerly dominant manufacturing centers in their efforts to create new images and a twenty-first-century economy.

II. The Crisis of Confidence

A. Racial Conflict and White Flight

The crisis of confidence in Cleveland's future began with an extraordinary population shift. During the 1960s and 1970s, the number of people moving out of

Cleveland was equal to 34.5 percent of its 1960 population. The desire for a suburban lifestyle replete with newer houses initially steered some people away from Cleveland and into dozens of surrounding cities. The slow but steady outflow of people became a torrent after two riots rooted in the city's long-standing racial conflict figuratively divided the city. The first riot occurred in the summer of 1966 in the Hough area, a predominantly African-American neighborhood on the city's northeast side, and lasted for six nights. The riot began with a confrontation between a white bar owner and two or three black patrons.[1] The confrontation spilled into the streets and led to wide-scale attacks against businesses owned by whites. Hundreds of fires were set and the violent attacks led to four deaths. The riots and looting spread across more than 20 blocks and unleashed simmering frustrations between blacks and whites.

In 1968, a second and more violent riot engulfed another eastside neighborhood, Glenville, from July 23 to 27. In the initial confrontation, three police officers and four African-Americans were killed. The exchange of gunfire and the subsequent fires, looting, and destruction of property gave Cleveland an image that it was not safe and was at war with itself. It was later revealed that some of the guns used in the riot had been purchased with funds donated by business leaders to help advance the city in the aftermath of Carl Stokes' election as mayor. Stokes was the first African-American elected mayor of a major American city. The business community donated $4 million to a "Cleveland Now" development campaign and placed the resources at the disposal of the new mayor. It was hoped these funds would help Mayor Stokes initiate new programs to unify residents and advance community and economic development. It was later discovered that a city employee authorized the use of some of these funds to buy the guns used by rioters.[2] Cleveland's image was now one of complete disarray and racial conflict. The resulting white flight left Cleveland's east side as a predominantly black community. In the aftermath of the riots, the large Jewish community that had lived on Cleveland's east side for decades began a systematic move to the region's eastern suburbs. By 1990, almost all of Cleveland's Jewish religious and cultural centers had moved to different eastern suburbs.[3]

The eastern part of Cleveland was soon completely separated by race and economic class from its western half and from the adjacent eastern suburbs. In later years, the divide would be predominantly economic as the growing black middle and upper class also moved to the eastern suburbs. Family median income in the eastern part of Cleveland would be less than half of that of families living in the adjacent suburbs. Cleveland's school system that was once the pride of the region fell into failure and was annually ranked among the poorest in Ohio. Most people who could afford to live in other cities moved out of Cleveland. The resulting racial and economic segregation would scar the city and region for decades and led to Cleveland losing more than half of its 1950 population base. Between 1960 and 1970, more than 125,000 people left and then another 177,000 people moved out in the 1980s. The decline continued into a third decade with the loss of another

Table 7.1 Population Changes in Cleveland and Cuyahoga County

	Cleveland		Cuyahoga County	
Year	Population	Change	Population	Change
1920	796,841		943,945	
1930	900,429	103,588	1,201,445	257,500
1940	878,336	–22,093	1,217,250	15,805
1950	914,808	36,472	1,389,532	172,282
1960	876,050	–38,758	1,647,895	258,363
1970	750,903	–125,147	1,720,835	72,940
1980	573,822	–177,081	1,498,400	–222,435
1990	505,616	–68,206	1,412,140	–86,260
2000	478,403	–27,213	1,393,978	–18,162
2006	444,313	–34,090	1,314,241	–79,737

Source: U.S. Bureau of the Census, various years.

68,000 residents in the 1980s. In the aftermath of the urban riots, most people simply moved to nearby suburban areas and Cuyahoga County's population steadily increased. Then, the population declines that plagued Cleveland spread and by 2006 the county had lost almost one-quarter of its residents from the 1970 high-water mark (Table 7.1).

B. *Economic Contraction and Fiscal Default*

If racial tensions and economic segregation were not enough to tarnish the region's image and weaken confidence in the city's future, the 1970s also ushered in a prolonged period of economic change that led to the loss of more than 200,000 manufacturing jobs. These job losses continued through 2008 and even with new jobs in other sectors of the economy, in the first decade of the twenty-first century northeast Ohio lost more than 77,000 jobs.[4] The rapid restructuring of the economy and the loss of so many jobs contributed to a growing lack of confidence in the future. As the economic restructuring began to shake the city's foundation, Cleveland endured another fiscal–political crisis that while encouraging even more people to leave the city would also set in motion the events that began the revitalization effort.

A young reformer, Dennis Kucinich (now a member of the U.S. House of Representatives) was elected mayor in 1978 for a two-year term.[5] The young and idealistic reformer assumed leadership of the city as its fiscal problems were increasing and deficits were becoming an annual occurrence. To balance the budget, the city frequently borrowed money and during Kucinich's tenure the banks demanded the sale of the municipal power company to repay several loans (the principal amount was due and the banks wanted full payment). Mayor Kucinich refused to sell the asset and the banks refused to "roll over" the debt (or extend the loan). With no other revenues available to repay the loan, Cleveland became the first major city to default on loan payments since the Great Depression. Infuriated, a sufficient number of residents signed a petition to demand a recall election that Mayor Kucinich narrowly survived. Mayor Kucinich retained the confidence of many westside residents and other residents of Cleveland in his "battle" with the banks. The business community lost complete confidence in the mayor's leadership abilities and a standoff existed even after Kucinich survived the recall vote. There was also a high level of frustration with the city's failure to deal with the national publicity describing Cleveland's brush with bankruptcy that was supplying additional evidence of a disintegrating city.

In this cauldron of population decline, confrontations between the business sector and the mayor, and the beginnings of a substantial economic restructuring in the region, a handful of leaders from the city's largest remaining companies sought a candidate to replace Mayor Kucinich. George Voinovich, a resident of Cleveland and the Republican Lieutenant Governor, had lost an earlier election for mayor. He agreed to run again and vacate his statewide office if the business community would agree to help him reform the city's finances and administration, and then join in an effort to advance the city and region's economy. Voinovich wanted the business community to be a long-term partner fiscally and emotionally committed to rebuilding Cleveland's finances, image, downtown, and its future.

III. Cleveland's "Hail Mary" Pass: Downtown Revitalization as Symbols of Confidence

A. *Playhouse Square and a Citizen-Driven Public/Private Partnership*

In some ways, George Voinovich and Cleveland's leadership actually "backed into" a focus on entertainment, culture, and sports to rebuild confidence in the city. In the throes of the confrontation between Mayor Kucinich and the banks (and business community), an historic preservation effort led by community activists was launched to protect an extraordinary part of Cleveland's gloried past. Through the 1950s, downtown Cleveland had a thriving theater district anchored by five grand facilities built in the 1920s for live performances and movies. By 1969, all the theaters had closed. As more and more people left the city, entertainment facilities were built in the suburbs. The racial riots gave people additional justification for avoiding the "unsafe" city and downtown. In the 1970s, plans were afoot to raze the theaters.

A group of citizen-activists concerned with preservation and restoration orga- nized a nonprofit corporation, the Playhouse Square Foundation, to save the the- ater district. With the assistance of the community's large private foundations (the Cleveland Foundation and the Gund Foundation), individual donors, and eventu- ally Cuyahoga County itself (but in the absence of strong or committed leadership from the public sector), each theater was restored. Today the Playhouse Square Foundation operates the largest theater district outside of New York City and more than 1 million tickets are sold annually for shows, plays, concerts, speeches, and other performances. To advance real estate development in the adjacent area, leader- ship from the Playhouse Theatre Foundation created the Cleveland Theater District Development Corporation. This community development corporation (CDC) has restored some buildings and built new commercial space, parking facilities, a hotel, and a public plaza for performances, celebrations, and concerts. For a city search- ing for a success story and evidence that downtown life could again be restored, Playhouse Square became a symbol of what was possible and the value of partner- ships between community groups, leading foundations, and private benefactors. The crowds that attended shows and other events created a lively atmosphere in a part of the downtown area that had been largely abandoned. Entertainment and attractions emerged as a vehicle for rebuilding confidence and optimism. Playhouse Square's success in attracting crowds and financial commitments for its restoration by foundations, businesses, and from people across the region amid dismal news for Cleveland, created a blueprint for a revitalization strategy. Cleveland would follow Indianapolis and focus on entertainment, sports, and culture, and cultivate public/ private partnerships to achieve its goals. Three of Playhouse Square's theaters along a restored Euclid Avenue are seen in Figure 7.2.

B. Public/Private Partnership Mayoralty of George Voinovich and the Reinvigoration of a Regime[6]

George Voinovich needed no prompting or convincing that the city and region's future was linked to the fate of downtown and strong partnerships between the pub- lic and private sectors. He recognized that a massive rebuilding effort was needed to restore confidence in the city and generate excitement about its future.[7] During Mayor Voinovich's tenure, the Flats, a declining industrial area adjacent to down- town and located along the Cuyahoga River, was redeveloped as an entertainment destination with restaurants and pubs. A perfect complement to the attractions at Playhouse Square, the Flats, unfortunately, was located more than a mile from the theaters. The Flats would go through a second decline and, after 2003, it would become the site of a new residential development and a planned new neighborhood (which, in turn, was delayed by the credit and financial crisis of 2008 and 2009). Focusing on the Flats was a logical extension of the success of Playhouse Square. If people would return to the city for unique entertainment venues, a restored Flats

Figure 7.2 Playhouse Square: Theaters and restored buildings, products of a public/private partnership on the eastern edge of the downtown area. (Photo courtesy of Mark S. Rosentraub.)

area that turned abandoned warehouses and industrial properties into restaurants, clubs, and pubs together with some new condominiums and apartments might continue to breathe life and vitality into the downtown area.

Mayor Voinovich was focused on projects, which could rapidly change impressions that the city's best days had already passed. In addition to the redevelopment of the Flats, the Voinovich administration and its private business partners focused on a new ballpark for the city's MLB team, the Indians. In 1984, a proposal for a domed stadium financed by a property tax increase was defeated by a 2 to 1 margin. Undeterred, in 1986, the Greater Cleveland Domed Stadium Corporation acquired the land and buildings that housed the deteriorating Central Market, providing a de facto location for a new ballpark. To purchase the land, the Domed Stadium Corporation received a $6 million grant from the State of Ohio and borrowed $18 million from area banks. With no revenue streams to repay the debt, the Domed Stadium Corporation turned to Cleveland Tomorrow. Cleveland Tomorrow was created and funded by the city's business leaders as part of their commitment to help Mayor Voinovich in his efforts to restore the city's luster. Cleveland Tomorrow assumed responsibility for the debt and this initiated the first of many neighborhood and downtown real estate development deals that would be financed by the city's leading businesses through Cleveland Tomorrow and other organizations that its board would create. (The role of Cleveland's business leaders in redeveloping downtown and the entire city is addressed later in this chapter).

Cleveland's Central Market mirrored the downtown area as it too was in a state of decline. By 1981, it had fewer than 40 tenants and was but a shell of its former prominence as a retail and wholesale produce, meat, and fish market for the region. Some buildings were completely dilapidated. The private acquisition of the land was an effort to reengage the process to build a new downtown ballpark and to remove the stumbling block of assembling the land needed for the project. The 28-acre site was actually large enough to accommodate a ballpark and an arena as advocates for changing downtown Cleveland into a sports and entertainment center also wanted to convince the region's NBA team (the Cavaliers) to return from its suburban home in distant Richfield. In 1988, a new proposal was presented to voters to build a ballpark and arena. This time property taxes would not be raised, but taxes would be increased on the sale of alcohol and tobacco. It too failed as voters again refused to support higher taxes for sports and entertainment facilities.

Disappointment with the public vote for a domed stadium and then a ballpark and arena did not stop interest in other redevelopment efforts. A public/private partnership was created to remodel a deteriorating and abandoned train station affixed to the city's landmark Terminal Tower (railroad station). Reopened as a mall in 1990, new commercial space was added in 1991 that included a Ritz-Carlton Hotel. The BP America Building opened in 1985 in the downtown area (without any tax abatements) and the adjacent Key Tower opened in 1991, but work on this structure was initiated during George Voinovich's administration.[8]

C. Mayor Michael White and the Ballpark and Arena Proposal's Redux

In November 1989, Michael White was elected mayor. A surprise winner, the city's second African-American mayor (and Cleveland's longest serving mayor with three four-year terms) was not a sports fan, but indicated he would be inclined to urge voters to support a tax increase for a ballpark and arena if he could be convinced the facilities would advance the economic development of downtown. Impressed with the possibility that the arena could return a large number of events from the suburbs to the city, Mayor White endorsed and strenuously campaigned to increase taxes to build two sports facilities. Framed as an economic development and revitalization program, the proposal focused on the investments by the teams, the commitments of support from Cleveland Tomorrow, and the changes for downtown from the presence of sports and entertainment events all year. Voters were again asked to support higher taxes on the sale of alcohol and tobacco products to build a 42,000-seat, open-air ballpark for the Indians and a 20,000-seat arena for the

Figure 7.3   Quicken Loans Arena was part of the Gateway Development Authority and one of three sports facilities built in downtown Cleveland. (Photo courtesy of Mark S. Rosentraub.)

Cavaliers and myriad other entertainment events. The Cleveland Arena, built in the 1930s with 10,000 seats, was razed in 1977, after the Cavaliers moved to Richfield.

With Mayor White's enthusiastic endorsement, the countywide referendum to build both facilities passed with support from 51.6 percent of the voters. A majority of the voters who lived in Cleveland, 56 percent, voted against the tax increase illustrating the inability of both white and black mayors to secure support for the concept from the city's voters. Support for the new ballpark and an arena to move the Cavaliers back to downtown Cleveland came from suburban residents. It took six years to secure public approval for a new ballpark and arena (Figure 7.3).[9] While the plans for the new facility were advanced by business leaders, the defeat of two previous proposals and the time it took to secure public support suggests local politics were not as firmly controlled by downtown business interests as some critics of the role of corporate leaders in urban economic development have argued.[10]

The 1990 campaign for the tax increase for the two facilities was conducted amid an implied threat from MLB that it would approve any request from the Indians to relocate if the new ballpark was not built. The Indians' ownership never said it would move the team if a new ballpark were not built. MLB's commissioner,

Fay Vincent, in testimony before Cleveland's city council declared that the team's situation satisfied the criteria the league used to approve relocation requests. The intent of his message was clear.[11] Without a new ballpark, the Indians would be supported in their efforts to join other corporations that had left Cleveland.

Voters' concerns with the deal for the new facilities that produced their relatively modest levels of support was a result of four concerns, none of which dealt with opposition to an investment by the public to restore confidence in the region and city's future. Strong action to improve the image of and confidence in the region was supported. The concerns raised during the campaign were nothing if not prescient. First, firm agreements with both teams regarding the cost of the facilities and the teams' contributions and financial responsibilities did not exist. As a result, the public sector's actual financial responsibility or investment was unclear. Second, leases had not been negotiated with either team meaning there was no agreement regarding responsibilities for ongoing and long-term maintenance expenses. Third, voters were not presented with a plan that explained how the sports facilities would be included in any revitalization effort. Fourth, neither team was asked to make any commitment for real estate development adjacent to the facilities to complement or advance the revitalization effort.

D. Large Subsidies and the Dispersion of Assets

Asking voters to approve a tax increase before leases, firm construction estimates, and a memorandum of understanding regarding responsibilities for maintenance existed gave the team owners substantial negotiating advantages when it came time to create leases and construction agreements. With a tax increase approved by voters, elected officials had to deliver a deal with the teams or face public criticism for campaigning to raise taxes and then being unable to secure the agreements necessary to retain and attract the teams. The approach taken—get the money and then finalize the plans—actually destroyed any political leverage the public sector had to secure larger investments from the teams or any commitment from them for related real estate development. Convincing reluctant voters to support tax increases for sports facilities is usually easier when there is a firm commitment from the teams to pay designated amounts of money. Voters had already rejected two different proposals for new taxes to pay for sports facilities. Those actions created an environment in which leaders could have asked for commitments from the teams to reduce voters' opposition to higher taxes. With voter approval secured, the owners could strive to reduce their financial responsibilities and force elected and other community leaders to endure any criticism for having campaigned to raise taxes and then failing to get the teams to commit to Cleveland. The teams used this bargaining strength to secure extraordinary lease arrangements and minimize their financial responsibilities for capital and operating costs.[12]

The excessive subsidies did not end with the sports facilities. Cleveland also added big-ticket museums to its quest to create a new image and those were also heavily subsidized. In 1983, music company executives in New York City created The Rock and Roll Hall of Fame and chose its first members even before a home for the Hall was identified. After considering New York and Memphis as possible locations, Cleveland was selected. Cleveland's link to the history and evolution of rock and roll was limited to legendary disc jockey Alan Freed who popularized the term "rock and roll" to describe the new, emerging music style. Freed also organized numerous rock and roll concerts that provided a showcase for emerging performers at several Midwest venues. Cleveland's selection, however, was not related to this limited or loose connection to rock and roll's history, but to the public sector's willingness to provide $65 million in tax money to build the new hall of fame.

The Hall of Fame's leadership had recruited renowned architect I. M. Pei to design the facility and had expended a great deal of time to convince him to accept the commission. Pei was not attracted to any of the more central locations for the Hall. He preferred a more dramatic and dynamic location for his forthcoming masterpiece and chose a site on the shores of Lake Erie at the northern most part of the downtown area. The spectacular building is, as a result, distant from the center of downtown and contributed to the dispersed nature of the buildings that anchored the revitalization effort. After several delays, construction was begun in 1993 and the Rock and Roll Hall of Fame and Museum opened in 1995. A science museum located nearby opened in 1996 establishing for downtown Cleveland a "minimuseum" area on what was initially described as America's "north coast." It too was paid for by the public sector.

The new ballpark and arena opened in 1994 and, with construction of the Rock and Roll Hall of Fame and Museum and the Science Center underway, there was some hope that the revitalization effort might be enhancing confidence in the city and region's future. That feeling lasted only for a short period of time. In 1995, Cleveland and the region were traumatized when Art Modell, owner of the Cleveland Browns, announced he was moving the team (a Cleveland icon) to Baltimore. Modell was frustrated by the deals given the Indians and Cavaliers while his team continued to play in a stadium built in the early 1930s and commonly referred to as "the mistake by the lake." In contrast, Maryland and Baltimore agreed to build a new stadium for the Browns and give the team control of most if not all revenues without asking Modell to accept any financial responsibilities for building the new facility.

Losing the Browns was as traumatic for Cleveland as the loss of the Dodgers for Brooklyn. Leadership in the stunned city and region mobilized support and the NFL decided to create a new Cleveland Browns franchise *if* a new stadium was ready for the 1999 season. To meet this condition, Cleveland would need to use the foundations of the existing facility, meaning the new stadium would also be on the northern edge of the downtown area (adjacent to the Science Center and the Rock and Roll Hall of Fame and Museum). This location, distant from the other sports facilities, also used very valuable lakefront property, reducing the public's access and opportunities to use this asset. Assembling land for a stadium located closer to the two other sports facilities would have taken too long to satisfy the NFL's schedule. It was also possible that environmental and construction challenges at other sites would have substantially increased the cost for the stadium at a more central location. Cleveland accepted the NFL's condition and Cuyahoga County taxpayers assumed responsibility for more than 70 percent of the cost of building the new stadium in exchange for a new franchise that would retain the name and colors of the beloved Browns.

Cleveland's "Hail Mary" pass to revitalize its downtown, change its image, and instill confidence in the city and region's future included:

1. Building three new sports facilities (Figure 7.3)
2. Restoration of the five theaters that constitute Playhouse Square
3. Opening two retail venues/shopping centers
4. Building The Rock and Roll Hall of Fame and Museum
5. Building the Science Center and IMAX Theater
6. Building several new commercial office towers, each supported with property tax abatements

The next section focuses on what was achieved from this investment in an image of confidence in the future.

IV. Results of Cleveland's "Hail Mary" Pass

The major goal for the big-ticket investments was to create sufficient confidence in Cleveland's future that private investments in commercial and residential developments would follow as people returned to the downtown area for entertainment. In "jump starting" private investment in the city, it was also hoped that corporations would retain the jobs located in the downtown area and perhaps other firms would also consider expanding or locating in Cleveland. Finally, if the big-ticket items were successful in building confidence in the city perhaps downtown Cleveland could become a residential neighborhood and offer some of the amenities and housing options readily available in thriving areas. It is important to underscore that it is not possible to see if a single amenity or even if the combined effect of all the new facilities encouraged private investments. One could ask developers how important the public's investments were for creating confidence and attracting them to projects in the downtown area, but the private sector has a clear incentive to suggest that without the public sector's activities it would not have invested its own money. Indicating that public subsidies for big-ticket items was critical for building confidence would establish an environment where developers could advocate for additional support to reduce their risks for each and every project. In looking at investment patterns, job location changes, and residential growth before and after the building of the big-ticket items, any improvements must be described as correlated with, but not caused by, the presence of the new amenities. Insight can be gained, however, from a comparison of private sector investment levels, job locations, and residential choices prior to and after the building of the sports and entertainment venues, but causality cannot be statistically inferred as numerous other macro- and micro-economic factors also affect outcomes.[13]

A. *Private Investment Levels in Cleveland:*
Nonresidential Projects

A view of private sector investments in Cleveland was produced through an analysis of construction data collected by the FW Dodge Corporation. This firm tabulates construction costs for all nonresidential projects. Data for Cleveland and Cuyahoga County were available for the years 1994 through 2003. This information was analyzed at the zip code and neighborhood level so that figures for downtown Cleveland could be tabulated. To compare outcomes in the years after many of the big-ticket items were built with those figures for the 1980s, information was collected from Cuyahoga County government offices in association with staff from the Greater Cleveland Partnership. This information, however, could not be classified by neighborhood or zip code area, but exists only as totals for each city. Finally, as FW Dodge data do not include residential construction, data from the Cuyahoga County tax files were used to tabulate private sector investment in residential properties.

Between 1994 and 2003, there was a total of $3.6 billion in construction activity in nonresidential projects throughout Cleveland and $632.3 million in construction activity in the downtown area. This period corresponds to the initiation and completion of several of the sports and cultural amenities. The year-by-year totals for the downtown area and Cleveland, as well as the value of the projects in constant dollars are contained in Table 7.2. Construction figures for 1980 through 1989—the years immediately before the investment in several big-ticket amenities—are also tabulated.

Comparisons across time periods are always difficult in that national and regional economic conditions vary and contribute to any observed differences. Further, there are myriad tangible and intangible factors that influence investor confidence. In the absence of any binding agreements that firms would make specific investments if a particular public/private partnership was created, it is not possible to attribute any observed outcomes to the building of a particular asset.

With these caveats in mind, from 1980 to 1989 (a 10-year period), Cuyahoga County reported that private construction projects in the city of Cleveland had a value of slightly more than $1 billion. When these figures are converted to 2004 dollars, the value of the construction projects is $1.85 billion. For the period 1995 through 2003 (a nine-year period), the present value of the nonresidential

Table 7.2 Construction Costs for All Nonresidential Projects in Cleveland and Downtown Cleveland (2004 dollars)

Year	Yearly Construction Costs		Construction Costs (2004 Dollars)	
	Downtown	Cleveland	Downtown	Cleveland
1995	38,923,393	118,108,363	47,961,493	145,533,392
1996	82,521,064	149,483,906	98,982,520	179,303,234
1997	46,646,432	156,259,076	54,298,675	181,893,029
1998	90,953,454	2,359,125,487	104,236,260	2,703,651,239
1999	184,384,537	306,025,561	207,839,417	344,953,949
2000	64,695,993	120,163,442	72,925,733	135,448,992
2001	60,159,490	169,771,013	63,629,569	179,563,630
2002	55,949,990	120,443,538	58,508,968	125,952,249
2003	8,051,997	115,529,928	8,207,099	117,755,326
Total	632,286,350	3,616,060,311	716,589,734	4,114,055,040
1980–1989	Not Available	1,006,959,500	Not Available	1,842,735,885

Sources: Data from 1995 through 2003 from the FW Dodge Corporation. With permission. Data from 1980 to 1989 from Cuyahoga County public records and reports collected and maintained by Greater Cleveland Partnership.

construction projects was $4.1 billion or more than twice the figure for the 1980s. In downtown Cleveland alone, an area marked by the loss of many businesses in the 1980s, $717 million (in 2004 dollars) was spent for new construction (see Table 7.2).

B. Private Investment in Residential Properties

From 1980 to 1989, Cuyahoga County records indicate that $54.8 million was invested in residential properties in Cleveland; the value of these expenditures in 2004 dollars was $100.3 million. From 1990 through 2002, almost four times as much was invested in residential real estate in Cleveland (Table 7.3). Baade, among others, has noted that some large civic projects, such as sports facilities, have no positive effects on regional economic development.[14] These same facilities, however, can move economic activity within a region, and in many instances that is an important policy objective. The movement of economic activity to the center city can improve the tax base of that community and reduce sprawl by increasing

**Table 7.3   Construction Costs for Residential Projects
in Cleveland, Property Tax Abatements Received**

Years	Annual Construction Cost	Construction Cost (2004 Dollars)
1980–1989	$ 54,827,800	$ 100,334,874
1990	10,880,991	15,817,579
1991	7,574,744	10,422,307
1992	6,968,739	9,345,478
1993	14,592,407	18,951,710
1994	26,992,227	34,192,616
1995	24,257,806	29,890,523
1996	32,109,205	38,514,409
1997	30,389,211	35,374,493
1998	35,767,450	40,990,914
1999	40,869,604	46,068,476
2000	33,711,063	37,999,324
2001	35,278,693	37,313,615
2002	39,325,609	41,124,239
Total	**$338,717,749**	**$396,005,683**

Sources: Data from 1980 to 1989 from Cuyahoga County public
   records and reports collected and maintained by
   Greater Cleveland Partnership; data from 1990 through
   2002 from the Maxine Goodman Levin College of
   Urban Affairs, Cleveland State University.

the reuse of existing infrastructure. It is important to note after the building of a
number of big-ticket items, during a period of substantial expansion of the U.S.
economy and of a very low level of population growth in Northeast Ohio, there
was a large increase in private sector investment in both nonresidential and residential properties in Cleveland and in the downtown area. These investments, and
the tax revenues that resulted for Cleveland and its public schools, are the returns
from the public/private partnerships that were formed. In reviewing these data,
causality (that the new private sector investments are a result of the public/private
partnerships) is not implied. However, in an analysis of private sector job retention in the downtown areas of Cincinnati, Cleveland, Columbus, and Indianapolis,

it was found that Cleveland did far better than the other areas and actually had job growth despite the prevailing decentralization trends in the Midwest and the United States.[15] Those jobs in Cleveland and the resulting tax increases for the city and public school system were one of the returns from the public's investments.

The residential development that took place in Cleveland was also aided by the city's creation of a program to grant property tax abatements to owners of new homes. Cleveland's program requires owners to pay the full taxes due as a result of increments to the value of land. The program established the value of all land at 20 percent of the purchase price with the remaining portion of the home's sale price removed from the calculation of property tax liabilities for 15 years. The property tax abatement could be transferred to subsequent buyers. Many other cities in Cuyahoga County also provide tax abatements to buyers of new homes. Cleveland hoped that investment in the sports facilities and other amenities combined with a competitive abatement program would bring new residents to the city, or attract existing residents to buy a new and more expensive home in the city. Prior to the existence of the abatement program, some had observed that the virtual absence of new homes with values in excess of $150,000 forced residents seeking new and larger homes to leave Cleveland.

A report card on the performance of the property tax abatement program is contained in Table 7.4. The number of properties returning 100 percent of their value to the property tax rolls by year beginning in 2007 will produce (in constant or present value dollars) $53.8 million in new property taxes for Cleveland each year beginning in 2020. A survey of people who bought these homes found that 60 percent would have lived elsewhere if the abatements were not available.[16] This suggests that the amenities in Cleveland likely produced $21.5 in new annual property taxes with the balance of the gain attributed to the presence of the abatements and the other amenities in Cleveland (see Table 7.4).

There was also a general upswing in private sector investment activity (residential and nonresidential) in the years after the opening of the sports facilities. While the new investments took place during a time of a general expansion in the national economy, Northeast Ohio was still in the throes of the severe economic restructuring that gripped the manufacturing sector and Cleveland and Cuyahoga County were still suffering from population losses. While it is impossible to answer whether or not this level of private sector investment would have taken place if the public sector had not made its investments in the sports facilities, interviews with community leaders indicated that several believed the public sector investments were critical especially given the substantial job losses in the manufacturing sector.[17]

C. Tax Revenue Changes

The existence of the earnings tax as the largest source of revenue for Cleveland is why the city's policies and practices are focused on securing and maintaining jobs. Regional growth that involves new jobs outside of the city does not directly enhance Cleveland's fiscal situation. However, the redevelopment of downtown—with its

Table 7.4   Property Tax Revenues to Cleveland, the Cleveland Public Schools, and Cuyahoga County From Homes That Received Abatements

Year Taxed	Number	Assessed Value	Cumulative Assessed Value	New Property Taxes	Cumulative New Property Taxes
2007	65	$2,695,595	$2,695,595	$170,410	$170,410
2008	132	5,980,835	8,676,430	374,460	544,870
2009	96	4,038,895	12,715,325	252,875	797,745
2010	53	2,377,340	15,092,665	148,845	946,591
2011	35	1,125,075	16,217,740	70,441	1,017,032
2012	273	10,364,935	26,582,675	648,949	1,665,980
2013	237	10,218,565	36,801,240	639,784	2,305,765
2014	147	8,221,150	45,022,390	514,726	2,820,491
2015	288	17,089,450	62,111,840	1,138,714	3,959,205
2016	261	15,705,305	77,817,145	1,021,551	4,980,755
2017	270	22,937,250	100,754,395	1,602,706	6,583,462
2018	181	11,306,540	112,060,935	731,434	7,314,895
2019	481	34,615,105	146,676,040	2,270,324	9,585,220
2020	327	22,671,810	169,347,850	1,485,638	11,070,858
Total	2,846				53,763,279
Taxes paid, properties bought because of abatements					32,257,967
Taxes paid, properties probably bought without abatement					21,505,312

Source: Cuyahoga County Auditor's Office; Mikelbank, B., M. Rosentraub, and C. Post. 2009. *Residential property tax abatements and rebuilding in Cleveland, Ohio.* Unpublished paper. Cleveland: Maxine Goodman Levin College of Urban Affairs.

majority financial support from Cuyahoga County—if it contributes to job attraction and retention in Cleveland, has the potential to substantially protect and perhaps enhance revenue streams for the city. Corporations are also subject to a 2 percent tax on their earnings.

As illustrated in Figure 7.4, Cleveland enjoyed real growth in its earning tax levels from 1992 through 2000. There was a sharp decline from 2000 to 2003, and then some restored growth from 2003 through 2007. The absolute increase

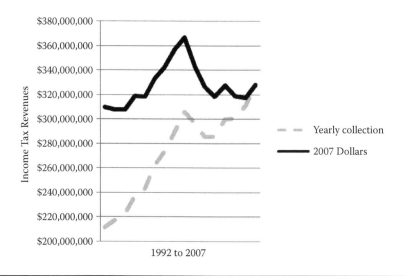

Figure 7.4 Income tax receipts for Cleveland, 1992–2007. (From City of Cleveland Comprehensive Annual Financial Report, various years.)

(from 1992 to 2007) was $116.8 million. In real (adjusted for inflation) terms, the growth was $18.3 million. Some would suggest that such a relatively small increment—a real increase of 8.7 percent—was a bit modest and hardly worth the funds expended for the sports and entertainment facilities that assisted in this growth. Others could suggest that stabilization and even a modest increase in income taxes was an impressive achievement given the population losses suffered and economic decline (loss of manufacturing jobs and the restructuring underway). Under those circumstances, the stabilization and increase of Cleveland's main source of revenue can be seen as a notable if not extraordinary accomplishment.

As should be expected given the economic restructuring taking place and outmigration, the situation regarding property tax receipts was not as favorable. Large manufacturing plants traditionally generated high levels of property taxes and as these facilities closed or were downsized revenues declined. Greater Cleveland lost more than 43 percent of its 500,000+ manufacturing jobs between 1980 and 2007[18] and the closing of plants left the city with a declining property tax base. Lastly, in those sectors of the economy that are expanding, some of the facilities (hospitals) are exempt from local property taxes. While there was an absolute increase in property taxes collected (an increase of $11.9 million), in real (adjusted for inflation) terms the city collected $14.6 million *less* in 2007 than it did in 1992. This represents a real decline of 25.6 percent. As illustrated in Figure 7.5, there has been a relatively steady decline in real (or constant dollar) property tax collections since 1992. In some years, there was an increase, but the slope of the line is clear and consistent.

The Indians, Cavaliers, and Browns were permitted to retain all the revenue generated at the ballpark, arena, and stadium, but to ensure that some tax benefits

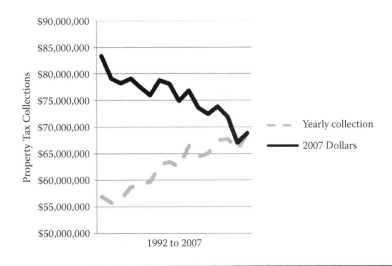

Figure 7.5 Property tax receipts for Cleveland, 1992–2007. (From City of Cleveland Comprehensive Annual Financial Report, various years.)

accrued to Cleveland to help offset the investment made by its residents through the higher taxes, the teams agreed to support the creation of an amusement tax. An 8 percent tax is applied against all tickets sold for all events held at the ballpark, the arena, and at the stadium. Economists have repeatedly underscored that ticket taxes represent foregone income for teams.[19] In the absence of an amusement tax, ticket prices do not decline. Teams simply price at the highest level the market will support. A tax does not increase the price. If the government passes a tax, it shares in the revenue. If the tax does not exist, then the team realizes additional revenue.

In 1995, Cleveland collected $7.2 million from the amusement taxes and this grew to $13.9 in 2007. In constant dollars, the increment was approximately $4.3 million. The differences from year to year reflect changes in attendance levels that are linked to the teams' performance. In the years that the Indians and Cavaliers have been in their respective playoffs, revenues rose, and when the teams had less success, revenues declined. The Browns have not played a home playoff game since their return to the NFL (Table 7.5).

D. Job Retention and Employment Changes

Another view of changes in Cleveland after the investments in the big-ticket items is provided in Table 7.6. The total payrolls of all businesses in Cleveland for the entire city and for the two largest employment centers, downtown and the University Circle area, are included in the table. University Circle is home to the Cleveland Clinic and University Hospitals, two of the region's largest employers. Both healthcare centers are also at the center of Ohio's strategic plans focused on

Table 7.5   Amusement Tax Revenue Collections

| Year | Amusement Tax Revenues | | Playoffs |
	Annual Revenues	In 2007 Dollars	
1995	$7,173,059	$9,659,529	Indians; Cavaliers
1996	7,505,426	9,838,719	Indians; Cavaliers
1997	9,977,427	12,692,843	Indians
1998	8,932,106	11,187,242	Indians; Cavaliers
1999	9,750,710	12,011,830	Indians
2000	13,249,323	15,886,629	
2001	12,067,391	13,948,829	Indians
2002	12,581,373	14,378,712	
2003	11,291,310	12,577,662	
2004	10,071,768	11,007,159	
2005	11,082,443	11,762,383	
2006	11,879,154	12,124,764	Cavaliers
2007	13,930,166	13,930,166	Indians; Cavaliers

Source: Department of Finance, City of Cleveland.

Table 7.6   **Payroll Earnings in Cleveland, 1993 and 2007 (in millions of dollars; all figures in 2007 dollars)**

| Cleveland Community | 1993 | | 2007 | | |
	Amount ($)	Percent	Amount ($)	Percent of Total	Percent of Change
Downtown	6,758	53.5	6,808	48.1	3.3
University Circle	1,211	9.6	1,988	14.1	51.9
Elsewhere in Cleveland	4,674	36.9	5,344	37.9	4.7
Total	12,643	100	14,140	100	11.8

Source: Department of Finance, City of Cleveland.

bioengineering, research into new therapies, procedures, and equipment, and new systems for the delivery of care. It is also important to look at these data in light of the population losses suffered by Cleveland and the state's overall lower economic growth rates. Payroll levels in Cleveland rose, in real terms, by almost $1.5 billion from 1993 to 2007. The concentration of payroll dollars in the downtown area grew by a modest $50 million. Most importantly, however, there was no real decline even as population levels in the city and county declined. Given the growing importance of the healthcare sector for the region, it is not surprising that the real increase in wages in the University Circle area was equal to $777 million (see Table 7.6).

V. Extra Benefits from Building Amenities: Regional Cooperation

In Cleveland as in many areas, when economic contraction and restructuring occurs, there are calls for greater regional cooperation among local governments.[20] There have been repeated claims that the failure to have higher levels of regional cooperation has contributed to the economic declines for Cleveland. Too often the countywide levels of cooperation achieved through the building of the amenities in downtown Cleveland are ignored.[21] The big-ticket projects were undertaken to maintain some degree of centrality and vibrancy for Cleveland, but were financed at the county level requiring cooperation for development from residents of 57 different cities.

Cuyahoga County, and not Cleveland, was responsible for most of the public investment in the big-ticket items. This meant that the wealthier residents of suburban cities paid the majority of the costs for the big-ticket items. Cleveland residents also saw their taxes increase. However, since there are twice as many people living in the suburbs as in the city, a majority of the burden for rebuilding downtown Cleveland is shifted to nonresidents. Cuyahoga County's main source of revenue is the property tax. Because the county's residents are far wealthier, the value of residential property in the county is also far greater, which further shifts the burden of financing the rebuilding of downtown Cleveland to nonresidents. Countywide taxing instruments were used for the public's investment in all three sports facilities, the Rock and Roll Hall of Fame and Museum ($65 million), Playhouse Square ($18.7 million), and the Tower City retail center ($7 million). What makes these investments and the tax base sharing more notable is that all of the tax revenue generated by the facilities and the income tax paid by employees and the athletes accrues to Cleveland.[22] In addition, a substantial majority of the earnings' taxes paid to Cleveland comes from commuters who work in the city, but live in one of the suburban communities.[23] The revitalization of downtown Cleveland is an unheralded example of regionalism and intergovernmental cooperation among a county's taxpayers.

VI. Amending Cleveland's Major League Loser Status: New Leases

The efforts to improve Cleveland and Cuyahoga County were not limited to attracting private sector investments after the subsidies were provided. Community leaders also sought to reduce the subsidies and successfully renegotiated the leases with the teams for their use of the ballpark and the arena. To oversee the building, maintenance, and operation of the ballpark, the arena, the related parking garages, and the two public plazas, Cleveland and Cuyahoga County created the Gateway Economic Development Corporation of Greater Cleveland (Gateway). This non-profit corporation was also responsible for ensuring that property tax payments were made. Even though the sports facilities were owned by a public nonprofit organization (Gateway), they were exclusively used to generate profit for the two teams. From the revenues it received from the rents paid by the teams, it was agreed that Gateway would pay property taxes to support the Cleveland Public Schools and hold the school district "harmless" from the tax effects of removing the land from the property tax rolls.

Five volunteer commissioners lead Gateway. Cleveland's mayor appoints two of these individuals and each of Cuyahoga County's three elected county commissioners also make an appointment to Gateway's board. The five commissioners have the authority to hire the needed professional staff (general manager and accountant) and attorneys to represent the board in its negotiations with the teams. The rent paid by the teams was to generate sufficient revenues for Gateway to meet its responsibilities to maintain the facilities, hire the needed staff, and also to pay the facilities' property taxes. To appreciate why the rental payments were not sufficient and the political environment within which the leases could be substantially renegotiated, some of the history surrounding the negotiations of the leases is required.[24]

A. Provision of Extraordinary Subsidies

Separate deals were negotiated with each team. The Indians agreed to immediately pay $20 million for the ballpark's construction and to make annual payments of $2.9 million until the construction bonds were retired. These funds were to be used to reduce the public sector's financial responsibilities for constructing the ballpark. The present value of this commitment is $31 million. It was originally anticipated that the ballpark could be built for approximately $130 million, but the total cost was $193 million, and the public sector was responsible for all of the additional costs. The Indians paid 26.4 percent of the capital cost of the new ballpark.

The Cavaliers agreed to pay 27.5 percent of their annual revenue from the leasing of suites and 48 percent of the revenue from the sale of club seats for the new arena. The Cavaliers also provided an "up front" payment of $4 million, which was to be credited against their required annual payments. These annual payments were to be their contribution toward the construction cost of the arena. Originally expected to cost $75 million, the arena's price tag ended up being $154 million. The public sector was also responsible for this cost overrun. Voters were told that the arena and ballpark would cost approximately $200 million. The final price for both facilities was 71 percent more ($142 million) than the voters were told to expect and the public sector was responsible for paying for all of the extra costs. These extraordinary cost overruns would plague local politics and issues involving the facilities for years. With the tax on alcohol and tobacco sales unable to retire the debt associated with a combined capital cost of more than $340 million, Cuyahoga County had to rely on property tax receipts to cover the extra costs. In essence, this meant that while voters opposed a property tax for a domed stadium in 1984, in the end, property tax revenues collected by the county had to be used to finance part of the cost for building the ballpark and arena.

Both teams also agreed to pay rent based on attendance and those were to be the funds that Gateway used to meet all of its financial responsibilities. When both facilities opened, Gateway had enough revenue to meet its obligations. Capacity crowds attended 454 consecutive games played by the Indians. By 2002, attendance dropped to 2.6 million and then to 1.7 million in 2003. With the Indians' winning the division in 2007, attendance rose to 2.3 million, but in 2008 fell to less than 2.2 million. Gateway now had less money to meet its obligations.

The situation with the Cavaliers was quite different and even contentious. The Cavaliers embarked on a strategy of changing several things at the arena and then arguing that their investments were tantamount to rental payments and should be subtracted from any required fees. Their calculations led them to conclude that the public sector owed them several million dollars. The team also took the position that they had the unilateral right to make the changes they deemed necessary and then to deduct these expenses from any required rent payments. The expenses they incurred were so high that they annually presented the public sector with a statement indicating the balance owed to them. As a result, the Cavaliers never paid rent for use of the arena and only made the required capital construction payments. Gateway soon did not have enough money to meet its expenses. Initially the teams wanted the public sector to simply transfer funds from their budgets to meet Gateway's responsibilities. Gateway's board refused to ask either the county or city for more money especially given the public sector's responsibility for 100 percent of the cost overruns associated with both facilities.

Negotiations to modify the leases to ensure that Gateway's financial responsibilities could be met and the facilities maintained were initiated. However, the situation was quite different as new owners were now involved. The original lease for the Indians and the deal for the building of the ballpark were negotiated with Richard Jacobs. A resident of the Greater Cleveland area and an extremely wealthy developer and businessman, Jacobs purchased the team in 1986. George and Gordon Gund owned the Cleveland Cavaliers when the new arena was built and the original lease created. When the Cavaliers began play in 1970, they used the aging Cleveland

Arena. Built in 1937 and located just east of the downtown area, the facility hosted more than 300 events each year during the late 1940s and 1950s. With Cleveland's population declining, team owner Nick Mileti built a new arena in suburban Richfield, 25 miles south of Cleveland and in the middle of the Cleveland–Akron region. The Richfield Coliseum opened in 1974 and was among the first to contain luxury suites, but these premium seats were at the top of the seating bowl or above all the seats in the arena, providing a less than intimate view of games and events. Without any public transit options, fans were forced to pay for parking along with their tickets. The Cavaliers and The Richfield Coliseum were sold in 1980 to Ted Stepien—another long-term resident of the region—and three years later he sold the team and the arena to George and Gordon Gund. Under the Gunds' tenure, the Cavaliers enjoyed some of their most notable success. Despite the remote location from Cleveland, traffic problems created by the narrow county roads around the facility, and the cost of parking, capacity crowds frequented The Coliseum.

Cleveland and Cuyahoga County faced an important challenge in their efforts to attract the Cavaliers back to downtown Cleveland. The Cavaliers were drawing sellout crowds generating robust parking and other revenues for the Gunds. The Cavaliers' owners made it appear that they were quite content to remain at their suburban location at the geographic center of the region especially given current demographic trends. What Cleveland's leadership may not have appreciated was that the Richfield Coliseum had become economically obsolete. As teams grew more reliant on luxury seating, the coliseum had too few of the amenities that would allow the team to charge the higher prices other teams could in their in newer facilities. The Cavaliers were in need of a new arena and might have been more flexible in their negotiations if Cleveland and Cuyahoga County had threatened to cancel construction of the arena. But with Cleveland's leadership worried about the need to instill confidence in the future, the Cavaliers were able to secure a very favorable lease.[25]

B. New Owners, New Possibilities

While Richard Jacobs and the Gunds exploited the advantages of their negotiating positions, the new owners of the franchises were more concerned with maintaining and advancing the image of both teams as they were locked into long-term leases and unable to relocate. The new ownership was also hard-pressed to make a case for more public subsidies given the substantial profits made by Richard Jacobs and the Gund brothers when they sold their teams.

The Indians were sold to Larry Dolan (and several Dolan family trusts). Charles Dolan, Larry's brother, founded HBO and also owns Cablevision in New York City, Madison Square Garden, and the Knicks and Rangers. The Dolan family is from the Greater Cleveland area and the brothers were interested in buying an Ohio-based sports franchise. After making an unsuccessful effort to purchase the Cincinnati Reds, the Dolans turned their attention to the Indians when Jacobs made it clear he was interested in selling the team.

Jacobs had positioned the Indians for sale through the building of a championship franchise. In the years after acquiring the team, Jacobs increased the team's payroll, but the fiscal losses mounted due to playing in the antiquated Municipal Stadium (opened in 1931). In 1992, with a new facility on the horizon, Jacobs slashed the payroll making strategic investments in new and younger players. Then, with the new revenue streams from the ballpark available in 1994, the team's payroll grew by 20 percent or more each year (except 1998) and in some years the increase was more than 50 percent. The Indians responded by winning their division in each year from 1995 through 1999. The team also made the playoffs in 2000 and won its division in 2001, the two seasons immediately after the Dolans assumed control (Table 7.7).

How did this strategy position the team for sale? Revenues were at record levels during this period as each game was sold out and the team's popularity was at an all-time high. The new ballpark offered many new revenue streams (luxury seating, state-of-the art retail facilities, electronic displays), and Jacobs could demonstrate the team's revenue potential to any prospective owner. It was also a good time to sell the team. The players who gave the Indians their winning series were becoming more expensive and getting older (less productive). A decline in performance was likely for some, and retaining others was going to cost quite a bit of money. Jacobs found the Dolans to be very interested buyers and sold the franchise for $323 million.

Richard Jacobs acquired the team for $35.5 million in 1986 and assumed $12 million of the team's debt for a total purchase price of $47.5 million. That investment in 1999 dollars was $74 million and with a sale price of between $320 and $323 million, the gross profit was between $246 million and $249 million. An argument could be made that the team might have had operating losses in some years before and after the move to the new ballpark, thus reducing the gross profit figure. However, it is safe to assume that Jacobs made a substantial return on his investments and enjoyed extraordinary financial benefits as a result of the level of the public sector's investment in the ballpark. Simply put, that investment reduced his costs in securing the new revenue streams that increased the value and profitability of the team. General knowledge of the profitable return also made it politically dangerous to argue for additional subsidies.

The Gund brothers bought the Cavaliers and The Richfield Coliseum (together with Ted Stepien's advertising business and a cable television station) for $20 million in 1983. However, this was not their only cost. Prior to selling the team, Ted Stepien had traded away or sold the team's first-round draft picks for successive years and the NBA allowed the Gunds to buy those rights back from other teams. The value of the advertising business and the cable station are unknown, but for a conservative estimate of the profit made by the Gunds when they sold the team, the value of those assets can be placed at zero. A generous estimate of the cost to reacquire the draft picks is $2 million.

In 2005, the Gunds sold the Cavaliers to Dan Gilbert for $375 million. In 2005 dollars, their initial investment was $42.9 leaving a gross profit of $332.1 million.

**Table 7.7   The Cleveland Indians' Payrolls and Winning
Percentages: 1988–2008**

Season	Opening Day Payroll	In 2008 Dollars	Percent Change	Winning Percentage
2008	$78,970,066	$78,970,066	22.8	
2007	$61,673,267	$64,324,242	7.8	**.593**
2006	$56,031,500	$59,648,258	29.8	.481
2005	$41,502,500	$45,942,201	17.4	.574
2004	$34,319,300	$39,118,813	−30.7	.494
2003	$48,584,834	$56,446,111	−40.0	.420
2002	$78,909,449	$94,058,637	−15.8	.457
2001	$92,660,001	$111,710,601	16.8	**.562**
2000	$76,508,334	$95,680,742	0.8	.566
1999	$73,857,962	$94,896,018	23.1	**.599**
1998	$59,033,499	$77,116,161	7.4	**.549**
1997	$54,130,232	$71,822,074	15.9	**.534**
1996	$45,317,914	$61,959,920	25.4	**.615**
1995	$35,185,500	$49,418,889	20.1	**.694**
1994	$28,490,167	$41,137,307	76.8	.584
1993	$15,717,667	$23,267,879	84.8	.469
1992	$8,236,166	$12,589,824	−56.1	.469
1991	$18,270,000	$28,653,767	14.1	.352
1990	$15,152,000	$25,106,650	49.3	.475
1989	$8,928,500	$16,813,616	17.8	.451
1988	$7,819,500	$14,267,039		.481

Note: Bold indicates seasons in which a division championship
was won. The Indians also won the American League pennant, but lost the 1995 (Atlanta) and 1997 (Florida) World
Series.

Source: Salary figures adapted from *USA Today*'s database.

There were likely other expenses and losses incurred by the Gunds, but even if those had a 2005 value of $25 million or $50 million, the profit levels produced for them by the public sector's subsidies were clearly quite robust. This is not to suggest that other factors including the desire to own a team did not also contribute to the price Dan Gilbert was willing to pay. At the same time, however, the team's value would have been dramatically lower if the Gund brothers paid for the building of a new arena or a larger portion of the facility's costs. On a very positive note, the Gunds did bring respectability back to the franchise in the 1980s when the team regularly competed for the conference's championship. That was quite a reversal from the team's performance under previous owners. However, in the years immediately before the sale, the team again faltered and the Gund brothers' most significant achievement might well have been winning the draft rights to LeBron James. The marquee value and talent of this one player not only carried the team to the NBA Finals, but has elevated demand for tickets and team paraphernalia. Again, the substantial return earned by the Gunds made it politically difficult to ask the public sector for more money to maintain the facilities.

After purchasing the Indians and Cavaliers, both of the new owners made substantial improvements to the ballpark and arena and did so without any financial contributions from the public sector. Through the 2007–2008 season, Dan Gilbert spent slightly more than $31 million to enhance the arena.[26] The Dolan family has spent $8.5 million for a new scoreboard and other electronic displays. The Cavaliers have also spent $20 million for a new practice facility to ensure that the team has the assets to attract and retain the best players in an effort to build and maintain a championship-caliber franchise. Both of the new owners were also very willing to discuss Gateway's needs and resolve its financial crisis.

C. New Leases for the Ballpark and Arena

After lengthy negotiations and exchanges of proposals and ideas (and implied public positions that could be taken if the matter was not resolved), the teams agreed to assume responsibility for all maintenance of the arena and ballpark for projects that cost $500,000 or less. Projects could not be amalgamated to subvert the $500,000 cap. In other words, as with repairing the carpet in the luxury seat areas, each suite was an independent project, as was any enhancement to different parts of the club seating area or throughout the ballpark. When the speakers were to be replaced throughout the ballpark (there are more than 150 individual speakers in the facility), each was treated as a separate project requiring the Indians to assume responsibility for the entire cost (estimated at $2.6 million). Further, if the teams wanted to make any new capital investments in the facilities, they had to assume full responsibility for those expenses. The teams also agreed to guarantee that Gateway had sufficient funds to pay the taxes due and to support the corporation's administrative budget.

In turn, Gateway agreed that its annual budget would be subject to review by the teams, but that its responsibilities for ensuring that the facilities are maintained was something that would be kept independent of the teams' leadership. In addition to the capital investments made by the teams in the facilities, this agreement raised their annual costs or contributions to the facilities by more than $2 million (for each team). In essence, the public sector is left with financial responsibility for the roof of the arena, the air-conditioning and heating system in the arena, the arena's ice-making system, and the foundation and steel supports for both facilities.

While these new arrangements substantially reduced the public sector's exposure, the teams wanted something of value in exchange for their assumption of the financial costs of maintaining the facilities. Each team was given authority to place more advertising on the outside of the ballpark and arena, and the authority to lease advertising on additional spaces inside each facility. The limits placed on advertising in the original leases were eliminated in exchange for a new agreement regarding substantially increased annual responsibilities for maintenance and operation of the facilities and the surrounding property (concrete repairs, for example, to the areas adjacent to the facilities and for all security expenses related to new requirements established by the leagues in the aftermath of 9/11).

One issue lingered involving the Cavaliers that Gateway's leadership wanted to resolve. Prior to selling the team, the Gund brothers had their administrative staff continue to record all of the expenses the team incurred to improve the facility. The brothers believed these were construction expenses that were the public sector's responsibility. Rather than challenge the accounting, it was agreed with the new owner that these expenses could be counted toward any excess rental income that needed to be offset (if attendance exceeded 1.6 million people at all events held in the arena) during the term of the team's lease. However, at the end of the lease period, the debt would be erased and the public sector would have no responsibility to make any payments to the Cavaliers or their owner. Since the Cavaliers had also agreed to pay for all of the needed maintenance at the arena (excluding the roof and the machine that makes ice for hockey and other events), there was little need to press the issue of extra rental payments for higher attendance levels and to let any possible liabilities for the team be offset by the accrued list of expenses prepared by the previous owners.

The new lease arrangements and the responsibilities assumed by the teams have saved the public sector millions of dollars. The teams are now responsible for annual maintenance expenses that currently exceed $4 million each year.[27] The teams also accepted all financial responsibility for the improvements made that make sure the ballpark and arena continue to be considered state-of-the-art. By accepting responsibility for the annual maintenance of the facilities and complete responsibility for the property taxes and Gateway's administrative costs, the team owners accepted the challenge of raising the revenues needed to meet these expenses and reduce the burden on Cuyahoga County's taxpayers.

VII. Business Leaders and Downtown and Community Development

Before summarizing the results from the amenities constructed in downtown Cleveland, the building of these assets permits a brief review of the activities of the business leaders recruited by Mayor George Voinovich to help him reform the city after his election in 1978. These leaders created Cleveland Tomorrow to sustain their work and contributions. In later years, Cleveland Tomorrow would merge with two other organizations to form the Greater Cleveland Partnership (GCP). GCP is now the conduit for the business community's work with Cleveland and the Cleveland Public Schools. Cleveland Tomorrow and GCP assumed the lead roles in championing the use of public money for several of the big-ticket items. Were these activities typical of those feared by many social scientists?[28] Or, did business leaders also orchestrate a wide-ranging set of activities that included community development projects as well as countywide financing schemes to stabilize Cleveland?

Voinovich clearly wanted to link corporate leaders to Cleveland's future. He made their participation a condition of his candidacy. He only agreed to stand for election as mayor if the corporate community would agree to reengage and help improve the operations of the city. He also wanted the corporate leaders to be partners in the rebuilding of Cleveland. Cleveland in 1980 lacked a group of business leaders committed and involved with civic affairs as many had effectively disengaged as a result of the conflicts with Dennis Kucinich. Hanson, Wolman, and Connolly concluded that the detachment was a product of the staggering problems Cleveland faced including huge population losses, racial tensions, a deteriorating school system, the staggering loss of manufacturing jobs, and the "famed fire on the Cuyahoga River."[29] There was not only no engaged business leaders, but in the aftermath of the Kucinich administration, substantial disinterest and a desire to distance businesses from Cleveland's civic affairs. Several corporations had relocated to the suburbs and their leaders were all too eager to turn away from the complex problems Cleveland faced. In the midst of this chaotic situation—population declines, businesses leaving for the suburbs or other regions, and a destructive relationship between the private sector and the Kucinich administration—a small group of leaders from some of Cleveland's remaining large corporations convinced Voinovich to run for mayor. Then, fulfilling their commitment to him, these same leaders convinced other business executives to get reengaged and help the new administration rebuild Cleveland.

A team of local business executives was recruited to review the city's operations and made more than 700 recommendations and several hundred were implemented by the new mayor's administration.[30] Eight business executives honored the commitment to Mayor Voinovich to lead the reengagement of the business community sector, and this group called themselves the Cleveland Tomorrow Project Committee. It would become Cleveland Tomorrow and membership was limited to the city's leading corporate executive officers. This was not a group to represent the business community, but "was to provide a forum where the CEOs of the major companies can come together to discuss what they see as the critical issues and try to develop a focused agenda for action."[31] Projects that would affect the city and region's economy were chosen and for each there had to be a champion. The champion was a CEO who would agree to lead the effort. A venture capital fund was created, as was an organization to improve management–labor relations.[32]

To counter the severe contractions in the manufacturing sector, an advanced manufacturing program was also created. Each of the new organizations was designed to increase employment opportunities and advance the local and regional economy. Cleveland Tomorrow had three objectives: (1) make manufacturing competitive, (2) foster the creation of new companies, and (3) assist in rebuilding the city center.[33] These objectives did not conflict with any community goals. Cleveland Tomorrow then worked with local foundations to create Neighborhood Progress, Incorporated (NPI). NPI worked with community development corporations to rehabilitate existing homes and build new ones in Cleveland where the housing stock in several neighborhoods was rapidly deteriorating and abandoned houses were becoming commonplace. Cleveland Tomorrow led the effort to raise $50 million to be used to help finance housing and retail development projects in the city's neighborhoods. Cleveland Tomorrow also worked to convince ShoreBank to open offices in Cleveland. ShoreBank, which was founded in Chicago, is a commercial bank committed to community development and now has offices in Cleveland and Detroit. In Cleveland, the bank has assumed a leadership role in rebuilding neighborhoods and funding new residential programs in several inner city neighborhoods. Cleveland Tomorrow's (and its successor organization's) success in securing new market tax credits has also led to the building of new retail centers in neighborhoods. In some neighborhoods, there were few if any retail outlets as many stores closed after the riots and entrepreneurs preferred more suburban locations. Cleveland Tomorrow's decision to expand its focus to include redevelopment of inner city neighborhoods has led to the building of several shopping centers and new apartments and houses in the areas that were destroyed by the riots in the 1960s and adversely impacted by the outmigration. More recently Cleveland Tomorrow's successor organization, the GCP, has led the redevelopment of an arts district in another inner city neighborhood.

When Cleveland Tomorrow merged with two other organizations (one formed to address minority inclusion and the region's chamber of commerce), education and workforce development became a primary focus of the GCP. Partnerships with the public schools actually began in 1986 and the corporate community's more formal involvement with education expanded as the challenges for the Cleveland Public Schools increased. The business community supported Mayor White's (1990–2002) call for the schools to be placed under the mayor's authority in an effort to increase accountability and improve performance. Corporate leaders also created and funded new programs. One of these encouraged businesses to adopt a school and have their employees serve as tutors and mentors in the schools to improve reading and math skills. Cleveland's corporate leadership also committed to the creation of an annual fund of $1 million to support new initiatives to enhance the management and administrative skills of teachers and principals in the Cleveland schools. These funds were given to the superintendent to use for any special initiatives that would enhance teaching skills or the administrative expertise of teachers, principals, or other school district employees. These discretionary funds in the cash-strapped district were sometimes the only resources available to augment professional development within the district.

The GCP also supported and financed each of the campaigns to increase local taxes to support the Cleveland Public Schools. This is notable since the largest proportion of the local taxes for the schools is paid by the businesses located in downtown Cleveland. In essence, what this meant was that the GCP was paying for a campaign to raise its own taxes. Businesses in Cleveland account for more than 60 percent of the school district's tax base. If voters agreed to support an increase in the tax rate, the largest increase would fall on the business sector. Rather than opposing any increment and claiming that higher taxes would make a Cleveland location an impediment to expansion or the attraction of new firms, the GCP funded the campaign to secure passage of every tax increase sought by the district.

Cleveland Tomorrow and its successor organization focused on job creation, the attraction and retention of businesses, enhancing the competitiveness of the manufacturing sector, and the redevelopment of downtown. To that extensive agenda was added neighborhood development and then a commitment to public education. To be sure, Cleveland Tomorrow was led by the region's major corporations, as is its successor organization. It is fair to recognize that the goals of the organization may well have served the self-interests of its members, but it also needs to be acknowledged that job retention, programs to enhance the manufacturing sector, and venture capital funds each had the potential to create needed jobs in a region losing a substantial number of employment opportunities. Cleveland's business leadership was not narrowly focused on enhancements that only created direct benefits for its members.[34]

VIII. Conclusions

Cleveland and Cuyahoga County provided extraordinarily large public subsidies for three sport facilities and two museums. The investments were made without any assurances from the private sector. Political pressure from the NFL and the trustees of the Rock and Roll Hall of Fame led to the new assets being built in locations distant from the other amenities anchoring the revitalization effort. In addition, there was no coordinated strategic plan for revitalization of the downtown area.

Why were large subsidies provided and the wishes of the teams, league, and the Rock and Roll Hall of Fame's board indulged? Simply put, decades of population losses in Cleveland and in Cuyahoga County, two devastating racial riots, and the severe economic restructuring that led to the loss of more than 200,000 jobs had shaken, if not destroyed, confidence in the city's future. Leaders believed dramatic actions were needed to create an air of optimism to attract investors and restore residents' confidence in the city's future. In the immediate aftermath of the opening of all of the facilities, there was indeed reason to conclude that Cleveland and Cuyahoga County were indeed "major league losers" when it came to the public's investments in sports and cultural amenities for revitalization.

An additional decade of experience suggests the original assessment was too harsh. Private sector investment—while not pledged or assured at the time the public sector subsidies were provided—did dramatically increase in the years after the facilities opened. Causality cannot be determined, thus it is not possible to conclude that the private sector investments were a result of the public sector subsidies of the sports facilities and museums. In addition, there were other subsidies provided including property tax abatements for new home construction. In addition, the late 1990s and the early years of the twenty-first century were "boom times" for America. Some might argue that the private sector investment would have taken place even if the public sector subsidies for sports, culture, entertainment, and new homes were not provided.

While such a claim cannot be statistically rejected, it is important to point out that in the years of substantial increments in private sector investments in real estate in downtown Cleveland and in its neighborhoods, the city continued to lose residents. At the same time that job levels were stabilized in the downtown area and earnings tax revenues increased, Cleveland and Cuyahoga County continued to shrink. This suggests that in a very demonstrable way, the public sector investments in the downtown area's future did create some confidence that the city's future was going to improve and be different from its immediate past. Faced with extraordinary declines in its population and job base, Cleveland and Cuyahoga County made a decision to invest in specific amenities to change the look and feel of the area. The subsequent investment in real estate could well lead many to observe that the subsidies were appropriate and in retrospect prudent investments that generated appropriate returns in private sector investments. The returns on these large subsidies were the large private sector investments in projects that began in 1995.

It is also important to acknowledge that the public sector was able to undo part of the subsidies through new leases with the Indians and Cavaliers. While the city and county did give the teams expanded opportunities for exterior advertising, the teams not only assumed responsibility for most of the maintenance expenses associated with both facilities, but have made their own investments to update the ballpark and arena. In total, the teams have invested more than $40 million to enhance the facilities. The new lease arrangements now make the teams responsible for the facilities except for major structural items.

The outcome for Cleveland—in the absence of assurances and commitments—does not mean that other cities should follow in their footsteps and enter into deals without substantial private sector assurances and investments. There are cities that may find themselves in a similar position where there is crisis of confidence in the future as a result of population and job losses. In that regard, there is good news from Cleveland's experiences. Building on its assets and making important commitments in sports, culture, and the arts did lead to new and far higher levels of private investment in real estate projects. This outcome suggests that redevelopment efforts, which are associated with sports, do have a potential for elevating private sector investments.[35]

The positive outcomes for Cleveland, which include (1) new leases with the Indians and Cavaliers that eliminated ongoing subsidies to the teams, (2) substantial commitments from the Indians and Cavaliers to invest in the ballpark and arena without any public funds involved in the enhancements, and (3) higher levels of private sector investments in revitalization after the extensive subsidies to raise confidence in Cleveland's future, do not obscure two distracting negative outcomes. First, the original subsidies, even understanding the need to generate confidence in Cleveland's future, created extraordinary profits for the owners of the Cavaliers and Indians. These profits were a direct result of the public sector's assumption of a large portion of the cost to build the new facilities. Far more aggressive negotiations by the public sector should have established a cap on these profits given the subsidies provided. Second, and, more importantly, despite clear success in attracting private sector capital to help revitalize downtown and other parts of the city and county, the population outflow has not ended. Indeed, Cleveland and Cuyahoga County continue to lose residents creating the possibility that the public sector cannot win or create the kind of change desired (higher family incomes and stable or expanding population bases) from success with its big-ticket investments. Critics may well still bristle at the notion that the big-ticket strategy had any level of success. If success is measured by stronger levels of private sector investment, a stabilized level of jobs in the downtown area, and improving earnings' tax revenues at a time when the city continued to lose residents (as compared to outcomes prior to the big-ticket strategy), then it is appropriate to recognize some level of success was achieved. Disappointment reigns in that even becoming a Major League Winner from its sports, entertainment, and downtown development strategy at some levels still left Cleveland and Cuyahoga County's residents and leaders scrambling for ideas to reverse population declines. It may well be possible that an amenity policy—even when successful—is not sufficient to reverse population trends and that cities and regions cannot win when they are losing residents, jobs, and wealth.

Finally, Cleveland's story also sheds important light on the role of business leaders in redevelopment efforts. While a region's corporate community may be initially focused on big-ticket items, they are not adverse to more neighborhood-based initiatives. The evidence from Cleveland's experiences suggest that business leadership groups clearly understand the need for and supports initiatives to enhance public education systems and the quality of life in inner-city neighborhoods. Few if any of the new retail centers in Cleveland's inner-city neighborhoods would exist without the funding provided by Cleveland Tomorrow and then the GCP. The GCP has also provided some level of fiscal flexibility for the superintendent of the Cleveland Public Schools while also financing all of the campaigns to raise public support for public education. More recently, downtown businesses raised their own taxes to create a Business Improvement District (BID) and new programs for the homeless. While critics might still argue that the capitalized value of the subsidies for the sports and entertainment facilities exceeds these commitments, it is also true that the suburban areas and their wealthier residents and the business community pay a far larger proportion of the taxes used to build the amenities. At a minimum, then, some of the negative images conveyed about the motives and objectives of the corporate community must be amended based on the work of Cleveland Tomorrow and the GCP. Their work should encourage other cities to engage their business communities in downtown and neighborhood revitalization efforts.

Endnotes

1. Lackritz, M. E. 1968. *The Hough riots of 1966*. Cleveland: Regional Church Planning Office.
2. Hanson, R. H., H. Wolman, and D. Connolly. 2006. *Finding a new voice for corporate leaders in a changed urban world: The Greater Cleveland Partnership*. Washington, D.C: The Brookings Institution Metropolitan Policy Program.
3. In September 2008, the Greater Jewish Federation, citing the need to be located closer to the Jewish community, announced that its primary headquarters building also would be located in Beachwood (one of the area's eastern suburbs). This action removed the last remaining Jewish facility from the city of Cleveland, as the last remaining congregation had already announced its intention to also relocate to the suburbs.
4. Austrian, Z. 2008. *Manufacturing brief*. Center for Economic Development, Maxine Goodman Levin College of Urban Policy and Public Administration, Cleveland State University, Cleveland, Ohio.
5. Cleveland's mayors served two-year terms at this point in history. There was a failed recall movement to remove Mayor Kucinich. The term of office was changed to four years during his successor's tenure.
6. Regime is a term Professor Clarence Stone uses to describe the groups of business leaders, elected officials, and executives from nonprofit organizations that meet to discuss and advance a region's economic future. Many social scientist have long noted the role of elites in shaping policy. Professor Stone's use of the term *regime* described situations where the same sets of actors participated in decisions impacting a region's development across a prolonged period of time. The importance of these organizations and their role in building sports facilities, museums, and other amenities was discussed in Chapter 2. That discussion also highlighted the concerns expressed by some that elites might ignore community needs while steering public funds into big-ticket items. Other researchers have noted that while elites and regimes are attracted to large-scale projects, they also led community development efforts. In this chapter and the next,

the activities of regimes in Cleveland and Reading are analyzed to provide insight into how these groups led efforts to build large-scale facilities while also funding community development efforts.

7. Position restated in discussion and presentation by now U.S. Senator George Voinovich in interviews and presentations, September 2008, in his Washington office.

8. Hanson, Wolman, and Connolly. *Finding a new voice for corporate leaders in a changed urban world.*

9. Stoffel, J. 1990. New sports complex for Cleveland. *The New York Times,* June 13: http://www.nytimes.com/1990/06/13/business/real-estate-new-sports-complex-for-cleveland.html (accessed April 27, 2009).

10. Squires, G. 1989. ed. *Unequal partnerships: Political economy of urban redevelopment in postwar America.* New Brunswick, NJ: Rutgers University Press.

11. Rosentraub, M. S. 1997a. *Major league losers: The real cost of sports and who's paying for it.* New York: Basic Books.

12. Ibid.

13. The limitations inherent in using even complex regression models to isolate the effects of amenity package investments on economic development are discussed in Rosentraub, M. S. 2006. The local context of a sports stategy for economic development. *Economic Development Quarterly* 20 (3): 278–291; and Rosentraub, M. S. and M. Jun. 2009.

14. See, for example, Baade, R. A. 1996. Professional sports as catalysts for metropolitan economic development. *Journal of Urban Affairs* 18 (1): 1–17; see also Noll, R. G. and A. Zimbalist. 1997. Build the stadium—create the jobs! In *Sports, jobs, and taxes: The economic impact of sports teams and stadiums,* ed. R. G. Noll and A. Zimbalist, 1–54. Washington, D.C.: The Brookings Institution.

15. Austrian, Z. and M. S. Rosentraub. 2002. Cities, sports and economic change: a retrospective assessment. *Journal of Urban Affairs* 24 (5): 549–565.

16. Mikelbank, B., M. Rosentraub, and C. Post. 2008. Residential property tax abatements and rebuilding in Cleveland, Ohio. Unpublished paper. Cleveland: Maxine Goodman Levin College of Urban Affairs.

17. Business leaders that would each be described as members of Cleveland's regime underscored the importance of the public investments in making people think there was a future for the downtown area. While it could easily be argued many of them or their companies benefitted from the presence of the sports and entertainment facilities, they would respond that as national companies they are expanding elsewhere and needed reasons to convince their boards and shareholders that continued investments and presence in downtown Cleveland were in the company's best interests. Exchanges like that, as well as the inevitable self-interest issues, make it difficult to predict causality, but underscore the pressure on Cleveland's civic leaders. The outcomes at least give those leaders some comfort that their investments were not a waste of the public sector's money.

18. Austrian, *Manufacturing brief.*

19. Sandy, R. P., J. Sloane, and M. S. Rosentraub, 2004. *The economics of sports: An international perspective.* New York: Palgrave McMillan.

20. Leland, S. and M. S. Rosentraub. 2009. Consolidated and fragmented governments and regional cooperation: Surprising lessons from Charlotte, Cleveland, Indianapolis, and Kansas City. In *Who will govern metropolitan regions in the 21st Century?* ed. D. Phares, Armonk, NY: M. E. Sharpe, (forthcoming)

21. Rosentraub, M. S. and W. Al-Habil. 2009. Why metropolitan governance is growing as is the need for flexible governments. In *Who will govern metropolitan regions in the 21st Century?* ed. D. Phares, Armonk, NY: M. E. Sharpe (forthcoming).

22. In 2007, Cleveland and the suburban city of Independence agreed to an earnings tax sharing plan when the Cavaliers decided to build a practice facility separate from what was available at the arena. With that facility located in Independence, the city is entitled to the proportion of the earnings tax that results from the players and coaches "working" within their city limits. The tax-sharing agreement protects Cleveland's long-term interest while allowing the team to build the needed facility and offices. An earnings tax is a tax on income and is paid to the city where an employee works, not the city where the employee lives.

23. Mikelbank, Rosentraub, and Post, Residential property tax abatements and rebuilding in Cleveland, Ohio.

24. During the time the leases were negotiated, the author was one of the five commissioners serving on the board of the Gateway Economic Development Corporation of Greater Cleveland and a participant in the process. The author was first recruited as an advisor to the board as the renegotiations began and was then appointed to a vacant seat by one of Cuyahoga County's commissioners.

25. Delaney, K. J. and R. Eckstein. 2003. *Public dollars, private stadiums: The battle over building sports stadiums.* New Brunswick, NJ: Rutgers University Press.

26. Confirmed through e-mail exchanges with John Wolf, vice president for Finance and Administration, Cleveland Cavaliers, September 2008.

27. Gateway Economic Development Corporation of Greater Cleveland. 2008. *Resolution No. 2008-5 regarding authorization and approval of annual operating budget for 2009.* Cleveland: Gateway Economic Development Corporation of Greater Cleveland.

28. Squires, *Unequal partnerships.*

29. Hanson, Wolman, and Connolly, *Finding a new voice for corporate leaders in a changed urban world.*

30. Harvard Business School. 1996a. *The Cleveland turnaround (A): Responding to the crisis, 1978–1988.* N9-796-151, Cambridge: Harvard University.

31. Ibid., p. 1.

32. Cleveland Development Advisors (CDA) was established in 1989 to manage the real estate investment funds raised by Cleveland Tomorrow. These funds were used for economic and community development projects in the downtown area and in other neighborhoods. The community projects funded through CDA include retail centers, arts and entertainment centers, and new construction as well as the rehabilitation of existing residential properties. The Arbor Park Place Shopping Center, for example, is a 39,000-square-foot retail center in the midst of an eastside neighborhood abandoned by store owners decades ago. The Gordon Arts project is an investment designed to stabilize and enhance a westside neighborhood.

33. Hanson, Wolman, and Connolly. *Finding a new voice for corporate leaders in a changed urban world,* p. 7.

34. Harvard Business School. 1996b. *The Cleveland turnaround (B): Building on progress, 1989–1996.* N9-796-152, Cambridge: Harvard University.

35. Rosentraub, M. S. and M. Joo. 2009. Tourism and economic development: Which investments produce gains for regions? *Tourism Management* (forthcoming).

Chapter 8

Stagnation, Crime, and Population Change: Reading's Volunteer Leadership Group and a Focus on Sports, Entertainment, the Arts, and Culture to Revitalize a Small City

I. Introduction: Economic Change in a Small City

The economic changes that transformed large metropolitan areas and their central cities across the Midwest and elsewhere have also had a drastic effect on numerous smaller regions and cities. As leadership in some smaller cities focused on revitalization strategies, they usually encountered the additional challenge of more limited wealth that sometimes constrained options. Smaller cities are less likely to be home to large community or private foundations that could make investments in assets, such as Playhouse Square in Cleveland. Smaller communities were also likely to have been home to fewer large corporations. If one or more of these businesses moved to other regions, the economic effects were frequently devastating in terms of the loss of jobs and the resulting depreciation in land values. Of equal significance, however, was the loss of executive talent and that often meant the availability of fewer people to work with public leaders and involve the private sector in the design and implementation of a revitalization strategy. The loss of corporations in smaller towns can also result in a shortage of leadership for positions on the boards of arts and cultural organizations, weakening the ability of these institutions to participate in redevelopment efforts. The loss of executive talent for these organizations is often a staggering setback when communities strive to maintain amenities to underscore their attractiveness and potential as locations for new and expanding businesses. If some of the arts and cultural organizations fail, then the ability to attract other businesses is further constrained as new companies could well fear the absence of amenities that could reduce their ability to attract and retain the human capital needed to be competitive and profitable. The acquisition of local businesses by out-of-town corporations can also reduce the availability of local executive talent to help a smaller city with its revitalization strategies. If a community is seen as a place where younger executives stay for a short period of time before resuming their climb on the parent company's corporate ladder, they might be less likely to participate in community-building activities. These are just some of the challenges that confronted Reading, Pennsylvania.

II. Changes in a Small City: Economic and Racial Separation

A. *Reading in Brief*

Located 58 miles northwest of Philadelphia and 81 miles northeast of Baltimore, Reading is too far from either city to be a suburban or ex-urban part of their economies. In addition, there is no passenger rail connection to either city making it very inconvenient for residents in Reading or surrounding Berks County to work in either of those metropolitan areas. Reading was founded prior to the Revolutionary War and the city's iron industry provided arms to George Washington's army. The city's manufacturing base and role in the coal industry attracted immigrants and created its first wave of wealth and growth in the early nineteenth century. In later years (last half of the nineteenth and the early part of the twentieth century), the production of clothing and eyewear propelled Reading and it became the home for one of eastern Pennsylvania's most successful department store chains. Reading continued to grow and by the onset of the Great Depression the city's population

Table 8.1 Population Changes in Reading, Pennsylvania

Year	Population	Percent Change
1880	43,278	
1890	58,661	35.5
1900	78,961	34.6
1910	96,071	21.7
1920	107,784	12.2
1930	111,171	3.1
1940	110,568	–0.5
1950	109,320	–1.1
1960	98,061	–10.3
1970	87,643	–10.6
1980	78,686	–10.2
1990	78,380	–0.4
2000	81,207	3.6
2007	80,769	–0.5

Sources: U.S. Bureau of the Census, various years; Berks County, Pennsylvania Planning Department.

exceeded 110,000. A period of general decline began in the post-1950s and, by 1990, the city had almost 30 percent fewer residents than it did in 1930. Then, in the 1990s and the first part of the twenty-first century the city enjoyed a small population increment (Table 8.1).

At first, the population decline was part of the general suburbanization trends taking place in the post-World War II environment as families with increasing wealth sought a more suburban lifestyle, newer large homes, and homes with large front and back yards. The expansion of some manufacturing and other businesses in the suburban areas of surrounding Berks County also brought increased prosperity to other parts of region. Berks County has continued to grow and by 2000 had more than 350,000 residents. The county's planning department has estimated that a population of 400,000 residents by 2020 is expected if current employment and population growth trends are sustained (Figure 8.1).

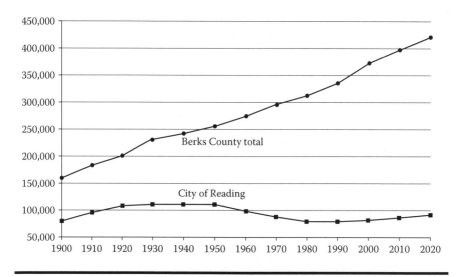

Figure 8.1 Population trends in Reading and Berks County, 1900 to 2020. (From Berks County, Pennsylvania Planning Department.)

B. Reading and Berks County Today

The future population projections may be a bit optimistic. From 2000 to 2006, the entire Reading Metropolitan Statistical Area (MSA) added but 1,112 jobs. Over this seven-year period, the private sector payroll increased by less than 1 percent (Table 8.2). Expanding the view back to 1998, the economic restructuring that has so severely impacted the Midwest becomes more obvious. Since 1998, the Reading MSA has lost 10,300 manufacturing jobs (loss of 24.8 percent of the 1998 manufacturing job base) while the number of professional, scientific, and technical jobs also declined, but by a more modest 3.1 percent. The largest employment increases were in healthcare and social assistance positions (5,522) and in the finance and insurance sector (3,820). The financial crisis of 2008 and 2009 might well lead to the loss of some of these jobs. Since 1998, the real increase in payrolls has been but 1.5 percent (Table 8.3).

While a cursory look at these population and employment trends would suggest that Reading and Berks County are adjusting well to the changing economic environment and the resulting population trends affecting the Rust Belt, a closer look at the characteristics of Reading's residents highlights the issues that have led to a serious level of deterioration in the city. First, there is a growing and pronounced lower income population in Reading. The median household income of the city's residents declined 36 percent (in real terms) from $39,924 in 1989 (in 2007 dollars) to $25,536 in 2007. Median household income of people living in Berks County, but outside of Reading, was double that of Reading's residents by 2007. In another measure of income levels in the city, *City-Data* reported that in 2000 there were

Table 8.2   Changing Employment by Sector and Overall Payroll Levels, Reading MSA, 2000–2006

Employment/ Payroll	Year						
	2000	*2001*	*2002*	*2003*	*2004*	*2005*	*2006*
Total employment	148,863	151,116	145,505	143,162	144,424	146,678	149,975
Payroll[a]	4,615	4,701	4,610	4,805	4,870	5,259	5,505
Manufacturing	39,102	39,293	33,550	31,167	31,255	31,741	31,296
Prof./ Scientific/ technical	6,885	7,470	7,113	7,596	5,438	6,056	5,991
Corporate management	3,402	3,078	3,279	3,086	3,042	2,958	3,741
Administrative support	9,068	8,083	6,263	6,865	7,754	8,088	8,734
Education	2,382	2,465	2,743	2,404	2,232	2,345	2,374
Healthcare	16,108	17,147	17,594	18,523	20,022	21,123	21,216
Arts, entertainment	2,057	2,102	2,524	2,286	2,501	2,614	2,452
Hotels, food	10,220	9,842	10,099	10,377	11,080	10,271	10,443
Other services	7,570	7,767	7,876	8,458	8,032	7,813	7,825
Information	2,058	2,086	2,345	2,194	2,224	2,013	1,908
Finance, insurance	6,009	8,360	9,337	8,480	8,168	8,360	9,494
CPI adjusted payroll[b]	5,422	5,324	5,162	5,244	5,214	5,469	5,505

[a] In millions of dollars.
[b] In 2006 dollars.
Source: U.S. Bureau of the Census, County Business Patterns, http://www.census.gov/econ/cbp/index.html, accessed October 16, 2008.

only 132 owner-occupied houses with a market value of $200,000 or more and in 2007 there were only 132 apartments or houses where contract rents exceeded $1,000 per month.

Second, the dropout rate from the Reading public schools is extremely high. The Pennsylvania Department of Education places the dropout rate at 7.5 percent; no

Table 8.3   Employment Changes in Reading MSA, 1998–2006

Employment Sector/Payroll	Change	
	From 1998 to 2006	*Percent*
Employment	6,526	4.5
Payroll (in millions of constant dollars)	1,366	33.0
Manufacturing	–10,300	–24.8
Professional, scientific, technical	–221	–3.6
Management of companies	1,080	40.6
Administration, support	2,006	29.8
Education	278	13.3
Healthcare and social assistance	5,522	35.2
Arts, entertainment, and recreation	340	16.1
Accommodations and food services	510	5.1
Other Services	476	6.5
Information	–33	–1.7
Finance and Insurance	3,820	67.3

Source: U.S. Bureau of the Census, County Business Patterns data files, various years.

other school district in Berks County had a dropout rate of more than 2.2 percent.[1] *The Washington Post*, however, reported that 67 percent of the students enrolled in Reading High School do not graduate.[2] Regardless of which rate is accurate, this higher dropout level contributes to a poor image for Reading's schools and the greater confidence that exists in the public education systems available in suburban Berks County.

Third, crime rates in Reading have risen. Despite its small-town appearance and status, statistically, crime rates in Reading are far above national averages. For example, in 2003, FBI statistics indicate that the murder rate in Reading was 2.59 times the national rate. The rate at which forcible rape crimes were reported was almost double the level for the United States, and the overall violent crime rate was also almost twice (1.96) the national level (Table 8.4). These rates contributed to an image that Reading was an unsafe and dangerous place to live, work, shop, or visit for entertainment and its downtown area and neighborhoods were places to be avoided.

Fourth, Reading's population growth has been driven by an influx of lower income Hispanic households and accompanying migration of whites to suburban

Table 8.4   Crime Rates in Reading, 2003

Crime	Local Rate Compared to National Levels
Murder	2.59
Rape	1.91
Robbery	2.46
Aggravated assault	1.50
All Violent Crime	1.96
Burglary	1.66
Larceny or theft	1.03
Car theft	2.16
Arson	2.30
All property crime	1.30

Note: Rates adjusted per 100,000; U.S. national rates equal 1.0. Numbers greater than 1 indicate rates above the U.S. averages and a number of 2.59 would mean a rate more than 2.5 times the national rate.

Source: Federal Bureau of Investigation.

Berks County. This has created a highly segregated situation. In 1990, 14,486 residents of Reading or 18.5 percent of the city's population described themselves as Hispanic. In 2000, 30,302 residents or 37.3 percent of Reading's residents indicated they were Hispanic. The number of nonminority residents of Reading decreased by more than 29,000 people between 1990 and 2000. By 2000, almost 80 percent of the residents of Reading described themselves as members of other racial groups (nonwhites). There was an increase of 3,367 residents of Berks County living outside of Reading who described themselves as Hispanic and accounted for 2.1 percent of the county's population in 2000 (excluding Reading). Minorities accounted for just 9.3 percent of the residents of suburban Berks County (Table 8.5). By 2000, Reading and Berks County had become two very different communities, defined and separated from each other by high degrees of racial and economic segregation.

Finally, Reading's housing stock has deteriorated and there are blighted properties throughout most neighborhoods. A 2004 study for the city found 1,241 vacant buildings of which 1,088 were single-family homes. The study observed that "Reading has critical problems: many vacancies in the downtown area; some residential blocks overwhelmed by vacant houses and lots; abandoned or mostly-vacant

Table 8.5   Demographic Change in Reading and Suburban Berks County, 1990–2000

Race	City of Reading		Berks County	
	1990	*2000*	*1990*	*2000*
Nonminority	47,154	17,757	250,233	265,127
Black	7,607	9,947	2,396	3,831
Native American	113	356	220	255
Asian	1,114	1,296	1,632	2,489
Islander		32		45
Other	7,906	18,125	974	12,411
Multiracial		3,392		2,218
Hispanic	14,486	30,302	2,688	6,055
Total	78,380	81,207	258,143	292,431

Note: Berks County figures exclude residents of Reading. Nonminority refers to respondents who did not indicate they were Hispanic or members of any other racial group.

Source: U. S. Bureau of the Census; Berks County Planning Department.

factories; graffiti; and evidence of drug sales and other criminal activity."[3] The report also strongly recommended a renewed commitment to code enforcement. Community and government leaders noted that in the 1980s and 1990s the city had reduced its code enforcement activities.[4] The city also lacked a housing counseling service and the Fels Institute of Government (University of Pennsylvania) study noted that, as early as 2004, approximately 12 houses per month were lost to foreclosures. These homes added to the larger number of vacant properties and it was recommended that Reading establish a housing counseling service to work with homeowners to prevent foreclosures.[5]

III. Into the Breach: A Volunteer Leadership Group and Its Focus on Entertainment

The effort to revitalize Reading is clearly tied to a group of older business leaders (hereafter, leadership group). Unlike some of the groups in other cities, however, there was no direct economic return that any of these individuals or their firms would receive if the city's stature were revived. Most of the members of Reading's leadership group were retired or had sold their main businesses years ago. Each had amassed their personal fortunes or achieved their financial stability decades ago. Several had homes and new businesses or offices (ventures started during their retirement years after selling their main businesses) in Berks County, near Reading's airport. These individuals were not the rentiers described by Logan and Molotch[6] as they had long ago sold the businesses that generated their wealth or retired as executives from the region's largest firms.

The commitment of this group to Reading was tied to their psychological attachments to the city and a lifetime of memories. Several members of the group had grown to maturity in Reading and as immigrants to the United States or the children of immigrants yearned to restore to the city the quality of life they remembered. Other members of this small group had relocated to the area decades ago when they joined some of the area's growing and successful manufacturing concerns. These individuals grew to love the city and decided to spend their active retirement years committed to efforts to revitalize Reading. Each member of the group could have chosen to live his or her retirement years in other parts of the country or could have simply spent their retirement years doting on children and grandchildren. Instead each decided to spend a substantial portion of his active retirement years as a steward of a pronounced redevelopment effort for Reading. In addition, each had committed personal capital and, in some instances, substantial amounts of money to projects designed to revitalize downtown Reading. Prominent among these projects is a hoped-for hotel and several new cultural assets. Group members have also made a commitment to underwrite the operational expenses of one or more of the arts and cultural organizations at the heart of the revitalization effort. Through 2008, that annual obligation alone is in excess of $1 million. Group members also used their personal political power and influence (undoubtedly linked to campaign contributions and efforts on behalf of state and federal office seekers) to present the city's case for grants and assistance. Members of the leadership group were also willing to commit their private funds to efforts that had received state assistance, in essence, providing the needed or required "matching funds" that the city could not provide. Even the most stringent analysis of this group's activities would be hard-pressed to conclude that any member could or would realize a financial return on the personal funds they had spent.[7]

With a customer-oriented business approach from their years of private sector success, this group of community leaders recognized that, if Reading could not again become a center of activity through the attraction of people to the city, it would be difficult if not impossible to stop the decline in most neighborhoods and the downtown area. One of the business group's members had made his fortune through a very successful string of department stores. Attracting customers to safe and exciting venues was ingrained in his personal and business philosophy. As he looked at Reading, it had lost its excitement and was perceived as an unsafe place to visit.

For decades Penn Street from 4th to 8th Streets was the retail and social hub of Reading and Berks County. The legendary stories that people tell of the "good old days for Reading" describe trips to this part of downtown for shopping, dining, and entertainment.[8] Middle and upscale retail shopping now takes place in two suburban malls. The Berkshire Mall is located approximately three miles west of downtown Reading and surrounded by acres of free parking. Vanity Fair's Outlet Mall is located less than two miles west of the downtown area and 1.2 miles east of the Berkshire Mall. It too is surrounded by parking lots removing the need to venture downtown for retail shopping. As Reading's demography changed, the stores that now fill Penn Street cater to lower income families. Just as the Fels Institute study noted, the business group members knew that without a venue to bring some level of economic integration to Reading, the city's decline would continue. The initial hope was not to attract higher income families to return as residents to stem the outmigration. To be sure, if that did occur it would be an exceptional benefit. The goal was more limited. What the city wanted was an attraction or venue that would bring people into the city for entertainment. The small group of retired business leaders understood that they needed to reinstill a sense of security and confidence in people that downtown Reading was a safe and fun place to visit. Reading needed the middle and upper class from throughout Berks County and the region to have faith in its future and it needed a new image. Without something different, Reading would continue to be seen as crime-laden and filled with cut-rate stores and venues catering only to its growing lower income population. In many ways, the challenges for Reading in the early years of the new century were similar to that which Cleveland addressed through the successful renovation of the theaters that became Playhouse Square. These theaters attract approximately 1 million visits each year to a downtown area once seen as crime-ridden. Reading didn't need nearly that many visitors, but it needed something quite unique and special to change its image and something that would make people venture into a downtown area viewed as dangerous.

Reading's leadership group also decided to focus on sports, entertainment, and culture to remake the city's image and attract people to the downtown area. The projects selected would not include retail development. Downtown Reading was not going to be able to successfully compete with the nearby Berkshire and Vanity Fair Outlet malls. Those two venues were well established, convenient, surrounded by acres of free parking, and very close to Penn Street. Penn Street is not going to succeed as a retail center with these two far larger and more successful malls located so close to the downtown area. If people were going to be attracted to the downtown area, the focus would have to be on sports and entertainment and then, perhaps, the development of other unique or complementary activities. To be sure, there was substantial risk in focusing on sports, entertainment, and culture, and the building of new venues.

Allentown, a mere 26 miles northeast of Reading, opened a new arena in late 2000 and ground was broken for Hershey's Giant Center (another arena) complete with luxury suites and club seats in November 2000. The Giant Center is located 55 miles from downtown Reading and residents of Berks County can easily drive to events at that facility in about one hour. Moving forward with a new arena for Reading would mean that there would then be three venues within a relatively short driving distance of each other competing to attract events and attendees. Could three facilities similar in scale and purpose survive serving a combined market of approximately 1.5 million people? Some people could have reasonably feared that one or more of these facilities would need large public subsidies to survive.[9]

Despite these risks and concerns, Reading and Berks County moved forward with plans for a new arena, and the Sovereign Center, costing $32 million, opened in September 2001. A grant from the State of Pennsylvania provided $14.5 million toward the project's cost. Sovereign Bank paid $2 million for the naming rights (and the right to erect an advertising pylon in front of the facility) and the bank provided a $12 million loan to the Berks County Convention Center Authority. The loan was secured by a 5 percent tax on hotel rooms charged at all facilities located within 15 miles of the Sovereign Center. A total of $3.5 million was secured through private donations from members of the leadership group focused on revitalization and the sale of sponsorships and advertising inside the facility. There is also an admissions tax that is charged on tickets sold for all events held at the Center with the revenues accruing to Reading. The Center has 7,083 seats for hockey and more for concert events. The arena is home to a minor league hockey team and an arena league football team. A minor league basketball team is part of a league that suspended operations for the 2008/2009 season, but there is hope that the team will return in the future.

The Sovereign Center was not the only facility that opened in the downtown area to give Reading its concentrated focus on sports, arts, and entertainment. The Berks County Convention Center Authority also oversaw the acquisition and renovation of the historic Rajah Theater. The theater was built in the early 1900s to host vaudeville and other live entertainment events. The facility was completely renovated in the late 1990s. With concert and theater seating for more than 1,500 patrons, the performance hall is now the home of the Reading Symphony Orchestra and the "Broadway on 6th Street" theater series. The renovation cost $10 million with funds coming from state grants and the proceeds from a loan also guaranteed by the Convention Center Authority from its hotel room receipts.

Despite the stiff competition from the arenas in Allentown and Hershey and other venues for live performance, both of Reading's new entertainment venues have been a financial success. In every year but one the facilities have generated more revenues than they need to meet their capital and operating expenses. "The

Sovereign Center on Penn Street reported $193,000 in profits for the year ending June 30 (2008), and the Performing Arts Center on North Sixth Street reported a smaller-than-expected loss of $29,000. Authority Treasurer Carl Herbein said that's a combined operating profit of $164,000, according to unaudited figures and compares with an operating profit of $40,000 for the prior year."[10]

Both facilities are managed by SMG (one of the nation's leading facility management businesses) and they have been successful in bringing leading entertainers to both venues. In the last few years Elton John, Neil Diamond, Jerry Seinfeld, Dolly Parton, and Cher have each appeared in Reading. Few if any members of the leadership group that convened to change Reading's image or residents of the region who had long ago given up on the city would have believed that such an impressive roster of entertainers would appear in downtown Reading. That was as improbable an outcome when one looked at downtown Reading in the late 1990s as holding a Super Bowl in Indianapolis was when leaders there put forward a strategy for revitalization in the late 1970s.

To make attendance at events easier, convenient, and safe, parking is available behind, in front of, and diagonally across from the arena. In this regard, leaders in Reading followed the same strategy used in revitalizing Cleveland's Playhouse Square. There too people were afraid of crime levels and, to reduce that anxiety, parking facilities were built adjacent to the theater complex. Reading's placement of convenient and abundant parking in very close proximity to the arena helped to respond to the fears some might have had in attending events in a downtown area thought to be crime-ridden. With attendance at the arena increasing, a surface lot across from the facility is being made available for a new hotel if that financing can be secured. Until the hotel is built, the lot will continue to be used for parking. By having sufficient parking for all attendees adjacent to the arena, the city and the leadership group of retired business leaders and entrepreneurs wanted to ensure that any safety concerns would be immediately addressed. The availability of close-in parking, however, reduced the ability, in the short run, to increase pedestrian traffic on the streets that could patronize local businesses. The higher priority, as with the building of Playhouse Square in Cleveland, was to guarantee that attendees were comfortable and willing to come to events in downtown Reading. To further enhance safety and attractiveness, the facility, as well as all of the others built to make downtown Reading a destination, are also ringed with high-power streetlights. These lights have sufficient candlepower to keep the area and its parking facilities well lighted, generating an additional feeling of safety (Figure 8.2). With more than 100,000 visits each year to events hosted at the Sovereign Center, that objective has been achieved. The advertising pylon available on Penn Street is also illustrated in the photo. Reading—at an obviously smaller level as compared to Los Angeles—was able to capitalize on advertising to reduce the public subsidy required through the granting of permission to erect the advertising tower (see Figure 8.2).

Figure 8.2 Reading's Sovereign Center, the powerful new street lights, and the center's advertising pylon. (Photo courtesy of Mark S. Rosentraub.)

IV. Reimaging Reading: From the Outlet Capital to a Mid-Atlantic Arts Center

Sports and entertainment helped to bring people back to downtown Reading, but the leadership group was interested in a new image for the city. Reading was a railroad and manufacturing center for decades earning it a legendary spot on *Monopoly* gaming boards. When that part of its legacy passed, the city became known for its outlet malls, but that unique aspect of its identity has been lost among the proliferation of similar retail centers across the nation. The leadership group wanted a more compelling image and one that would draw people from the region to the downtown area on a regular basis. Reading's mall did nothing to aid in revitalizing the city.

Inspired by Alexandria, Virginia's *Torpedo Factory* and Bethlehem, Pennsylvania's *Banana Factory*, the group's leader, Albert Boscov, envisioned a much larger arts center as an anchor for a mixed-use Entertainment Center for the southern part of downtown Reading. A complex of factory buildings where safety goggles, glasses, and sunglasses were long manufactured was closed in 2002. Alexandria's *Torpedo*

Factory Art Center is, as its name implies, the home of a center for the creative arts in a former torpedo factory. Since the factory to be used as the arts center in Reading was used to make safety goggles, its name became *goggleWorks* and it too was envisioned as a center for the creative arts. Boscov wanted a center that would be more than a studio, he wanted a center for the arts that attracted people throughout the day, every day. Such a facility in his mind would have opportunities for classes that would be part of the curriculum of the public schools. There could also be classes from the local colleges taught at goggleWorks and adult education in the afternoon and evenings. To oversee the transformation of the former factory into studios for artists, a movie theater, numerous classrooms, and rehearsal space for the performing arts, Boscov hired the director of the *Banana Factory* and gave her the financial support and authority to make the center a far larger and grander version of Bethlehem's center. Some financial support was secured from the state, but the leadership group not only funded the remaining capital costs, but continues to provide sufficient funding to sustain any shortfalls in goggleWorks' operating budget.

GoggleWorks has sufficient space to be home to more than 34 artists. Each artist who is leasing space is expected to use the facility to produce his/her work (with opportunities for the public to watch the "artist at work") and showcase his/her pieces. As part of the lease, each artist agrees to be present for at least 20 hours per week and on the second Sunday of each month when the entire facility is open all day to attract more visitors. GoggleWorks was envisioned to be far more than a showroom for art. It was to be a place where people could watch artists at work and talk to them about their style, techniques, and works of art, and where students of all ages attended classes in both the creative and performing arts. GoggleWorks also has a small restaurant, coffee shop, and showroom where works of art by the resident artists can be purchased. In this way, the artists also receive exhibition space for their work when they are not present.

The executive director was also successful in convincing many of the region's performing arts schools (ballet and dance) to relocate and now these students fill the halls of goggleWorks every day. The Reading public high schools use the facility for their art classes ensuring that there is activity in the building every school day from 9 a.m. until 3 p.m. The performing arts schools maintain a flow of students in the late afternoon and classes for adults as well as films shown in the theatre each night attract visitors to goggleWorks until 10 p.m. The building is open to visitors and artists from 9 a.m. until 10 p.m. Attendance reports indicate that there are 80,000 visits per year to goggleWorks. In 2008, there were 25 different arts organizations as well as 34 artists in residence (Figure 8.3).

GoggleWorks cost $12 million. The State of Pennsylvania provided a $3 million grant for its development. The members of the leadership group raised $7 million in donations and also paid the additional $2 million. To meet the center's operating expenses, the plan is to raise one-third of needed revenues from programs; one-third from rent paid by the artists, organization, and schools; and then to raise sufficient money through gifts and donations to cover the balance. At the current

Figure 8.3   Reading's goggleWorks. (Photo courtesy of Mark S. Rosentraub.)

time, members of the group of community leaders provide sufficient money to meet any revenue shortfalls.

Boscov's dream or vision was to have the art center anchor an Entertainment Square around which new condominiums and townhouses could be built. His hope was that an arts center and other entertainment amenities could become a lure to encourage higher income individuals and families to live once again in downtown Reading. Two other amenities were planned by the leadership group in a coordinated fashion with the city to complete this Entertainment Square. Group members assumed responsibility for arranging the financing for a new movie multiplex complete with the region's first IMAX theater. Another member of the group provided support for the building of a performing arts center for the Reading Area Community College that is within three short blocks of goggleWorks. By 2008, the two new parts of the Entertainment Square were open. The Miller Center for the Arts is home to a 512-seat theater and provides the needed classrooms of the community college and space for performing arts seminars (Figure 8.4 and Figure 8.5). In the background of the Miller Center (Figure 8.4), the IMAX theater can be seen and Figure 8.5 illustrates the movie complex and the street lighting. A multistory parking garage across from the theaters and goggleWorks serves visitors to each of the venues in Reading's new Entertainment Square.

Figure 8.4   Reading area community college's Miller Center for the Arts. (Photo courtesy of Mark S. Rosentraub.)

V. Reading's Leadership Group and Community Development

The ability to attract residents to a city with so many abandoned homes was another issue that concerned the group of community leaders. To reduce the number of dilapidated properties in the city, the group established *Our City Reading* to finance the reconstruction of some of the abandoned residential properties. Group members paid all of the expenses associated with rehabilitating these houses and then sold them at below market rates so that lower income families could afford the mortgages. Basically, the goal was to ensure that lower income families could be homeowners of a quality house for the same money that they paid for rent. Through October 2008, the group had paid for the renovation of and sold 375 homes to lower income families that formerly rented apartments in the city. Only two of the new owners have defaulted on their payments. The average loss or cost to the group is approximately $20,000 per home and buyers are required to provide a down payment of just $500. Group members have contributed $7.5 million to the *Our City Reading* program (through October 2008). That figure is the result of the loss of

Figure 8.5 Downtown Reading's new 11-screen movie theater and IMAX center across from goggleWorks and part of Entertainment Square. (Photo courtesy of Mark S. Rosentraub.)

$20,000 per unit sold to each of the 375 lower income families. The Pennsylvania Housing Financing Agency provides public support for the program by paying for the closing costs associated with the issuance of the mortgage. In effect, the $20,000 expenditure by the group of civic leaders in each house becomes the down payment, leaving mortgage balances of approximately $29,500 on each home (accounting for the $500 down payment provided by each new owner).

VI. Measures of Success

The assets that comprise the sports, entertainment, and arts amenities that anchored Reading's revitalization effort have been open for just a few years. The movie and IMAX theater complex opened its doors for the 2008 holiday season. As a result, their cumulative effect on longer-term development trends will not be known for a few years. The credit crisis and recession of 2008 and 2009 will also postpone some of the anticipated benefits. As a result, it is too soon to note if the revitalization is a success and if the amenities can increase the economic integration in Reading and reverse the deterioration of many of the city's neighborhoods. There are, however, a few very encouraging signs of improvements.

Table 8.6 Hotel and Admission Tax Receipts Through 2007

Year	Hotel Tax		Admissions Tax	
	Receipts ($)	Percent Change	Receipts ($)	Percent Change
2007	1,677,537	8.3	665,000	6.4
2006	1,548,341	6.9	625,000	15.6
2005	1,448,340	10.9	540,587	–12.8
2004	1,306,154	–7.1	620,202	22.0
2003	1,406,733	6.5	508,472	14.8
2002	1,320,880		442,892	43.4
2001			308,913	

Source: City of Reading.

First, there have been steady increases in both the hotel and admission tax receipts through 2007 indicating rising demand for hotel rooms and for the events held in the arena and performing arts centers. The facilities, then, have been successful in bringing people to downtown Reading for events. Many of these people had probably avoided the downtown area for entertainment for years, meaning the goal of bringing people into the city for entertainment activities is being achieved. The rising admission tax receipts combined with the fiscal performance of the sports and performing arts centers also indicate that both facilities are viable despite the presence of other arenas and theaters for live performances within one to two hours driving time of the Reading MSA (Table 8.6).

Second, goggleWorks is attracting 80,000 visits each year and on the special "second Sundays" when all artists are present, attendance averages 1,500 people. The small theater permits films that would not normally be seen in Reading to be available and demand has reached the point where the films are shown each night. Capacity crowds are routine on the weekends in the 131-seat auditorium. With the relocation of performing arts schools to the downtown facility and the availability of evening classes, the amenity attracts people to the downtown area from 9 a.m. to 10 p.m. four days a week and on weekends.

There is no evidence yet available that the attraction of people to the new downtown amenities has translated into a substantial uptick in new residential or commercial development projects (even in advance of the credit crisis of late 2008 and 2009). Throughout 2008, there was considerable discussion of a $2 billion project along the Schuylkill Riverfront, a short distance from Entertainment Square. The financial crisis in 2008/2009 and the recession may well delay the project or change its scale. The continued discussion of the project and the interest shown by investors from outside of Reading suggests that there is a potential for new, higher-end or market-rate residential development. Community leaders disappointed in the pace of this development's progress are still impressed that there is even discussion of a multibillion development within the city's limits. That discussion is often noted as an extraordinary success that should be credited to the investments in the arena, performance center, and Entertainment Square. The community group that has led the revitalization strategy is also committed to the building of a new Doubletree Hotel across from the Sovereign Center. They are prepared to invest $8 million if the balance of the needed funds can be secured from the state or the federal government. The group also has purchased and prepared land across from goggleWorks to build an apartment and condominium complex. To offer below market prices, they believe $11.5 million in grants from the state or the federal government will be needed. A grant of that magnitude will ensure that their losses are minimized. So far no commitments have been made by either the state or any federal agency and it is likely that this project's future will also be delayed. Some other observers in Reading believe that in addition to any grants received the leadership group will also need a $40 million loan from the Federal Housing Administration for the dream of an economically integrated residential project at Entertainment Square to be realized. In the current economic environment, a loan of that magnitude might be difficult to secure.

Amid these as yet unrelated possibilities, a review of the value of approved building permits for Reading from 2004 through September 2008 illustrates the challenges confronting the civic group and Reading's public leaders. The value reported in 2004 has never again been reached, and the projected value of new construction in 2008, based on activity through September 2008, suggests that the credit crisis and recession was already taking a substantial toll on the city (Table 8.7). The steady decline in the value of building permits from 2004 sug-

Table 8.7 Total Value of Building Permits Issued for Reading, 2004–2008	
Year	Value ($)
2004	149,652,000
2005	129,742,000
2006	133,486,000
2007	118,308,000
2008	58,623,000

Source: www.Economagic.com.

gests that changing Reading will be a multiyear process. However, had the project on the river been approved, that trajectory change might have been sufficient to reverse the city's fortunes. That level of success is still a future goal.

VII. Conclusions

There is little doubt that in the absence of a civic group of former corporate executives and company owners led by Albert Boscov, Michael Ehlerman, Carl Herbein, Marlin Miller, and others, few if any of the projects built to change Reading's development would exist. These individuals have not only pledged resources from

their own personal wealth, but they have used their political capital to secure financial support from Pennsylvania and the federal government for the needed projects.
The local tax burden to sustain the projects is limited to a hotel tax that while
paid by visitors inevitably has a slight negative impact on hotel operators and other
businesses. That short-term loss, however, may well be offset by higher levels of
consumption generated by attendance at the events hosted by the Sovereign Center.
For example, if more out-of-town visitors stay at hotels and eat at nearby restaurants
as a result of their attendance, then it is possible that any economic losses generated
by the higher priced room costs are compensated by a higher number of visitors.
Assuming that the entire hotel tax is negatively capitalized, the local investment
amounts to less than $1.7 million per year. The balance of the funding for the assets
has come from the personal wealth of individuals or through grants from the state
or federal agencies. This should be properly identified as net gains to the local
economy as those resources could have easily been invested in other communities
or elsewhere in the international economy.

Members of this group have also committed personal funds for an important
community development program. Neither Reading nor Pennsylvania had sufficient resources to rebuild abandoned or dilapidated houses, remodel them, and
then sell them to lower income households at a per unit cost (loss) of approximately
$20,000. With 375 homes revitalized and sold through this program through
2008, at least $7.5 million has been set aside for community development focused
on housing for lower or moderate income households.

There also is little doubt that the new amenities have achieved the two most
important goals. First, large numbers of people (for a small city and region) are
coming to downtown Reading for entertainment. Downtown areas that people
avoided for decades because of crime rates and the fears generated by economic
and racial segregation, are now frequently visited by families, and by middle-aged
and older residents of the region. The fiscal performance of the Sovereign Center
attests to the number of people frequenting that part of the downtown area. The
number of people visiting goggleWorks each day and on each "second Sunday" is
another example of the success of the amenities in changing Reading's image and
appeal. Second, while it might be too early to proclaim that Reading has completely
changed its image or that it has a new image, things have certainly improved from
the time that the downtown area was avoided. The city might not yet be an arts
capital, but its reputation has prompted attention from *The Washington Post*,[11] US
Airways,[12] *American Craft*,[13] and *American Style*.[14] Such attention was not directed
toward the city prior to the investment in the amenities. The appearance of leading
entertainers also has an effect of the city's image in the minds of people throughout
the region.

It is extremely likely that the retired business executives and owners who
led this effort will never earn any economic returns on their investments. The
investments made by them fit Nowak's description of investments designed to be

market-building efforts.[15] In essence, the group is trying to revitalize Reading into a market for private investment. While Nowak points to the need for market-building commitments to earn market-based rates of returns—or some appropriate financial return—it is highly unlikely that a level of financial success will be realized by members of the leadership group that planned the revitalization strategy. It is possible that some future residential development might be profitable, but the time horizon on that is difficult to project. The return to the members of this group of civic leaders will be largely intangible—making the city worthy of private investments in new homes and businesses. Tangible returns would come if the assets built achieve the hoped-for levels of success and the members of the group then capitalize on that excitement created with additional investments in residential or commercial investments. Because of the commitment and motives of the individuals in the civic group that focused on rebuilding the city, Reading is an example of where minor league sports, entertainment, arts, and culture have led a successful revitalization effort. While more time is needed to determine if the city becomes more financially integrated, its image is being changed and crowds are again part of the downtown life of a small city. In that regard, the city is indeed a Major League Winner sporting a new image, new crowds, new confidence, and even rebuilt homes for more growth.

Endnotes

1. Heister, M. 2008. *Public secondary school dropouts, 2006-2007.* Harrisburg, PA: Pennsylvania Department of Education.
2. Montgomery, D. 2008. The engine of change: Reading, Pa. has proven it's deft at switching tracks. As residents head to the polls, the question is: Where to next? *The Washington Post,* April 22, C01.
3. Fels Institute of Government. 2008. *Vacancy inventory and reinvestment strategies for Reading, PA.* Philadelphia: University of Pennsylvania, p. 18. (Available online, http://www.readingpa.gov/documents/fels_report.pdf (accessed November 1, 2008).
4. Confirmed in interviews conducted in October 2008 with city employees, private sector business leaders, and leaders of nongovernmental economic and housing development organizations by the author.
5. Fels Institute of Government, *Vacancy inventory and reinvestment strategies for Reading, PA,* p.18.
6. Logan, J. R. and H. L. Molotch. 1987. *Urban fortunes: The political economy of place.* Berkeley: University of California Press.
7. The number of individuals involved in the leadership group is small and their identities and names widely known. Some members of the group have been portrayed in regional and national publications. To honor the commitment made regarding confidentiality, the names of the group's members interviewed are not included in this text relative to specific statements or actions taken by the group.

8. Interview with Cindy Herninitz, chief of staff to Mayor Thomas McMahon, City of Reading, October 2008.
9. Some hotel operators in Reading filed a lawsuit against the imposition of a tax on room nights to pay for part of its cost. Experts testified that there was indeed substantial risk that multiple arenas in close proximity to each other could lead to operating losses for one or more of these facilities. The court ruled that there was nothing irregular in the procedures followed by Berks County and Reading and the case was dismissed.
10. Spatz, D. 2008. Reading's two civic centers combine for $164,000 profit. *Reading Eagle*, August 21, online ed.: https://www.readingeagle.com (accessed September 6, 2008).
11. Fidler, J. 2006. Reading: It's not just outlet malls anymore. *The Washington Post,* July 19, C2.
12. US Airways. 2006. The man with a plan. *US Airways Magazine*, November 2006, p. 136.
13. American Craft. 2006. goggleWorks, Reading, PA. *American Craft*, October/November 6.
14. Tiger, C. 2008. See for yourself: A former eyeglass factory brings a Pennsylvania city's vision to life. *American Style* August: 70–75.
15. Nowak, J. 2008. The market-building potential of development finance in older industrial cities. In *Retooling for growth: Building a 21ˢᵗ century economy in America's older industrial areas.* ed. McGahey R. C. and J. S. Vey, 373–410. Washington, D.C.: The Brookings Institution.

Chapter 9

Sports, Culture, Entertainment and Revitalization: Turning Subsidies into Strategic Investments

I. Introduction

Each of the six cities studied tied sports, entertainment, or arts and culture to a revitalization strategy. The obvious size, locational, and demographic differences between the communities did not substantially change the goals and hopes leadership had for the rebuilding efforts. Each city wanted to rebuild a deteriorating or stagnant part of its downtown area. Leaders in each city also recognized the need to attract and retain highly skilled workers to advance economic development, and a revitalized downtown was part of the effort to increase or extend a region's attractiveness. Each of the cities looked to new amenities as tools to restore confidence in its downtown area as a place to visit, work, or live, and within the city. Leaders in each of the communities also wanted the new amenities to attract crowds to offset the impression that their downtown area had become a dangerous or uninviting place. In most of the cities, increasing racial and economic segregation between core

and suburban areas had also fostered prejudices and it was hoped that the new amenities could also initiate a process that would lead to more integration. The revitalization strategies for several of the cities were also designed to counter the view that
economic restructuring had created a destiny of decline that could not be reversed.

In pursuit of revitalized downtowns, some cities relied only on their own tax
money to build amenities in an effort to convince entrepreneurs to make related
private investments. Other communities tied their expenditure of tax dollars to
commitments or guarantees by private investors to build residential and commercial properties. In some cities, major league teams were required to pay for only a
small part of the construction costs of the facilities they would use without having to make any other investments. The teams were then given control of all of
the revenue streams from the new ballparks or arenas. Columbus, Los Angeles,
and San Diego added their power of eminent domain to the incentive packages to
facilitate the development guarantees made by Nationwide Insurance, AEG, and
JMI. The outcomes in each of the case studies in which different approaches were
used to reach similar goals provide other communities with important insights into
the ways in which partnerships can be formed to ensure subsidies become strategic
investments to revitalize downtown areas. Each city adopted tactics to fit their local
situation. These variations on a common theme produce the recommendations and
guidance for other communities that face similar or the same challenges to economic and social development.

Cleveland and Reading engaged in activities designed to bolster confidence in
their community's future. San Diego and Columbus entered into partnerships to
build new downtown communities that included sports and entertainment facilities and both cities gave extensive control over development to their private sector
partners. Los Angeles gave extensive control over development to AEG and, by
also permitting the firm to build advertising pylons visible from two freeways, the
city was able to leverage more than $2.8 billion in private investment. Reading's
activities were led by a group of retired executives and older entrepreneurs who had
sold their businesses. They invested substantial sums of their personal wealth and
provided the leadership for the revitalization effort. In each of the other communities, there was substantial leadership from the public sector as well as participation
by regime members. Lastly, Indianapolis became a broker city and secured extraordinary levels of private, nonprofit, and state government funds in exchange for its
investment of local tax dollars.

II. Subsidies to Investments in the Aftermath of the Credit Crisis

Discussing these strategies as recommendations to avoid or minimize subsidies in
the aftermath of the credit crisis of 2008 and 2009 and the collapse of real estate

values might appear to be tainted with some irony. For some people, the collapse of real estate values and the credit crisis might be seen as synonymous with an over reliance on revitalization strategies that included or even catered to the building of sports, entertainment, and cultural facilities with adjoining residences, hotels, and commercial space. The fiscal tools used in the revitalization strategies, the assembly of land for real estate redevelopment, and the resulting construction linked teams, governments, cultural organizations, and entertainment firms with some of the financial organizations and banks at the center of the collapse of the credit markets in 2008. Does that association mean the revitalization of downtown areas through the creation of new neighborhoods and an emphasis on entertainment, sports, and culture to attract human capital and bring people back to cities is wrongheaded?

In addition, the credit crisis delayed some revitalization projects and reduced the value of properties that were to be the revenue sources for the repayment of the public's investment in San Diego's partnership with the Padres. In the New York metropolitan area, the Atlantic Yards project in Brooklyn, which includes a new arena for the NBA's Nets as well as residential and commercial properties (designed by legendary architect Frank Gehry) was delayed, and the mixed-use project adjoining the new stadium being built by the New York Giants and Jets in New Jersey's Meadowlands was threatened after the required construction and longer-term financing could not be secured. The redevelopment of Cleveland's Flats Area along the Cuyahoga River immediately west of downtown was postponed. The demand for and value of downtown housing near Los Angeles' STAPLES Center and L.A. LIVE has also declined. Two large residential developments in Reading's downtown area have also been postponed. Do these disappointments imply that a focus on real estate development linked to sports, entertainment, and culture for revitalization is the latest example of a search for "fool's gold" or an elixir to cure the ills in many core urban areas? Have community leaders been seduced by a siren's call regarding the value of amenities while turning attention from other core strategies that might have a greater likelihood of enhancing economic development?

It might be tempting to extend concerns with too little regulation of the credit markets and the issuance of mortgages to homeowners who could not make the required payments to an inappropriate or invalid focus on amenities for revitalization and economic development. Such a position, however, would ignore other important trends and their impact on cities. Before proceeding to the lessons learned from the case studies, it is useful to summarize these trends and their linkage to the conceptual framework presented earlier. Ignoring the success that turned subsidies into investments for revitalization would be to reject these more permanent societal changes as guides for prudent policies and approaches to redevelopment and revitalization. It is these trends, discussed below, that are more permanent than the credit crisis created by inappropriate lending policies, inadequate oversight controls, and the failure of rating agencies and accountants to properly perform their jobs and fulfill their responsibilities.

A. Value of Amenities for Economic Development and Revitalization

Businesses are increasingly dependent on human capital for their growth and expansion. Successful firms will locate in the regions with the largest concentrations of the most talented and skilled workers. This means firms locate where people want to live, changing older business–labor linkages where workers moved to those locations that were best for a business. This shifting in the relationship between businesses and labor is a result of the importance and value of highly skilled and educated workers for innovation and the changing structure of the American economy. Within this new structure, research, services, healthcare, computing, information technology, robotics, and advanced manufacturing assume larger roles than does the manufacturing processes that produced millions of jobs in the twentieth century. The expanding sectors of today's economy are less dependent on the traditional factors that affected location decision and the economic development that dominated America's growth and expansion in the nineteenth and twentieth centuries.

Highly skilled workers place a great deal of value on the mix and availability of amenities when choosing a place to live. Areas with fewer amenities are seen as less desirable. One important amenity is a lively downtown area that capitalizes on the potential to be a residential neighborhood for the increasing numbers of people enjoying long and active periods of their lives after fulfilling their child-rearing responsibilities. The desire of young professionals for cities with dynamic downtown areas is also part of the attraction that propels the growth of Boston, Charlotte, Chicago, and New York. As these proportions of the population increase, the popularity of safe downtown and urban neighborhoods with a large number of amenities will continue to increase.

B. Urban Tourism

The temporary downturn in the economy—while substantial and the most severe since the Great Depression—will not substantially shift the importance of tourism and entertainment as robust and growing portions of the world's economy. The demand for and interest in entertainment, tourism, and travel overcame the substantial contractions that took place in the aftermath of the 9/11 attacks and terrorist incidents in Spain, England, and Israel. A similar pattern is likely to be repeated in response to the recession in 2008 that extends into 2009 and even into 2010. Unemployment will increase during this economic contraction, but a recovery, even if delayed until the last half of 2010 or into 2011, will not change the longer-term trend of increasing demand for experiences as part of tourism and recreation. While there is debate over the relative value of different amenity packages for economic development and their causal connection to economic development and revitalization, there is little disagreement that areas lacking in amenities will increasingly find themselves less likely locations for growth, expansion, and the attraction and retention of younger and high-value workers.[1] Add to all of these factors the changes in technology that accelerates the declining period of time that comparative advantages in production can be sustained and the emphasis on amenities is more easy to understand as communities strive to achieve a competitive advantage based on human capital.[2] As a result, the lessons learned from the six cases can help communities include amenities as part of a revitalization and economic development strategy.

III. Lessons Learned: Similarities within Differences

Before focusing on nine recommended strategies for communities to consider based on the six case studies, it is useful to point to similarities in the challenges confronting the cities studied regardless of differences in size, economic diversity, and regional growth patterns. For example, each city had a declining area that was increasingly avoided by people and was being bypassed by investors. In some instances, these depressed areas constituted part of a downtown area, the entire downtown area, or an entire city. What is important to note is that the challenges that Los Angeles faced in revitalizing its downtown area were more similar than different from the challenges before Reading as it tackled a problem that spanned its entire downtown area as well as numerous neighborhoods. Columbus, too, had a deteriorating section of its downtown area, and Indianapolis' leadership watched as people and economic activity moved to more outlying areas within its boundaries, but still distant from its downtown core community.

In Cleveland, Los Angeles, and Reading, there was a perception that parts or all of their downtown areas were dangerous and crime-ridden places that should be avoided. All three cities needed strategies to change images and to attract crowds back to areas that were once the center of their region's retail and entertainment activity. Indianapolis, and Columbus' downtown areas might have been seen as less dangerous, but businesses and people had been relocating to more suburban areas for decades. Increasingly in these cities, there was also no reason or need to be downtown after business hours. Indianapolis and Columbus are their state's capitols so there was a certain concentration of state workers. When the legislatures were in session, there was additional activity in and around the state government's buildings. When the legislatures were not in session or after the business day, both downtown areas were increasingly deserted. The number of people living in each downtown area was also declining each year. The area that became San Diego's Ballpark District was also less dangerous, but development levels were stagnant.

Only in San Diego did some believe that the area targeted for development could or might have revived or become vital *without* a large-scale development plan. In the other cities, trends indicated the downtown areas were far more likely to deteriorate or stagnate. There was little or no evidence of development taking place or imminent in most of the downtown areas before the revitalization efforts were launched. Columbus had made a large investment in a new downtown mall, but it was struggling against two new and far larger retail centers on the city's northeast and northwest borders. The Arena District had languished for decades. At the time of Cleveland's big-ticket investments, there was a substantial shift of the region's population away from the city, a trend also evident in Indianapolis. Reading was able to avoid a loss of residents, but similar to Cleveland, its residents had incomes substantially lower than those of people living outside its boundaries. Population growth was also concentrated in suburban Columbus and adjacent counties. Those residents who remained in downtown Los Angeles also had incomes far below people living in other parts of the city.

A lack of confidence in a city's future was probably most evident or pressing in Cleveland and Reading, but there were serious reservations about what was possible compared to new development in downtown Los Angeles, Indianapolis, and Columbus. In these three areas as revitalization plans were put forward, most people were looking to the suburban areas for their region's future and there was considerable skepticism that redevelopment efforts would have any impact or change longer-term trends. Because of their small sizes, Cleveland and Reading were becoming economically and racially segregated within their respective counties and metropolitan regions. In Columbus, Indianapolis, and Los Angeles, there was confidence in the future for other parts of the city and certainly in the region, but not in the core or central parts of the downtown area. It is important to underscore these similarities and to keep them in mind as community leaders from other cities and regions seek to benefit from the lessons learned in efforts to rely on amenities to anchor revitalization and economic development strategies.

IV. Lessons Learned: Advice for Other Cities Looking to Sports, Entertainment, and Cultural Amenities for Revitalization

Each city in the case studies in this book decided that investments in sports, entertainment, arts, and cultural amenities should anchor revitalization efforts. Several important lessons emerge from their experiences that will help other cities as they consider public/private partnerships to minimize and avoid subsidies.

A. Recommendation 1: Value of Advertising

Communities sometimes overlook the value of advertising and how particular locations because of commuting patterns or the attraction of crowds at events can generate advertising revenue. These locations if appropriately marketed and then leased to businesses that can sell opportunities for advertising to other firms can generate substantial revenues for the public sector. These funds—or the revenue streams given to the firms that lease the advertising space—can reduce the need for tax dollars in a revitalization effort. Los Angeles' decision to allow AEG to build two advertising pylons with direct visual access from two freeways was a centerpiece of its ability to form a partnership that led to that firm paying for most of the construction and maintenance costs of the STAPLES Center. With Los Angeles receiving other revenues from the STAPLES Center's operations, the arena was built without any public subsidies. The value of the advertising streams was also integral to Los Angeles' ability to get AEG to build a new hotel adjacent to the convention center and the arena as part of its $2.5 billion investment in L.A. LIVE. Some might counter that assets or opportunities available to Los Angeles because of its market size are not options for other cities. Yet, as the picture of the Sovereign Center in Reading readily demonstrates, a small city with a facility not adjacent to a freeway was still able to secure $2 million for its revitalization effort by leasing naming rights to an arena and permitting an advertising tower to be built on its main thoroughfare (just outside the new arena). Reading has other locations that are also equally valuable as a result of traffic flows and it might well be advised to consider other advertising marquees near goggleWorks to generate needed revenues.

Cleveland also capitalized on expanded advertising options for the Indians and Cavaliers at the ballpark and arena to renegotiate leases with both teams. In exchange for the teams receiving broader rights to lease space for advertising inside and on the outside of both facilities, the franchises agreed to assume responsibility for annual maintenance expenses and to make additional improvements in the arena and ballpark. In terms of the annual maintenance costs, the public sector is saving more than $4 million a year[3] and each team also has made other substantial investments to upgrade each facility. In this manner the additional advertising permitted by Cleveland can be thought of as generating a revenue stream of more than $60 million across a 15-year period. That revenue reduces the need for any additional tax money to sustain the facilities.

Some might object to expanded advertising in public space considering such practices to be too commercially oriented and inappropriate for a city. Others could object to the additional advertisement's contribution to a form of pollution of the visual aesthetics or vistas in a city. Over the past several years, transportation systems have sold advertising on buses, and cities and other governments have leased advertising space at venues that attract large crowds (bus and train stations, transit stops, airport terminals, publicly owned sports facilities, etc.). There are legitimate reasons to object to this level of commercial activity and to government policies that embrace market-oriented approaches to finance revitalization or community development activities. These concerns can be amplified if inappropriate advertising is permitted. Los Angeles has set guidelines to ensure that some businesses viewed as inappropriate relative to the public interest (e.g., businesses selling tobacco products, firearms, or some forms of alcohol) are not able to advertise in public spaces. But, Los Angeles did agree to permit Budweiser's name to appear on the pylons.

While focusing on these concerns, it is also important to underscore that one way to avoid public subsidies and higher taxes for amenities, community development, and revitalization strategies is to take advantage of the marketing value created when large numbers of people are attracted to and use the facilities built by the public sector. Cleveland, Los Angeles, and Reading reduced the public sector's fiscal responsibilities for the building of amenities by permitting advertising and the value of this option should be considered by other communities to reduce the costs of their investments in revitalization efforts. Cities interested in building new amenities need to analyze the value of the public space they control and then consider if that revenue would be helpful in securing revitalization or community development goals. As the evidence illustrates, this option exists for the largest cities and smaller ones as well and does reduce the fiscal cost to taxpayers while ensuring an amenity is built and maintained.

B. Recommendation 2: Concentrate Amenities and Make Detailed Plans

Indianapolis, San Diego, Los Angeles, and Columbus concentrated their revitalization efforts in a tightly defined geographic space. Cleveland's revitalization effort is spread across a large downtown area and Reading's redevelopment projects are diffused across a much smaller core area. One clear advantage from a concentrated approach is that it is far easier to successfully complete a revitalization effort in a tightly designed area and ensure that all of the buildings or land within the district are redeveloped. This creates an image of success and vitality contrasted with a previous period of decline and deterioration. Placing a number of amenities in a small and defined space also concentrates activities making it easier to create the presence of crowds that are essential to enhance impressions of safety. The absence (or far smaller presence) of abandoned, dilapidated, or vacant building or properties also creates an image of vitality and feelings of safety for visitors and pedestrians. If amenities are dispersed across a broad area, it requires far more resources to redevelop all properties within the revitalized district to create the image of the successful rebuilding of a portion of the downtown area. Dispersed amenities risks the impression that each is an isolated island of activity in a larger sea of deteriorating properties.

Cleveland's extraordinary assets are located in different parts of a large downtown area. The large number of buildings and properties between these amenities requires a substantial amount of investment if all signs of blight are to be eliminated. While robust, development levels in Cleveland have not been sufficient to eliminate all of the vacant or abandoned properties between its sports, entertainment, and arts and cultural amenities in the downtown area. As a result, there is still an appearance of substantial levels of deterioration as well as abandoned buildings among the splendor and architectural significance of five theaters for the performing arts, three sports facilities, and two great museums. While Indianapolis' leadership may be frustrated that more development has not taken place to the north of its entertainment district, within the large area that is the redevelopment district there is a robust convention center, three new sports facilities, a successful retail mall, two theaters for the performing arts, an Arts Garden, a new multiplex movie theater as part of the mall, several hotels, several museums, two park areas, and dozens of restaurants. Across three decades, virtually all evidence of deterioration has been erased. Visitors from the region or from other cities when in the midst of this redeveloped entertainment center are part of a vibrant downtown that now has several thousand residential units. The image of success and vitality that Indianapolis' revitalized core area projects stands in sharp contrast to the abandoned buildings and storefronts that are interlaced within the new amenities built in Cleveland.

Los Angeles created an extraordinary entertainment zone with the STAPLES Center and L.A. LIVE, and the Ballpark District in San Diego and the Arena District in Columbus are far smaller than the entertainment district in Indianapolis, but they too are complete and create an image of vibrancy, excitement, and safety. Reading, having also dispersed its new assets within a relatively small downtown area will be challenged to refine its strategy to eliminate vacant and dilapidated buildings adjacent to or near its vibrant new assets. Its Sovereign Center is several blocks from the Sovereign Performing Arts Center, and both of those facilities are at the opposite end of the small downtown area from goggleWorks and the emerging Entertainment Center. Efforts to fill in development to connect these areas—a central component of the Penn Corridor Development Plan developed for the city—will require substantial investment and a long-term commitment.[4]

The lesson learned is clear. Revitalization strategies have a greater potential to achieve their objectives and goals if there is commitment to concentrate the assets in close proximity to one another. Some of the success that Indianapolis, Los Angeles, San Diego, and Columbus have realized is a function of their planning decisions not to diffuse the location of strategic assets. That concentration helps to create a crowding effect that produces an image of vitality and safety. All communities considering the use of sports and cultural amenities to revitalize a downtown area would be well-served to follow in the footsteps of Indianapolis, Los Angeles, San Diego, and Columbus and concentrate all of the new assets in a zone and then build out from the center. Trying to connect separated nodes of activities, as economies continue to decentralize, seems to be a far harder goal to achieve.

Circumstances directed Cleveland and Reading to rely on a more diffused strategy. I. M. Pei wanted a majestic vista to match the breathtaking design of the Rock and Roll Hall of Fame and Museum and, to satisfy the NFL's schedule, the new home for the Cleveland Browns could only be built in one location. Reading capitalized on the availability of abandoned factory space for goggleWorks despite its more distant location from the legacy locations where the Sovereign Center (arena) and the Performing Arts Center would operate. The Performing Arts Center, similar to Cleveland's Playhouse Square District, is a rebuilt older theater. The Sovereign

Center is located on the former site of the city's grand Astor Theatre and no land assembly was needed to facilitate its construction.

While it may not be possible to have as clear a plan and vision as did Indianapolis or Columbus, documents that allow the public and private investors to clearly understand a city's redevelopment goals and what the completed projects will produce helps to create confidence that the dream can become a reality. The presentation of a vision and plan enables private investors to determine how a related project that they would create would complement and benefit from the overall strategy and interconnections among all of the planned assets. Indianapolis' plans and vision was probably deemed unrealistic, but doubts also existed that downtown Los Angeles or Reading could attract crowds to events. Columbus relied on architects hired by Nationwide Insurance, but the vision for the Arena District, subsequently approved by the city, helped people understand the direction that was being taken on behalf of the community. Los Angeles succeeded without a plan and relied on AEG for a vision, and things were still successful. Other private developers understood what AEG envisioned and their subsequent investments in residential and other properties helped to substantially improve the image of the area and achieve the city's goal of an attractive and dynamic area surrounding the convention center. There is a great benefit to a widely circulated and clear plan and no revitalization effort should move forward without an easily understood vision.

C. Recommendation 3: Build Neighborhoods or Iconic Architecture

The success of revitalization efforts in Indianapolis, San Diego, and Columbus is related to the fit of anchor facilities in and with new neighborhoods. The scale of the large amenities was carefully crafted and their exteriors designed to ensure that even with their required size these capital assets would still fit as anchor tenants for the new neighborhoods. The resulting designs, whether inspired by Wrigley Field or Fenway Park or not, accomplished a similar purpose. The new facilities made the new neighborhoods built around them instantly popular places to live and work. Indianapolis' Conseco Fieldhouse, Columbus' Nationwide Arena, and San Diego's Petco Field have been great assets for the revitalization of their downtown areas. Some of the design elements that facilitate neighborhood integration include street-level entrances and open-air vistas or glass walls that allow people inside and outside of the facility to observe what is taking place on the street and inside the venue. The construction materials and the scale (height) of the facilities also need to fit into the neighborhood's design so that neither an arena nor a ballpark is the tallest structure. Indianapolis' Conseco Fieldhouse has a wall of glass that allows people inside to gaze at downtown Indianapolis and Petco Park has open space that allows people enjoying a public park outside the right field fence to peer into the ballpark. Cleveland's Progressive Field has a similar vista with a public street and pedestrian promenade passing behind its left field home run porch. The neighborhood design framework has been a success for several communities and that framework for revitalization to encourage pedestrian traffic and the development of residential and neighborhood amenities around a facility can be a very successful revitalization tool.

Los Angeles, while including street-level access for the STAPLES Center and a large public square for L.A. LIVE (a sort of Times Square West), was attracted to an alternative perspective, one also adopted in the plans for Brooklyn's Atlantic Yards. Described by *New York Times* writer Charles Bagli as "STARchitecture," Los Angeles and New York have favored the use of renowned architects or spectacular facilities to create iconic and controversial exteriors that excite passions and create instant celebrity status for an area. L.A. LIVE and the STAPLES Center are anchors for a new downtown neighborhood, but there is nothing neighborhood-like in their design. Instead, bathed in pastel lighting and larger-than-life video boards and advertisements, these facilities are designed to create the impression of instant celebrity status. That status appeals to a certain segment of the residential and commercial markets in several cities. The decision to focus on "STARchitecture" has clearly been successful for Los Angeles and if the full measure of Frank Gehry's design for Atlantic Yards is built, the image of downtown Brooklyn will be inexorably changed. The protests surrounding Gehry's designs and some of the opposition to L.A. LIVE attest to the passions stirred by the designs.

The value from building facilities that fit comfortably into the design of new or emerging downtown neighborhoods is obvious when a city and developer agree on plans and then integrate the amenity to create areas similar to what exists around Wrigley Field in Chicago and adjacent to Fenway Park in Boston. San Diego and Columbus have realized that goal. The alternative approach, the building of an iconic structure, is the best strategy when a new facility must either stand out in its competition with other regional venues for attractions, or when a decidedly different image is desired. The location of Cleveland's Rock and Roll Hall of Fame and Museum was not ideal relative to a revitalization program that concentrated new assets in a designated area. Its iconic design by I M. Pei, however, assured that building would not be simply an efficient structure that would be seen as just another in a series of halls of fame. The building itself became an attraction as a result of its effects on visitors. The building was as much of a tourist attraction as was the Rock and Roll Hall of Fame and Museum. Cleveland also placed value on the possible impact an iconic design would have on its civic image and in that sense Pei's design was a "game changer" in terms of its impact on people and the city.

Frank Gehry's dramatic design of an arena for Atlantic Yards in Brooklyn shares an important similarity with the philosophy behind the design of the STAPLES Center and L.A. LIVE. In the New York and Los Angeles market areas, there are many venues competing to attract events. New York has Madison Square Garden in Manhattan and there is a new arena in downtown Newark, New Jersey. On Long Island, east of New York City, there are also venues that can host events.

Across the Los Angeles region and into Orange County, there are also many venues where concerts and events can be held. If developers simply put another facility in Brooklyn or downtown Los Angeles that was indistinguishable from other venues, few entertainers or events would see any difference from appearing at one place or another. The unique aspects of Gehry's design for Brooklyn and the spectacle aspects built into the STAPLES Center and L.A. LIVE ensure that the venues become the places where entertainers want to appear. Los Angeles had to attract fans and entertainers to an area that was viewed as dangerous. Brooklyn needs to attract people and events from Manhattan. Iconic facilities become places people want to visit and where entertainers want to be seen while also changing an area's image. Those factors are integral to the decision to pursue an iconic versus a purely functional design for a facility.

The recommendation from these two different approaches to the design and the integration of assets into a revitalization strategy is to choose one framework or another. If a community's interest lies in the development of a new neighborhood, a facility has to be designed to complement and anchor a neighborhood and be part of the daily life of the area. Avoiding only functional designs is critical if an iconic structure is needed to make an amenity the chosen place for events or to create an entirely new image for a community. When iconic structures are built, the site chosen must be a vista or location that permits the special nature of the architecture to be clearly visible. Iconic facilities can lose their ability to have an effect on people when the special or different aspects of their design are difficult for people to appreciate. This occurs when iconic facilities are nestled into areas where more functional and or traditional buildings surround the structure. As one developer observed, a truly iconic structure creates its reputation and image from the effect it has on people. If the location works against its ability to effect people's image of a city or community, an innovative design will have a far less dramatic impact.

Iconic facilities can also create their own neighborhoods. L.A. LIVE and the STAPLES Center made an area that was once avoided into one that attracts visitors from the region and tourists alike. Its "STARchitecture" elements have attracted people who want to live near the celebrity status created by the facilities. Columbus, Indianapolis, and San Diego created new neighborhoods and the demand for housing in these areas attests to the success of that approach too. The failure to either pursue a neighborhood design or a focus on iconic architecture wastes the opportunities available when amenities are built. Clear direction and a distinct choice of the framework—neighborhood or "star power"—should be made and then followed.

D. Recommendation 4: Link Private Sector Investments to a Commitment of Tax Money

San Diego, Los Angles, and Columbus created models that provide substantial guidance and benchmarks for other communities that want to link big-ticket items to revitalization strategies. Each of these cities secured commitments from private sector partners for new investments that supported the revitalization program and generated new tax revenues. The new taxes produced by the related real estate development were to be sufficient to repay any debt assumed by the public sector to pay for their part of the new facility or the needed infrastructure. Nationwide Insurance Company agreed to pay for a substantial portion of any shortfall related to the bonds issued by Columbus for the Arena District if property tax revenues from the new development in the Arena District were insufficient to repay the loan. Columbus has been fully protected by Nationwide's guarantee. Los Angeles had similar protections for its investments that made the STAPLES Center possible, and the revenues the city receives created a positive return. The investment from Los Angeles to ensure that L.A. LIVE was built will also be more than offset by new taxes generated by the facility and the nearby residential development. Los Angeles' investment is classified as cash positive in that its returns exceed the costs of repaying the bonds it sold to finance its investment. Columbus' investment may also be cash positive by 2010 and the guarantee from Nationwide ensures that the city never had to invest any of its tax money to repay the bonds it sold.

San Diego also received guarantees regarding real estate investment that turned the plan for the Ballpark District into a reality. JMI Realty has built more than three times the promised $311 million in new development in the Ballpark District. While a single, large headquarter hotel was not constructed, the number of new hotel rooms that JMI built satisfied its commitment to San Diego. San Diego, however, did not receive the same level of complete fiscal protection that was secured by Los Angeles and Columbus. In the long run, the Ballpark District might not generate sufficient new taxes to offset all of the bonds sold by the city to build Petco Park. If property values rise over the next 20 years by rather modest levels (an outcome made a bit more uncertain by the credit crisis and resulting decline in property values), San Diego's return on its investment could exceed $1 billion (in constant dollars). The city has assumed some risk that its financial returns might not exceed its costs. It is also possible for the city to earn a substantial return on its investment in addition to having a new neighborhood built where it wanted with a large number of new hotel rooms. San Diego does have the opportunity to earn a larger return on its investment if the full potential of the Ballpark District is realized.

Two lessons are learned from the experiences of these three cities. First, both a large (Los Angeles) and medium-sized (Columbus) city were able to avoid the provision of or even a hint of fiscal subsidies for the building of facilities used by professional sports teams. Each made an investment, but both received guarantees from their private sector partner that taxpayers' money would not be used if new revenues were not generated to repay the bonds sold. By providing partners with site control and by using their power of eminent domain to assemble the land needed for the arena and related amenities, residences, and commercial space, both cities secured a new sports facility and neighborhood without any tax subsidies. Some people criticize the use of the public sector's power of eminent domain to transfer land from one set of private owners to another that promises to build what the city wants. To be sure, the use of eminent domain to transfer land to other private developers can lead to abuses. In bargaining with teams or others to avoid subsidies, the offer of land assembly and site control are valuable assets. Cities have to weigh the ability to secure benefits against the possible abuse of its power to seize land and then transfer it to other owners (or lease it to the other developers for their use). As Columbus and Los Angeles learned, agreeing to assemble land and providing site control to a single developer led to the building of new amenities without public subsidies. Second, San Diego's use of eminent domain and its investment permitted it to have Petco Park and a new neighborhood built even though it accepted more risk. San Diego, however, may end up with substantial returns on its investment, but the final outcome rests on the demand for downtown homes.

E. Recommendation 5: Organizations Needed to Succeed as a Broker City

Securing guaranteed investments is not always possible. Indianapolis provides a model for cities that must use their own tax revenues to leverage investments from others to ensure that any subsidies for big-ticket amenities become strategic investments. Without any advanced agreements from developers, Indianapolis actually secured more investments from private, nonprofit, and state government sources for new facilities and buildings (residential, commercial, and public) than any other city. The total private sector investments in Columbus, Los Angeles, and San Diego as part of the Arena District, L.A. LIVE, and the Ballpark District were smaller in value than those made in downtown Indianapolis. As a result of Indianapolis' success, a large portion of its downtown has been completely rebuilt and revitalized. Indianapolis accomplished its goals by following a focused strategy across four decades. Economically obsolete venues built with public subsidies (Market Square Arena and the RCA Dome) were replaced with new ones that were also heavily subsidized (Conseco Fieldhouse and Lucas Oil Stadium). To leverage its public investments, Indianapolis became "the broker city" aggressively negotiating for events and investments from the private and nonprofit sectors, as well as the state of Indiana, to ensure that the subsidies it provided became strategic investments.

Two organizations assumed important roles in helping Indianapolis leverage its investments. The Indiana Sports Corporation was charged with responsibility for attracting events (athletic competitions) and sports organizations (headquarters of associations and other groups) to the downtown area. Indianapolis Downtown Incorporated was responsible for recruiting and then advocating for businesses located in the downtown area. These organizations were part advocate, part dealmaker, and part business recruiter for the downtown revitalization strategy. The consolidated city/county's Department of Metropolitan Development also provided needed assistance. In 1985, Indianapolis created the Indianapolis Local Improvement Bond Bank to be the financing conduit for critical downtown redevelopment projects. The lesson to be learned from Indianapolis' effort was that a coordinated focus on downtown revitalization by numerous organizations made invaluable contributions to the efforts to secure investments by others in the downtown area. Revitalizing downtown was not a part-time activity of the mayor's office or even the responsibility of a small group of private leaders. The revitalization program was also not part of a "build it and they will come" process. Indianapolis did not just hope other investments would be made. Instead, a group of organizations and departments focused their staff on the downtown's revitalization. The lesson from Indianapolis' success is that, if there are not guaranteed commitments for development linked to the building of a sport, arts, culture, or entertainment amenity, then a focused effort by an array of organizations is required to increase the likelihood that subsidies become strategic investments.

If a city directs so much attention to its downtown area, does it run the risk of ignoring the needs of other communities? A criticism directed toward the administration of Indianapolis' four-term mayor (16 years) William Hudnut was that he put too much focus on downtown and did not pay sufficient attention to other communities and their needs.[5] While the pattern of private sector investment in Indianapolis suggests there never was a deflection of attention from the other parts of the city, it is possible that some inner city neighborhoods did not receive the attention needed to achieve their development goals. Communities that follow Indianapolis' model need to simultaneously provide focused leadership for efforts in other inner city areas.

The organizations created to bolster and support Indianapolis' revitalization strategy raise important questions regarding Reading's efforts. Community leaders who have limited staff to support their efforts are leading Reading's revitalization program. As a result, they have very few resources available to focus on successfully leveraging the commitments to secure investments by others. The Berks County Economic Partnership, as well as city and county agencies, is assuming some or all of the responsibilities performed by organizations, such as the Indiana Sports Commission and Indianapolis Downtown Incorporated, but none is as large and each seems to lack the needed resources and expertise to be as successful. If Reading is to capitalize on the investments made by its community leaders, elected officials will need to be sure the work associated with attracting events and businesses to the downtown area is performed. The elected leaders must also be sure sufficient staff resources are available to advocate for and ensure that businesses that relocate to the downtown area receive the services and attention they need to thrive and advance the region's economy. Any city that follows Indianapolis' model must make sure that appropriate investments are made to create and staff the supporting institutions. Without that investment, it is likely there will be fewer events and lower levels of private, nonprofit, and public investments.

F. Recommendation 6: Prudent Risk-Taking for Confidence Building

Cleveland's public sector embarked on its revitalization strategy to restore confidence in the city's future. It committed approximately three-quarters of a billion dollars to the effort, and there was a subsequent and pronounced uptick in private sector investment in the years after the building of several big-ticket amenities. In that regard, Cleveland's risk-taking was rewarded and the outcome was quite positive. What must be viewed with concern and caution is the overall lack of change. Despite extensive investments from private sector developers and an improved image, the region's economy still faltered and population losses for the city and county continued through 2008. Cleveland took needed risks, but two or three decades into its effort the city still cannot "win for losing" people and economic vitality.

What Lesson Does This Offer?

Changes in the larger economy can swamp or thwart successful revitalization efforts. No community can simply rely on new buildings and amenities or a completely revitalized section of its downtown to restructure economic outcomes. The public sector through big-ticket items and other investments in amenities can establish a framework for private sector activity, but economic development is inexorably related to business innovation and entrepreneurship. These innovations and advancements can be supported by the public sector, but leadership for economic advancement comes from the private sector. Successful revitalization efforts that lead to economic advancement require the existence of attractive amenities, the elimination of blight, and a focus on entrepreneurial activity and innovation by the private sector.

These observations are particularly important for cities like Reading. Its revitalization effort has been largely financed by a group of people committing their personal wealth to a dream of what the city again could be while using their political capital to secure assistance from state and federal agencies. Their extraordinary success and the impressive nature of their commitment will not change the city or region's future without new business development. Creating jobs will require a strong partnership that must be led by the public sector, these committed community leaders, and other businesses from throughout the region.

Even with a partnership of that magnitude, the sobering lesson from outcomes in Cleveland is that with regard to regional growth, even when there is a commitment to build amenities and other coordinated efforts, success is not guaranteed. Cleveland's effort united a small group of business leaders (Cleveland Tomorrow), local governments, and the broader business and university communities in a revitalization effort with each making a substantial commitment to advance the region through programs to aid business formation and entrepreneurship. Yet, Cleveland and Cuyahoga County continue to lose people and jobs. The enhancement of the physical infrastructure, the availability of amenities, and the attraction of people to downtown locations are foundation elements for longer-term changes and economic development. In Cleveland's case, while the city and county are still losing residents, there is now an unprecedented level of venture capital committed to the health and advanced manufacturing sectors. That change took place two decades after the implementation of the amenity enhancement focus and its rewards may not be evident for another decade. Reading has taken the steps to build a secure foundation for the future and that involved great risk. More risk and investment must be taken to advance the work of corporations and entrepreneurs if successful economic revitalization is to lead to new jobs and higher incomes for residents.

G. Recommendation 7: "Über-Plans" Unifying Public and Private Capital

All of the cities studied shared two elements in their revitalization strategies. Each emphasized amenities for its role in the attraction of human capital and each rejected an evolutionary approach to urban change in favor of large-scale plans. In every instance, years of stagnation or decline that had turned into decades led to a loss of confidence in perspectives that emphasized Jane Jacobs' approach to the life–death–life cycle of urban space and neighborhoods. Most community leaders by their actions believed that revitalization had to be "jump started" and that there would only be more decline if substantial resources were not injected into downtown areas. Each city had seen their downtown centers decline. Rising crime levels and economic and social segregation separated the downtown areas (and, in some instances, the entire city itself) from suburban areas or other parts of the cities. These conditions suggested that without focused and concentrated actions stagnation and decline would continue. In larger and smaller cities, leaders were convinced that in the absence of coordinated action and a mega-plan laid over the area there were simply too many more attractive locations where investors would prefer to invest their private capital. In Los Angeles, that private capital was focused on other parts of the city or region. For Reading, private capital was being invested in the suburban parts of the county or in other regions. San Diego's and Columbus' leadership also watched as development patterns pushed farther and farther away from the downtown area.

Revitalization in each of these cities involved the hyper-injection of coordinated public and private capital, a sort of "über-planning" view for the management and oversight of redevelopment that transformed an area almost overnight. This does not mean that the ideas put forward by Jane Jacobs and others are wrong. What it does imply is that a spatial component has been added to Joseph Schumpeter's theory of creative destruction. Public and private leaders do agree that innovation replaces shop-worn technologies and creates more jobs. But, in an era when these new jobs can be located distant from the ones eliminated, cities must compete to ensure that new opportunities occur within their boundaries. To create an inviting environment for the new jobs, cities are rushing to revitalize deteriorating core areas as quickly as possible while also providing the amenities thought to appeal to entrepreneurs and talented workers. The focus on amenity theory is a progressive effort to create viable spaces within which the new technologies will develop and flourish. In its essence, the "über-planning" or instant transformation approaches that led to the Arena or Ballpark Districts are efforts to spatially direct the life cycle of innovation into the area where jobs, businesses, and technologies have been displaced. Rather than rejecting ideas related to Jane Jacobs' ideas, the activities of leaders from Reading to Los Angeles and San Diego could be seen to be efforts to capture the positive outcomes from creative destruction.

The recommendation that emerges from each of the case studies is that revitalization efforts that involve a large-scale infusion of public and private money can revitalize downtown areas that for decades had declined. Some critics will argue that before such a conclusion can be sustained, comparisons need to made with areas that pursued a more naturally occurring revitalization strategy to determine whether or not that approach would lead to a new downtown area. While it is possible that allowing parts of a downtown area to go through a revival driven by naturally occurring market forces will lead to new buildings, residences, and businesses the evidence from each of the case studies was that downtown areas or sections of downtown areas were locked into protracted periods of decline or stagnation. In the absence of "über-plans," it seems reasonable to conclude that substantial or significant change was unlikely and development would continue to be attracted to other parts of a region or other regions.

H. Recommendation 8: Constructively Involve Business Leaders in Downtown and Community Development

A number of analysts viewed with dismay the roles played by business leaders in championing an emphasis on big-ticket items as anchors for revitalization strategies. Many correctly identified the benefits that big-ticket items typically produced for the corporations represented by the involved business leaders. The extraordinary profits earned by team owners as a result of the public sector's use of tax dollars to pay for facilities provided additional evidence of the substantial gains realized by already wealthy individuals when sport facilities were built with public money. Public subsidies for arts and cultural facilities also create benefits for those patrons who enjoy the new venues and they are typically wealthier than the residents of many inner city communities. These subsidies lower the cost of enjoying the arts and performances in the new museums and theaters. In the absence of a public subsidy, the cost of amenities would require higher ticket prices to ensure that facilities and events occur. This underscored the possibility that public subsidies for big-ticket items advanced the self-interest of business leaders or of higher income residents of regions.

It is impossible to study the role of amenities in revitalization efforts and not address the role of local corporations and their leaders. Special attention was directed toward this issue in Cleveland and Reading and the evidence there illustrates the complexity in putting forward any single set of observations regarding elite behavior with regard to redevelopment efforts. Cleveland's business leaders initially focused on advancing the region's economy through a focus on job and business creation and expanding the supply of venture capital in the region. These activities were initiated in response to the loss of thousands of manufacturing positions and a desire to create new jobs and foster growth for the region. To be sure, the region's corporations would have benefited from these activities, but job creation was the number one concern for all residents of the area and the small groups of business leaders was focused on providing leadership for economic development with benefits for the region. It would be hard to argue that those activities were only, or largely, self-serving advancements for limited pecuniary interests.

At the same time that Cleveland Tomorrow (and then the GCP) were making investments in big-ticket items, professional staff working for the organizations created by the corporate leaders argued for and secured resources to make a series of investments to rebuild inner city communities. Their work began with the funding of several neighborhood retail centers. With the population losses in Cleveland, most retailers had moved to suburban locations. Cleveland Tomorrow's investments helped to build several neighborhood shopping centers and attract stores to these projects. Cleveland Tomorrow and the GCP also took the lead in establishing organizations to advance the building of residential properties in the city's neighborhoods while organizing corporate support for public education. The corporate leaders provided all of the financial support for the campaigns to raise taxes to increase support for the Cleveland Public Schools. The corporations located in downtown Cleveland pay more than 60 percent of the local taxes assessed by the Cleveland Public Schools. Campaigning for higher school tax increases was tantamount to campaigning for higher corporate taxes. Other community development initiatives put forward include an annual discretionary fund for the head of the Cleveland Public Schools and the provision of volunteers for tutoring in numerous schools. Neighborhood Progress, Inc. (NPI) continues to assist numerous community development corporations involved in building new affordable homes in neighborhoods across the city. The business community created NPI, and corporate leaders still serve on its board and provide needed capital for new residential projects.

It could be argued that the value of these investments was far less than the public's expenditures for the big-ticket items. Following that line of thought, had the public sector assumed responsibility for the corporate community's investment portfolio and the private sector made the investments in the big-ticket items, overall tax levels would be far less. That logic cannot be refuted even if its political efficacy is unrealistic. In Cleveland, financial responsibility for the big-ticket items was assumed by the county meaning that at least two-thirds if not three-quarters of the fiscal burden was assumed by the wealthier residents of suburban areas. The direct tax revenue gains from the sports, entertainment, and arts facilities all accrue to Cleveland. While suburbanites voted for this arrangement, a willingness to support countywide responsibility for issues related to Cleveland's public schools or neighborhood-level retail and residential development would be harder to imagine. It is also unlikely that residents in other cities that were also supporting tax abatement to advance housing in their own cities would have agreed to help support housing projects in Cleveland.

These issues could be endlessly debated. What is clear, however, was that the corporate leaders in Cleveland had a large focus on community development illustrating the role of economic elites is not limited to self-serving activities. The review of revitalization efforts in Reading adds another layer of complexity. There a group of volunteers led the revitalization effort and is investing a substantial amount of their personal wealth with no clear path visible for it to recoup or directly benefit from the investments in amenities. The evidence in Reading suggests that, in the absence of the leadership from business leaders (or retired executives and entrepreneurs), revitalization plans for the downtown area might never have been launched. The existence of goggleWorks and Entertainment Square is a result of the efforts of a small group of volunteers. At this time, this group is also responsibility for ensuring that goggleWorks has sufficient revenue to meet its operating expenses.

This suggests that any community looking at a revitalization effort would be well served to involve business leaders in the effort. Elected officials and community organizers must be vigilant in protecting the public interests and ensuring that the activities are not designed to only advance a corporate agenda. The evidence from Cleveland and Reading suggests this will be a far easier task than may have been previously recognized. The evidence also indicates the view that corporate leaders are only focused on advancing their limited self-interest is not supported by a careful review of the complete range of their activities. It is still possible to suggest the private sector should assume more responsibility for the cost of big-ticket items. At the same time, it must be recognized that corporations are often involved in community development activities and programs to advance a region's overall economic development.

I. Recommendation 9: Level the Negotiating Table

Including sports facilities and other amenities in revitalization strategies was presented as one approach to offset the advantages the sports cartel have accrued. Several of the case studies illustrate that large and medium-sized markets have been able to offset some of the control exercised by teams that leads to subsidies by securing real estate investments that permitted some revitalization goals to be realized. However, the playing field has not been made completely level. San Diego did break new ground with its Ballpark District by getting the owner of the San Diego Padres to guarantee that more than $300 million in new real estate development would occur if the ballpark were built. More than three times that guaranteed level of new development has been built, but a positive final verdict on San Diego's fiscal gains will be realized only if there is continuing growth in real estate values. San Diego also got a new neighborhood built where it wanted and the extra hotel rooms it deemed necessary for its convention center. Columbus was also able to level the negotiating table and did not subsidize the building of an arena for a new hockey franchise. Nationwide Insurance paid for the arena, built a new neighborhood, and guaranteed that, if new property taxes were not sufficient to repay the bonds sold to build the needed infrastructure, it would be responsible for any shortfalls. Indianapolis has a new image and a new downtown. Its acceptance of a role as a broker city has leveraged more money for revitalization than was ever imagined and while it still has provided large subsidies to retain two professional sports teams. In 2012, Indianapolis will host a Super Bowl while continuing to be a perennial home for several high-profile NCAA championship events. Cleveland used a focus on sports and entertainment to overcome a crisis in confidence regarding its future and Los Angeles used aspects of advertising to rebuild part of its downtown once seen as a crime-laden zone to be avoided.

The negotiating table between cities and the interests that control amenities is not level. But, several cities through their incorporation of sports, culture, the arts, and entertainment in revitalization efforts achieved several important goals. To be sure, teams and other interests were enriched. So too were the cities and their downtown areas, and in that regard the steps they took created benefits, excitement, and new images. Subsidies can be avoided or the effects minimized by including team owners, the arts, and entertainment amenities into revitalization strategies. Indianapolis was only able to avoid losses from the excessive subsidies through its activities as a broker city, but its activities have produced extraordinary outcomes and an entirely new image. Columbus, Los Angeles, and San Diego received the benefits they wanted in exchange for their investments. Cleveland advanced its image and enjoyed substantial private sector investments in the aftermath of the provision of subsidies.

V. Conclusion

Sports, the arts, culture, and entertainment underscore the centrality of downtown areas. These amenities also contribute to the attractiveness of a region and in an era where businesses locate where people prefer to live, those communities with fewer amenities will likely enjoy less economic development. The six cities studied here have applied these ideas in efforts to create jobs and underscore their centrality. Each turned subsidies into strategic investments and created a level of success for themselves and their regions. Not all goals were achieved and some areas are still frustrated by their inability to reach the desired levels of economic development. Cleveland struggles with population growth and Reading still seeks to achieve a level of improved economic integration in its residents, but each city still has a safer downtown attracting crowds where once few would venture. They, too, have become Major League Winners joining Columbus,[6] Indianapolis, Los Angeles, and San Diego in providing examples of the ways in which revitalization can be achieved.

Endnotes

1. Clark, T. N., ed. 2004. *The city as an entertainment machine*. Amsterdam: Elsevier-JAI Press; Rosentraub, M. S. and M. Joo. 2009. Tourism and economic development: Which investments produce gains for regions? *Tourism Management* (forthcoming).
2. Berks County Economic Partnership, Sasaki Architects PC, and The Brookings Institution. 2006. *Penn corridor development plan*. Reading, PA: Berks County Economic Partnership; Hill, E. W. and J. F. Brennan. 2000. Methodology for indentifying the drivers of industrial clusters: The founding of regional competitive advantage. *Economic Development Quarterly* 14 (1): 65–96; Markusen, A. and G. Schrock. 2008. Placing labor center stage in industrial city revitalization. In *Retooling for growth: Building a 21st century economy in America's older industrial areas*, ed. R. M. McGahey and J. S. Vey, 179–210. Washington, D.C.: The Brookings Institution.
3. Gateway Economic Development Corporation. 2008. *Board of Directors Meeting Agenda*. November 12.
4. Berks County Economic Partnership, Sasaki Architects PC, and The Brookings Institution, *Penn corridor development plan*.
5. Hudnut, W. 1995. *The Hudnut years in Indianapolis, 1976–1991*, Indianapolis: Indiana University Press.
6. In May 2009 the Columbus Blue Jackets and Nationwide Insurance informed Columbus' leadership that both the team and the arena were losing money. Similar to the situation confronting Indianapolis, the recession had reduced the demand for tickets to the team's games and events held at the arena. The existence of a second arena—the one built by The Ohio State University—created additional competition to host a declining number of events in the greater Columbus region. To reduce the financial pressures on the team and the arena's operator, a proposal was made to have the public sector buy Nationwide Arena for $125 million. The proceeds would be used to bolster the team's balance sheet and cover the operating losses at the arena. This outcome did not mean the Columbus model for building an arena did not work. Rather what it underscored was that the failure of The Ohio State University and Columbus to build only one arena to serve the needs of the university and the metropolitan area left the region with two arenas, both struggling in the severe recession that gripped the nation throughout 2009 and into 2010.

References

American Craft. 2006. goggleWorks, Reading, PA. *American Craft*, October/November 6.

Andrews, D. 2004. Sports in the late capitalist movement. In *The commercialization of sport*, ed. Trevor Slack, 3–28. London: Routledge.

Austrian, Z. 2008. *Manufacturing Brief*. Center for Economic Development, Maxine Goodman Levin College of Urban Policy and Public Administration, Cleveland State University.

Austrian, Z. and M.S. Rosentraub. 2002. Cities, sports and economic change: A retrospective assessment. *Journal of Urban Affairs* 24 (5): 549–565.

Baade, R.A. 1996. Professional sports as catalysts for metropolitan economic development. *Journal of Urban Affairs* 18 (1): 1–17.

Baade, R.A. 2003. *Los Angles City Controller's report on economic impact: Staples Center*. Los Angeles: City of Los Angeles, Office of the Controller.

Baade, R.A. and R. Dye. 1988. Sports stadiums and area development: Assessing the reality. *Heartland Policy Study*, Number 68. Chicago: The Heartland Institute.

Bach, A. 2007. Arena District. *Urban Land*. Case Number C037003, January–March, Washington, D.C.: The Urban Land Institute.

Barnes, B. 2008. A film year full of escapism, flat in attendance. *New York Times,* January 2: http://www.nytimes.com/2008/01/02/movies/02year.html (accessed July 6, 2008).

Berks County Economic Partnership, Sasaki Architects PC, and The Brookings Institution. 2006. *Penn corridor development plan*. Reading, PA: Berks County Economic Partnership.

Birch, E. 2005. *Who lives downtown?* Washington, D.C.: The Brookings Institution, Metropolitan Policy Program.

Broderick, P. 2006. It takes a baseball park to raise a village. *San Diego Business Journal*, October 9, 27 (43): 40.

Brown, G. and M. Morrison, ed. 2008. *ESPN sports almanac 2008*. Lake Worth, FL: Sports Almanac.

Burns, M. 2007. Nationwide, schools settle arena valuation dispute. *Columbus Business First*, December 5, online ed.: http://columbus.bizjournals.com/columbus/stories/2007/12/03/daily22.html (accessed April 3, 2008).

Bush, B. 2008. Rivals to this day: As Ohio State's Schottenstein Center turns 10, its bumpy history with Nationwide Arena hasn't been forgotten. *Columbus Dispatch;* http://www.crainscleveland.com/apps/pbcs.dll/section?category=fram...es_2008_11_17_arena_anniv.ART_ART_11-17-08_A1_KOBTM3E.html_sid=101 (accessed November 17, 2008).

Cagan. J. and N. deMause. 1998. *Field of schemes: How the great stadium swindle turns public money into private profit*. Monroe, ME: Common Courage Press.

Chalip, L. 2002. Using the Olympics to opitmise tourism benefits: University lecture on the Olympics. Barcelona: Centre d'Estudies Olympics: http://olympicstudies.uab.es/lectures/web/pdf/chalip.pdf (accessed December 21, 2008).

Chapin, T. 2002. Beyond the entrepreneurial city: Municipal capitalism in San Diego. *Journal of Urban Affairs* 24 (5): 565–581.

Chema, T. 1996. When professional sports justify the subsidy: A reply to Robert A. Baade. *Journal of Urban Affairs* 18 (1): 19–22.

Children's Museum of Indianapolis. 2005. *The economic impact and value of The Children's Museum to the central Indiana economy.* Indianapolis: The Children's Museum.

City of Columbus. 1998. *Capital improvements project development and reimbursement agreement for Nationwide Arena District, September 15.* City of Columbus: Office of the Mayor.

Clark, T.N., ed. 2004. *The city as an entertainment machine.* Amsterdam: Elsevier-JAI Press.

Coates, D. and B.R. Humphreys. 1999. The growth effects of sports franchises, stadia, and arenas. *Journal of Policy Analysis and Management* 14 (4): 601–624.

Curry, T.J., K. Schwirian, and R.A. Woldoff. 2004. *High stakes: Big time sports and downtown redevelopment.* Columbus: Ohio State University Press.

Dahl, R.A. 1961. *Who governs? Democracy and power in an American city.* New Haven: Yale University Press.

Danielson, M.N. 1997. *Home team: Professional sports and the American metropolis.* Princeton, NJ: Princeton University Press.

Davies, J.S. 2002. Urban regime theory: A normative-empirical critique. *Journal of Urban Affairs* 24 (1): 1–17.

Deady, T. 1994. L.A. County hotel room occupancy shows a significant increase in 1993. *Los Angeles Business Journal,* March 7, as cited in *High-Beam Encyclopedia,* online ed.: http://www.encyclopedia.com/doc/1G1-15277102.html (accessed April 1, 2008).

Delaney, K.J. and R. Eckstein. 2003. *Public dollars, private stadiums: The battle over building sports stadiums.* New Brunswick, NJ: Rutgers University Press.

Duke, V. and L. Crolley. 1996. *Football, nationality, and the state.* London: Addison Wesley Longman.

Eisinger, P. 2000. The politics of bread and circuses. *Urban Affairs Review* 35 (3): 316–333.

Elkins, D.R. 1995. The structure and context of the urban growth coalition: The view from the chamber of commerce. *Policy Studies Journal* 23 (4): 583–601.

Euchner, C.C. 1994. *Playing the field: Why sports team move and cities fight to keep them.* Baltimore: Johns Hopkins University Press.

Farmer, S. 2007. SC, Coliseum Commission still trying to find solution. *Los Angeles Times.* December 14. Internet ed.: http://articles.latimes.com/2007/dec/14/sports/sp-newswire14 (accessed March 10, 2008).

Fels Institute of Government. 2008. *Vacancy inventory and reinvestment strategies for Reading, PA.* Philadelphia: University of Pennsylvania: http://www.readingpa.gov/documents/fels_report.pdf (accessed November 1, 2008).

Fidler, J. 2006. Reading: It's not just outlet malls anymore. *The Washington Post,* July 19, C2.

Florida, R. 2002. *The rise of the creative class.* New York: Basic Books.

Fogarty, M.S., G.S. Garofalo, and D.C. Hammack. 2002. *Cleveland from startup to the present: Innovation and entrepreneurship in the 19th and early 20th centuries.* Cleveland: Center for Regional Economic Issues, Weatherhead School of Business, Case Western Reserve University, http://generationfoundation.org/pubs/ClevelandFromStartupToPresent.pdf.

Forbes. 2008. NFL team valuations, http://www.forbes.com/lists/2008/30/sportsmoney_nfl08_NFL-Team-Valuations_Rank.html (accessed December 1, 2008).

Forbes 2008. NBA team valuations. http://www.forbes.com/lists/2008/32/nba08_NBA-Team-Valuations_MetroArea.html (accessed December 4, 2008).

Garmise, S. 2006. *People and the competitive advantage of place: Building a workplace for the 21ˢᵗ century.* Armonk, NY: M.E. Sharpe.

Gateway Economic Development Corporation of Greater Cleveland. 2008. *Resolution No. 2008-5 regarding authorization and approval of annual operating budget for 2009.* Cleveland: Gateway Economic Development Corporation of Greater Cleveland.

Gottdiener, M. 2001. *The theming of America: American dreams, media fantasies, and themed environments.* Boulder, CO: Westview Press.

Gronbjerg, K.A. and R. Clerkin. 2003. Indianapolis nonprofit sector: Management capacities and challenges. (Unpublished paper.) Indianapolis: Center on Philanthropy and the School of Public and Environmental Affairs, Indiana University.

Hamashige, H. 1994. Downtown L.A. office rents tumble more than 30%, but high-rise towers ride out quake with little damage—Los Angeles, California—Special Report: Quarterly Real Estate. *Los Angeles Business Journal,* January 31, online ed.: http://findarticles.com/p/articles/mi_m5072/is_n4_v16/ai_15125486 (accessed March 8, 2008).

Hannigan, J. 1998. *Fantasy city: Pleasure and profit in the postmodern metropolis.* London: Routledge Press.

Hanson, R.H., H. Wolman, and D. Connolly. 2006. *Finding a new voice for corporate leaders in a changed urban world: The Greater Cleveland Partnership.* Washington, D.C: The Brookings Institution Metropolitan Policy Program.

Harrison, B. and B. Bluestone. 1988. *The great u-turn: Corporate restructuring and the polarizing of America.* New York: Basic Books.

Harvard Business School. 1996a. *The Cleveland turnaround (A): Responding to the crisis, 1978-1988.* N9-796-151, Cambridge, MA: Harvard University.

Harvard Business School. 1996b. *The Cleveland turnaround (B): Building on progress, 1989-1996.* N9-796-152, Cambridge, MA: Harvard University.

Heister, M. 2008. *Public secondary school dropouts, 2006–2007.* Harrisburg, PA: Pennsylvania Department of Education.

Hill, E.W. and J.F. Brennan. 2000. Methodology for identifying the drivers of industrial clusters: The founding of regional competitive advantage. *Economic Development Quarterly* 14 (1): 65–96.

Hirschman, A.O. 1958. *The strategy of economic development.* New Haven: Yale University Press.

Hobbs, F. and N. Stoops. 2002. *Demographic trends in the 20ᵗʰ century: Census 2000 special reports.* Washington, D.C.: U.S. Department of Commerce, Bureau of the Census.

Hoffman, L., S.S. Fainstein, and D.R. Judd eds. 2003. *Cities and visitors: Regulating people, markets, and city space.* New York: John Wiley & Sons.

Home Box Office (HBO). 2008. *Nine innings from ground zero: The healing of a nation began with the swing of a bat.* http://www.hbo.com/sports/nineinnings/ (accessed October 8, 2008).

Hoyman, M. and C. Faricy. 2009. It takes a village: A test of the creative class, social capital, and human capital theories. *Urban Affairs Review* 44 (3): 311–333.

Hudnut, W. 1995. *The Hudnut years in Indianapolis, 1976-1991.* Indianapolis: Indiana University Press.

Humphrey, B. and D.R. Howard, eds. 2008. *The business of sports: Economic perspectives.* New York: Praeger Publishers.

Hunter, F. 1953. *Community power structure: A study of decision makers.* Chapel Hill: University of North Carolina Press.

Iarns, A., P. Kaplan, A. Bauerfeind, J. Huestis, and K. Quilliman. 2006. *Economic development and smart growth: 8 case studies on the connections between smart growth development and jobs, wealth, and quality of life in communities.* Washington, D.C.: International Economic Development Council.

Imbroscio, D.L. 1998. Reformulating urban regime theory: The division of labor between state and market reconsidered. *Journal of Urban Affairs* 20 (3): 233–248.

Indianapolis Downtown, Incorporated. 2007. *Annual report.* Indianapolis: Indianapolis Downtown, Incorporated.

Jacobs, J. 1969. *The economy of cities.* New York: Penguin Books.

Jacobs, J. 1993. *The death and life of great American cities.* New York: Modern Library.

Jennings, M.K. 1964. *Community influentials: The elites of Atlanta.* New York: Free Press.

Johnson, A. 2000. Minor league baseball: Risks and potential benefits for communities large and small. In *The economics and politics of sports facilities.* ed. W.C. Rich, 141–151. Westport, CT: Quorum Books.

Judd, D.R. and S.S. Fainstein, eds. 1999. *The tourist city.* New Haven, CT: Yale University Press.

Kang, Y.S. and R. Perdue. 1994. Long-term impact of a mega-event on international tourism to the host country: A conceptual model and the case of the 1988 Seoul Olympics. In *Global tourist behavior,* ed. M. Uysal, 205–226. New York: Haworth Press.

Kennedy, S. and M.S. Rosentraub. 2000. Public-private partnerships, professional sports teams, and the protection of the public's interests. *The American Review of Public Administration* 30 (4): 436–459.

Kotler, P.D., H. Haider, and I. Rein. 1993. *Marketing places: Attracting investment, industry, and tourism to cities, states, and nations.* New York: Free Press.

Kurtzman, J. 2005. Economic impact: Sport tourism and the city. *Journal of Sport Tourism* 10 (1): 47–71.

L.A. Arena Company, LLC. 1996. Proposal for L.A. Arena Company LLC to Los Angeles City Council, Mayor Richard Riordan, Los Angeles Convention and Exhibition Center, and the Los Angeles Community Redevelopment Agency. Los Angeles: Office of City Council.

Lackritz, M.E. 1968. *The Hough riots of 1966.* Cleveland: Regional Church Planning Office.

Larkin, B. 2008. How Cleveland fumbled away Eaton corporation. *The Plain Dealer,* October 5, D1 3.

Lefebvre, H. 1996. *Writings on cities.* Malden, MA: Blackwell Publishers.

Lefebvre, H. 1991. *The production of space.* Malden, MA: Blackwell Publishers.

Leland, S. and M.S. Rosentraub. 2009. Consolidated and fragmented governments and regional cooperation: Surprising lessons from Charlotte, Cleveland, Indianapolis, and Kansas City. In *Who will govern metropolitan regions in the 21st century?* ed. D. Phares, Armonk, NY: M.E. Sharpe (forthcoming).

Levine, M. 2000. A third world city in the first world: Social exclusion, racial inequality, and sustainable development in Baltimore, Maryland. In *The social sustainability of cities.* eds. M. Polese and R. Stren 123–156. Toronto: University of Toronto Press.

Levine, P. 1993. *From Ellis Island to Ebbets Field: Sport and the American Jewish experience.* Cary, NC: Oxford University Press.

Logan, J.R. and H.L. Molotch. 1987. *Urban fortunes: The political economy of place.* Berkeley: University of California Press.

Longworth, R.C. 2007. *Caught in the middle: America's heartland in the age of globalism.* New York: Bloomsbury USA.

Los Angeles, City of. 1997a. Proposed arena at the Los Angles Convention Center—memorandum to the ad hoc committee on the sports arena from Keith Comrie, City Administrative Officer and Ronald Deaton, Chief Legislative Analyst. Los Angeles: Office of the City Council.

Los Angeles, City of. 1997b. Los Angeles Convention Center Arena: Proposal summary. Internal Memorandum, City Council. Los Angeles: Office of the City Council.

Los Angeles, City of. 1998. Gap funding agreement between city of Los Angeles and L.A. Arena Company, LLC (Los Angeles Arena Project). March 26. Los Angeles: Office of the City Council.

Malanga, S. 2004. The curse of the creative class. *City Journal,* Winter, 36 (40): 36–45.

Markusen, A., and G. Schrock. 2008. Placing labor center stage in industrial city revitalization. In *Retooling for growth: building a 21st century economy in America's older industrial areas*, eds. R.M. McGahey and J.S. Vey, 179–210. Washington, D.C.: The Brookings Institution.

Marshall, A. 1920. *Principles of economics,* 8th ed. London: Macmillan and Company.

Mason, D.S. 2008. Synecdochic images and city branding. Unpublished paper presented at *The Role of Sports and Entertainment Facilities in Urban Development Conference,* Edmonton, Alberta, February 12. Faculty of Physical Education and Recreation, University of Alberta (and the Edmonton Chamber of Commerce).

McGahey, R. and J.S. Vey. eds. 2008. *Retooling for growth: Building a 21st Century economy in America's older industrial areas.* Washington, D.C.: The Brookings Institution.

McGovern, S.J. 2003. Ideology, consciousness, and inner city redevelopment: The case of Stephen Goldsmith's Indianapolis. *Journal of Urban Affairs* 25 (1): 1–26.

Mikelbank, B., M. Rosentraub, and C. Post. 2008. Residential property tax abatements and rebuilding in Cleveland, Ohio. Unpublished paper. Cleveland: Maxine Goodman Levin College of Urban Affairs, Cleveland, Ohio.

Misener, L. and D.S. Mason. 2006. Creating community networks: Can sporting events offer meaningful sources of social capital? *Managing Leisure* 11: 39–56.

Molotch, H. 1979. Capital and neighborhood in the United States: Some conceptual links. *Urban Affairs Quarterly* 14: 289–312.

Molotch, H. 1993. The political economy of growth machines. *Journal of Urban Affairs* 15 (1): 29–53.

Montgomery, D. 2008. The engine of change: Reading, Pa. has proven it's deft at switching tracks. As residents head to the polls, the question is: Where to next? *The Washington Post,* April 22, C01.

Moret, S., M. Fleming, and P.O. Hovey. 2008. Effective chambers of commerce: A key to regional economic prosperity. In *Retooling for growth: Building a 21st century economy in America's older industrial areas,* eds. R.M. McGahey, and J.S. Vey, 119–148, Washington, D.C.: Brookings Institution.

Money Magazine, 2008. 100 best places to live and launch. http://money.cnn.com/galleries/2008/fsb/0803/gallery.best_places_to_launch.fsb/index.html (accessed September 9, 2008).

Nelson, A.C. 2002. Locating major league stadiums where they can make a difference. *Public Works Management and Policy* 7 (2): 98–114.

Nicholson, M. and R. Hoye. eds. 2008. *Sport and social capital*. London: Elsevier.

Newman, M. 2006. The neighborhood that the ballpark built. *The New York Times*, April 26, 10.

Noll, R.G. and A. Zimbalist. 1997. Build the stadium— create the jobs! In *Sports, jobs, and taxes: The economic impact of sports teams and stadiums,* eds. R.G. Noll and A. Zimbalist, 1–54. Washington, D.C.: The Brookings Institution.

Nowak, J. 2008. The market-building potential of development finance in older industrial cities. In *Retooling for growth: building a 21ˢᵗ century economy in America's older industrial areas.* eds. R.C. McGahey and J.S. Vey, 373–410. Washington, D.C.: The Brookings Institution.

Peck, J. 2005. Struggling with the creative class. *International Journal of Urban and Regional Research* 29 (4): 74–770.

Perroux, F. 1955. Note sur la notion de pole de croissance. *Economique Appliquée* 1–2: 307–22.

Pierce, N.R. 2000. Ohio looks hard at what's lost through business subsidies. In *Readings in urban economic issues and public policy.* ed. R.W. Wassner, 151–153, Malden, MA: Blackwell Publishers.

Pine, J. and J.H. Gilmore. 1999. *The experience economy: Work is theatre and every business a stage.* Cambridge, MA: Harvard Business Press.

Porter, M.E. 1985. *Competitive advantage: Creating and sustaining superior performance.* New York: The Free Press.

Porter, M.E. 1990. *The competitive advantage of nations.* New York: Free Press.

Porter, P.R. and D. Sweet. 1984. *Rebuilding America's cities: Roads to recovery.* New Brunswick, NJ: Rutgers University, Center for Urban Policy Research.

Pramik, M. 2007. City Center might close once Macy's leaves. *Columbus Dispatch*, September 27: http://www.dispatch.com/live/content/local_news/stories/2007/09/27/city_center.html (accessed April 5, 2008).

Reese, L.A. and D. Fasenfest. 2004. *Critical evaluations of economic development policies.* Detroit: Wayne State University Press.

Riley-Katz, A. 2007. Nokia Theatre ready for its close-up: construction of AEG's $120 million project down-to-wire. *Los Angeles Business Journal,* October 15, Internet ed.: http://findarticles.com/p/articles/mi_m5072/is_42_29/ai_n21080011 (accessed March 9, 2008).

Rose, M.M. 2008. Forlorn downtown mall waits, *Columbus Dispatch*, August 1, p. 1.

Rose, M.M. and M. Pramik. 2009. Goodbye, City Center. *Columbus Dispatch*, February 4, p. 1.

Rosentraub, M.S. 1997a. *Major league losers: The real cost of sports and who's paying for it.* New York: Basic Books.

Rosentraub, M.S. 1997b. Stadiums and urban space. In *Sports, jobs, and taxes: The economic impact of sports teams and stadiums,* eds. R.G. Noll and A. Zimbalist, 178–207. Washington, D.C.: The Brookings Institution.

Rosentraub, M.S. 1998. *The San Diego Padres and the proposed ballpark and redevelopment plan: An assessment of business, economic, and spatial issues.* San Diego: San Diego Padres Baseball Club.

Rosentraub, M.S. 1999a. Are public policies needed to level the playing field between cities and teams? *Journal of Urban Affairs* 21 (4): 377–395.

Rosentraub, M.S. 1999b. *Major league losers: The real cost of sports and who's paying for it*, rev. ed. New York: Basic Books.

Rosentraub, M.S. 2000. Sports facilities, redevelopment, and the centrality of downtown areas: Observations and lessons from experiences in a rustbelt and sunbelt city. *Marquette University Sports Law Journal* 10 (2): 219–236.

Rosentraub, M.S. 2006. The local context of a sports strategy for economic development. *Economic Development Quarterly* 20 (3): 278–291.

Rosentraub, M.S., D. Swindell, M. Przybylski, and D. Mullins. 1994. Sports and a downtown development strategy: If you build it will jobs come? *Journal of Urban Affairs* 16 (3): 221–239.

Rosentraub, M.S. and P. Helmke. 1996. Location theory, a growth coalition, and a regime in a medium-sized city. *Urban Affairs Review* 31 (4): 482-507.

Rosentraub, M.S. and M. Joo. 2009a. Tourism and economic development: Which investments produce gains for regions? *Tourism Management* (forthcoming).

Rosentraub, M.S., D. Swindell, and S. Tsvetkova. 2009b. Justifying public investments in sports: measuring the intangibles. *Journal of Tourism* (forthcoming).

Rosentraub, M. S. and W. Al-Habil. 2009c. Why metropolitan governance is growing as is the need for flexible governments. In *Who will govern metropolitan regions in the 21ˢᵗ century?* ed. D. Phares, Armonk, NY: M.E. Sharpe (forthcoming).

Rother, C. 2002. Chargers offered to explore dropping ticket guarantee. *San Diego Union Tribune*: www.sandiego.gov/chargerissues/documents/explore.shtml (accessed March 30, 2008).

Rubenstein, H.M. 1992. *Pedestrian malls, streetscapes, and spaces*. New York: John Wiley & Sons.

Saito, L.T. 2007. Economic revitalization and the community benefits program: A case study of the L.A. Live project, a Los Angeles sports and entertainment district. Los Angles: Department of Sociology, University of Southern California.

Sanders, H. 2002. Convention myths and markets: A critical review of convent center feasibility studies. *Economic Development Quarterly* 16 (3): 195–210.

Sanders. H. 2005. *Space available: The realities of convention centers as economic development strategy*. Washington, D.C.: The Brookings Institution.

San Diego, City of. 1998. *Memorandum of understanding between the City of San Diego, the Redevelopment Agency of the City of San Diego, the Centre City Development Corporation, and Padres, L.P. concerning a ballpark district, construction of a baseball park, and a redevelopment project*. City of San Diego: Resolution R-291450, Attachment A.

San Diego, City of. 1999. *Manager's report*. City of San Diego, Report No. 99-64.

San Diego Union-Tribune. 2004. Change the mix: A vibrant downtown now needs more offices. March 31, B8.

Sandy, R.P., J. Sloane, and M.S. Rosentraub. 2004. *The economics of sports: An international perspective*. New York: Palgrave McMillan.

Schneider, K. 2008. A waterfront revival in the Midwest: Home and businesses enliven an old industrial district in Columbus, Ohio. *New York Times,* December 3, B4.

Schoettle, A. 2009. Fieldhouse flop? Pacers: We've lost money 9 of last 10 years. *Indianapolis Business Journal*, February 7: https://www.ibj.com (accessed February 7, 2009).

Scully, G. 1995. *The market structure of sports*. Chicago: The University of Chicago Press.

Searle, G. 2002. Uncertain legacy: Sydney's Olympic stadiums. *European Planning Studies* 10 (7): 845–860.

Sheban, J. 2004. Rise in urban housing cheered. *The Columbus Dispatch*, June 3, 1E.

Sloane, P.J. 1971. The economics of professional football: The football club as a utility maximiser. *Scottish Journal of Political Economy*. 18 (2): 121–146.

Snider, M. 2008. DVD feels first sting of slipping sales. *USA Today.* January 7: http://www. usatoday.com/life/movies/news/2008-01-07-dvd-sales-slippage_N.htm (accessed January 5, 2008).

Spatz, D. 2008. Reading's two civic centers combine for $164,000 profit. *Reading Eagle,* August 21 online ed.: https://www.readingeagle.com (accessed September 6, 2008).

Squires, G., ed. 1989. *Unequal partnerships: Political economy of urban redevelopment in post-war America.* New Bruswick, NJ: Rutgers University Press.

Stoffel, J. 1990. New sports complex for Cleveland. *New York Times,* June 13: http://query. nytimes.com/gst/fullpage.html?res=9C0CE2DC1F31F930A25755C0A966958260 (accessed September 9, 2008).

Stolarick, K. and R. Florida. 2006. Creativity, connections and innovation: A study of linkages in the Montreal region. *Environment and Planning A* 38: 1799–1817.

Stone, C. 1989. *Regime politics: Governing Atlanta, 1946-1988.* Lawrence, KS: University of Kansas Press.

Swiatek, J. 2008. A work in progress: Even before designs are finalized, massive JW Marriott project is forging ahead. *The Indianapolis Star,* October 5, D1, 4.

Swindell, D. 2000. Issue representation in neighborhood organizations: Questing for democracy at the grassroots. *Journal of Urban Affairs* 22 (2): 123–137.

Swindell, D. and M.S. Rosentraub. 2009. Doing better: Sports, economic impact analysis, and schools of public policy and administration. *Journal of Public Administration Education* (forthcoming).

Swindell, D., M. Rosentraub, and A. Tsvetkova. 2009. Public dollars, sports facilities, and intangible benefits: The value of a team to a region's residents and tourists. *Journal of Tourism.* 9 (2): 133–159.

Tiger, C. 2008. See for yourself: A former eyeglass factory brings a Pennsylvania city's vision to life. *American Style.* August: 70–75.

Timmons, A. 2006. Winning on the field and at the ballot box: The effect of the fan base on stadium subsidies. Unpublished public policy thesis. Stanford University: Department of Economics.

Trumpbour, R. 2007. *The new cathedrals: Politics and the media in the history of stadium construction.* Syracuse, NY: Syracuse University Press.

Turner, D. 1995. Police crackdown causes crime rate to plummet in downtown LA. *Los Angeles Business Journal,* April 3 online ed. contained at BNET: http://findarticles. com/p/articles/mi_m5072/is_n14_v17/ai_17015000 (accessed March 10, 2008).

US Airways Magazine. 2006. The man with a plan. November 2006, 136.

Viles, Peter. 2008. L.A. Land: Downtown blues. *Los Angeles Times,* o-line ed.: https:// latimesblogs.latimes.com/laland/2008/03/downtown-blues.html (accessed December 10, 2008).

Vogelsang-Coombs, V. 2007. Mayoral leadership and facilitative governance. *American Review of Public Administration* 37 (2): 198–225.

Warren, S. 1994. Disneyfication of the metropolis: Popular resistance in Seattle. *Journal of Urban Affairs* 16 (2): 89–108.

Williams, J. 2004. Warehouse rejuvenation transformed East Village. *San Diego Union-Tribune,* December 12: http://www.signonsandiego.com/uniontrib/20041212/news_ mz1j12buss.html (accessed March 28, 2008).

Wilson, D. 1996. Metaphors, Growth coalition discourses, and black poverty neighborhoods in a U.S. city. *Antipode.* 28 (1): 72–96.

Wilson, J. 1994. *Playing by the rules: Sport, society, and the state*. Detroit: Wayne State University Press.

Wojan, T.R., D.M. Lambert, and A. McGranahan. 2007. Emoting with their feet: Bohemian attraction to creative milieu. *Journal of Economic Geography* 31: 711–736.

Zahniser, David. 2005. L.A. Live promoters tout Times Square West. *Daily Breeze*, September 18 online ed." http://www.joelkotkin.com/Commentary/DB%20LA%20Live%20 promoters%20tout%20Times%20Square%20West.htm (accessed March 8, 2008).

Zimbalist, A. 2006. *The bottom line: Observations and arguments on the sports business*. Philadelphia: Temple University Press.

Zimbalist, A. and J.G. Long. 2006. Facility finance: Measurement, trends and analysis. *International Journal of Sport Finance* 1: 201–211.

Index

A

Advertising revenues, 20
    benefits to public sector, 250
    ethical issues, 251–252
    Los Angeles pylon agreements, 135, 140,
        141, 142
    in Reading, PA, 234, 235
    value to development, 250–252
Allentown, PA, 233
Amateur sports strategy, in Indianapolis, 68
Amenities. *See also* Big-ticket amenities
    ability to change distribution of human
        capital, xiv, 44
    correct mix of, 41
    failure to change regional economic
        development, 23, 219, 260
    as fool's gold, 247
    importance of, 43–44
    linkage to economic development, 22–23
    regional cooperation in building, 207
    and sports/entertainment/culture triad,
        12–13
    supply of, 42–43
    value for economic revitalization, 248
Amenity theory, 262
American Idol competition, at Nokia Theatre,
    150
Amusement taxes, in Cleveland, 206
Ancient Rome, importance of sports/culture/
    entertainment in, 13
Anshutz Entertainment Group (AEG), 133,
    155, 251
    share of redevelopment costs, 143
    transfer of land via eminent domain, 148
Arena District, 178–180

actual development, 176–177
Columbus plan, 167–168
comparisons with San Diego Ballpark
    District, 176
development in, 174
early assessment, 171–176
financial arrangements, 168–171
master plan, 173
private sector investment, 175
property tax exemptions for, 167
total cost, 170–171
Arlington, Texas, failures from planned
    redevelopment, 46
Artificial scarcity, role of sports leagues in
    creating, 57
Atlantic Yards project, 247, 255
Austin, Texas, music scene in, 36–38

B

Baltimore, 19
    Harborfront development, 16
    population changes, 7
    team relocation, 59
Banana Factory, Bethlehem, PA, 235, 236
Barnstorming, 56
Baseball, role in socializing U.S. immigrants,
    15–16
Berks County
    contemporary outlook, 226–230
    population change in, 225, 226
    racial and economic segregation, 229
    suburbanization trends, 224, 225
    white flight in, 228–229
Berkshire Mall, 232
Best places to live lists, 12

Bidding environment, 33, 54
Big-ticket amenities
    attracting human capital with, 34
    and city image, 35–36
    Cleveland's image-focused investment in,
        188
    controversy over role in attracting talented
        workers, 39
    and creative class, 36–38
    and economic development, 39–42
    framework for investment, 31–33, 34
    and human capital, 39–42
    as iconic architecture, 34
    importance of, 43–44
    in Indianapolis, 66
    and neighborhood revitalization, 47–48
    participation modes for planning, 34
    private sector need to assume cost for, 264
    real value of, 31
    and redevelopment orientation, 34
    supply issues, 42–43
    unbalanced negotiations over, 34
    uniting with neighborhood amenities, 40
    value and appropriateness, 35
    vs. neighborhood development, 38–39
Boscov, Albert, 235
Boston
    festival marketplaces, 8
    population changes, 7
Broadcast revenue deals, cartels' control over,
        58
Broker city
    Indianapolis as, 65, 94–96, 246
    organizations necessary for success as,
        258–259
Brooklyn
    Atlantic Yards project, 247, 255
    gentrification, 48
Building permits, total value in Reading, 241
Business-labor relationships, shift in, 248
Business leaders, 32
    civic initiatives, 33
    contributions to education in Cleveland,
        215, 217
    control over policymaking, 32–33
    disinterest and detachment in Cleveland,
        215
    empowerment by Mayor Voinovich, 188
    importance of involving in community
        development, 262–264
    limited control of development, 50
    paucity in smaller cities, 224

personal commitment in Reading, PA, 231
    private funds committed by, 231
    in Reading, Pennsylvania, 230
    role in Cleveland redevelopment, 188,
        215–217, 219–220
    role in Reading, PA, 241–242
    and urban redevelopment, 49–51
    Voinovich's emphasis on, 191, 192–194
Business location, and human capital issues, 23
Business relocation
    factors in, 41
    and growth poles, 47

C

Cartels, sports leagues as, 33, 51
Case studies, 9–10
    Columbus, 161–182
    Indianapolis, 65–96
    Los Angeles, 129–157
    overview, 24–26
    Reading, Pennsylvania, 223–243
    San Diego, 99–127
    similarities between cities, 249–250
Central cities
    economic contraction and population
        declines in, 6
    loss of quality of life, 11
Central Indiana market, team support stresses,
        92
Centrality
    historical end of, 5
    in Indianapolis, 78–87
    loss of, 1–2
Charlotte, failures from planned redevelopment,
        46
Chicago
    iconic structure building, 35
    population changes, 7
    Soldier Field, 54–55
Chicago White Sox, 54
Chichen-Itza, Great Ball Court, 14
Cincinnati
    population changes, 7
    sports league placements in, 164–165
Cincinnati Reds, 164
City-team relationships, unbalanced, 25
Cleveland, 26
    advanced manufacturing program, 216
    advertising options, 251
    alcohol and tobacco taxes, 194
    amusement tax revenue collection, 206

assessment of development results, 198–207
ballpark and Arena lease renegotiations, 213–214
Browns relocation, 197
building of sports facilities, 195
business leaders' role in development, 215–217
Central Market decline, 194
construction costs for nonresidential projects, 200
construction costs for residential projects, 201
continued loss of residents, 218, 219, 260
corporate tax losses, 204–205
crisis of confidence, 188–191
dispersion of new facilities, 186, 196–198, 252–253
Domed Stadium Corporation, 193
downtown revitalization as symbol of confidence, 191–198
drop in sports attendance, 209
east-west economic division, 189
economic contraction and fiscal default in, 190–191
failure to focus development in single neighborhood, 186
fiscal defaults, 190–191
Flats redevelopment, 192, 247
Gateway Development Authority, 195
Glenville riots, 189
Greater Cleveland Partnership, 66
healthcare industry, 205, 207
Hough area riots, 189
iconic structure building in, 35
income tax receipts, 204
Indians' payrolls and winning percentages, 212
job losses, 185–188
job retention and employment changes, 205–207
lack of coordinated development strategy, 185
linking of Browns franchise to stadium building, 197
new leases with sports leagues, 208–214
new property tax sources, 202
overall lack of economic change, 260
payroll earnings, 206
Playhouse Square, 191–192, 193
population changes, 7, 190, 266
population declines, 185–188

private investment for nonresidential projects, 199–200
private investment for residential projects, 200–202
property tax abatements, 198, 201, 202, 204, 218
property tax receipts, 205
public-private partnerships, 191–192
public sector responsibilities for cost overruns, 208–209
Quicken Loans Arena, 195
racial conflict and white flight in, 188–190
regional cooperation in building amenities, 207
renegotiations with new team owners, 210–213
residential development, 192
retention of private sector payrolls, 83–84
revival of ballpark and arena referendum, 194–196
Rock and Roll Hall of Fame, 196–197
role of business leaders, 33
sports/cultural/entertainment facilities building, 185–188
sports league placements in, 164–165
struggle to retain highly skilled workers, 38
subsidization of sports facilities, 190–198, 208–210
suburban support for new facilities, 195, 220, 264
successful urban neighborhoods, 39
tax revenue changes, 202–205
team investments in new facilities, 218
ticket taxes, 205
unfocused negotiations with teams, 196
unsafe image, 189, 191
Voinovoch's mayoralty, 192–194
voter rebellion, 21, 194, 195
White's mayoralty, 194–196
Cleveland Browns, 164–165
team relocation, 197
Cleveland Cavaliers, 194, 195
commitments to invest in ballpark, 219
contentious negotiations with government, 209
relocation to downtown, 210
Cleveland Clinic, 205
Cleveland Foundation, 192
Cleveland Indians, 164
new commitments to invest in ballpark, 219
payrolls and winning percentages, 212
renegotiation of lease, 208

Cleveland Orchestra, 43
Cleveland Theater District Development
    Corporation, 192
Cleveland Tomorrow, 193, 216, 220, 263
Club owners, benefits from subsidization,
    18–20
Colosseum, 13, 35
Columbus, 25
    actual development, 176–177
    Arena District, 26, 45, 178–180
    Arena District assessment, 171–176
    Arena District plan, 167–168
    avoidance of tax increases, 177
    development in Arena District, 174
    Dispatch Ice Haus, 171–172
    education benefits from development, 168,
        177, 181
    environmental restoration responsibilities,
        169
    exercise of eminent domain, 168, 171
    failed initiatives in, 161–163, 173
    failures from planned redevelopment, 46
    financial arrangements, Arena district,
        168–171
    franchise fee, 165, 166, 170
    Germantown development, 39
    growth in private sector employment, 86
    growth of Delaware County, 173–174
    infrastructure improvement responsibilities,
        167
    integrated development in, 181
    lack of income guarantees, 168
    major league sports in, 161–163
    master vision, Arena District, 173
    minor league baseball in, 181
    Nationwide Arena, 177
    need for professional sports team, 163–166,
        165–166
    neighborhood revitalization in, 161–163
    percentage public and private investments,
        170
    and population changes in Central Ohio,
        175
    private sector financial risk, 167, 169, 170
    privately built arena in, 161–163, 166–171
    property tax exemptions for Arena area, 167
    property tax expectations and
        commitments, 175
    public/private partnership in, 166–171, 170
    public sector investment, 169, 170
    quality of life investments, 12

    real estate development in, 166–171
    Short North community, 172, 173
    total public investment, 169
    voter rebellion, 21, 50, 161–163, 165
Columbus Blue Jackets, 168
Columbus Dispatch Ice Haus, 171–172
    comparisons with San Diego Ballpark
        District, 172
Community benefits agreements, 156
    in Los Angeles, 152–153, 156–157
Community development
    core *vs.* other neighborhoods, 259
    importance of involving business leaders in,
        262–264
    in Reading, Pennsylvania, 238–239
    role of economic elites in, 264
Competition, minimization by cartels, 57
Concentrated amenities, value of, 252–254
Confidence building, 250, 261. *See also* Crisis of
        confidence
    prudent risk-taking for, 260–261
Conseco Fieldhouse, 70, 88, 254
Consolidated city-county government, 65–66
Constantinople, Hippodrome, 14
Cost overruns, in Cleveland, 208–209
Creative class, 12, 25, 41, 60
    attracting in Indianapolis region, 78
    attracting through amenities, 36–38
Creative destruction theory, 261–262
Credit crisis, 125
    and continued loss of manufacturing jobs,
        226
    and downtown L.A. real estate decline, 157
    effects on Reading development, 239, 240
    effects on revitalization projects and
        property taxes, 247
    effects on San Diego tax revenues, 116, 257
    effects on strategic investments, 246–249
    rebuilding cities amid, xiii
Crime rates
    issues for all cities, 249
    Reading, PA, 228, 229, 232
Crisis of confidence, 250, 261. *See also*
        Confidence building
    in Cleveland, 188–191
    in Reading, PA, 232
    redevelopment to resolve, 191–198
Cultural centers. *See also* Sports/entertainment/
        culture triad
    as opportunity for development, 9

Cuyahoga County
    continued population loss, 218
    cost overruns and property tax receipts, 209
    population changes, 190

D

Dallas Cowboys, 20
Damage clauses, 58
Debt levels, due to subsidization, 2–3
Decapolis, sport facilities in ancient, 14
Democratic participation
    issues in Indianapolis, 67
    undermining of, 70
Demographic changes, in Reading, PA, 230
Detroit, population changes, 7
Development
    as alternative to legal action against teams, 60
    as alternative to subsidies, 60
    Arena District, Columbus, 174
    failure of amenities to change, 23
    human capital approach to, 41
    links to new facilities, 3
    role of big-ticket amenities, 39–42
    stagnation as cost of delay, 45–47
Disney Hall, 35, 154, 155
Disney World, and tourism planning concept, 134
Disneyfication, of sports, 134–135
Dispersed revitalization
    in Cleveland, 186, 187, 197
    risks of, 252–254
Diversification, and economic recovery, xiii–xiv, xv
Dolan, Larry, 210
Downtown redevelopment, 1–2
    assessment of results in Cleveland, 198–207
    in Columbus, 171
    and crisis of confidence in Cleveland, 191–198
    failure to transform Indianapolis region, 96
    leveraging by new facilities, 3
    in Los Angeles, 129–130, 136–139, 146–147, 171
    in Reading, PA, 223
    and rise of sports and culture for revitalization, 9–10
    in San Diego, 99–100, 107, 111, 112, 171
    sports/entertainment/culture as trinity for, 16–22
    turning subsidies into strategic investments with, 245–246

E

Economic contraction, in Cleveland, 190–191
Economic development. *See also* Development
    role of sports and culture in, xiii
    using sports/entertainment/culture for, 4–5
    value of amenities for, 248
Economic elites, role in community development, 264
Economic recovery, diversification and, xiii–xiv, xv
Education
    benefits from development in Columbus, 168, 177, 181
    business leaders' contributions in Cleveland, 215
    decay in Cleveland, 189
    Gateway support in Cleveland, 208
    importance for true economic development, 23, 40
    investment by business leaders in Reading, 236
    as investment in human capital, xiv
    private sector investment in Cleveland, 201–202
    and property taxes in Cleveland, 203
    in Reading, Pennsylvania, 227–228
    school adoption program in Cleveland, 216–217
Elitist model
    of redevelopment, 34, 67
    skewing of civic agenda by, 70
Eminent domain, 34, 246
    attempts to seize team assets by, 22
    ethical issues, 258
    use in Columbus, 168, 171
    use in Los Angeles, 130, 140, 148
Employment concentrations
    in Cleveland, 205–207
    in Indianapolis, 81, 96
    private sector employment, 82
    in Reading, PA, 227
English theater, historical importance, 15
Entertainment venues. *See* Sports/ entertainment/culture triad
Evolutionary change theory, 32, 34, 44–49
    and destruction of neighborhood character, 124
    San Diego implementation and challenges, 117
Experience economy, 12, 23

F

Fabulous Forum, 131–132, 137
    limitations, 132–133
Fairness in Antitrust in National Sports Act
        (FANS), 59
Famous architects, use of, 255
Faneuil Hall, 8
Festival marketplaces, 6–7
    lessons learned, 7–8
    replacement by sports and entertainment
        venues, 9
Foreclosure rates, in Reading, Pennsylvania,
        230
Franchise fees, for Columbus NHL
        membership, 165
Franchise values, 20–22, 51–54
Franklin County Convention Facilities
        Authority (FCCFA), 165
    eminent domain acquisitions, 168
Free markets
    failure of, 54
    sports leagues' domination of, 51

G

Gateway development, 172, 208
    reduced financing, 209
Gehry, Frank, 255
Gilbert, Dan, 211
Gladiatorial games, 14
GoggleWorks, 236, 237, 253
    success of, 240
Grammy Awards, 150
Growth coalitions, 49
    in Columbus, 165
    in Indianapolis, 66, 67, 68, 74, 94
Growth poles, 32, 47–49
Growth regimes, 50
    in Cleveland, 192–194
    in Indianapolis, 94
Gund Foundation, 192

H

Hippodrome, 14
Historical buildings, remodeling, 7
Hockey leagues, 162
Hollywood Park Raceway, 137
Home ownership subsidization, in Reading, PA,
        238, 242
Human capital, 23, 32, 38

ability of amenities to change distribution,
        44
    amenities attracting, 36
    attracting and retaining, xiv
    attracting with big-ticket amenities, 34, 249
    attracting with sports/entertainment/culture
        development, 4–5, 11–12
    and big-ticket amenities, 39–42
    and choice of community, xv
    competitive advantages based on, 249
    as driver of economic development, 24
    investment through education, xiv
    reliance of business development on, 248
    and sports/entertainment/culture triad,
        12–13

I

Iconic architecture, 34
    big-ticket items as, 34
    creating city identity through, 35
    importance to development efforts, 254–256
    in Los Angeles redevelopment, 153–154
Idea generators, 12, 41, 43, 60
Identity, creating through iconic architecture,
        35
Image
    effect of abandoned properties on, 187
    issues in Los Angeles, 129–130, 132, 136
    issues in Reading, Pennsylvania, 228, 232
    as motivation for new facility investment,
        4–5
    and new museums in Cleveland, 196–197
    role in Cleveland redevelopment, 185–188,
        188
    role in Reading, PA, 235–237
    strategies for all cities, 249
    and value of big-ticket items, 35
Income inequality, between central cities and
        suburbs, 6
Income statistics, metropolitan areas with MLB
        teams, 103–104
India-No-Place, 87
Indiana Repertory Theatre, 16, 89
Indiana Sports Corporation, 95, 258
Indianapolis, 19, 24
    amateur sports strategy, 68
    approved and funded projects, 73
    balanced approach to development, 39
    as broker city, 65, 94–96
    changes due to redevelopment strategy, 75
    changing employment concentrations, 81

civic image strategy, 8–9
commercial investment in downtown, 76
concentration of jobs, 84
Conseco Fieldhouse, 71, 75, 88, 91
decline in local visitors, 89–90
Department of Metropolitan Development, 95
development goals, objectives, and history, 65–69
downtown bike path, 40
downtown comparisons, 87–88
downtown maintenance, 75–77
downtown payroll dollars concentration, 82
failure to greatly increase jobs and payrolls, 87, 96
Fountain Square neighborhood, 39
future challenges, 90–94
goal of becoming amateur sports capital, 16–17
health sector expansion, 81
hospitality sector employment, 78
iconic structure building in, 35
idea generators in, 43
IDI, 74
image changes, 87, 94
income levels, 78–80
investments from nonprofit and state government sources, 258
job concentrations in Marion County, 83
lessons learned, 25–26
Lucas Oil Stadium, 71, 72, 73, 75, 90, 91
Market Square Arena, 71, 91
median family income levels, 79
modest population growth, 77
music scene in, 36–38
nonimage of, 68
percent change, private sector payroll dollars, 86
population changes, 7
private sector employment, 82, 85
public and private investments in, 72–73
public and private sector jobs, 83
quality of life investments, 12
regional economic changes and centrality, 78–87
remaking of downtown residential neighborhood, 72
residential units built, 75, 76, 86
revitalization examples, 48–49
safety rating, 90
specific facilities, 70–72
sports and redevelopment, 69–70

struggle to retain highly skilled workers, 38
subsidies and revenues challenges, 90–94
success of planned redevelopment, 46
as Super Bowl host city, 87–90
uniting big-ticket items with neighborhood amenities, 40
Indianapolis 500, 68, 69
Indianapolis Arts Garden, 48
Indianapolis Colts, 69, 73, 89
effort to secure revenue protection, 90–94
Indianapolis Downtown Incorporated (IDI), 74, 89, 95, 258
Indianapolis Pacers, 162, 165
Indianapolis Symphony, 8, 16, 71
Industry clusters, 45
Inner city schools, advancement of, 10
Innovations
origin in social interactions, 44
role in job growth, 41
Intellectual capital, attracting, 11–12

J

Jacobs, Richard, 210
James, LeBron, 213
JMI Realty, 125, 126, 257
Job concentrations
midwestern cities, 84
retention efforts in Cleveland, 201–202
Job creation, 10
efforts in Cleveland, 217
failure of Indianapolis sports strategy, 78
Job losses, in Cleveland, 185–188
Job relocation
midwestern manufacturing jobs, 11
and suburbanization, 6
Job retention, in Cleveland, 205–207

K

Kansas City
growth in private sector employment, 86
increase and declines in employment, 81
population changes, 7
Kroc, Joan, 101
Kroc, Ray, 101
Kucinich, Dennis, 190, 191, 215

L

L.A. Arena Company, 140
L.A. Kings

and Fabulous Forum, 131–132
need for new facility, 131
relocating to downtown, 130–135
L.A. Lakers, 155
and Fabulous Forum, 131–132
need for new facility, 131
relocating to downtown, 130–135
L.A. LIVE, 16, 35, 45, 129–130, 130, 139,
148–151, 154, 155, 251, 253, 256
and community redevelopment, 152–153
public sector investment, 149
schematic view, 151
Legal actions
to eliminate subsidies, 33
against teams, 34, 58–60
Lessons learned
broker city requirements, 258–259
business leader involvement, 262–264
concentrated *vs.* dispersed amenities, 252
festival marketplaces, 8
iconic architecture, 254–256
Indianapolis, 65
leveling negotiation leverage, 264–265
linking private sector investments to tax
money commitments, 256–258
planned development linking public/private
capital, 261–262
prudent risk-taking for confidence building,
260–261
similarities of case study cities, 249–250
value of advertising, 250–252
value of planning, 252–254
Lilly Endowment, 66, 68
Liquidated damages, legal attempts to enforce,
58
Living wage guarantees, 152
Location
and freeway access, 139
issues in downtown Los Angeles, 138
and L.A. redevelopment, 129–130
Los Angeles, 25, 32
advertising pylon agreements, 140, 141, 142
appeal of downtown, 133–135
area economics, 133–135
city investment and returns, 141–147
community development and L.A. LIVE,
152–153
comparative population density, 138
debate over need for additional
entertainment facilities, 149
destructive tendencies of planners, 44
deterioration of downtown areas, 156

Disneyfication of sports, 134–135
downtown housing redevelopment,
146–147, 147
downtown liabilities and assets, 136–139
downtown occupancy rates, 136
efforts to resuscitate convention center,
154–155
emphasis on tourism and consumption, 152
Fabulous Forum, 131–132
failures from planned redevelopment, 46
Forum limitations, 132–133
freeway access issues, 138, 139, 140
housing value increases, 147
iconic structure building in, 35, 153–154
image of violence and lawlessness, 129–130,
132, 136
investment repayment to L.A. Community
Reinvestment Agency, 147
investments in STAPLES Center, 143
L.A. Lakers, 131–132
L.A. LIVE, 148–151
land and location issues, 138
location issues, 137, 138–139
new property taxes generated, 146
Nokia Center, 151
payments to city for STAPLES Center, 145
private sector share of costs, 141, 143
protection of public interest, 142
public/private partnership, 140–141
public/private partnerships, 51
quality of life investments, 12
real estate declines, 157
STAPLES Center, 26, 45, 138
success of planned redevelopment, 46
taxpayer protection, 144, 146
team relocation to downtown, 130–135
use of eminent domain, 130, 140, 148
voter opposition to sports subsidies, 165
Los Angeles Community Reinvestment Agency
investment repayments, 147
share of redevelopment costs, 143
Los Angeles Convention Center
comparisons to San Diego and Orange
County, 131
deterioration, 130
efforts to resuscitate, 154–155
hotel for, 139, 149
share of development costs, 141, 143
as white elephant, 129, 130
Los Angeles Philharmonic Orchestra, 153
Louisville, consolidated government in, 66
Low-income population

home ownership subsidization for, 238–239, 242
in Reading, PA, 226, 228
Low-rent areas, potential economic value, 44–45
Luxury seating, 99, 133
in Cleveland ballpark, 208
and Disneyfication, 134
in Los Angeles, 133
as new revenue stream in Cleveland, 211
in Roman Colosseum, 14
San Diego ranking, 102

M

Major League Baseball
changes in player salaries, 20
controlled distribution of teams, 53–54
estimated team earnings, 105
franchise values, 52–53
history, 56–57
metropolitan areas population, income, and GDP, 103–104
Major league image, 4
Major League Soccer (MLS), Columbus Crew, 163
Manufacturing jobs
losses in Cleveland, 190, 202, 204
losses in Reading, PA, 224–225, 226
shift to other sectors from, 248
Market controls, arguments against, 53
Market forces. *See also* Free markets
sports leagues' control over, 33
Median family income
in Indianapolis, 80
midwestern cities, 79
Middle/upper income population
attracting with sports/entertainment/culture venues, 11
challenges of luring, 24
Midwestern cities
concentration of jobs, 84
downtown payroll dollars in, 82
economic restructuring, 226
median family income levels, 79
Migration trends, 42
Miller Center for the Arts, 237, 238
Minneapolis Lakers, 131–132
Minor league teams
move to attract, 4
in Reading, PA, 243

Moores, John, 101, 106, 108
JMI Realty, 125, 126

N

Naming rights, 2, 20, 99, 107
in Columbus, 168
minor league ballpark in Columbus, 181
Nashville, iconic structure building in, 35
National Basketball Association (NBA), 8, 162
history, 57
National Football League (NFL), 162
franchise values, 18, 19, 52–53
power over market forces, 54
protection for small market teams, 90
team movements, 4
National Hockey League (NHL), 163
franchise fees, 165
Nationwide Insurance Company, 161, 163, 257
commitment to develop without tax monies, 167
development guarantees to Columbus, 166
further development, 180
incentives to build, 178–179
naming rights, 168
property tax commitments to Columbus, 175
Nationwide Realty Investors, 161
Native Americans, importance of lacrosse, 15
Neighborhood Progress, Incorporated (NPI), 216, 263
Neighborhood revitalization, 4, 34, 42
as alternative to subsidies, 60
Columbus Dispatch Ice Haus and, 171–172
dependence on larger economic factors, 260
in downtown Los Angeles, 146–147, 147, 155
as driver, 36
and L.A. LIVE, 152–153
linking to sports facilities in Columbus and San Diego, 181
local amenities and, 36–38
with loss of Bohemian character, 124
in Reading, PA, 223
in San Diego's East village, 113–115, 122
simultaneously with big-ticket development, 39
through sports and culture, xiv
value of amenities for, 248
vs. big-ticket amenities, 38–39
New York
cartel control over number of teams, 53–54
population changes, 7

Nicholson, Jack, 133
Nokia Theatre, 130, 139, 148, 151
    events hosted, 150

O

Ohio
    Delaware County population changes, 175
    excessive facility competition in, 182
    Franklin County population changes, 175
    Franklin County voter referendum
        rejection, 161–162
    population changes
        central state, 175
        metropolitan areas, 162
Ohio State University (OSU), 171
    Gateway development, 172
    new basketball arena, 182
    sports at, 163
Olympic Games, 15
    historical importance, 14
Organic urban change, *vs.* planned
        redevelopment, 44–49
Our City Reading, 238
Our Lady of the Angels Cathedral, 153, 154
Outsourcing, 41

P

Parking issues, 8
    in Los Angeles redevelopment area, 152
    in Reading, PA, 234
Participation modes, 34
Pei, I.M., 197, 255
Performing arts centers, naming rights, 2
Petco Park, 26, 109
    development surrounding, 123, 124
    naming rights, 107
Pittsburgh Penguins, 162
Planned redevelopment, 34
    failure and success examples, 46
    and growth poles, 47–49
    importance of, 254
    value of, 252–254
    vs. organic urban change, 44–49
Player salaries, 18
    increases due to subsidization, 18
    major league baseball, 20
    real increases, 19
Players, benefits from subsidization, 18–20
Playhouse Square, 191–192, 192, 193, 198
    countywide taxing instruments for, 207

Population change
    in Cleveland, 185–188, 188–189, 190
    continuation in Cleveland and Cuyahoga
        County, 218, 219
    in Cuyahoga County, 190
    in Indianapolis, 77
    Ohio metropolitan areas, 162
    in Reading, PA, 223, 225, 226
    selected central cities, 7
    and suburbanization, 5–7
Private sector
    assumption of risks by, 4
    attraction by public sector spending in
        Cleveland, 198
    extraordinary profits realized by, 262
    importance of planned development linking
        public and, 261–262
    increased investment after public sector
        building, 201, 218, 219
    investment in Cleveland's nonresidential
        projects, 199–200
    investment in Cleveland's residential
        projects, 200–202
    linking investments to tax commitments,
        256–258
    timing of investment in Cleveland, 187
Private sector employment
    in Indianapolis, 82, 83, 85
    in midwestern cities, 85
    percent change, 86
Profit maximization, 42
Property tax abatements, in Cleveland, 201,
        202, 203, 218
Property taxes, effects of credit crisis on, 247
Public benefits
    generation in San Diego, 107
    protecting in Los Angeles, 142
    and stigma of subsidies, 107–112
Public engagement
    limitations in Indianapolis, 67
    limiting through political decision
        processes, 50
    in redevelopment, 34
Public/private partnerships, 2, 4, 10, 257
    in Cleveland, 188, 191–192
    in Columbus, 26, 161, 165, 166–171, 170,
        177
    in Indianapolis, 69–70
    inherently unequal nature of, 69–70
    in Los Angeles, 51, 140–141, 150, 157
    and mayoralty of George Voinovich,
        192–194

risk/benefit relationships, 43
in San Diego, 51, 101, 124–127
shared risk, 108
STAPLES Center investments, 143

Q

Qualcomm Stadium, 108
remodeling agreement, 104
trigger clause, 104
Quall, 101
Quicken Loans Arena, 195
Quincy Market, 8

R

Racial conflict, 245, 246
in Cleveland, 188–190
Racial separation, in Reading, PA, 224–230
Railroad stations, conversion to marketplaces, 8
Reading, Pennsylvania, 25
advertising pylon use, 234, 235
building permits total value, 241
city image transformation, 235–237
community development, 238–239
contemporary outlook, 226–230
crime rates, 228, 229
demographic changes, 230
deteriorating housing stock, 229
dropout rate, 227–228
and economic change in small cities,
223–224
economic integration issues, 266
education benefits, 236
employment changes by sector and payroll,
227, 228
Entertainment Square, 239
foreclosure rates, 230
goggleWorks, 236, 237, 239
historic Rajah Theater, 233
as historical outlet capital, 235–237
history, 224–225
home ownership subsidization, 238–239
hotel and admission tax receipts, 240
hotel developments, 241
investment risk issues, 259
leadership group, 238–239
loss of executive talent, 224
low-income population, 226, 228
measures of success, 239–241
as mid-Atlantic arts center, 235–237
Miller Center for the Arts, 237, 238
movie theater and IMAX center, 237, 239
need for new business development, 260
Our City Reading, 238
Performing Arts Center, 234
population change in, 223, 225
racial and economic segregation, 229
residential and commercial development
possibilities, 240
role of business leaders, 33
Sovereign Center, 233, 234, 235
state and federal funding, 242
struggle to retain highly skilled workers, 38
success of entertainment venues, 234
vacant buildings, 229, 230
Vanity Fair Outlet Mall, 232
volunteer leadership group, 230–234
Redevelopment. *See also* Downtown
redevelopment
business leaders' role in, 49–51
comprehensive approaches to, 10
criticism of subsidized, 10
evolutionary change *vs.* planned approach,
34
in Indianapolis, 69–74
orientation approaches, 34
participation modes for planning, 34
Regional cooperation, in Cleveland area, 207
Regional economy
failure to change by new facilities, 2
in Indianapolis, 75–77, 78–87
Return on investment
Columbus Arena District, 178
L.A. Community Reinvestment Agency, 147
in Los Angeles, 141–147, 144
as motivator for development, 42
San Diego Ballpark District, 117
Revenue challenges, in Indianapolis, 90–94
Revenue guarantees, to Indianapolis Colts,
90–92
Revenue sharing, in Los Angeles, 142
Richfield Coliseum, 210, 211
Riordan, Richard, 129–130
as champion of market-based approach, 131
Risk-taking, importance of prudence, 260–261
Rock and Roll Hall of Fame, 196–197, 198
countywide taxation policies, 207
Rodney King case, 129, 136
Rosentraub, Mark, xxi
Roski, Edward, 133
Rouse, James W., 6
Rust Belt cities, 47, 226
lack of neighborhood-level entertainment, 37

S

Safety issues, 245, 248, 249
  in Cleveland, 189
  in Reading, PA, 223, 234
  in Reading, Pennsylvania, 228
San Diego, 25, 32
  actual completed building, 112–115
  ballpark costs for Padres and city, 109
  Ballpark District, 45, 110, 112–115,
    117–124, 124–127, 125, 127, 172,
    176
  as broker, 126
  Charger ticket sales guarantee, 104–105
  contentious legal relations with Chargers,
    100
  Convention Center, 107, 109, 125, 131
  destructive tendencies of planners, 44
  development, land use, 117–124
  development near Petco Park, 123, 124
  East Village, 107, 109, 111, 126
  fiscal needs for new ballpark, 102
  guarantees from private sector, 257, 265
  inconsistent sales tax revenues from Ballpark
    District, 116
  investment and tax gain estimates, 118–121
  lack of fiscal protection, 257
  legal battles against sports teams, 22, 102,
    104
  linking sports facility to neighborhood
    development in, 181
  mini baseball field development, 126
  Mission Valley convenience, 108
  new construction associated with ballpark,
    113–114
  new residential and commercial
    development, 126
  Padres' fiscal challenges, 100
  Padres' need for new ballpark, 101–102
  Padres' revenue limitations, 102
  Petco Park, 109
  private investment commitment, 264–265
  public benefits and stigma of subsidies,
    107–112
  public/private partnerships, 51
  Qualcomm Stadium, 108
  quality of life investments, 12
  residential redevelopment, 112, 117, 122
  shared risks and returns in, 99–100, 109,
    124–127
  small base of high-income residents, 100

  sports world politics, 102–107
  success of planned redevelopment, 46
  Task Force II and public benefits generation,
    107
  taxes generated, 115–117
  TR Produce building redevelopment, 122,
    123
  transient occupancy tax revenues, 115
  trigger clause with Chargers, 104, 106
  use of eminent domain, 258
  voter opposition to sports subsidies,
    100–101, 104, 165
San Diego Chargers, 22
  control over Padres' stadium rental and
    income, 100, 101
  legal problems with city, 102, 104
  ticket guarantees from city, 104, 106
  training relocation to Los Angeles, 106
  trigger clause, 104, 106
San Diego Padres, 26
  dependence on Chargers, 100, 101
  fiscal challenges, 100
  need for new ballpark, 101–102
  ownership history, 101
  revenue limitations, 102
Schottenstein Center, 182
Segregation, racial and economic, 229
Shared risk, in San Diego, 99–100, 124–127
Short North community, 172, 179
  total private sector investment, 175
Small cities, 264
  economic and racial separation, 224–230
  economic change in, 223–224
  limited wealth base, 223
  loss of executive talent in, 224
Small market teams, NFL protection for, 90
Social capital, 15
  congressional failure to protect, 60
  importance in attracting people, 24
  produced by sports teams, 56
  role of sports in, 15
Southern states, migration trends, 42
Sovereign Center, 233, 234, 235
Sports/entertainment/culture triad, 2
  and amenities, 12–13
  attracting human capital via, 4–5
  city image enhancement with, 4–5
  in Cleveland, 192
  diversifying city offerings via, xiii
  economic development with, 4–5
  historical importance of, 13–16

and human capital, 12–13
in Indianapolis, 69–74, 94–96
neighborhood revitalization through, xiv
rationale for cities' pursuit of, 10–16
in Reading, 223
role as socializing institutions, 15
role in retention of human capital, 32
as trinity for redevelopment, 16–22
turning subsidies into strategic investments
   with, 245–246
Sports facilities
   ability to move economic activity, 200
   city subsidization of, 16–17
   controversial financing of, 2
   importance in American society, 53
Sports leagues
   antitrust exemptions for, 5
   area saturation issues, 162
   artificial scarcities created by, 57
   assumption of maintenance and
      improvements in Cleveland, 213
   as cartel, 51
   city undervaluation of worth to, 54
   Columbus case study, 161–163, 163–166
   historical development of power, 56–58
   implications of control over supply, 54–55
   minimization of financial responsibilities
      by, 196
   placement of teams in Cincinnati and
      Cleveland, 164–165
   power to control supply, 58
   underwriting of facilities building, 208
St. Louis, population changes, 7
St. Petersburg, failure to obtain public support,
   22
Stagnation, 245, 249
   and delayed development, 45–47
   and dispersed *vs.* centralized development,
      252
STAPLES Center, 26, 45, 130, 138, 150, 154,
   251, 253, 256
   advertising pylons, 135
   investments in, 143
   location, 139
   payments to city, 145
   public sector share of costs, 142, 143
   revenues generated by, 156
STARchitecture, 255, 256
State and local governments
   challenges to leagues' power, 58–60
   higher debt levels, 2

legal actions, 58–60
redefinitions of, 10–11
subsidization of facilities by, 2–3
Strategic investments
   and credit crisis aftermath, 246–249
   turning subsidies into, xv, 245–246
   and urban tourism, 248–249
   value of amenities as, 248
   vs. subsidization, 3–4
Subsidization, 99, 246
   avoidance by anchoring development with
      sports facility, 180
   and business self-interest, 262–263
   in Cleveland, 196–198, 208–210, 217
   in Columbus, 176
   era of, 2–3
   ethical issues, 262–263
   financial effects on owners and players,
      18–20
   and franchise values, 20–22
   future challenges for Indianapolis, 90–94
   importance of linking private sector
      investments to, 256–258
   Indianapolis example, 92–94
   issues in Columbus, 166
   minimizing, 246–247
   and misplaced revenues/values, 22–24
   opposition in Los Angeles, 131
   opposition in San Diego, 100–101
   reductions in Cleveland, 208
   revitalization and development as
      alternatives to, 60
   risks in Indianapolis, 96
   sports facilities, 16–17
   stigma in San Diego, 107–112
   team owner enrichment through, 18
   and unbalanced power, 50
   voter rebellions, 21
   vs. strategic investments, 3–4, 25
Suburbanization, 1, 11
   in central Ohio, 174
   in Cleveland, 189
   and decline of Reading, PA, 225
   and festival marketplace experiments, 7–8
   historical development, 5
   Indianapolis' civic image strategy, 8–9
   and population change, 5–7
   and rise of sports/culture for revitalization,
      9–10
   of sports facilities, 68

T

Tax-and-build frenzy, disappointing results, 17–18
Tax revenues
    amusement taxes in Cleveland, 206
    dependence on private sector investment, 263
    enhancement by growth coalitions, 74
    generated by STAPLES Center, 156
    investment to AEG, 148–149
    in Los Angeles, 146
    offsetting public investment with, 3–4
    policies in Cleveland, 202–205
    in Reading, Pennsylvania, 240
    in San Diego Ballpark District, 107
    and taxpayer protection in Los Angeles, 144, 146
Team auctions, 5
Team moves, competitive nature of, 17
Team owners
    renegotiations in Cleveland, 210–213
    subsidization of, 2
Team relocations
    Cleveland Browns, 197
    Indianapolis threats, 92–93
    within Los Angeles, 130–135
    Minneapolis Lakers, 131–132
    to Ohio, 165
    as shows of league power, 57
    from suburb to city, 194
    threats of, 53–55, 106, 195
Team values. *See also* Franchise values
    increase through subsidization, 99–100
Teams, generation of economic activity by, 22
Ticket purchases, 21
Torpedo Factory, Alexandraia, VA, 235, 236
Tourism planning concept, 134
Transient occupancy tax (TOT), 110
    in San Diego, 115

U

Unbalanced negotiations, 33, 34
    between teams and cities, 51
Unequal partnerships, in Indianapolis, 69–70
UniGov, 65–66. *See also* Consolidated city-county government
University of Michigan, xxii
Upper-income residents. *See* Middle/upper income population
Urban change, 1–2
Urban decay, 245
    amid redevelopment in Cleveland, 187
    in Reading, PA, 224–225, 232
Urban tourism, 248–249

V

Vanity Fair Outlet Mall, 232
Vincent, Fay, 196
Voinovich, George, 188, 191
    emphasis on business leadership, 192–194
Volunteer leadership group
    and community development, 238–239
    focus on entertainment, 230–234
    in Reading, PA, 223
Voter rebellions, 21, 22, 50
    in Cleveland, 194, 195
    in Columbus, 161–162, 165
    in San Diego, 100–101, 104

W

Welfare maximization, 42
Western states, migration trends, 42
White flight
    in Cleveland, 188–190
    in Reading, Pennsylvania, 228